The Complete Poems and Songs of

Robert Burns

The Complete Poems and Songs of

Robert Burns

This edition published 2000 by Geddes & Grosset, an imprint of
Children's Leisure Products Limited

© 2000 Children's Leisure Products Limited, David Dale House,
New Lanark ML11 9DJ, Scotland
Reprinted 2001

Cover portrait of Robert Burns and Highland Mary by Thomas Faed,
courtesy of Glasgow Museums

ISBN 1 85534 982 5

Printed and bound in Indonesia

Introduction

Robert Burns is unique among poets. There is no other literary figure in whose name, and on whose birthday each year, thousands of people, across the world, sit down and enjoy a ceremonial meal. The phenomenon of the Burns cult is truly remarkable. But the essential thing about Robert Burns is that he was a great poet. When he died, in 1796, in debt, aged 37, worn out by hard work and illness, well loved but far from being a cult figure, he was already a great poet. If, improbably, the 'Burns Suppers' ceased to take place, it would make no difference to the stature of the writer whom they celebrate. The truest way to appreciate and honour a poet is to read his work.

The passage of time and the stifling of the Scots language by modern English have put some obstacles in the way of our reading of Burns. The 'lyart haffets' of the cottar in *The Cottar's Saturday Night* are not immediately obvious as 'grey sidewhiskers'. The 'hawkie' beyond the 'hallan' does not immediately suggest the white-faced cow beyond the partition wall separating house from byre. But these are isolated examples. In *To a Mouse*, the phrase 'a damon icker in a thrave' may not mean much to us on its own, but when we go straight on to read that it is a 'sma request,' and 'I'll get a blessing wi' the lave, And never miss't', then we don't need any glossary to get the sense. Anyone who wants to check can find that it means an occasional ear of corn from a bundle of sheaves, but the context of the poem has already made the meaning sufficiently plain. And this happens all the time with Burns. Put your trust in the poet, read him – especially read him aloud – and you will be greatly rewarded.

Burns's poems are full of memorable thoughts and images. Among his lyrics are phrases and verses so universally known that their source is half-forgotten:

'The best-laid schemes o' mice, and men
Gang aft agley'
'O wad some Pow'r the giftie gie us
To see oursel's as others see us'
'Nae man can tether time or tide'

One of the most remarkable things about Burns is his versatility. He is a superb love poet, and for him 'Love and Poesy' always went together. As a boy of fifteen he began to write love poems, and he never stopped falling in love and writing about it:

'Till a' the seas gang dry, my dear.
And the rocks melt wi' the sun!
I will love thee still, my dear,
While the sands o' life shall run.'

But Burns was the master of many forms of verse. Picking up on a Scottish tradition, he developed the verse epistle, a poem in letter form to a friend, often another poet. In an epistle he could write about anything he pleased; in the *Epistle to J. Lapraik* he wrote about himself:

'Gie me ae spark o' Nature's fire,
That's a' the learning I desire;

Then though I drudge through dub an' mire
    At pleugh or cart,
My Muse, though hamely in attire,
    May touch the heart.'

This did himself less than justice. As a child he had been well taught, and he was an avid reader all his life. But the poverty of his father had prevented him from a college education, and he felt the lack of it, less in himself than in other people's attitudes towards him. Sometimes he played up to the 'heaven-taught' ploughman-poet image that was bestowed on him; often he resented it. Resentment at religious oppressiveness and hypocrisy sharpened his gift for satire. After the publication of *Holy Willie's Prayer*, many others as well as its victim, Mr William Fisher, must have taken care to show a less sanctimonious face to the world:

'Yet here am I, a chosen sample,
To show Thy grace is great and ample...'

With his satiric gift went the ability to make a swift epigram, as in one of his mock-epitaphs on a schoolteacher:

'Here lie Willie Michie's banes: Satan, when ye tak' him,
Gie him the schoolin of your weans,
For clever de'ils he'll mak 'em.'

Burns is perhaps most famous for his nature poetry, after his love songs. As a hard-working countryman, he did not idolise the country, but he fell in with the poetical habit of the day, beginning with description, and then bringing the subject of the poem round to his own state, of happiness or gloom, as in *And Maun I Still on Menie Doat*:

'The wanton coot the water skims,
Amang the reeds the ducklings cry,
The stately swan majestic swims,
And ev'rything is blest but I.'

For his native country, he had a burning fervour. He read all he could find of Scottish history; even as a boy Wallace had been one of his heroes, along with another soldierly leader, Hannibal. His poem *Robert Bruce's March to Bannockburn*, with its stirring lines, became the anthem of Scotland:

'Scots, wha hae wi' Wallace bled,
Scots, wham Bruce has aften led,
Welcome to your gory bed,
    Or to Victorie!'

With his Scottish patriotism went a slightly quixotic symapthy for the Jacobite cause, which had been finally defeated in 1746, thirteen years before he was born. For Burns, as for others, hostility to the Hanoverian monarchy and its corrupt administration of Scotland added something more than nostalgia:

'The injured Stuart line is gone,
A race outlandish fills their throne;
An idiot race, to honour lost: know them best despise them most.'

He scratched these lines on the window-pane of an inn in Stirling, looking up towards the then-ruinous castle which had cradled the Stewart kings.

It is not likely that Robert Burns would have long approved of a Stewart restoration. In politics, he was a radical. He supported the American War of Independence, and wrote, in his *Ode for General Washington's Birthday*:

'But come, ye sons of Liberty,
Columbia's offspring, brave as free,
In danger's hour still flaming in the van,
Ye know, and dare maintain, the Royalty of Man!'

Like his slightly younger English contemporaries, Wordsworth and Coleridge, he heard with joy in 1789 of the French Revolution. But by 1795, when war with post-revolutionary France was imminent, he was writing *Does Haughty Gaul Invasion Threat?* His sympathy for the exploited comes out in works like *The Slave's Lament* (not one of his most memorable poems) and his deep and genuine feeling of the brotherhood of man is most often recalled in *A Man's a Man for A' That*:

'The rank is but the guinea's stamp,
The Man's the gowd for a' that.'

though it recurs in many other poems.

In what were to be his last years, Burns spent much of his time gathering all he could find of the remaining folk-songs, and fragments of folk-songs, in Scots. This was a true labour of love, for which he received no payment. The long hostility of the Church to any form of popular song or music had taken a heavy toll on the self-expression of country people. Burns rescued and rewrote many. Such an exercise rarely improves on the original, but in his case, such was his intimacy with the material, his sense for what was true and valid, and his respect for the work of the unknown original authors, that he gave to Scotland one of the finest collections of folk-song of any European country. One example, out of many, is *For the Sake of Somebody*, with its beautiful melody, which Burns changed from a rather coarse country song for a man, into a haunting love song for a girl:

'My heart is sair – I dare na tell,
My heart is sair for Somebody;
I could wake a winter night
For the sake o' Somebody.
O-hon for Somebody! for Somebody! could range the world aroun'
For the sake o' Somebody.'

If Burns's preoccupation with songs gives cause for any regret as we look back on his work, it may be that it deprived us of more poems like *Tam o' Shanter*. This splendid, galloping, eldritch midnight adventure was written in 1791, on the request for a 'witch tale'. Beautifully paced, its mock-heroic style giving full reign to the comedy, it draws on all of Burns's powers:

'The wind blew as 'twad blawn its last;
The rattling showers rose on the blast;
The speedy gleams the darkness swallow'd;
Loud, deep and lang the thunder bellow'd: night, a child might understand
The deil had business on his hand.'

Burns's variety of themes and styles is outstanding. He is a poet for all moods and all seasons. His own humanity as an individual, and his extended feeling for a wider humanity, shine through everything he wrote. He wrote fast, often under difficult circumstances, and the quality of his work is uneven. His poems in 'Augustan English' often seem stilted and artificial beside his poems in Scots. Some of his poems are 'occasional' in the sense that they were written in response to a particular event, not necesssarily for the critical eye of posterity. But these are trifling criticisms against the treasury of his complete work. If there are some farthings, 'placks and bodles' among the gold he has left us, we are still a little richer for each word from his pen.

Chronology

1759   Birth at Alloway in Ayrshire of Robert Burns on 25 January, eldest son of William Burness and Agnes Broun.

1765   Robert attends Alloway school until his father and some neighbours employ a young teacher, John Murdoch.

1766   The family moves to Mount Oliphant, southeast of Alloway.

1768   John Murdoch leaves for a better post and the little school is closed down. William Burness looks after his sons' education.

1772   Robert and his brother Gilbert go to Dalrymple school in the summer months, week about.

1773   Robert goes to Ayr to study grammar, French and Latin under John Murdoch.

1774   Robert writes *O Once I Lov'd*, his first song, in the autumn after falling in love with his harvest partner, Nelly Kilpatrick.

1777   The family moves inland to Lochlea, a larger farm near Tarbolton.

1778   Robert attends school at Kirkoswald for the summer to learn mensuration and surveying. Here he falls in love with Peggy Thompson.

1780   Robert and his friends establish the Bachelors' Club in Tarbolton.

1781   Robert becomes a freemason and goes to Irvine to learn flax dressing.

1782   In March Robert returns from Irvine to Lochlea after the premises where he worked are destroyed by fire.
        William Burness takes a legal case against his landlord to the Court of Session.

1783   Robert first keeps a commonplace book in which he records and revises his early poems.

1784   In January the Court of Session finds in favour of William Burness but by this time he is ill and the case has exhausted his savings. He dies on 13 February.
        In March Robert and Gilbert take on the lease of the farm at Mossgiel.
        Robert meets and falls in love with Jean Armour.

1785   On 22 May Elizabeth Paton, Mrs Burns's servant, has a child, Elizabeth, by Robert, his first child.
        Robert records *The Death and Dying Words of Poor Mailie* in his commonplace book.

1786   In February it is revealed to her family that Jean Armour is pregnant by Robert. Jean is sent to relatives in Paisley.
        Robert meets and falls in love with Mary Campbell but she dies in Greenock.
        Robert decides to go to Jamaica but postpones it when the Kilmarnock Edition of his *Poems Chiefly in the Scottish Dialect* is published in July.
        In September Jean Armour gives birth to twins, a boy and a girl.
        On 17 November Burns leaves for Edinburgh to arrange a second edition of his poems, encouraged by blind poet Thomas Blacklock. He arrives on 28 November.

1787   The expanded Edinburgh Edition of his poems is published on 21 April.
        In May Burns tours the Border country and northern England. At Dumfries he learns that Meg Cameron, a servant girl in Edinburgh, is pregnant by him.
        On 9 June Burns returns to Mossgiel and renews his love affair with Jean Armour.
        At the end of June he embarks on a tour of the West Highlands on his own, visiting Inveraray and Dumbarton.
        On 25 August Robert sets off with William Nicol on a tour of the Northern Highlands, returning to Edinburgh on 16 September.
        In October Burns tours the Ochils. He stays at Harvieston House when he courts Margaret Chalmers and proposes marriage but is refused.
        Volume One of Johnson's *Scots Musical Museum* is published containing three songs by Burns.

Jenny Clow, a servant girl in Edinburgh, has a child by Burns.

In December Burns meets Mrs Maclehose.

1788 Volume Two of Johnson's *Museum* is published in February containing thirty-five songs by Burns.

In February Robert returns to Ayrshire. In March Jean Armour has twin girls but they die within a month. In August their marriage is regularized by the Kirk Session in Mauchline.

Robert enters the Excise and completes a six-week training course.

In the summer he moves in to Ellisland and is joined there by Jean and their son (the girl twin having died late in 1787) in December.

1789 At the end of February he pays a hurried visit to Edinburgh.

On 18 August Jean has a son, Francis Wallace.

1790 Volume Three of Johnson's *Museum* is published in February with forty songs by Robert. *Tam o' Shanter* is completed in the autumn.

1791 On 31 March Anna Park, a barmaid at the Globe Tavern in Dumfries, has a baby daughter by Robert; the child, Elizabeth, is taken in by Jean.

On 9 April Jean has a son, William Nicol.

In November Robert gives up Ellisland and the family moves to a house in the Wee Vennel, Dumfries.

He meets Maria Riddell at Friars Carse, the home of Robert Riddell, Maria's brother-in-law.

At the end of November Robert pays his last visit to Edinburgh.

On 6 December Robert meets and parts for the last time with Nancy Maclehose.

1792 Volume Four of Johnson's *Museum* is published in August with fifty songs by Burns.

In September Burns begins a correspondence with George Thomson with a view to contributing to his *Select Collection of Original Scottish Airs*.

On 21 November Jean gives birth to a daughter, Elizabeth.

Burns is suspected of being a 'Friend of the People' and his conduct is investigated by the Board of Excise.

1793 An enlarged edition of Thomson's collection is published in two volumes on 18 February.

In April a new edition of Burns's poems is published.

In May Burns and Jean move to a larger house in Mill Vennel, Dumfries.

In July Burns travels through Galloway and Wigtonshire.

1794 On 12 August Jean has a baby boy, James Glencairn.

In December Burns is promoted to acting supervisor of the Excise.

1795 Elizabeth, Robert's daughter by Jean, dies just before her third birthday.

Robert contracts rheumatic fever.

1796 Robert dies on 21 July.

Jean gives birth to a son, Maxwell, on 25 July, the day of his father's funeral.

Volume Five of Johnson's *Museum* is published with thirty-seven songs by Robert, one of them being *Auld Lang Syne*.

Poems & Songs

HANDSOME NELL

'I never had the least thought or inclination of turning Poet till I got once heartily in love, and then rhyme and song were, in a manner, the spontaneous language of my heart. The following composition was the first of my performances. It is, indeed, very puerile and silly; but I am always pleased with it, as it recalls to my mind those happy days when my heart was yet honest, and my tongue was sincere'—*Commonplace Book*, August 1783.

O, once I lov'd a bonnie lass,
    Ay, and I love her still;
And whilst that virtue warms my breast,
    I'll love my handsome Nell.

As bonnie lasses I hae seen,
    And monie full as braw;
But for a modest gracefu' mien,
    The like I never saw.

A bonnie lass, I will confess,
    Is pleasant to the e'e;
But without some better qualities,
    She's no a lass for me.

But Nelly's looks are blythe and sweet,
    And what is best of a',
Her reputation is complete,
    And fair without a flaw

She dresses aye sae clean and neat,
    Both decent and genteel;
And then there's something in her gait
    Gars onie dress look weel.

A gaudy dress and gentle air
    May slightly touch the heart;
But it's innocence and modesty
    That polishes the dart.

'Tis this in Nelly pleases me,
    'Tis this enchants my soul;
For absolutely in my breast
    She reigns without control.

O TIBBIE, I HAE SEEN THE DAY
Tune—*Invercauld's reel*

Chorus: O Tibbie, I hae seen the day,
    Ye wadna been sae shy;
For laik o' gear ye lightly me,
    But, trowth, I care na by.

Yestreen I met you on the moor,
Ye spak na, but gaed by like stour;
Ye geck at me because I'm poor,
    But fient a hair care I.

When coming hame on Sunday last,
Upon the road as I cam past,
Ye snufft and ga'e your head a cast—
    But, trowth, I care't na by.

I doubt na, lass, but ye may think,
Because ye hae the name o' clink,
That ye can please me at a wink,
    Whene'er ye like to try.

But sorrow tak' him that's sae mean,
Altho' his pouch o' coin were clean,
Wha follows onie saucy quean,
 That looks sae proud and high.

Altho' a lad were e'er sae smart,
If that he want the yellow dirt,
Ye'll cast your head anither airt,
 And answer him fu' dry.

But if he hae the name o' gear,
Ye'll fasten to him like a brier,
Tho' hardly he, for sense or lear,
 Be better than the kye.

But, Tibbie, lass, take my advice:
Your daddie's gear maks you sae nice;
The deil a ane wad speir your price,
 Were ye as poor as I.

There lives a lass beside yon park,
I'd rather hae her in her sark,
Than you wi' a' your thousand mark;
 That gars you look sae high.

I Dream'd I Lay

I dream'd I lay where flowers were springing
 Gaily in the sunny beam;
List'ning to the wild birds singing,
 By a falling crystal stream:
Straight the sky grew black and daring;
 Thro' the woods the whirlwinds rave;
Trees with agéd arms were warring,
 O'er the swelling drumlie wave.

Such was my life's deceitful morning,
 Such the pleasures I enjoyed:
But lang or noon, loud tempests storming
 A' my flowery bliss destroy'd.
Tho' fickle fortune has deceiv'd me—
 She promis'd fair, and perform'd but ill,
Of monie a joy and hope bereav'd me—
 I bear a heart shall support me still.

In The Character Of A Ruined Farmer
Tune—Go from my window, love, do

The sun he is sunk in the west,
All creatures retiréd to rest,
While here I sit, all sore beset,
 With sorrow, grief and woe:
And it's O fickle Fortune, O!

The prosperous man is asleep,
Nor hears how the whirlwinds sweep;
But Misery and I must watch
 The surly tempests blow:
And it's O fickle Fortune, O!

There lies the dear partner of my breast;
Her cares for a moment at rest:
Must I see thee, my youthful pride,
 Thus brought so very low?
And it's O fickle Fortune, O!

There lie my sweet babies in her arms;
No anxious fear their little hearts alarms;
But for their sake my heart does ache,
 With many a bitter throe:
And it's O fickle Fortune, O!

I once was by Fortune caresst:
I once could relieve the distrest:
Now life's poor support, hardly earn'd
 My fate will scarce bestow:
And it's O fickle Fortune, O!

No comfort, no comfort I have!
How welcome to me were the grave!
But then my wife and children dear—
 O, wither would they go?
And it's O fickle Fortune, O!

O whither, O whither shall I turn?
All friendless, forsaken, forlorn!
For, in this world, Rest or Peace
 I never more shall know:
And it's O fickle Fortune, O!

TRAGIC FRAGMENT

All villain as I am—a damnéd wretch,
A hardened, stubborn, unrepenting sinner—
Still my heart melts at human wretchedness;
And with sincere but unavailing sighs
I view the helpless children of distress:
With tears indignant I behold the oppressor
Rejoicing in the honest man's destruction,
Whose unsubmitting heart was all his crime—
Ev'n you, ye hapless crew! I pity you;
Ye, whom the seeming good think sin to pity;
Ye poor, despised, abandoned vagabonds,
Whom Vice, as usual, has turn'd o'er to ruin.
O! but for friends and interposing Heaven,
I had been driven forth like you forlorn,
The most detested, worthless wretch among you!
O injured God! Thy goodness has endow'd me
With talents passing most of my compeers,
Which I in just proportion have abused—
As far surpassing other common villains
As Thou in natural parts has given me more.

THE TARBOLTON LASSES

If ye gae up to yon hill-tap,
 Ye'll there see bonnie Peggy;
She kens her father is a laird,
 And she forsooth's a leddy.

There Sophy tight, a lassie bright,
 Besides a handsome fortune:
Wha canna win her in a night,
 Has little art in courtin.

Gae down by Faile, and taste the ale,
 And tak a look o' Mysie;
She's dour and din, a deil within,
 But aiblins she may please ye.

If she be shy, her sister try,
 Ye'll maybe fancy Jenny;
If ye'll dispense wi' want o' sense—
 She kens hersel she's bonnie.

As ye gae up by yon hillside,
 Speir in for bonnie Bessy;
She'll gie ye a beck, and bid ye light,
 And handsomely address ye.

There's few sae bonnie, nane sae guid,
 In a' King George' dominion;
If ye should doubt the truth o' this—
 It's Bessy's ain opinion!

AH, WOE IS ME, MY MOTHER DEAR
Paraphrase of Jeremiah 15, Verse 10

Ah, woe is me, my mother dear!
 A man of strife ye've born me:
For sair contention I maun bear;
 They hate, revile and scorn me.

I ne'er could lend on bill or band,
 That five per cent might blest me;
And borrowing, on the tither hand,
 The deil a ane wad trust me.

Yet I, a coin-deniéd wight,
 By Fortune quite discarded;
Ye see how I am, day and night,
 By lad and lass blackguarded!

MONTGOMERIE'S PEGGY
Tune—*Galla Water*

Altho' my bed were in yon muir,
 Amang the heather, in my plaidie;
Yet happy, happy would I be,
 Had I my dear Montgomerie's Peggy.

When o'er the hill beat surly storms,
 And winter nights were dark and rainy;
I'd seek some dell, and in my arms
 I'd shelter dear Montgomerie's Peggy.

Were I a baron proud and high,
 And horse and servants waiting ready;
Then a' 'twad gie o' joy to me—
 The sharin't with Montgomerie's Peggy.

THE MERRY PLOUGHMAN

As I was a-wand'ring ae morning in spring,
I heard a young ploughman sae sweetly to sing;
And as he was singin', thir words he did say—
There's nae life like the ploughman's in the month o' sweet May.

The lav'rock in the morning she'll rise frae her nest,
And mount i' the air wi' the dew on her breast;
And wi' the merry ploughman she'll whistle and sing,
And at night she'll return to her nest back again.

THE RONALDS OF THE BENNALS

In Tarbolton, ye ken, there are proper young men,
    And proper young lasses and a', man:
But ken ye the Ronalds that live in the Bennals,
    They carry the gree frae them a', man.

Their father's a laird, and weel he can spare't,
    Braid money to tocher them a', man;
To proper young men, he'll clink in the hand
    Gowd guineas a hundred or twa, man.

There's ane they ca' Jean, I'll warrant ye've seen
    As bonnie a lass or as braw, man;
But for sense and guid taste she'll vie wi' the best,
    And a conduct that beautifies a', man.

The charms o' the min', the langer they shine,
    The mair admiration they draw, man;
While peaches and cherries, and roses and lilies,
    They fade and they wither awa', man,

If ye be for Miss Jean, tak this frae a frien',
    A hint o' a rival or twa, man;
The Laird o' Blackbyre wad gang through the fire,
    If that wad entice her awa', man.

The Laird o' Braehead has been on his speed,
    For mair than a towmond or twa, man;
The Laird o' the Ford will straught on a board,
    If he canna get her at a', man.

Then Anna comes in, the pride o' her kin,
    The boast of our bachelors a', man:
Sae sonsie and sweet, sae fully complete,
    She steals our affections awa', man.

If I should detail the pick and the wale
    O' lasses that live here awa', man,
The faut wad be mine if she didna shine
    The sweetest and best o' them a', man.

I lo'e her mysel, but darena weel tell,
    My poverty keeps me in awe, man;
For making o' rhymes, and working at times,
    Does little or naething at a', man.

Yet I wadna choose to let her refuse,
    Nor hae't in her power to say na, man:
For though I be poor, unnoticed, obscure,
    My stomach's as proud as them a', man.

Though I canna ride in weel-booted pride,
    And flee o'er the hills like a craw, man,
I can haud up my head wi' the best o' the breed,
    Though fluttering ever so braw, man.

My coat and my vest, they are Scotch o' the best,
    O' pairs o' guid breeks I hae twa, man;
And stockings and pumps to put on my stumps,
    And ne'er a wrang steek in them a', man.

My sarks they are few, but five o' them new,
    Twal' hundred, as white as the snaw, man,
A ten-shillings hat, a Holland cravat;
    There are no monie poets sae braw, man.

I never had freens weel stockit in means,
    To leave me a hundred or twa, man;
Nae weel-tocher'd aunts, to wait on their drants,
    And wish them in hell for it a', man.

I never was cannie for hoarding o' money,
    Or claughtin 't together at a', man;
I've little to spend, and naething to lend,
    But deevil a shilling I awe, man.

HERE'S TO THY HEALTH
Tune—*Logan Burn*

Here's to thy health, my bonnie lass,
    Guid nicht and joy be wi' thee;
I'll come nae mair to thy bower door,
    To tell thee that I lo'e thee.
O dinna think, my pretty pink,
    But I can live without thee:
I vow and swear I dinna care,
    How lang ye look about ye.

Thou'rt aye sae free informing me,
    Thou hast nae mind to marry;
I'll be as free informing thee,
    Nae time hae I to tarry:
I ken thy frien's try ilka means
    Frae wedlock to delay thee;
Depending on some higher chance,
    But fortune may betray thee.

I ken they scorn my low estate,
    But that does never grieve me;
For I'm as free as any he;
    Sma' siller will relieve me.
I'll count my health my greatest wealth,
    Sae lang as I'll enjoy it;
I'll fear nae scant, I'll bode nae want,
    As lang's I get employment.

But far off fowls hae feathers fair,
    And, aye until ye try them,
Tho' they seem fair, still have a care:
    They may prove as bad as I am.
But at twal at night, when the moon shines bright,
    My dear, I'll come and see thee;
For the man that loves his mistress weel,
    Nae travel makes him weary.

THE LASS OF CESSNOCK BANKS
A Song of Similes
Tune—*If he be a butcher neat and trim*

On Cessnock banks a lassie dwells;
    Could I describe her shape and mien;
Our lasses a' she far excels,
    An' she has twa sparkling roguish een.

She's sweeter than the morning dawn,
    When rising Phoebus first is seen,
And dew-drops twinkle o'er the lawn;
    An' she has twa sparkling roguish een.

She's stately like yon youthful ash,
    That grows the cowslip braes between,
And drinks the stream with vigour fresh;
    An' she has twa sparkling roguish een.

She's spotless like the flowering thorn,
    With flowers so white and leaves so green,
When purest in the dewy morn;
    An' she has twa sparkling roguish een.

Her looks are like the vernal May,
    When evening Phoebus shines serene,
While birds rejoice on every spray;
    An' she has twa sparkling roguish een.

Her hair is like the curling mist,
    That climbs the mountain-sides at e'en,
When flower-reviving rains are past;
    An' she has twa sparkling roguish een.

Her forehead's like the show'ry bow,
    When gleaming sunbeams intervene
And gild the distant mountain's brow;
    An' she has twa sparkling roguish een.

Her cheeks are like yon crimson gem,
    The pride of all the flowery scene,
Just opening on its thorny stem;
    An' she has twa sparkling roguish een.

Her bosom's like the nightly snow,
    When pale the morning rises keen,
While hid the murm'ring streamlets flow;
    An' she has twa sparkling roguish een.

Her lips are like yon cherries ripe,
    That sunny walls from Boreas screen;
They tempt the taste and charm the sight;
    An' she has twa sparkling roguish een.

Her teeth are like a flock of sheep,
    With fleeces newly washen clean,
That slowly mount the rising steep;
    An' she has twa sparkling roguish een.

Her breath is like the fragrant breeze,
    That gently stirs the blossom'd bean,
When Phoebus sinks behind the seas;
    An' she has twa sparkling roguish een.

Her voice is like the ev'ning thrush,
    That sings on Cessnock banks unseen,
While his mate sits nestling in the bush;
    An' she has twa sparkling roguish een.

But it's not her air, her form, her face,
    Tho' matching beauty's fabled queen;
'Tis the mind that shines in ev'ry grace,
    An' chiefly in her roguish een.

BONNIE PEGGY ALISON
Tune—*The Braes o' Balquhidder*

Chorus: And I'll kiss thee yet, yet,
    And I'll kiss thee o'er again:
And I'll kiss thee yet, yet,
    My bonnie Peggy Alison

When in my arms, wi' a' thy charms,
    I clasp my countless treasure, O!
I seek nae mair o' Heaven to share
    Than sic a moment's pleasure, O!

Ilk care and fear, when thou art near[1]
 I ever mair defy them, O!
Young kings upon their hansel throne
 Are no sae blest as I am, O!

And by thy een sae bonnie blue,
 I swear I'm thine for ever, O!
And on thy lips I seal my vow,
 And break it shall I never, O!

[1] This stanza was omitted when this song was first published.

MARY MORISON
Tune—*Duncan Davidson*

O Mary, at thy window be,
 It is the wish'd, the trysted hour!
Those smiles and glances let me see,
 That make the miser's treasure poor:
How blythely wad I bide the stour,
 A weary slave frae sun to sun,
Could I the rich reward secure,
 The lovely Mary Morison.

Yestreen, when to the trembling string
 The dance gaed thro' the lighted ha',
To thee my fancy took its wing,
 I sat, but neither heard nor saw:
Tho' this was fair, and that was braw,
 And yon the toast of a' the town,
I sigh'd, and said among them a',
 'Ye are na Mary Morison.'

Oh, Mary, canst thou wreck his peace,
 Wha for thy sake wad gladly die?
Or canst thou break that heart of his,
 Whase only faut is loving thee?
If love for love thou wilt na gie,
 At least be pity to me shown;
A thought ungentle canna be
 The thought o' Mary Morison.

WINTER—A DIRGE

The wintry west extends his blast,
 And hail and rain does blaw;
Or the stormy north sends driving forth
 The blinding sleet and snaw:
While, tumbling brown, the burn comes down,
 And roars frae bank to brae;
And bird and beast in covert rest,
 And pass the heartless day.

'The sweeping blast, the sky o'ercast,'
　　The joyless winter day,
Let others fear, to me more dear
　　Than all the pride of May:
The tempest's howl, it soothes my soul,
　　My griefs it seems to join;
The leafless trees my fancy please,
　　Their fate resembles mine!

Thou Power Supreme, whose mighty scheme
　　These woes of mine fulfil,
Here firm I rest; they must be best,
　　Because they are Thy will!
Then all I want—(Oh do Thou grant
　　This one request of mine!)
Since to enjoy Thou dost deny,
　　Assist me to resign!

A PRAYER UNDER THE PRESSURE OF VIOLENT ANGUISH

O Thou Great Being! what Thou art,
　　Surpasses me to know;
Yet sure I am, that known to Thee
　　Are all Thy works below.

Thy creature here before Thee stands,
　　All wretched and distrest;
Yet sure those ills that wring my soul
　　Obey Thy high behest.

Sure, Thou, Almighty, canst not act
　　From cruelty or wrath!
O, free my weary eyes from tears,
　　Or close them fast in death!

But, if I must afflicted be,
　　To suit some wise design,
Then man my soul with firm resolves
　　To bear and not repine!

PARAPHRASE OF THE FIRST PSALM

The man, in life wherever plac'd,
　　Hath happiness in store,
Who walks not in the wicked's way,
　　Nor learns their guilty lore!

Nor from the seat of scornful pride
　　Casts forth his eyes abroad,
But with humility and awe
　　Still walks before his God.

That man shall flourish like the trees,
　　Which by the streamlets grow;
The fruitful top is spread on high,
　　And firm the root below.

But he whose blossom buds in guilt
　　Shall to the ground be cast,
And, like the rootless stubble, tost
　　Before the sweeping blast.

For why? that God the good adore,
　　Hath giv'n them peace and rest,
But hath decreed that wicked men
　　Shall ne'er be truly blest.

THE FIRST SIX VERSES OF THE NINETIETH PSALM VERSIFIED

O Thou, the first, the greatest friend
　　Of all the human race!
Whose strong right hand has ever been
　　Their stay and dwelling-place!

Before the mountains heav'd their heads
　　Beneath Thy forming hand,
Before this ponderous globe itself,
　　Arose at Thy command;

That Pow'r which rais'd and still upholds
　　This universal frame,
From countless, unbeginning time
　　Was ever still the same.

Those mighty periods of years
　　Which seem to us so vast,
Appear no more before Thy sight
　　Than yesterday that's past.

Thou giv'st the word: Thy creature, man,
　　Is to existence brought;
Again Thou say'st, 'Ye sons of men,
　　Return ye into nought!'

Thou layest them, with all their cares,
　　In everlasting sleep;
As with a flood Thou tak'st them off
　　With overwhelming sweep.

They flourish like the morning flow'r,
　　In beauty's pride array'd;
But long ere night cut down it lies
　　All wither'd and decay'd.

A PRAYER IN THE PROSPECT OF DEATH

O Thou unknown, Almighty Cause
　　Of all my hope and fear!
In whose dread presence, ere an hour,
　　Perhaps I must appear!

If I have wander'd in those paths
  Of life I ought to shun,
As something, loudly, in my breast,
  Remonstrates I have done;

Thou know'st that Thou hast forméd me
  With passions wild and strong;
And list'ning to their witching voice
  Has often led me wrong.

Where human weakness has come short,
  Or frailty stept aside,
Do Thou, All-Good-for such Thou art—
  In shades of darkness hide.

Where with intention I have err'd,
  No other plea I have,
But Thou art good, and Goodness still
  Delighteth to forgive.

Stanzas On The Same Occasion

Why am I loth to leave this earthly scene?
  Have I so found it full of pleasing charms?
Some drops of joy with draughts of ill between;
  Some gleams of sunshine 'mid renewing storms,
Is it departing pangs my soul alarms?
  Or death's unlovely, dreary, dark abode?
For guilt, for guilt, my terrors are in arms;
  I tremble to approach an angry God,
And justly smart beneath His sin-avenging rod.

Fain would I say, 'Forgive my foul offence!'
  Fain promise never more to disobey;
But should my Author health again dispense,
  Again I might desert fair Virtue's way;
Again in Folly's path might go astray;
  Again exalt the brute and sink the man;
Then how should I for Heavenly Mercy pray,
  Who act so counter Heavenly Mercy's plan?
Who sin so oft have mourn'd, yet to temptation ran?

O Thou, great Governor of all below!
  If I may dare a lifted eye to Thee,
Thy nod can make the tempest cease to blow,
  Or still the tumult of the raging sea:
With that controlling pow'r assist ev'n me,
  Those headlong, furious passions to confine,
For all unfit I feel my pow'rs to be,
  To rule their torrent in th' allowed line;
O, aid me with Thy help, *Omnipotence Divine*!

FICKLE FORTUNE—A FRAGMENT

Though fickle Fortune has deceived me
    (She promis'd fair and perform'd but ill),
Of mistress, friends and wealth bereav'd me,
    Yet I bear a heart shall support me still.

I'll act with prudence as far 's I'm able,
    But if success I must never find,
Then come misfortune, I bid thee welcome,
    I'll meet thee with an undaunted mind.

RAGING FORTUNE—FRAGMENT OF SONG

O raging Fortune's withering blast
    Has laid my leaf full low, O!
O raging Fortune's withering blast
    Has laid my leaf full low, O!
My stem was fair, my bud was green,
    My blossom sweet did blow, O;
The dew fell fresh, the sun rose mild,
    And made my branches grow, O.
But luckless Fortune's northern storms
    Laid a' my blossoms low, O;
But luckless Fortune's northern storms
    Laid a' my blossoms low, O!

I'LL GO AND BE A SODGER

O why the deuce should I repine,
    And be an ill foreboder?
I'm twenty-three, and five feet nine—
    I'll go and be a sodger!

I gat some gear wi' mickle care,
    I held it weel thegither;
But now it's gane, and something mair—
    I'll go and be a sodger!

NO CHURCHMAN AM I
Tune—*Prepare, my dear brethren, to the tavern let's fly*

No Churchman am I for to rail and to write,
No Statesman nor Soldier to plot or to fight,
No sly man of business contriving a snare,
For a big-belly'd bottle's the whole of my care.

The Peer I don't envy, I give him his bow;
I scorn not the Peasant, though ever so low;
But a club of good fellows, like those that are here,
And a bottle like this, are my glory and care.

Here passes the Squire on his brother—his horse;
There Centum per Centum, the Cit with his purse;
But see you the Crown how it waves in the air,
There a big-belly'd bottle still eases my care.

The wife of my bosom, alas! she did die;
For sweet consolation to church I did fly;
I found that old Solomon prov'd it fair,
That a big-belly'd bottle's a cure for all care.

I once was persuaded a venture to make;
A letter inform'd me that all was to wreck;
But the pursy old landlord just waddl'd upstairs,
With a glorious bottle that ended my cares.

'Life's cares they are comforts'[1]—a maxim laid down
By the Bard, what d'ye call him, that wore the black gown;
And faith I agree with th' old prig to a hair,
For a big-belly'd bottle's a heav'n of a care.

A Stanza Added in a Mason Lodge

Then fill up a bumper and make it o'erflow,
And honours masonic prepare for to throw;
May ev'ry true Brother of th' Compass and Square
Have a big-belly'd bottle when harass'd with care.

[1] Young's 'Night Thoughts'—R.B.

MY FATHER WAS A FARMER
Tune—*The weaver and his shuttle, O*

My father was a farmer upon the Carrick border, O,
And carefully he bred me in decency and order, O;
He bade me act a manly part, though I had ne'er a farthing, O;
For without an honest manly heart, no man was worth regarding, O.

Then out into the world at length my course I did determine, O;
Tho' to be rich was not my wish, yet to be great was charming, O;
My talents they were not the worst, nor yet my education, O:
Resolv'd was I, at least to try, to mend my situation, O.

In many a way, and vain essay, I courted Fortune's favour, O;
Some cause unseen still stept between, to frustrate each endeavour, O;
Sometimes by foes I was o'erpower'd, sometimes by friends forsaken, O;
And when my hope was at the top, I still was worst mistaken, O.

Then sore harass'd, and tir'd at last, with Fortune's vain delusion, O,
I dropt my schemes, like idle dreams, and came to this conclusion, O;
The past was bad, and the future hid, its good or ill untriéd, O;
But the present hour was in my pow'r, and so I would enjoy it, O.

No help, nor hope, nor view had I, nor person to befriend me, O;
So I must toil, and sweat, and moil, and labour to sustain me, O:
To plough and sow, and reap and mow, my father bred me early, O;
For one, he said, to labour bred, was a match for Fortune fairly, O.

Thus all obscure, unknown, and poor, thro' life I'm doom'd to wander, O,
Till down my weary bones I lay in everlasting slumber, O:
No view nor care, but shun whate'er might breed me pain or sorrow, O;
I live today as well 's I may, regardless of tomorrow, O.

But cheerful still, I am as well as a monarch in a palace, O,
Tho' Fortune's frown still hunts me down, with all her wonted malice, O:
I make indeed my daily bread, but ne'er can make it farther, O;
But as daily bread is all I need, I do not much regard her, O.

When sometimes by my labour, I can earn a little money, O,
Some unforeseen misfortune still comes gen'rally upon me, O—
Mischance, mistake, or by neglect, or my good-natur'd folly, O—
But come what will, I've sworn it still, I'll ne'er be melancholy, O.

All you who follow wealth and power with unremitting ardour, O,
The more in this you look for bliss, you leave your view the farther, O:
Had you the wealth Potosi boasts, or nations to adore you, O,
A cheerful honest-hearted clown I will prefer before you, O.

John Barleycorn—A Ballad[1]

There was three kings into the east,
 Three kings both great and high,
And they hae sworn a solemn oath
 John Barleycorn should die.

They took a plough and plough'd him down,
 Put clods upon his head,
And they hae sworn a solemn oath
 John Barleycorn was dead.

But the cheerful Spring came kindly on,
 And show'rs began to fall;
John Barleycorn got up again,
 And sore surpris'd them all.

The sultry suns of Summer came,
 And he grew thick and strong,
His head weel arm'd wi' pointed spears,
 That no one should him wrong.

The sober Autumn enter'd mild,
 When he grew wan and pale;
His bending joints and drooping head
 Show'd he began to fail.

His colour sicken'd more and more,
 He faded into age;
And then his enemies began
 To show their deadly rage.

[1] This is partly composed on the plan of an old song known by the same name.—R.B.

They've taen a weapon, long and sharp,
    And cut him by the knee;
Then tied him fast upon a cart,
    Like a rogue for forgerie.

They laid him down upon his back,
    And cudgell'd him full sore;
They hung him up before the storm,
    And turned him o'er and o'er.

They filled up a darksome pit
    With water to the brim;
They heaved in John Barleycorn,
    There let him sink or swim.

They laid him out upon the floor,
    To work him farther woe;
And still, as signs of life appear'd,
    They toss'd him to and fro.

They wasted, o'er a scorching flame,
    The marrow of his bones;
But a miller us'd him worst of all,
    For he crush'd him between two stones.

And they hae taen his very heart's blood,
    And drank it round and round;
And still the more and more they drank,
    Their joy did more abound.

John Barleycorn was a hero bold,
    Of noble enterprise;
For if you do but taste his blood,
    'Twill make your courage rise.

'Twill make a man forget his woe;
    'Twill heighten all his joy;
'Twill make the widow's heart to sing,
    Tho' the tear were in her eye.

Then let us toast John Barleycorn,
    Each man a glass in hand;
And may his great posterity
    Ne'er fail in old Scotland!

THE DEATH AND DYING WORDS OF POOR MAILIE
The Author's Only Pet Yowe—An Unco Mournfu' Tale

As Mailie, an' her lambs thegither,
Was ae day nibbling on the tether,
Upon her cloot she coost a hitch,
An' owre she warsl'd in the ditch:

There, groaning, dying, she did lie,
When Hughoc[1] he cam doytin by.

Wi' glowrin een, and lifted han's
Poor Hughoc like a statue stan's;
He saw her days were near-hand ended,
But, wae's my heart! he could na mend it!
He gapéd wide, but naething spak,
At langth poor Mailie silence brak.

'O thou, whase lamentable face
Appears to mourn my woefu' case!
My dying words attentive hear,
An' bear them to my Master dear.

'Tell him, if e'er again he keep
As muckle gear as buy a sheep,
O, bid him never tie them mair,
Wi' wicked strings o' hemp or hair!
But ca' them out to park or hill,
An' let them wander at their will:
So, may his flock increase an' grow
To scores o' lambs, an' packs o' woo'!

'Tell him, he was a Master kin',
An' aye was guid to me an' mine;
An' now my dying charge I gie him,
My helpless lambs, I trust them wi' him.

'O, bid him save their harmless lives,
Frae dogs, an' tods, an' butchers' knives!
But gie them guid cow-milk their fill,
Till they be fit to fend themsel;
An' tent them duly, e'en an' morn,
Wi' taets o' hay an' ripps o' corn.

'An' may they never learn the gaets,
Of ither vile, wanrestfu' Pets!
To slink thro' slaps, an' reave an' steal
At stacks o' pease, or stocks o' kail!
So may they, like their great forbears,
For monie a year come thro' the shears:
So wives will gie them bits o' bread,
An' bairns greet for them when they're dead.

'My poor toop-lamb, my son an' heir,
O, bid him breed him up wi' care!
An' if he live to be a beast,
To pit some havins in his breast!
An' warn him—what I winna name—

[1] A neibour herd-callant, about three-fourths as wise as other folk.—R.B.

To stay content wi' yowes at hame;
An' no to rin an' wear his cloots,
Like ither menseless, graceless brutes.

'An' neist, my yowie, silly thing,
Gude keep thee frae a tether string!
O, may thou ne'er forgather up,
Wi' onie blastit, moorland toop;
But aye keep mind to moop an' mell,
Wi' sheep o' credit like thysel!

'And now, my bairns, wi' my last breath,
I lea'e my blessin wi' you baith:
An' when you think upo' your mither,
Mind to be kind to ane anither.

'Now, honest Hughoc, dinna fail,
To tell my master a' my tale;
An' bid him burn this cursèd tether,
An' for thy pains thou'se get my blather.'

This said, poor Mailie turn'd her head,
And clos'd her een amang the dead!

POOR MAILIE'S ELEGY

Lament in rhyme, lament in prose,
Wi' saut tears trickling down your nose;
Our Bardie's fate is at a close,
            Past a' remead!
The last, sad capestane o' his woes;
            Poor Mailie's dead!

It's no the loss o' warl's gear,
That could sae bitter draw the tear,
Or make our Bardie, dowie, wear
            The mourning weed:
He's lost a friend an' neebor dear
            In Mailie dead.

Thro' a' the town she trotted by him;
A lang half-mile she could descry him;
Wi' kindly bleat, when she did spy him,
            She ran wi' speed:
A friend mair faithfu' ne'er cam nigh him,
            Than Mailie dead.

I wat she was a sheep o' sense,
An' could behave hersel wi' mense:
I'll say't, she never brak a fence,
            Thro' thievish greed.
Our Bardie, lanely, keeps the spence
            Sin' Mailie's dead.

Or, if he wanders up the howe,
Her living image in her yowe,
Comes bleating till him, owre the knowe,
    For bits o' bread;
An' down the briny pearls rowe
    For Mailie dead.

She was nae get o' moorlan tips,
Wi' tawted ket an' hairy hips;
For her forbears were brought in ships,
    Frae 'yont the Tweed.
A bonnier fleesh ne'er cross'd the clips
    Than Mailie's dead.

Wae worth the man wha first did shape
That vile, wanchancie thing—a raep!
It maks guid fellows girn an' gape,
    Wi' chokin dread;
An' Robin's bonnet wave wi' crape
    For Mailie dead.

O, a' ye Bards on bonnie Doon!
An' wha on Ayr your chanters tune!
Come, join the melancholious croon
    O' Robin's reed!
His heart will never get aboon—
    His Mailie's dead!

THE RIGS O' BARLEY
Tune—Corn rigs are bonnie

Chorus: Corn rigs, an' barley rigs,
    An' corn rigs are bonnie:
I'll ne'er forget that happy night,
    Amang the rigs wi' Annie.

It was upon a Lammas night,
    When corn rigs are bonnie,
Beneath the moon's unclouded light,
    I held awa to Annie;
The time flew by, wi' tentless heed,
    Till, 'tween the late and early,
Wi' sma' persuasion she agreed
    To see me thro' the barley.

The sky was blue, the wind was still,
    The moon was shining clearly;
I set her down, wi' right good will,
    Amang the rigs o' barley:
I ken't her heart was a' my ain;
    I lov'd her most sincerely;

I kiss'd her owre and owre again,
    Amang the rigs o' barley.

I lock'd her in my fond embrace;
    Her heart was beating rarely:
My blessings on that happy place,
    Amang the rigs o' barley!
But by the moon and stars so bright,
    That shone that hour so clearly!
She aye shall bless that happy night
    Amang the rigs o' barley.

I hae been blythe wi' comrades dear;
    I hae been merry drinking;
I hae been joyfu' gath'rin gear;
    I hae been happy thinking:
But a' the pleasures e'er I saw,
    Tho' three times doubl'd fairly,
That happy night was worth them a',
    Amang the rigs o' barley.

SONG COMPOSED IN AUGUST
Tune—*I had a horse, I had nae mair*

Now westlin winds and slaught'ring guns
    Bring Autumn's pleasant weather;
And the moorcock springs on whirring wings
    Amang the blooming heather:
Now waving grain, wide o'er the plain,
    Delights the weary farmer;
And the moon shines bright, when I rove at night,
    To muse upon my charmer.

The partridge loves the fruitful fells,
    The plover loves the mountains;
The woodcock haunts the lonely dells,
    The soaring hern the fountains:
Thro' lofty groves the cushat roves,
    The path of man to shun it;
The hazel bush o'erhangs the thrush,
    The spreading thorn the linnet.

Thus ev'ry kind their pleasure find,
    The savage and the tender;
Some social join, and leagues combine,
    Some solitary wander:
Avaunt, away! the cruel sway,
    Tyrannic man's dominion;
The sportsman's joy, the murd'ring cry,
    The flutt'ring, gory pinion!

But, PEGGY dear, the ev'ning's clear,
    Thick flies the skimming swallow,
The sky is blue, the fields in view,
    All fading-green and yellow:
Come let us stray our gladsome way,
    And view the charms of Nature;
The rustling corn, the fruited thorn,
    And ev'ry happy creature.

We'll gently walk, and sweetly talk,
    Till the silent moon shine clearly;
I'll grasp thy waist, and, fondly prest,
    Swear how I love thee dearly:
Not vernal show'rs to budding flow'rs,
    Not Autumn to the farmer,
So dear can be as thou to me,
    My fair, my lovely charmer!

MY NANIE, O
Tune—*My Nonie, O*

Behind yon hills where Stinchar[1] flows,
    'Mang moors an' mosses many, O,
The wintry sun the day has clos'd,
    And I'll awa' to Nanie, O.

The westlin wind blaws loud an' shill;
The night's baith mirk and rainy, O;
But I'll get my plaid an' out I'll steal,
    An' o'er the hill to Nanie, O.

My Nanie's charming, sweet an' young;
    Nae artfu' wiles to win ye, O:
May ill befa' the flattering tongue
    That wad beguile my Nanie, O.

Her face is fair, her heart is true;
    As spotless as she's bonnie, O:
The op'ning gowan, wat wi' dew,
    Nae purer is than Nanie, O.

A country lad is my degree,
    An' few there be that ken me, O;
But what care I how few they be,
    I'm welcome aye to Nanie, O.

My riches a's my penny-fee,
    An' I maun guide it cannie, O;
But warl's gear ne'er troubles me,
    My thoughts are a'—my Nanie, O.

Our auld guidman delights to view
    His sheep an' kye thrive bonnie, O;
But I'm as blythe that hauds his pleugh
    An' has nae care but Nanie, O.

Come weel, come woe, I care na by;
    I'll tak what Heav'n will sen' me, O:
Nae ither care in life have I,
    But live an' love my Nanie, O.

[1] In 1792, Burns gave George Thomson liberty to adopt this song in his collection and to alter the name of the river to Lugar for the sake of euphony, observing, at the same time, that Girvan would better suit the idea intended.

GREEN GROW THE RASHES

Chorus: Green grow the rashes, O;
    Green grow the rashes, O;
The sweetest hours that e'er I spent,
    Were spent amang the lasses, O.

There's nought but care on ev'ry han',
    In ev'ry hour that passes, O:
What signifies the life o' man,
    An 'twere na for the lasses, O.

The warly race may riches chase,
    An' riches still may fly them, O;
An' tho' at last they catch them fast,
    Their hearts can ne'er enjoy them, O.

But gie me a cannie hour at e'en,
    My arms about my dearie, O;
An' warly cares, an' warly men,
    May a' gae tapsalteerie, O!

For you sae douce, ye sneer at this,
    Ye're nought but senseless asses, O:
The wisest man the warl' e'er saw,
    He dearly lov'd the lasses, O.

Auld Nature swears, the lovely dears
    Her noblest work she classes, O:
Her prentice han' she try'd on man,
    An' then she made the lasses, O.

WHA IS THAT AT MY BOWER DOOR
Tune—*I had a horse*

'Wha is that at my bower door?'
    'O wha is it but Findlay!'
'Then gae your gate, ye'se nae be here:'
    'Indeed maun I,' quo' Findlay;

'What mak ye, sae like a thief?'
    'O come and see,' quo' Findlay;
'Before the morn ye'll work mischief;'
    'Indeed will I,' quo' Findlay.

'Gif I rise and let you in'—
    'Let me in,' quo' Findlay;
'Ye'll keep me waukin wi' your din;'
    'Indeed will I,' quo' Findlay;

'In my bower if ye should stay'—
    'Let me stay,' quo' Findlay;
'I fear ye'll bide till break o' day;'
    'Indeed will I,' quo' Findlay.

'Here this night if ye remain'—
    'I'll remain,' quo' Findlay;
'I dread ye'll learn the gate again:'
    'Indeed will I,' quo' Findlay.

'What may pass within this bower'—
    'Let it pass,' quo' Findlay;
'Ye maun conceal till your last hour:'
    'Indeed will I,' quo' Findlay.

REMORSE—A FRAGMENT

Of all the numerous ills that hurt our peace—
That press the soul, or wring the mind with anguish,
Beyond comparison the worst are those
That to our folly, or our guilt we owe:
In every other circumstance, the mind
Has this to say—'It was no deed of mine;'
But when to all the evil of misfortune
This sting is added—'Blame thy foolish self!'
Or, worser far, the pangs of keen remorse,
The torturing, gnawing consciousness of guilt—
Of guilt, perhaps where we've involvéd others,
The young, the innocent, who fondly lov'd us;
Nay more, that very love their cause of ruin!
O burning hell! in all thy store of torments
There's not a keener lash!
Lives there a man so firm, who, while his heart

Feels all the bitter horrors of his crime,
Can reason down its agonising throbs:
And after proper purpose of amendment,
Can firmly force his jarring thoughts to peace?
O happy, happy, enviable man!
O glorious magnanimity of soul!

Epitaph On James Grieve, Laird Of Boghead, Tarbolton

Here lies Boghead amang the dead,
   In hopes to get salvation;
But if such as he in Heav'n may be,
   Then welcome, hail! damnation.

Epitaph On An Innkeeper In Tarbolton

Here lies 'mang ither useless matters,
A. Manson[1] wi' his endless clatters.

[1] Andrew Manson.

Epitaph On William Hood, Senior, In Tarbolton

Here Souter Hood in death does sleep;
   To hell if he's gane thither,
Satan, gie him thy gear to keep;
   He'll haud it weel thegither.

Epitaph On My Own Friend And My Father's Friend, William Muir In Tarbolton Mill

An honest man here lies at rest
As e'er God with his image blest!
The friend of man, the friend of truth;
The friend of age, and guide of youth:
Few hearts like his, with virtue warm'd,
Few heads with knowledge so inform'd:
If there's another world, he lives in bliss;
If there is none, he made the best of this.

Epitaph On My Ever Honoured Father

O ye whose cheek the tear of pity stains,
   Draw near with pious rev'rence and attend!
Here lie the loving husband's dear remains,
   The tender father and the gen'rous friend;
The pitying heart that felt for human woe,
   The dauntless heart that fear'd no human pride;
The friend of man—to vice alone a foe;
   'For ev'n his failings lean'd to virtue's side.'[1]

[1] Goldsmith.—R.B.

BALLAD ON THE AMERICAN WAR
Tune—*Killiecrankie*

When Guilford good our pilot stood
    An' did our hellim thraw, man,
Ae night, at tea, began a plea,
    Within America, man:
Then up they gat the maskin-pat,
    And in the sea did jaw, man;
An' did nae less, in full congress,
    Than quite refuse our law, man.

Then thro' the lakes Montgomery[1] takes,
    I wat he was na slaw, man;
Down Lowrie's Burn[2] he took a turn,
    And Carleton did ca', man:
But yet, whatreck, he, at Quebec,
    Montgomery-like[3] did fa', man,
Wi' sword in hand, before his band,
    Amang his en'mies a', man.

Poor Tammy Gage within a cage
    Was kept at Boston-ha',[4] man;
Till Willie Howe took o'er the knowe
    For Philadelphia, man;
Wi' sword an' gun he thought a sin
    Guid Christian bluid to draw, man;
But at New York, wi' knife an' fork,
    Sir Loin he hackéd sma',[5] man.

Burgoyne gaed up, like spur an' whip,
    Till Fraser brave did fa', man;
Then lost his way, ae misty day,
    In Saratoga shaw, man.[6]
Cornwallis fought as lang 's he dought,
    An' did the Buckskins claw, man;
But Clinton's glaive frae rust to save,
    He hung it to the wa', man.

[1] General Richard Montgomery invaded Canada, autumn 1775, and took Montreal, the British commander, Sir Guy Carleton, retiring before him. In an attack on Quebec he was less fortunate, being killed by a storm of grape-shot in leading on his men at Cape Diamond.
[2] Lowrie's Burn, a pseudonym for the St Lawrence.
[3] A passing compliment to the Montgomeries of Coilsfield, the patrons of Burns.
[4] General Gage, governor of Massachusetts, was cooped up in Boston by General Washington during the latter part of 1775 and early part of 1776. In consequence of this inefficiency, he was replaced in October of that year by General Howe.
[5] Alluding to a foray made by orders of Howe at Peekskill, March 1777, when a large quantity of cattle belonging to the Americans was destroyed.
[6] Alluding to the active operations of Lord Cornwallis in Virginia, in 1780, all of which ended, however, in his surrender of his army at Yorktown, October 1781, while vainly hoping for reinforcements from General Clinton at New York.

Then Montague, an' Guilford too,
    Began to fear a fa', man;
And Sackville dour, wha stood the stour,
    The German chief to thraw, man:
For Paddy Burke, like onie Turk,
    Nae mercy had at a', man;
An' Charlie Fox threw by the box,
    An' lows'd his tinkler jaw, man.

Then Rockingham took up the game,
    Till death did on him ca', man;
When Shelburne meek held up his cheek,
    Conform to gospel law, man:
Saint Stephen's boys, wi' jarring noise,
    They did his measures thraw, man;
For North an' Fox united stocks,
    An' bore him to the wa', man.[1]

Then clubs an' hearts were Charlie's cartes,
    He swept the stakes awa', man,
Till the diamond's ace, of Indian race,
    Led him a sair *faux pas*, man:[2]
The Saxon lads, wi' loud placads,
    On Chatham's boy did ca', man;
An' Scotland drew her pipe an' blew,
    'Up, Willie, waur them a', man!'

Behind the throne then Granville's gone,
    A secret word or twa, man;
While slee Dundas arous'd the class
    Be-north the Roman wa', man:
An' Chatham's wraith, in heav'nly graith,
    (Inspiréd Bardies saw, man),
Wi' kindling eyes, cry'd, 'Willie, rise!
    Would I hae fear'd them a', man?'

But, word an' blow, North, Fox, and Co.
    Gowff'd Willie like a ba', man,
Till Suthron raise, an' coost their claise
    Behind him in a raw, man:
An' Caledon threw by the drone,
    An' did her whittle draw, man;
An' swoor fu' rude, thro' dirt an' blood,
    To mak it guid in law, man.[3]

---

[1] Lord North's administration was succeeded by that of the Marquis of Rockingham, March 1782. At the death of the latter in the succeeding July, Lord Shelburne became prime minister and Charles James Fox resigned his secretaryship. Under Shelburne, peace was restored, January 1783. By the union of North and Fox, Shelburne was soon after forced to resign in favour of his rivals, the heads of the celebrated coalition.

[2] Fox's India Bill, by which his ministry was brought down, December 1783.

[3] In the new parliament called by Pitt, after his accession to office in the spring of 1784, amid the many new members brought in for his support, and that of the king's prerogative, there was an exceeding proportion from Scotland.

REPLY TO AN ANNOUNCEMENT BY JOHN RANKINE
That a Girl in his Neighbourhood was with Child to the Poet

I am a keeper of the law
In some sma' points, altho' not a';
Some people tell me gin I fa',
      Ae way or ither,
The breaking of ae point, tho' sma',
      Breaks a' thegither.

I hae been in for 't ance or twice,
And winna say o'er far for thrice;
Yet never met wi' that surprise
      That broke my rest;
But now a rumour's like to rise—
      A whaup's i' the nest!

EPISTLE TO JOHN RANKINE
Enclosing Some Poems

O rough, rude, ready-witted Rankine,
The wale o' cocks for fun an' drinkin!
There's monie godly folks are thinkin,
      Your *dreams*[1] and tricks
Will send you, Korah-like, a-sinkin
      Straught to auld Nick's.

Ye hae saw monie cracks an' cants,
And in your wicked, drucken rants,
Ye mak a devil o' the *saunts*,
      An' fill them fou;
And then their failings, flaws, an' wants,
      Are a' seen thro'.

Hypocrisy, in mercy spare it!
That *holy robe*, O dinna tear it!
Spare 't for their sakes, wha aften wear it—
      The lads in *black*;
But your curst wit, when it comes near it,
      Rives 't aff their back.

Think, wicked Sinner, wha ye're skaithing:
It's just the *Blue-gown* badge an' claithing
O' saunts; tak that, ye lea'e them naething
      To ken them by
Frae onie unregenerate heathen,
      Like you or I.

I've sent you here some rhyming ware,
A' that I bargain'd for, an' mair;

---

[1] A certain humorous dream of his was then making a noise in the countryside.—R.B.

Sae, when ye hae an hour to spare,
      I will expect,
Yon *sang* ye'll sen 't, wi' cannie care,
      And no neglect.

Tho' faith, sma' heart hae I to sing!
My muse dow scarcely spread her wing;
I've play'd mysel a bonnie *spring*,
      An' *danc'd* my fill!
I'd better gaen an' sair 't the king,
      At Bunker's Hill.

'Twas ae night lately, in my fun,
I gaed a rovin' wi' the gun,
An' brought a *paitrick* to the *grun'*,
      A bonnie *hen*;
And, as the twilight was begun,
      Thought nane wad ken.

The poor, wee thing was *little hurt*;
I *straikit* it a wee for sport,
Ne'er thinkin they wad fash me for 't;
      But, Deil-ma-care!
Somebody tells the *poacher-court*
      The hale affair.

Some auld, us'd hands had taen a note,
That *sic a hen* had got a *shot*;
I was suspected for the plot;
      I scorn'd to lie;
So gat the whissle o' my groat,
      An' pay't the *fee*.

But by my *gun*, o' guns the wale,
An' by my *pouther* an' my *hail*,
An' by my *hen*, an' by her *tail*,
      I vow an' swear!
The *game* shall pay, o'er muir an' *dale*,
      For this, niest year.

As soon 's the *clockin-time* is by,
An' the *wee powts* begun to cry,
Lord, I'se hae sporting by an' by
      For my *gowd guinea*,
Tho' I should herd the *buckskin kye*
      For 't, in Virginia!

Trowth, they had muckle for to blame!
'Twas neither broken wing nor limb,
But twa-three *draps* about the *wame*,
      Scarce thro' the *feathers*;

> An' baith a *yellow George* to claim,
> An' *thole* their *blethers*!

> It pits me ay as mad 's a hare;
> So I can rhyme nor write nae mair;
> But *pennyworths* again is fair,
> When time's expedient:
> Meanwhile I am, respected Sir,
> Your most obedient.

A Poet's Welcome To His Love-Begotten Daughter
The First Instance that entitled him to the Venerable Appellation of Father

> Thou's welcome, wean, mishanter fa' me,
> If thought of thee, or of thy mammy,
> Shall ever daunton me or awe me,
> My sweet wee lady!
> Or if I blush when thou shalt ca' me
> Ti-ta or daddy.

> Tho' now they ca' me fornicator,
> An' tease my name in kintry clatter,
> The mair they talk, I'm kent the better,
> E'en let them clash;
> An auld wife's tongue's a feckless matter
> To gie ane fash.

> Welcome! my bonnie, sweet, wee dochter,
> Tho' ye come here a wee unsought for,
> And tho' your comin' I hae fought for,
> Baith kirk and queir;
> Yet, by my faith, ye're no unwrought for,
> That I shall swear!

> Sweet fruit o' monie a merry dint,
> My funny toil is now a' tint,
> Sin' thou came to the warl' asklent,
> Which fools may scoff at;
> In my last plack thy part's be in 't
> The better ha'f o't.

> Tho' I should be the waur bestead,
> Thou's be as braw and bienly clad,
> And thy young years as nicely bred
> Wi' education,
> As onie brat o' wedlock's bed,
> In a' thy station.

> Wee image o' my bonnie Betty,
> I, fatherly, will kiss and daut thee,
> As dear an' near my heart I set thee
> Wi' as guid will

As a' the priests had seen me get thee
 That's out o' hell.

Lord grant that thou may ay inherit
Thy mither's person, grace an' merit,
An' thy poor, worthless daddy's spirit,
 Without his failins,
'Twill please me mair to see thee heir it,
 Than stockit mailens.

For if thou be what I wad hae thee,
And tak the counsel I shall gie thee,
I'll never rue my trouble wi' thee,
 The cost nor shame o't,
But be a loving father to thee,
 And brag the name o't.

ROB MOSSGIEL

O leave novels, ye Mauchline belles,
 Ye're safer at your spinning wheel;
Such witching books are baited hooks
 For rakish rooks like Rob Mossgiel;

Your fine Tom Jones and Grandisons,
 They make your youthful fancies reel;
They heat your brains, and fire your veins,
 And then you're prey for Rob Mossgiel.

Beware a tongue that's smoothly hung,
 A heart that warmly seems to feel;
That feeling heart but acts a part,
 'Tis rakish art in Rob Mossgiel.

The frank address, the soft caress,
 Are worse than poisoned darts of steel;
The frank address, and politesse,
 Are all finesse in Rob Mossgiel.

THE MAUCHLINE LADY—A FRAGMENT
Tune—*I had a horse, and I had nae mair*

When first I came to Stewart Kyle,[1]
 My mind it was na steady;
Where'er I gaed, where'er I rade,
 A mistress still I had aye.

But when I came roun' by Mauchline toun,
 Not dreadin onie body,
My heart was caught, before I thought,
 And by a Mauchline lady.[2]

[1] That part of the central district of Ayrshire between the Rivers Irvine and Ayr. Burns was originally of King Kyle, between the Ayr and the Doon.
[2] Jean Armour.

MY GIRL SHE'S AIRY—A FRAGMENT
Tune—*Black Joke*

My girl[1] she's airy, she's buxom and gay;
Her breath is as sweet as the blossoms in May;
 A touch of her lips it ravishes quite:
She's always good-natur'd, good-humour'd and free;
She dances, she glances, she smiles with a glee;
 Her eyes are the lightenings of joy and delight;

[1] Elizabeth Paton with whom Burns had an affair in 1784

Her slender neck, her handsome waist,
Her hair well buckl'd, her stays well lac'd,
    Her taper white leg with an et and a c
For her a, b, e, d, and her c, u, n, t,
    And oh, for the joys of a long winter night!

The Belles Of Mauchline

In Mauchline there dwells six proper young belles,
    The pride of the place and its neighbourhood a';
Their carriage and dress, a stranger would guess,
    In Lon'on or Paris, they'd gotten it a'.
Miss Miller is fine, Miss Markland's divine,
    Miss Smith she has wit, and Miss Betty is braw:
There's beauty and fortune to get wi' Miss Morton,
    But Armour's[1] the jewel for me o' them a'.

[1] Jean Armour.

Epitaph On A Noisy Polemic

Below thir stanes lie Jamie's[1] banes;
    O Death, it's my opinion,
Thou ne'er took such a bleth'rin bitch
    Into thy dark dominion!

[1] James Humphrey, a fluent controversialist on matters beyond his understanding.

Epitaph On A Henpecked Country Squire

As father Adam first was fool'd,
    A case that's still too common,
Here lies a man a woman rul'd,
    The devil rul'd the woman.

Epigram On Said Occasion

O Death, had'st thou but spar'd his life,
    Whom we this day lament!
We freely wad exchang'd the *wife*,
    And a' been weel content.
Ev'n as he is, cauld in his graff,
    The *swap* we yet will do 't;
Tak thou the carlin's carcase aff,
    Thou'se get the *saul o' boot*.

Another

One Queen Artemisia, as old stories tell,
When depriv'd of her husband she lovéd so well,
In respect for the love and affection he show'd her,
She reduc'd him to dust and she drank up the powder.

But Queen Netherplace, of a diff'rent complexion,
When call'd on to order the fun'ral direction,
Would have *eat* her dead lord, on a slender pretence,
Not to show her respect but—*to save the expense*.

ON TAM THE CHAPMAN

As Tam the chapman on a day,
Wi' Death forgather'd by the way,
Weel pleas'd, he greets a wight sae famous,
And Death was nae less pleas'd wi' Thomas,
Wha cheerfully lays down his pack,
And there blaws up a hearty crack:
His social, friendly, honest heart
Sae tickled Death, they couldna part;
Sae after viewing knives and garters,
Death taks him hame to gie him quarters.

LINES ADDRESSED TO JOHN RANKINE

Ae day, as Death, that gruesome carl,
Was driving to the tither warl',
A mixie-maxie, motley squad,
And monie a guilt-bespotted lad;
Black gowns of each denomination,
And thieves of every rank and station,
From him that wears the star and garter,
To him that wintles in a halter:
Asham'd himsel' to see the wretches,
He mutters, glow'ring at the bitches:
'By God I'll not be seen behint them,
Nor 'mang the sp'ritual core present them,
Without, at least, ae honest man,
To grace this damn'd infernal clan!'
By Adamhill a glance he threw,
'Lord God!' quoth he, 'I have it now;
There's just the man I want, i' faith!'
And quickly stoppit Rankine's breath.

THREE LINES TO THE SAME
Written with Directions to be delivered to Rankine after the Poet's Death

He who of Rankine sang, lies stiff and dead,
And a green grassy hillock hides his head;
Alas! Alas! a devilish change indeed.

MAN WAS MADE TO MOURN—A DIRGE

When chill November's surly blast
Made fields and forests bare,
One ev'ning, as I wander'd forth
Along the banks of Ayr,

I spied a man, whose agéd step
  Seem'd weary, worn with care;
His face was furrow'd o'er with years,
  And hoary was his hair.

'Young stranger, whither wand'rest thou?'
  Began the rev'rend sage;
'Does thirst of wealth thy step constrain
  Or youthful pleasure's rage?
Or haply, prest with cares and woes,
  Too soon thou hast began
To wander forth, with me to mourn
  The miseries of man.

'The sun that overhangs yon moors,
  Out-spreading far and wide,
Where hundreds labour to support
  A haughty lordling's pride;
I've seen yon weary winter-sun
  Twice forty times return;
And ev'ry time has added proofs
  That man was made to mourn.

'O man! while in thy early years,
  How prodigal of time!
Mispending all thy precious hours,
  Thy glorious, youthful prime!
Alternate follies take the sway;
  Licentious passions burn;
Which tenfold force gives Nature's law.
  That man was made to mourn.

'Look not alone on youthful prime,
  Or manhood's active might;
Man then is useful to his kind,
  Supported is his right:
But see him on the edge of life,
  With cares and sorrows worn,
Then Age and Want—O! ill-match'd pair!
  Show man was made to mourn.

'A few seem favourites of fate,
  In pleasure's lap caresst;
Yet, think not all the rich and great
  Are likewise truly blest.
But O! what crowds in ev'ry land,
  All wretched and forlorn,
Thro' weary life this lesson learn,
  That man was made to mourn!

'Many and sharp the num'rous ills
  Inwoven with our frame!

More pointed still we make ourselves,
 Regret, remorse and shame!
And man, whose heav'n-erected face
 The smiles of love adorn,
Man's inhumanity to man
 Makes countless thousands mourn!

'See yonder poor, o'erlabour'd wight,
 So abject, mean and vile,
Who begs a brother of the earth
 To give him leave to toil;
And see his lordly fellow-worm
 The poor petition spurn,
Unmindful, tho' a weeping wife,
 And helpless offspring mourn.

'If I'm design'd yon lordling's slave,
 By Nature's law design'd,
Why was an independent wish
 E'er planted in my mind?
If not, why am I subject to
 His cruelty or scorn?
Or why has man the will and pow'r
 To make his fellow mourn?

'Yet, let not this too much, my son,
 Disturb thy youthful breast:
This partial view of humankind
 Is surely not the last!
The poor, oppresséd, honest man
 Had never, sure, been born,
Had there not been some recompense
 To comfort those that mourn!

'O Death! the poor man's dearest friend,
 The kindest and the best!
Welcome the hour my agéd limbs
 Are laid with thee at rest!
The great, the wealthy fear thy blow,
 From pomp and pleasure torn;
But, O! a blest relief for those
 That weary-laden mourn!'

THE TWA HERDS, OR THE HOLY TULYIE
An Unco Mournfu' Tale

'Blockheads with reason wicked wits abhor,
But fool with fool is barbarous civil war.'—Pope.

O a' ye pious godly flocks,
 Weel fed on pastures orthodox,
Wha now will keep you frae the fox
   Or worrying tykes?

Or wha will tent the waifs an' crocks,
    About the dykes?

The twa best herds in a' the wast,
The e'er ga'e gospel horn a blast
These five an' twenty simmers past—
    Oh, dool to tell!
Hae had a bitter black out-cast
    Atween themsel'.

O, Moodie, man, an' wordy Russell,[1]
How could you raise so vile a bustle,
Ye'll see how New-Light herds[2] will whistle,
    An' think it fine!
The Lord's cause ne'er gat sic a twistle,
    Sin' I hae min'.

O, sirs! whae'er wad hae expeckit
Your duty ye wad sae negleckit?
Ye wha were ne'er by lairds respeckit
    To wear the plaid,
But by the brutes themselves eleckit,
    To be their guide!

What flock wi' Moodie's flock could rank?—
Sae hale and hearty every shank!
Nae poison'd sour Arminian stank
    He let them taste;
Frae Calvin's well, aye clear, they drank—
    O, sic a feast!

The thummart, wil'cat, brock, and tod,
Weel kenn'd his voice thro' a' the wood,
He smelt their ilka hole and road,
    Baith out and in;
And weel he liked to shed their bluid,
    And sell their skin.

What herd like Russell tell'd his tale?
His voice was heard through muir and dale,[3]
He kenn'd the Lord's sheep, ilka tail,
    O'er a' the height;
And saw gin they were sick or hale,
    At the first sight.

He fine a mangy sheep could scrub,
Or nobly fling the gospel club,

---

[1] The Rev. Mr Moodie of Riccarton and the Rev. John Russell of Kilmarnock, two Calvinist pastors, friends for many years, who fell out after a practical joke.
[2] *New-light* is a cant phrase in the West of Scotland for those religious opinions which Dr Taylor of Norwich has defended so strenuously.—R.B.
[3] Russell's voice could be heard a mile off.

And New-Light herds could nicely drub
    Or pay their skin;
Could shake them o'er the burning dub,
    Or heave them in.

Sic twa—O! do I live to see't?—
Sic famous twa should disagreet,
And names, like 'villain', 'hypocrite',
    Ilk ither gi'en;
While New-Light herds wi' laughin' spite,
    Say neither's liein!

A' ye wha tent the gospel fauld,
There's Duncan[1] deep, an' Peebles[2] shaul,
But chiefly thou, apostle Auld,[3]
    We trust in thee,
That thou wilt work them, het and cauld,
    Till they agree.

Consider, sirs, how we're beset;
There's scarce a new herd that we get,
But comes frae 'mang that cursed set
    I winna name;
I hope frae heav'n to see them yet
    In fiery flame.

Dalrymple[4] has been lang our fae,
M'Gill[5] has wrought us meikle wae,
An' that curs'd rascal ca'd M'Quhae,[6]
    And baith the Shaws,[7]
That aft hae made us black and blae,
    Wi' vengefu' paws.

Auld Wodrow[8], lang has hatch'd mischief;
We thought ay death wad bring relief;
But he has gotten, to our grief,
    Ane to succeed him[9]—
A chield wha'll soundly buff our beef;
    I meikle dread him.

And monie a ane that I could tell,
Wha fain wad openly rebel,
Forby turn-coats amang oursel'—
    There's Smith[10] for ane—
I doubt he's but a grey nick quill,
    And that ye'll fin'.

[1] Dr Robert Duncan of Dundonald.
[2] Rev. William Peebles of Newton-on-Ayr.
[3] Rev. William Auld of Mauchline.
[4] Rev. Dr Dalrymple of Ayr.
[5] Rev. William M'Gill, colleague of Dr Dalrymple.
[6] Minister of St Quivox.
[7] Dr Andrew Shaw of Craigie and Dr David Shaw of Coylton.
[8] Dr Peter Wodrow of Tarbolton.
[9] Rev. John M'Math, a young assistant and successor to Wodrow.
[10] Rev. George Smith of Galston.

O! a' ye flocks o'er a' the hills,
By mosses, meadows, moors, and fells,
Come, join your counsel and your skills
    To cowe the lairds,
And get the brutes the power themsel's,
    To choose their herds.

Then Orthodoxy yet may prance,
And Learning in a woody dance,
An' that fell cur ca'd Common Sense,
    That bites sae sair,
Be banished o'er the sea to France:
    Let him bark there.

Then Shaw's and D'rymple's eloquence,
M'Gill's close nervous excellence,
M'Quhae's pathetic manly sense,
    And gude M'Math,
Wi' Smith, wha through the heart can glance,
    May a' pack aff.

EPISTLE TO DAVIE, A BROTHER POET[1]
January

While winds frae aff Ben Lomond blaw,
And bar the doors wi' driving snaw,
    An' hing us owre the ingle,
I set me down to pass the time,
And spin a verse or twa o' rhyme,
    In hamely, westlin jingle.
While frosty winds blaw in the drift,
    Ben to the chimla lug,
I grudge a wee the great-folk's gift,
    That live sae bien an' snug:
      I tent less, and want less
        Their roomy fire-side;
      But hanker, and canker,
        To see their cursed pride.

It's hardly in a body's pow'r
To keep, at times, frae being sour,
    To see how things are shar'd;
How best o' chiels are whyles in want,
While coofs on countless thousands rant,
    And ken na how to wair't:
But, Davie lad, ne'er fash your head,
    Tho' we hae little gear,

---

[1] David Sillar, also the son of a small farmer. He printed a volume of rhymes that appeared in 1789 and was helped by Burns in obtaining subscribers. He eventually became a schoolmaster, councillor and magistrate in Irvine. The poem shows Burns in the full blossom of attachment to his Jean. It was not the fate of Sillar to obtain the hand of his 'Meg' referred to in the Epistle. She was Margaret Orr, a servant at Stair House.

We're fit to win our daily bread,
  As lang's we're hale and fier:
    'Mair spier na, nor fear na,'[1]
      Auld age ne'er mind a feg;
    The last o't, the warst o't
      Is only but to beg.

To lie in kilns and barns at e'en,
When banes are craz'd, and bluid is thin,
  Is doubtless, great distress!
Yet then content could make us blest;
Ev'n then, sometimes, we'd snatch a taste
  Of truest happiness.
The honest heart that's free frae a'
  Intended fraud or guile,
However Fortune kick the ba',
  Has ay some cause to smile;
    And mind still, you'll find still,
      A comfort this nae sma';
    Nae mair then we'll care then,
      Nae farther can we fa'.

What tho', like commoners of air,
We wander out, we know not where,
  But either house or hal'?
Yet nature's charms, the hills and woods,
The sweeping vales, and foaming floods,
  Are free alike to all.
In days when daisies deck the ground,
  And blackbirds whistle clear,
With honest joy our hearts will bound,
  To see the coming year:
    On braes when we please then,
      We'll sit and sowth a tune;
    Syne rhyme till't we'll time till't,
      And sing't when we hae done.

It's no in titles nor in rank;
It's no in wealth like Lon'on bank,
  To purchase peace and rest;
It's no in makin muckle, mair:
It's no in books; it's no in Lear,
  To make us truly blest:
If happiness hae not her seat
  And centre in the breast,
We may be wise, or rich, or great,
  But never can be blest:
    Nae treasures, nor pleasures
      Could make us happy lang;
    The heart ay's the part ay
      That makes us right or wrang.

[1] Ramsay.—R.B.

Think ye, that sic as *you* and *I*,
Wha drudge and drive thro' wet and dry,
　　Wi' never-ceasing toil;
Think ye, are we less blest than they,
Wha scarcely tent us in their way,
　　As hardly worth their while?
Alas! how aft in haughty mood,
　　God's creatures they oppress!
Or else, neglecting a' that's guid,
　　They riot in excess!
　　　　Baith careless and fearless
　　　　　　Of either heaven or hell;
　　　　Esteeming and deeming
　　　　　　It's a' an idle tale!

Then let us cheerfu' acquiesce;
Nor make our scanty pleasures less,
　　By pining at our state:
And, ev'n should misfortunes come,
I, here wha sit, hae met wi' some,
　　An's thankfu' for them yet.
They gie the wit of age to youth;
　　They let us ken oursel;
They make us see the naked truth,
　　The *real* guid and ill:
　　　　Tho' losses, and crosses,
　　　　　　Be lessons right severe,
　　　　There's wit there, ye'll get there,
　　　　　　Ye'll find nae other where.

But tent me, Davie, Ace o' Hearts!
(To say aught less wad wrang the cartes,
　　And flatt'ry I detest)
This life has joys for you and I;
And joys that riches ne'er could buy,
　　And joys the very best.
There's a' the pleasures o' the heart,
　　The lover and the frien';
Ye hae your Meg, your dearest part,
　　And I my darling Jean!
　　　　It warms me, it charms me,
　　　　　　To mention but her name:
　　　　It heats me, it beets me,
　　　　　　An' sets me a' on flame!

O all ye Pow'rs who rule above!
O Thou, whose very self art *love*!
　　Thou know'st my words sincere!
The life blood streaming thro' my heart,
Or my more dear immortal part,
　　Is not more fondly dear!

When heart-corroding care and grief
  Deprive my soul of rest,
Her dear idea brings relief,
  And solace to my breast.
    Thou Being, All-seeing,
      O hear my fervent pray'r!
    Still take her, and make her
      Thy most peculiar care!

All hail! ye tender feelings dear!
The smile of love, the friendly tear,
  The sympathetic glow!
Long since, this world's thorny ways
Had number'd out my weary days,
  Had it not been for you!
Fate still has blest me with a friend,
  In ev'ry care and ill;
And oft a more endearing band—
  A tie more tender still.
    It lightens, it brightens
      The tenebrific scene,
    To meet with, and greet with,
      My Davie, or my Jean!

O, how that *name* inspires my style!
The words come skelpan, rank and file,
  Amaist before I ken!
The ready measure rins as fine,
As Phoebus and the famous Nine
  Were glowran owre my pen.
My spavet Pegasus will limp,
  Till ance he's fairly het;
And then he'll hilch, and stilt, and jimp,
  And rin an unco fit:
    But least then, the beast then,
      Should rue this hasty ride,
    I'll light now, and dight now
      His sweaty, wizen'd hide.

HOLY WILLIE'S PRAYER

'And send the godly in a pet to pray.'—Pope.

Argument—Holy Willie was a rather oldish bachelor elder, in the parish of Mauchline, and much and justly famed for that polemical chattering, which ends in tippling orthodoxy, and for that spiritualised bawdry which refines to liquorish devotion. In a sessional process with a gentleman in Mauchline—a Mr Gavin Hamilton—*Holy Willie* and his priest, Father Auld, after full hearing in the presbytery of Ayr, came off but second best; owing partly to the oratorical powers of Mr Robert Aiken, Mr Hamilton's counsel; but chiefly to Mr Hamilton's being one of the most irreproachable and truly respectable characters in the county. On losing the process, the muse overheard him [Holy Willie] at his devotions, as follows:—

O Thou that in the heavens dost dwell!
Wha, as it pleases best Thysel',
Sends ane to heaven and ten to hell,
   A' for Thy glory,
And no' for onie gude or ill
    They've done before Thee!

I bless and praise Thy matchless might,
When thousands Thou hast left in night,
That I am here before Thy sight,
   For gifts and grace,
A burning and a shining light
    To a' this place.

What was I, or my generation,
That I should get sic exaltation?
I, wha deserv'd most just damnation
   For broken laws,
Sax thousand years ere my creation,
    Thro' Adam's cause!

When from my mither's womb I fell,
Thou might hae plung'd me deep in hell,
To gnash my gums, and weep and wail,
   In burnin' lakes,
Where damnéd devils roar and yell,
    Chain'd to their stakes.

Yet I am here, a chosen sample,
To show Thy grace is great and ample;
I'm here, a pillar o' Thy temple,
   Strong as a rock,
A guide, a buckler and example
    To a' Thy flock.

O Lord, Thou kens what zeal I bear,
When drinkers drink and swearers swear,
And singin' there and dancin' here
   Wi' great an' sma';
For I am keepet by Thy fear,
    Free frae them a'.

But yet, O Lord! confess I must—
At times I'm fash'd wi' fleshly lust;
And sometimes too, in wardly trust,
   Vile self gets in;
But Thou remembers we are dust,
    Defil'd wi' sin.

O Lord! yestreen, Thou kens, wi' Meg—
Thy pardon I sincerely beg!

O! may 't ne'er be a livin' plague
    To my dishonour!
An' I'll ne'er lift a lawless leg
    Again upon her.

Besides, I farther maun allow,
Wi' Leezie's lass, three times I trow;
But Lord, that Friday I was fou,
    When I came near her;
Or else, Thou kens, Thy servant true
    Wad never steer her.

Maybe Thou lets this fleshly thorn
Buffet Thy servant e'en and morn,
Lest he o'er proud and high should turn,
    That he's sae gifted;
If sae, Thy han' maun e'en be borne,
    Until Thou lift it.

Lord, bless Thy chosen in this place,
For here Thou hast a chosen race:
But God, confound their stubborn face
    And blast their name,
Wha bring Thy elders to disgrace
    An' open shame.

Lord, mind Gaw'n Hamilton's deserts;
He drinks and swears an' plays at cartes,
Yet has sae monie takin' arts,
    Wi' great and sma',
Frae God's ain priest the people's hearts
    He steals awa'.

An' when we chasten'd him therefore,
Thou kens how he bred sic a splore,
As set the warld in a roar
    O' laughin' at us—
Curse Thou his basket and his store,
    Kail an' potatoes!

Lord, hear my earnest cry and pray'r,
Against that Presbyt'ry of Ayr!
Thy strong right hand, Lord, make it bare
    Upo' their heads!
Lord, visit them, and dinna spare,
    For their misdeeds!

O Lord, my God, that glib-tongu'd Aiken,
My very heart and flesh are quaking,
To think how I sat sweating, shaking,
    And pish'd wi' dread,

While he wi' hingin' lip and snakin',
  Held up his head.

Lord, in Thy day of vengeance try him!
Lord, visit them that did employ him!
And pass not in Thy mercy by them,
  Nor hear their prayer,
But for Thy people's sake, destroy them,
  And dinna spare!

But, Lord, remember me and mine
Wi' mercies temporal and divine,
That I for grace and gear may shine,
  Excell'd by nane,
And a' the glory shall be Thine,
  Amen, Amen!

EPITAPH ON HOLY WILLIE

Here Holy Willie's sair-worn clay
  Taks up its last abode;
His saul has ta'en some ither way,
  I fear, the left-hand road.

Stop! there he is, as sure's a gun,
  Poor, silly body, see him;
Nae wonder he's as black 's the grun',
  Observe wha's standing wi' him.

Your brunstane devilship, I see,
  Has got him there before ye;
But haud your nine-tail cat a wee,
  Till ance you've heard my story.

Your pity I will not implore,
  For pity ye have nane;
Justice, alas! has gi'en him o'er,
  And mercy's day is gane.

But hear me, sir, deil as ye are,
  Look something to your credit;
A coof like him wad stain your name,
  If it were kent ye did it.

DEATH AND DOCTOR HORNBOOK[1]
A True Story

Some books are lies frae end to end,
And some great lies were never penn'd:

---

[1] Based on John Wilson, parish school teacher at Tarbolton, who eked out his income by keeping a grocery shop where he also sold drugs and gave 'medical advice gratis'.

Ev'n ministers they hae been kenn'd,
    In holy rapture,
A rousing whid, at times, to vend,
    And nail 't wi' Scripture.

But this that I am gaun to tell,
Which lately on a night befell,
Is just as true 's the Deil's in hell
    Or Dublin city:
That e'er he nearer comes oursel
    'S a muckle pity.

The clachan yill had made me canty,
I was na fou but just had plenty;
I stacher'd whyles, but yet took tent ay
    To free the ditches;
An' hillocks, stanes an' bushes kenn'd ay
    Frae ghaists an' witches.

The rising moon began to glow'r
The distant Cumnock hills out-owre:
To count her horns, wi' a' my pow'r,
    I set mysel,
But whether she had three or four,
    I cou'd na tell.

I was come round about the hill,
And todlin down on Willie's mill,
Setting my staff wi' a' my skill,
    To keep me sicker;
Tho' leeward whyles, against my will,
    I took a bicker.

I there wi' Something does forgather,
That pat me in an eerie swither;
An awfu' scythe, out-owre ae shouther,
    Clear-dangling, hang;
A three-tae'd leister on the ither
    Lay, large an' lang.

Its stature seem'd lang Scotch ells twa,
The queerest shape that e'er I saw,
For fient a wame it had ava,
    And then its shanks,
They were as thin, as sharp an' sma'
    As cheeks o' branks.

'Guid-een,' quo' I; 'Friend! hae ye been mawin,
When ither folk are busy sawin!'[1]

[1] This recontre happened in seed-time, 1785.—R.B.

It seem'd to mak a kind o' stan'
   But naething spak;
At length, says I, 'Friend! whare ye gaun?
   Will ye go back?'

It spak right howe—'My name is Death,
But be na fley'd.'—Quoth I, 'Guid faith,
Ye're maybe come to stap my breath;
   But tent me, billie;
I red ye weel, tak care o' skaith
   See, there's a gully!'

'Gudeman,' quo' he, 'put up your whittle,
I'm no design'd to try its mettle;
But if I did, I wad be kittle
   To be mislear'd;
I wad na mind it, no that spittle
   Outowre my beard.'

'Weel, weel!' says I, 'a bargain be 't;
Come, gie's your hand, an' sae we're gree 't;
We'll ease our shanks an' tak a seat—
   Come, gie's your news;
This while ye hae been monie a gate,
   At monie a house.'[1]

'Ay, ay!' quo' he, an' shook his head,
'It's e'en a lang, lang time indeed
Sin' I began to nick the thread
   An' choke the breath:
Folk maun do something for their bread,
   An' sae maun Death.

'Sax thousand years are near-hand fled
Sin' I was to the butching bred,
And monie a scheme in vain's been laid,
   To stap or scar me;
Till ane Hornbook's[2] ta'en up the trade,
   And faith! he'll waur me.

'Ye ken Jock Hornbook i' the clachan,
Deil mak his king's-hood in a spleuchan!
He's grown sae weel acquaint wi' Buchan,[3]
   And ither chaps,
The weans haud out their fingers laughin,
   And pouk my hips.

[1] An epidemical fever was then raging in that country.—R.B.
[2] This gentleman, Dr Hornbook, is professionally a brother of the sovereign order of the ferula; but, by intuition and inspiration, is at once an apothecary, surgeon, and physician.—R.B.
[3] Buchan's *Domestic Medicine*.—R.B. Dr William Buchan died in 1805.

'See, here's a scythe and there's a dart,
They hae pierc'd monie a gallant heart;
But Doctor Hornbook, wi' his art
      And cursèd skill,
Has made them baith no worth a fart,
      Damn'd haet they'll kill!

''Twas but yestreen, nae farther gane,
I threw a noble throw at ane;
Wi' less, I'm sure, I've hundreds slain;
      But deil-ma-care!
It just play'd dirl on the bane,
      But did nae mair.

'Hornbook was by, wi' ready art,
And had sae fortify'd the part
That when I lookèd to my dart,
      It was sae blunt,
Fient haet o't wad hae pierc'd the heart
      Of a kail-runt.

'I drew my scythe in sic a fury,
I near-hand cowpit wi' my hurry,
But yet the bauld Apothecary
      Withstood the shock;
I might as weel hae tried a quarry
      O' hard whin rock.

'Ev'n them he canna get attended,
Altho' their face he ne'er had kend it,
Just shite in a kail-blade, and send it,
      As soon 's he smells 't,
Baith their disease, and what will mend it,
      At once he tells 't.

'And then a' doctor's saws and whittles,
Of a' dimensions, shapes an' mettles,
A' kinds o' boxes, mugs an' bottles,
      He's sure to hae;
Their Latin names as fast he rattles
      As A B C.

'Calces o' fossils, earths and trees;
True sal-marinum o' the seas;
The farina of beans and pease,
      He has't in plenty;
Aqua-fontis, what you please,
      He can content ye.

'Forbye some new, uncommon weapons,
Urinus spiritus of capons;

Or mite-horn shavings, filings, scrapings,
        Distill'd *per se*;
Sal-alkali o' midge-tail clippings,
        And monie mae.'

'Waes me for Johnie Ged's[1] Hole now,'
Quoth I, 'if that thae news be true!
His braw calf-ward whare gowans grew,
        Sae white an' bonnie,
Nae doubt they'll rive it wi' the plew;
        They'll ruin Johnie!'

The creature grain'd an eldritch laugh,
And says, 'Ye needna yoke the pleugh,
Kirkyards will soon be till'd eneugh,
        Tak ye nae fear:
They'll a' be trench'd wi' monie a sheugh,
        In twa-three year.

'Whare I kill'd ane, a fair strae-death,
By loss o' blood or want of breath,
This night I'm free to tak my aith,
        That Hornbook's skill
Has clad a score i' their last claith,
        By drap and pill.

'An honest wabster to his trade,
Whase wife's twa nieves were scarce weel-bred
Gat tippence-worth to mend her head,
        When it was sair;
The wife slade cannie to her bed
        But ne'er spak mair.

'A countra laird had ta'en the batts,
Or some curmurring in his guts,
His only son for Hornbook sets
        And pays him well:
The lad, for twa guid gimmer-pets,
        Was laird himsel.

'A bonnie lass—ye kend her name—
Some ill-brewn drink had hov'd her wame;
She trusts hersel, to hide the shame,
        In Hornbook's care;
Horn sent her aff to her lang hame,
        To hide it there.

'That's just a swatch o' Hornbook's way;
Thus goes he on from day to day,

[1] The grave-digger.—R.B.

Thus does he poison, kill an' slay,
      An' 's weel paid for 't;
Yet stops me o' my lawfu' prey,
      Wi' his damn'd dirt:

'But, hark! I'll tell you of a plot,
Tho' dinna ye be speakin o' 't;
I'll nail the self-conceited sot,
      As dead 's a herrin;
Neist time we meet, I'll wad a groat,
      He gets his fairin!'

But just as he began to tell,
The auld kirk-hammer strak the bell
Some wee short hour ayont the *twal*,
      Which rais'd us baith:
I took the way that pleas'd mysel,
      And sae did Death.

EPISTLE TO JOHN LAPRAIK,
An Old Scottish Bard—1 April 1785

While briers an' woodbines budding green,
An' paitricks scraichin loud at e'en,
And morning poossie whiddan seen,
      Inspire my Muse,
This freedom, in an *unknown* frien',
      I pray excuse.

On Fastene'en we had a rockin,
To ca' the crack and weave our stockin;
And there was muckle fun and jokin,
      Ye need na doubt;
At length we had a hearty yokin
      At *sang about*.

There was ae *sang*, amang the rest,
Aboon them a' it pleas'd me best,
That some kind husband had addrest
      To some sweet wife;
It thirl'd the heart-strings thro' the breast,
      A' to the life.

I've scarce heard ought describ'd sae weel,
What gen'rous, manly bosoms feel;
Thought I, 'Can this be *Pope*, or *Steele*,
      Or *Beattie*'s wark?'
They tauld me 'twas an odd kind chiel
      About *Muirkirk*.

It pat me fidgin-fain to hear 't,
An' sae about him there I speir 't;

Then a' that kent him round declar'd
      He had *ingine*;
That nane excell'd it, few cam near 't,
      It was sae fine:

That set him to a pint of ale,
An' either douce or merry tale,
Or rhymes an' sangs he'd made himsel,
      Or witty catches—
'Tween Inverness and Teviotdale,
      He had few matches.

Then up I gat an' swoor an aith,
Tho' I should pawn my pleugh an' graith,
Or die a cadger pownie's death,
      At some dyke-back,
A *pint* an' *gill* I'd gie them *baith*,
      To hear your crack.

But first an' foremost, I should tell,
Amaist as soon as I could spell,
I to the *crambo-jingle* fell,
      Tho' rude an' rough—
Yet crooning to a body's sel,
      Does weel eneugh.

I am nae *poet*, in a sense;
But just a *rhymer* like by chance,
An' hae to learning nae pretence;
      Yet, what the matter?
Whene'er my Muse does on me glance,
      I jingle at her.

Your critic-folk may cock their nose,
And say, 'How can you e'er propose,
You wha ken hardly *verse* frae *prose*,
      To mak a *sang*?'
But by your leaves, my learnéd foes,
      Ye're maybe wrang.

What's a' your jargon o' your schools—
Your Latin names for horns an' stools?
If honest Nature made you *fools*,
      What sairs your grammars?
Ye'd better taen up *spades* and *shools*,
      Or *knappin-hammers*.

A set o' dull, conceited hashes
Confuse their brains in *college classes*!
They *gang in* stirks, and *come out* asses,
      Plain truth to speak;

An' syne they think to climb Parnassus
      By dint o' Greek!

Gie me ae spark o' Nature's fire,
That's a' the learning I desire;
Then tho' I drudge thro' dub an' mire
      At pleugh or cart,
My Muse, tho' hamely in attire,
      May touch the heart.

O for a spunk o' ALLAN's glee,
Or FERGUSSON's the bauld an' slee,
Or bright LAPRAIK's, my friend to be,
      If I can hit it!
That would be *lear* eneugh for me,
      If I could get it.

Now, Sir, if ye hae friends enow,
Tho' *real friends*, I b'lieve, are few;
Yet, if your catalogue be fu',
      I'se no insist:
But gif ye want ae friend that's true,
      I'm on your list.

I winna blaw about *mysel*,
As ill I like my fauts to tell;
But friends an' folk that wish me well,
      They sometimes roose me;
Tho' I maun own, as monie still,
      As far abuse me.

There's ae *wee faut* they whiles lay to me,
I like the lasses—Gude forgie me!
For monie a plack they wheedle frae me
      At dance or fair:
Maybe some *ither thing* they gie me,
      They weel can spare.

But MAUCHLINE Race or MAUCHLINE Fair,
I should be proud to meet you there;
We'se gie ae night's discharge to *care*,
      If we forgather;
An' hae a swap o' *rhymin-ware*
      Wi' ane anither.

The *four-gill chap*, we'se gar him clatter,
An' kirs'n him wi' reekin water;
Syne we'll sit down an' tak our whitter,
      To cheer our heart;
An' faith, we'se be *acquainted* better
      Before we part.

Awa ye selfish, warly race,
Wha think that havins, sense an' grace,
Ev'n love an' friendship should give place
   To *catch-the-plack*!
I dinna like to see your face,
    Nor hear your crack.

But ye whom social pleasure charms,
Whose hearts the *tide of kindness* warms,
Who hold your *being* on the terms,
   'Each aid the others,'
Come to my bowl, come to my arms,
    My friends, my brothers!

But to conclude my lang epistle,
As my auld pen's worn to the gristle,
Twa lines frae you wad gar me fissle,
   Who am, most fervent,
While I can either sing or whissle,
    Your friend and servant.

SECOND EPISTLE TO JOHN LAPRAIK
21 April 1785

While new-ca'd kye rowte at the stake
An' pownies reek in pleugh or braik,
This hour on e'enin's edge I take,
   To own I'm debtor
To honest-hearted, auld LAPRAIK,
    For his kind *letter*.

Forjesket sair, with weary legs,
Rattlin the corn out-owre the rigs,
Or dealing thro' amang the naigs
   Their ten-hours' bite,
My awkart Muse sair pleads and begs
    I would na write.

The tapetless, ramfeezl'd hizzie,
She's saft at best an' something lazy:
Quo' she, 'Ye ken we've been sae busy
   This month an' mair,
That trowth, my head is grown right dizzie,
    An' something sair.'

Her dowff excuses pat me mad;
'Conscience,' says I, 'ye thowless jad!
I'll write, an' that a hearty blaud,
   This vera night;
So dinna ye affront your trade,
    But rhyme it right.

'Shall bauld LAPRAIK, the *king o' hearts*,
Tho' mankind were a *pack o' cartes*,
Roose you sae weel for your deserts,
       In terms sae friendly,
Yet ye'll neglect to shaw your parts
       An' thank him kindly?'

Sae I gat paper in a blink,
An' down gaed *stumpie* in the ink:
Quoth I, 'Before I sleep a wink,
       I vow I'll close it;
An' if ye winna mak it clink,
       By Jove, I'll prose it!'

Sae I've begun to scrawl, but whether
In rhyme, or prose, or baith thegither,
Or some hotch-potch that's rightly neither,
       Let time mak proof;
But I shall scribble down some blether
       Just clean aff-loof.

My worthy friend, ne'er grudge an' carp,
Tho' Fortune use you hard an' sharp;
Come, kittle up your *moorlan harp*
       Wi' gleesome touch!
Ne'er mind how Fortune *waft* an' *warp*;
       She's but a bitch.

She's gien me monie a jirt an' fleg,
Sin' I could striddle owre a rig;
But, by the Lord, tho' I should beg
       Wi' lyart pow,
I'll laugh an' sing, an' shake my leg,
       As lang's I dow!

Now comes the *sax-an'-twentieth* simmer
I've seen the bud upon the timmer,
Still persecuted by the limmer
       Frae year to year;
But yet, despite the kittle kimmer,
       I, Rob, am here.

Do ye envy the *city gent*,
Behint a kist to lie an' sklent;
Or purse-proud, big wi' cent per cent,
       An' muckle wame,
In some bit *brugh* to represent
       A *bailie*'s name?

Or is't the paughty, feudal *thane*,
Wi' ruffl'd sark an' glancin cane,
Wha thinks himsel nae *sheep-shank bane*,
      But lordly stalks;
While caps and bonnets aff are taen,
      As by he walks?

'O *Thou* wha gies us each guid gift!
Gie me o' *wit* an' *sense* a lift,
Then turn me, if *Thou* please, *adrift*,
      Thro' Scotland wide;
Wi' *cits* nor *lairds* I wadna shift,
      In a' their pride!'

Were this the *charter* of our state,
'On pain o' *hell* be rich an' great,'
Damnation then would be our fate,
      Beyond remead;
But, thanks to *Heav'n*, that's no the gate
      We learn our *creed*.

For thus the royal *mandate* ran,
When first the human race began;
'The social, friendly, honest man,
      Whate'er he be,
'Tis *he* fulfils *great Nature's plan*,
      And none but he.'

O *mandate*, glorious and divine!
The followers o' the ragged Nine,[1]
Poor, thoughtless devils! yet may shine
      In glorious light,
While sordid sons o' Mammon's line
      Are dark as night!

Tho' here they scrape, an' squeeze, an' growl,
Their worthless nievefu' of a *soul*,
May in some *future carcase* howl,
      The forest's fright;
Or in some day-detesting *owl*
      May shun the light.

Then may Lapraik and Burns arise,
To reach their native, kindred skies,
And sing their pleasures, hopes an' joys,
      In some mild sphere;
Still closer knit in friendship's ties,
      Each passing year!

---

[1] Although this line stands in all the editions published in Burns' lifetime, it should read: 'The ragged followers o' the Nine'.

To William Simpson
Schoolmaster, Ochiltree—May 1785

I gat your letter, winsome Willie;
Wi' gratefu' heart I thank you brawlie;
Tho' I maun say't, I wad be silly,
   An' unco vain,
Should I believe, my coaxin billie
    Your flatterin strain.

But I'se believe ye kindly meant it,
I sud be laith to think ye hinted
Ironic satire, sidelins sklented
   On my poor Musie;
Tho' in sic phraisin terms ye've penn'd it,
    I scarce excuse ye.

My senses wad be in a creel,
Should I but dare a *hope* to speel
Wi' Allan,[1] or wi' Gilbertfield,[2]
   The braes o' fame;
Or Fergusson, the writer-chiel,
    A deathless name.

(O Fergusson! thy glorious parts
Ill suited law's dry, musty arts!
My curse upon your whunstane hearts,
   Ye Enbrugh gentry!
The tithe o' what ye waste at cartes
    Wad stow'd his pantry!)

Yet when a tale comes i' my head,
Or lasses gie my heart a screed—
As whyles they're like to be my dead,
   (O sad disease!)
I kittle up my rustic reed;
    It gies me ease.

Auld Coila now may fidge fu' fain,
She's gotten poets o' her ain;
Chiels wha their chanters winna hain,
   But tune their lays,
Till echoes a' resound again
    Her weel-sung praise.

Nae poet thought her worth his while,
To set her name in measur'd style;
She lay like some unkenn'd-of isle
   Beside New Holland,

---

[1] Allan Ramsay. [2] William Hamilton of Gilbertfield.

Or whare wild-meeting oceans boil
      Besouth Magellan.

Ramsay an' famous Fergusson
Gied Forth an' Tay a lift aboon;
Yarrow an' Tweed, to monie a tune,
      Owre Scotland rings;
While Irwin, Lugar, Ayr an' Doon
      Naebody sings.

Th' Illissus, Tiber, Thames an' Seine,
Glide sweet in monie a tunefu' line:
But Willie, set your fit to mine,
      An' cock your crest;
We'll gar our streams an' burnies shine
      Up wi' the best!

We'll sing auld Coila's plains an' fells,
Her moors red-brown wi' heather bells,
Her banks an' braes, her dens and dells,
      Whare glorious Wallace
Aft bure the gree, as story tells,
      Frae Suthron billies.

At Wallace' name, what Scottish blood
But boils up in a spring-tide flood!
Oft have our fearless fathers strode
      By Wallace' side,
Still pressing onward, red-wat-shod,
      Or glorious died!

O sweet are Coila's haughs an' woods,
When lintwhites chant amang the buds,
And jinkin hares, in amorous whids,
      Their loves enjoy;
While thro' the braes the cushat croods
      With wailfu' cry!

Ev'n winter bleak has charms to me,
When winds rave thro' the naked tree;
Or frosts on hills of Ochiltree
      Are hoary grey;
Or blinding drifts wild-furious flee,
      Dark'ning the day!

O Nature! a' thy shows an' forms
To feeling, pensive hearts hae charms!
Whether the Summer kindly warms,
      Wi' life an light;
Or Winter howls, in gusty storms,
      The lang, dark night!

The Muse, nae poet ever fand her,
Till by himsel he learn'd to wander,
Adown some trottin burn's meander,
      An' no think lang:
O sweet, to stray an' pensive ponder
      A heart-felt sang!

The warly race may drudge an' drive,
Hog-shouther, jundie, stretch an' strive,
Let me fair Nature's face descrive,
      And I, wi' pleasure,
Shall let the busy, grumbling hive
      Bum owre their treasure.

Fareweel, 'my rhyme-composing' brither!
We've been owre lang unkenn'd to ither:
Now let us lay our heads thegither,
      In love fraternal:
May envy wallop in a tether,
      Black fiend, infernal!

While Highlandmen hate tolls an' taxes;
While moorlan herds like guid, fat braxies;
While terra firma, on her axis,
      Diurnal turns;
Count on a friend, in faith an' practice,
      In Robert Burns.

Postcript

My memory's no worth a preen;
I had amaist forgotten clean,
Ye bade me write you what they mean
      By this *new-light*,[1]
'Bout which our herds sae aft hae been
      Maist like to fight.

In days when mankind were but callans
At grammar, logic, an' sic talents,
They took nae pains their speech to balance,
      Or rules to gie,
But spak their thoughts in plain, braid lallans,
      Like you or me.

In thae auld times, they thought the moon,
Just like a sark, or pair o' shoon,
Wore by degrees, till her last roon
      Gaed past their viewin,
An' shortly after she was done
      They gat a new ane.

[1] New-light is a cant phrase in the West of Scotland for those religious opinions which Dr Taylor of Norwich has defended so strenuously.—R.B.

This past for certain, undisputed;
It ne'er cam i' their heads to doubt it,
Till chiels gat up an' wad confute it,
        An' ca'd it wrang;
An' muckle din there was about it,
        Baith loud an' lang.

Some herds, weel learn'd upo' the beuk,
Wad threap auld folk the thing misteuk;
For 'twas the auld moon turn'd a neuk
        An' out o' sight,
An' backlins-comin, to the leuk,
        She grew mair bright.

This was deny'd, it was affirm'd;
The herds and hissels were alarm'd
The rev'rend grey-beards rav'd an' storm'd,
        That beardless laddies
Should think they better were inform'd,
        Than their auld daddies.

Frae less to mair it gaed to sticks;
Frae words an' aiths to clours an' nicks;
An monie a fallow gat his licks,
        Wi' hearty crunt;
An' some, to learn them for their tricks,
        Were hang'd an' brunt.

This game was play'd in monie lands,
An' auld-light caddies bure sic hands,
That faith, the youngsters took the sands
        Wi' nimble shanks;
Till lairds forbad, by strict commands,
        Sic bluidy pranks.

But new-light herds gat sic a cowe,
Folk thought them ruin'd stick-an-stowe;
Till now amaist on ev'ry knowe
        Ye'll find ane plac'd;
An' some, their new-light fair avow,
        Just quite barefac'd.

Nae doubt the auld-light flocks are bleatin;
Their zealous herds are vex'd an' sweatin;
Mysel, I've even seen them greetin
        Wi' girnin spite,
To hear the moon sae sadly lied on
        By word an' write.

But shortly they will cowe the louns!
Some auld-light herds in neebor touns

Are mind't, in things they ca' balloons,
  To tak a flight;
An' stay ae month amang the moons
  An' see them right.

Guid observation they will gie them;
An' when the auld moon's gaun to lea'e them,
The hindmaist shaird, they'll fetch it wi' them,
  Just i' their pouch;
An' when the new-light billies see them,
  I think they'll crouch!

Sae, ye observe that a' this clatter
Is naething but a 'moonshine matter';
But tho' dull prose-folk Latin splatter
  In logic tulyie,
I hope we bardies ken some better
  Than mind sic brulyie.

ONE NIGHT AS I DID WANDER
A Fragment—May 1785
Tune—*John Anderson, my jo*

One night as I did wander,
  When corn begins to shoot,
I sat me down to ponder,
  Upon an auld tree root;
Auld Ayr ran by before me,
  And bicker'd to the seas,
A cushat crooded o'er me,
  That echoed through the braes

THO' CRUEL FATE SHOULD BID US PART
Tune—*The northern lass*

Tho' cruel fate should bid us part,
  Far as the pole and line,
Her dear idea round my heart,
  Should tenderly entwine.

Tho' mountains rise, and deserts howl,
  And oceans roar between;
Yet, dearer than my deathless soul,
  I still would love my Jean.

RANTIN', ROVIN' ROBIN
Tune—*Daintie Davie*

Chorus: Robin was a rovin' boy,
  Rantin', rovin', rantin', rovin',
Robin was a rovin' boy,
  Rantin', rovin' Robin!

There was a lad was born in Kyle,[1]
But whatna day o' whatna style,
I doubt it's hardly worth the while
    To be sae nice wi' Robin.

Our monarch's hindmost year but ane
Was five-and-twenty days begun,[2]
'Twas then a blast o' Jan'war' win'
    Blew hansel in on Robin.

The gossip keekit in his loof,
Quo' scho, 'Wha lives will see the proof,
This waly boy will be nae coof:
    I think we'll ca' him Robin.'

'He'll hae misfortunes great an' sma',
But ay a heart aboon them a',
He'll be a credit till us a',
    We'll a' be proud o' Robin.'

'But sure as three times three mak nine,
I see by ilka score and line,
This chap will dearly like our kin',
    So leeze me on thee, Robin.'

'Guid faith,' quo', scho, 'I doubt you, sir,
Ye gar the bonnie lasses lie aspar;
But twenty fauts ye may hae waur,
    So blessin's on thee, Robin!'

[1] The central district of Ayrshire.
[2] January 25, 1759, the date of my bardship's vital existence.—R.B.

ELEGY ON THE DEATH OF ROBERT RUISSEAUX[1]

Now Robin lies in his last lair,
He'll gabble rhyme, nor sing nae mair,
Cauld poverty, wi' hungry stare,
    Nae mair shall fear him;
Nor anxious fear, nor cankert care,
    E'er mair come near him.

To tell the truth, they seldom fash'd him,
Except the moment that they crush'd him;
For sune as chance or fate had hush'd 'em—
    Tho' e'er sae short—
Then wi' a rhyme or sang he lash'd 'em,
    And thought it sport.

Tho' he was bred to kintra wark,
And counted was baith wight and stark,
Yet that was never Robin's mark
    To mak a man;
But tell him he was learn'd and clark—
    Ye roos'd him then!

[1] Ruisseaux is French for rivulets or 'burns', a translation of his name.

EPISTLE TO JOHN GOLDIE, KILMARNOCK
Author of The Gospel Recovered—August, 1785

O Goudie, terror o' the Whigs,
Dread o' blackcoats and rev'rend wigs!
Sour Bigotry, on her last legs,
    Girns an' looks back,
Wishing the ten Egyptian plagues
    Wad seize you quick.

Poor gapin, glowrin Superstition!
Wae's me, she's in a sad condition;
Fie! bring Black Jock,[1] her state physician,
   To see her water;
Alas, there's ground o' great suspicion
    She'll ne'er get better.

Enthusiasm's past redemption,
Gane in a galloping consumption,
Not a' the quacks, wi' a' their gumption,
   Can ever mend her;
Her feeble pulse gies strong presumption,
    Death soon will end her.

Auld Orthodoxy lang did grapple,
For every hole to get a stapple;
But now she fetches at the thrapple,
   An' fights for breath;
Haste, gie her name up in the chapel,[2]
   Near unto death.

It's you an' *Taylor*[3] are the chief
To blame for a' this black mischief;
But, could the Lord's ain folk get leave,
   A toom tar barrel
An' twa red peats wad bring relief,
   And end the quarrel.

For me, my skill's but very sma',
An' skill in prose I've nane ava';
But quietlins-wise, between us twa,
   Weel may you speed!
And tho' they sud you sair misca',
   Ne'er fash your head.

E'en swinge the dogs, and thresh them sicker!
The mair they squeel ay chap the thicker;
And still 'mang hands a hearty bicker
   O' something stout;
It gars an owthor's pulse beat quicker,
   And helps his wit.

There's naething like the honest nappy;
Whare'll ye e'er see men sae happy,
Or women sonsie, saft an' sappy,
   'Tween morn and morn,
As them wha like to taste the drappie,
   In glass or horn?

---

[1] The Rev. J. Russell, Kilmarnock.—R.B.   [3] Dr Taylor of Norwich.—R.B.
[2] Mr Russell's Kirk.—R.B.

I've seen me dazed upon a time,
I scarce could wink or see a styme;
Just ae half-mutchkin does me prime—
      Ought less is little—
Then back I rattle on the rhyme,
      As gleg's a whittle.

THIRD EPISTLE TO JOHN LAPRAIK

      Sept. 13, 1785
Guid speed and furder to you, Johnie,
Guid health, hale han's, an' weather bonnie;
Now when ye're nickin down fu' cannie
      The staff o' bread,
May ye ne'er want a stoup o' bran'y
      To clear your head!

May Boreas never thresh your rigs,
Nor kick your rickles aff their legs,
Sendin' the stuff o'er muirs an' haggs
      Like drivin' wrack;
But may the tapmost grain that wags
      Come to the sack.

I'm busy, too, an' skelpin' at it,
But bitter, daudin showers hae wat it;
Sae my auld stumpie pen I gat it,
      Wi' muckle wark,
An' took my jocteleg an whatt it,
      Like onie clark.

It's now twa month that I'm your debtor,
For your braw, nameless, dateless letter,
Abusin' me for harsh ill-nature
      On holy men,
While deil a hair yoursel ye're better,
      But mair profane.

But let the kirk-folk ring their bells,
Let's sing about our noble sel's:
We'll cry nae jads frae heathen hills
      To help, or roose us,
But browster wives an' whisky stills,
      They are the muses.

Your friendship, sir, I winna quat it,
An' if ye mak objections at it,
Then, han' in neive some day we'll knot it,
      An' witness take,
An' when wi' usquabae we've wat it,
      It winna break.

But if the beast an' branks be spar'd
Till kye be gaun without the herd,
An' a' the vittel in the yard,
   An' theekit right,
I mean your ingle-side to guard
   Ae winter night.

Then muse-inspirin' aquavitae
Shall make us baith sae blythe an' witty,
Till ye forget ye're auld an' gutty,
   An' be as canty
As ye were nine years less than thretty—
   Sweet ane an' twenty!

But stooks are cowpet wi' the blast,
An' now the sinn keeks in the west,
Then I maun rin amang the rest,
   An' quat my chanter;
Sae I subscribe mysel in haste,
   Yours, RAB THE RANTER.

TO THE REV. JOHN MCMATH
Enclosing a Copy of 'Holy Willie's Prayer', which he had requested

        Sept. 17, 1785
While at the stook the shearers cow'r
To shun the bitter blaudin' show'r,
Or in gulravage rinnin scowr
   To pass the time,
To you I dedicate the hour
   In idle rhyme.

My musie, tir'd wi' monie a sonnet
On gown, an' ban', an' douse black bonnet,
Is grown right eerie now she's done it,
   Lest they shou'd blame her,
An' rouse their holy thunder on it
   An anathem her.

I own 'twas rash, an' rather hardy,
That I, a simple, country bardie,
Shou'd meddle wi' a pack sae sturdy,
   Wha, if they ken me,
Can easy, wi' a single wordie,
   Lowse hell upon me.

But I gae mad at their grimaces,
Their sighin', cantin', grace-proud faces,
Their three-mile prayers, an' half-mile graces,
   Their raxin' conscience,
Whase greed, revenge, an' pride disgraces
   Waur nor their nonsense.

There's Gaw'n, misca'd waur than a beast,
Wha has mair honour in his breast
Than monie scores as guid's the priest
   Wha sae abus'd him.
An' may a bard no' crack his jest
   What way they've us'd him?

See him, the poor man's friend in need,
The gentleman in word an' deed,
An' shall his fame an' honour bleed
   By worthless skellums,
An' not a muse erect her head
   To cowe the blellums?

O Pope! had I thy satire's darts
To gie the rascals their deserts,
I'd rip their rotten, hollow hearts,
   An' tell aloud
Their jugglin' hocus-pocus arts
   To cheat the crowd.

God knows, I'm no' the thing I should be,
Nor am I even the thing I cou'd be,
But twenty times, I rather wou'd be
   An atheist clean,
Than under gospel colours hid be,
   Just for a screen.

An honest man may like a glass,
An honest man may like a lass,
But mean revenge, an' malice fause,
   He'll still disdain,
An' then cry zeal for gospel laws,
   Like some we ken.

They take religion in their mouth;
They talk o' mercy, grace, an' truth,
For what?—to gie their malice skouth
   On some puir wight,
An' hunt him down, o'er right an' ruth,
   To ruin straight.

All hail, Religion! maid divine!
Pardon a muse sae mean as mine,
Who in her rough imperfect line
   Thus daurs to name thee;
To stigmatise false friends of thine
   Can ne'er defame thee.

Tho' blotch't an' foul wi' monie a stain,
An' far unworthy of thy train,

With trembling voice I tune my strain,
      To join with those
Who boldly dare thy cause maintain
      In spite of foes:

In spite o' crowds, in spite o' mobs,
In spite o' undermining jobs,
In spite o' dark banditti stabs
      At worth an' merit,
By scoundrels, even wi' holy robes,
      But hellish spirit.

O Ayr! my dear, my native ground,
Within thy presbyterial bound
A candid liberal band is found
      Of public teachers,
As men, as Christians too, renown'd,
      An' manly preachers.

Sir, in that circle you are nam'd;
Sir, in that circle you are fam'd;
An' some, by whom your doctrine's blam'd
      (Which gies you honour),
Even, sir, by them your heart's esteem'd,
      An' winning manner.

Pardon this freedom I have ta'en,
An' if impertinent I've been,
Impute it not, good sir, in ane
      Whase heart ne'er wrang'd ye,
But to his utmost would befriend
      Ought that belang'd ye.

SECOND EPISTLE TO DAVIE
A Brother Poet and Brother Fiddler

Auld Neibour,
I'm three times doubly owre your debtor,
For your auld-farrant, frien'ly letter;
Tho' I maun say't, I doubt ye flatter,
      Ye speak sae fair;
For my puir, silly, rhymin' clatter
      Some less maun sair.

Hale be your heart! hale be your fiddle!
Lang may your elbuck jink an' diddle,
To cheer you thro' the weary widdle
      O' warly cares;
Till bairns' bairns kindly cuddle
      Your auld grey hairs.

But Davie, lad, I'm red ye're glaikit;
I'm tauld the Muse ye hae negleckit;
An' gif it's sae, ye sud by lickit
      Until ye fyke;
Sic hauns as you sud ne'er be faikit,
      Be hained wha like.

For me, I'm on Parnassus' brink,
Rivin the words to gar them clink;
Whyles dazed wi' love, whyles dazed wi' drink,
      Wi' jads or masons;
An' whyles, but aye owre late, I think
      Braw sober lessons.

Of a' the thoughtless sons o' man,
Commen' to me the Bardie clan;
Except it be some idle plan
      O' rhymin' clink,
The devil-haet—that I sud ban—
      They ever think!

Nae thought, nae view, nae scheme o' livin',
Nae cares to gie us joy or grievin',
But just the pouchie put the neive in,
      An' while ought's there,
Then, hiltie-skiltie, we gae scrievin',
      An' fash nae mair.

Leeze me on rhyme! it's aye a treasure,
My chief, amaist my only pleasure:
At hame, a-fiel', at wark, or leisure,
      The Muse, poor hizzie!
Tho' rough an' raploch be her measure,
      She's seldom lazy.

Haud to the Muse, my daintie Davie:
The warl' may play you monie a shavie;
But for the Muse, she'll never leave ye,
      Tho' e'er sae puir,
Na, even tho' limpin' wi' the spavie
      Frae door tae door.

YOUNG PEGGY BLOOMS
Tune—*Loch Eroch-side*

Young Peggy blooms our bonniest lass,
    Her blush is like the morning,
The rosy dawn, the springing grass,
    With early gems adorning:
Her eyes outshine the radiant beams
    That gild the passing shower,

And glitter o'er the crystal streams,
    And cheer each fresh'ning flower.

Her lips, more than the cherries bright,
    A richer dye has grac'd them;
They charm th' admiring gazer's sight,
    And sweetly tempt to taste them:
Her smile is as the ev'ning mild,
    When feather'd pairs are courting,
And little lambkins wanton wild,
    In playful bands disporting.

Were Fortune lovely Peggy's foe,
    Such sweetness would relent her;
As blooming Spring unbends the brow
    Of surly, savage Winter.
Detraction's eye no aim can gain
    Her winning pow'rs to lessen;
And fretful Envy grins in vain
    The poison'd tooth to fasten.

Ye Pow'rs of Honour, Love and Truth,
    From ev'ry ill defend her!
Inspire the highly favour'd youth
    The destinies intend her:
Still fan the sweet connubial flame
    Responsive in each bosom;
And bless the dear parental name
    With many a filial blossom.

FAREWELL TO BALLOCHMYLE
Tune—The Braes o' Ballochmyle

The Catrine woods were yellow seen,
    The flowers decay'd on Catrine lea;
Nae lav'rock sang on hillock green,
    But nature sicken'd on the e'e.
Thro' faded groves Maria sang,
    Hersel in beauty's bloom the while;
And aye the wild-wood ehoes rang—
    Fareweel the braes o' Ballochmyle!

Low in your wintry beds, ye flowers,
    Again ye'll flourish fresh and fair;
Ye birdies dumb, in with'ring bowers,
    Again ye'll charm the vocal air;
But here, alas! for me nae mair
    Shall birdie charm, or floweret smile—
Fareweel the bonnie banks of Ayr!
    Fareweel! fareweel! sweet Ballochmyle!

HER FLOWING LOCKS

Her flowing locks, the raven's wing,
Adown her neck and bosom hing;
How sweet unto that breast to cling,
    And round that neck entwine her!

Her lips are roses wet wi' dew,
O, what a feast her bonnie mou'!
Her cheeks a mair celestial hue,
    A crimson still diviner!

HALLOWEEN[1]

The following poem will, by many readers, be well enough understood; but for the sake of those who are unacquainted with the manners and traditions of the country where the scene is cast, notes are added to give some account of the principal charms and spells of that night.

'Yes! let the rich deride, the proud disdain,
The simple pleasure of the lowly train;
To me more dear, congenial to my heart,
One native charm, than all the gloss of art.'
                                GOLDSMITH

Upon that *night*, when fairies light
    On *Cassilis Downans*[2] dance,
Or owre the lays, in splendid blaze,
    On sprightly coursers prance;
Or for *Colean*, the rout is taen,
    Beneath the moon's pale beams;
There, up the *Cove*,[3] to stray an' rove,
    Amang the rocks an' streams
                To sport that night;

Amang the bonnie winding banks,
    Where *Doon* rins, wimplin, clear;
Where Bruce[4] ance rul'd the martial ranks,
    An' shook his *Carrick* spear;
Some merry, friendly, countra folks
    Together did convene,
To burn their nits, an' pou their stocks,
    An' haud their *Halloween*
                Fu' blythe that night.

[1] Is thought to be a night when witches, devils, and other mischief-making beings are abroad on their baneful midnight errands; particularly those aerial people, the fairies, are said on that night to hold a grand anniversary.—R.B.

[2] Certain little, romantic, rocky, green hills, in the neighbourhood of the ancient seat of the Earls of Cassilis.—R.B.

[3] A noted cavern near Colean house, called the Cove of Colean; which, as well as Cassilis Downans, is famed, in country story, for being a favorite haunt of fairies.—R.B.

[4] The famous family of that name, the ancestors of Robert, the great deliverer of his country, were Earls of Carrick.—R.B.

The lasses feat, an' cleanly neat,
    Mair braw than when they're fine;
Their faces blythe, fu' sweetly kythe,
    Hearts leal, an' warm, an' kin':
The lads sae trig, wi' wooer-babs
    Weel-knotted on their garten;
Some unco blate, an' some wi' gabs
    Gar lasses' hearts gang startin
            Whyles fast at night.

Then, first an' foremost, thro' the kail,
    Their *stocks*[1] maun a' be sought ance;
They steek their een, and grape an' wale
    For muckle anes, an' straught anes.
Poor hav'rel *Will* fell aff the drift,
    An' wandered thro' the *bow-kail*,
An' pou't for want o' better shift,
    A *runt* was like a sow-tail
            Sae bow't that night.

Then, straught or crooked, yird or nane,
    They roar an' cry a' throw'ther;
The vera *wee-things*, toddlin, rin,
    Wi' stocks out owre their shouther:
An' gif the *custock*'s sweet or sour,
    Wi' joctelegs they taste them;
Syne coziely, aboon the door,
    Wi' cannie care, they've plac'd them
            To lie that night.

The lassies staw frae 'mang them a',
    To pou their *stalks o' corn*;[2]
But *Rab* slips out, an' jinks about,
    Behint the muckle thorn:
He grippit *Nelly* hard an' fast;
    Loud skirl'd a' the lasses;
But her *tap-pickle* maist was lost,
    Whan kiutlin in the *fause-house*[3]
            Wi' him that night.

[1] The first ceremony of Halloween is pulling each a 'stock,' or plant of kail. They must go out, hand in hand, with eyes shut, and pull the first they meet with: its being big or little, straight or crooked, is prophetic of the size and shape of the grand object of all their spells—the husband or wife. If any 'yird,' or earth, stick to the root, that is 'tocher,' or fortune; and the taste of the 'custock,' that is, the heart of the stem, is indicative of the natural temper and disposition. Lastly, the stems, or, to give them their ordinary appellation, the 'runts,' are placed somewhere above the head of the door; and the Christian names of the people whom chance brings into the house are, according to the priority of placing the 'runts,' the names in question.—R.B.

[2] They go to the barnyard, and pull each, at three different times, a stalk of oats. If the third stalk wants the 'top-pickle,' that is, the grain at the top of the stalk, the party in question will come to the marriage-bed any-thing but a maid.—R.B.

[3] When the corn is in a doubtful state, by being too green or wet, the stack-builder, by means of old timber, etc, makes a large apartment in his stack, with an opening in the side which is fairest exposed to the wind: this he calls a 'fause-house.'—R.B.

The auld guid-wife's weel-hoordit *nits*[1]
    Are round an' round divided,
An' monie lads' an' lasses' fates
    Are there that night decided:
Some kindle, couthie, side by side,
    And burn thegither trimly;
Some start awa, wi' saucy pride,
    An' jump out owre the chimlie
            Fu' high that night.

Jean slips in twa, wi' tentie e'e;
    Wha 'twas, she wadna tell;
But this is *Jock*, an' this is *me*,
    She says in to hersel:
He bleez'd owre her, an' she owre him,
    As they wad never mair part:
Till fuff! he started up the lum,
    An' *Jean* had e'en a sair heart
            To see 't that night.

Poor *Willie*, wi' his *bow-kail runt*,
    Was *brunt* wi' primsie *Mallie*;
An' *Mary*, nae doubt, took the drunt,
    To be compar'd to *Willie*:
Mall's nit lap out, wi' pridefu' fling,
    An' her ain fit, it brunt it;
While *Willie* lap, and swoor by *jing*,
    'Twas just the way he wanted
            To be that night.

Nell had the *fause-house* in her min',
    She pits hersel an' *Rob* in;
In loving bleeze they sweetly join,
    Till white in ase they're sobbin':
Nell's heart was dancin' at the view;
    She whisper'd *Rob* to leuk for't:
Rob, stownlins, prie'd her bonnie mou,
    Fu' cozie in the neuk for 't,
            Unseen that night.

But *Merran* sat behint their backs,
    Her thoughts on *Andrew Bell*:
She lea'es them gashin at their cracks,
    An' slips out-by hersel:
She thro' the yard the nearest taks,
    An' for the *kiln* she goes then,

---

[1] Burning the nuts is a favourite charm. They name the lad and lass to each particular nut, as they lay them in the fire; and according as they burn quietly together, or start from beside one another, the course and issue of the courtship will be.—R.B.

An' darklins grapit for the *bauks*,
    And in the *blue-clue*[1] throws then,
        Right fear't that night.

An' ay she *win't*, an' ay she swat,
    I wat she made nae jaukin;
Till something *held* within the *pat*,
    Guid Lord! but she was quaukin!
But whether 'twas the *deil* himsel,
    Or whether 'twas a *bauk-en*',
Or whether it was *Andrew Bell*,
    She did na wait on talkin'
        To spier that night.

Wee Jenny to her graunie says,
    'Will ye go wi' me, Graunie?
I'll *eat the apple* at the *glass*,[2]
    I gat frae Uncle Johnie:'
She fufft her pipe wi' sic a lunt,
    In wrath she was sae vap'rin,
She notic't na an aizle brunt
    Her braw, new, worset apron
        Out thro' that night.

'Ye little skelpie-limmer's face![3]
    I daur you try sic sportin',
As seek the *foul thief* onie place,
    For him to spae your fortune:
Nae doubt but ye may get a *sight*!
    Great cause ye hae to fear it;
For monie a ane has gotten a fright,
    An' liv'd an' died deleerit,
        On sic a night.

'Ae hairst afore the *Sherra-moor*,
    I mind't as weel 's yestreen—
I was a gilpey then, I'm sure
    I was na past fyfteen:
The simmer had been cauld an' wat,
    An' *stuff* was unco green;
An' aye a rantin *kirn* we gat,
    An' just on *Halloween*
        It fell that night.

---

[1] Whoever would, with success, try this spell, must strictly observe these directions: Steal out, all alone, to the kiln, and darkling, throw into the 'pot' a clue of blue yarn; wind it in a new clue off the old one; and, toward the latter end, something will hold the thread: demand, 'Wha hauds?' i.e. who holds? and answer will be returned from the kiln-pot, by naming the Christian and surname of your future spouse.—R.B.

[2] Take a candle and go alone to a looking-glass; eat an apple before it, and some traditions say you should comb your hair all the time; the face of your conjungal companion, to be, will be seen in the glass, as if peeping over your shoulder.—R.B.

[3] A technical term in female scolding.—R.B.

'Our *stibble-rig* was *Rab M'Graen*,
    A clever, sturdy fallow;
His sin gat *Eppie Sim* wi' wean,
    That lived in Achmacalla:
He gat *hemp-seed*,[1] I mind it weel,
    An' he made unco light o't;
But monie a day was *by himsel*,
    He was sae sairly frighted
            That vera night.'

Then up gat fechtin *Jamie Fleck*,
    An' he swoor by his conscience,
That he could *saw hemp-seed* a peck;
    For it was a' but nonsense:
The auld guidman raught down the pock,
    An' out a handfu' gied him;
Syne bad him slip frae 'mang the folk,
    Sometime when nae ane see'd him,
            An' try't that night.

He marches thro' amang the stacks,
    Tho' he was something sturtin;
The *graip* he for a *harrow* taks,
    An' haurls at his curpin:
And ev'ry now an' then, he says,
    'Hemp-seed I saw thee,
An' her that is to be my lass,
    Come after me an' draw thee
            As fast this night.'

He whistl'd up *Lord Lennox' march*
    To keep his courage cheery;
Altho' his hair began to arch,
    He was sae fley'd an' eerie:
Till presently he hears a squeak,
    An' then a grane an' gruntle;
He by his shouther gae a keek,
    An' tumbled wi' a wintle
            Out-owre that night.

He roar'd a horrid murder-shout,
    In dreadfu' desperation!
An' young an' auld come rinnin out,
    An' hear the sad narration:

[1] Steal out, unperceived, and sow a handful of hemp-seed, harrowing it with anything you can conveniently draw after you. Repeat now and then: 'Hemp-seed, I saw thee, hemp-seed, I saw thee; and him (or her) that is to be my true love, come after me and pou thee.' Look over your left shoulder, and you will see the appearance of the person invoked, in the attitude of pulling hemp. Some traditions say, 'Come after me and shaw thee,' that is, show thyself; in which case, it simply appears. Others omit the harrowing, and say: 'Come after me and harrow thee.'—R.B.

He swoor 'twas hilchin *Jean M'Craw*,
　　Or crouchie *Merran Humphie*—
Till stop! she trotted thro' them a';
　　And wha was it but *Grumphie*
　　　　Asteer that night!

Meg fain wad to the *barn* gaen,
　　To *winn three wechts o' naething*;[1]
But for to meet the deil her lane,
　　She pat but little faith in:
She gies the herd a pickle nits,
　　An' twa red-cheekit apples,
To watch, while for the *barn* she sets,
　　In hopes to see *Tam Kipples*
　　　　That vera night.

She turns the key wi' cannie thraw,
　　An' owre the threshold ventures;
But first on *Sawnie* gies a ca',
　　Syne baudly in she enters:
A *ratton* rattl'd up the wa',
　　An' she cry'd, Lord preserve her!
An' ran thro' midden-hole an' a',
　　An' pray'd wi' zeal and fervour,
　　　　Fu' fast that night.

They hoy't out Will, wi' sair advice;
　　They hecht him some fine braw ane;
It chanc'd the *stack* he *faddom't thrice*,[2]
　　Was timmer-propt for thrawin:
He taks a swirlie, auld *moss-oak*
　　For some black, grousome *carlin*;
An' loot a winze, an' drew a stroke,
　　Till skin in blypes cam haurlin
　　　　Aff's nieves that night.

A wanton widow *Leezie* was,
　　As cantie as a kittlen;
But och! that night, amang the shaws,
　　She gat a fearfu' settlin!
She thro' the whins, an' by the cairn,
　　An' owre the hill gaed scrievin;

---

[1] This charm must likewise be performed unperceived and alone. You go to the barn, and open both doors, taking them off the hinges, if possible; for there is danger that the being about to appear may shut the doors, and do you some mischief. Then take that instrument used in winnowing the corn, which in our country dialect we call a 'wecht,' and go through all the attitudes of letting down corn against the wind. Repeat it three times, and the third time an apparition will pass through the barn, in at the windy door and out at the other, having both the figure in question, and the appearance or retinue, marking the employment or station in life.—R.B.

[2] Take an opportunity of going unnoticed to a 'bear-stack,' and fathom it three times round. The last fathom of the last time you will catch in your arms the appearance of your future conjugal yoke-fellow.—R.B.

Whare *three lairds' lan's met at a burn*,[1]
    To dip her *left sark-sleeve* in,
            Was bent that night.

Whyles owre a linn the burnie plays,
    As thro' the glen it wimpl't;
Whyles round a rocky scar it strays,
    Whyles in a wiel it dimpl't;
Whyles glitter'd to the nightly rays,
    Wi' bickerin', dancin' dazzle;
Whyles cooket underneath the braes,
    Below the spreading hazel
            Unseen that night.

Amang the brachens, on the brae,
    Between her an' the moon,
The deil, or else an outler quey,
    Gat up an' ga'e a croon:
Poor *Leezie*'s heart maist lap the hool;
    Near lav'rock-height she jumpet,
But mist a fit, an' in the *pool*
    Out-owre the lugs she plumpet,
            Wi' a plunge that night.

In order, on the clean hearth-stane,
    The *luggies*[2] three are rangéd;
An' ev'ry time great care is taen
    To see them duly changéd:
Auld Uncle *John*, wha *wedlock's joys*
    Sin' *Mar's-year*[3] did desire,
Because he gat the toom dish thrice,
    He heav'd them on the fire
            In wrath that night.

Wi' merry sangs, an' friendly cracks,
    I wat they did na weary;
And unco tales, an' funnie jokes,
    Their sports were cheap an' cheery:
Till *butter'd sowens*,[4] wi' fragrant lunt,
    Set a' their gabs a-steerin;
Syne, wi' a social glass o' strunt,
    They parted aff careerin
            Fu' blythe that night.

---

[1] You go out, one or more (for this is a social spell), to a south-running spring, or rivulet, where 'three lairds' lands meet,' and dip your left shirt sleeve. Go to bed in sight of a fire, and hang your wet sleeve before it to dry. Lie awake, and, some time near midnight, an apparition, having the exact figure of the grand object in question, will come and turn the sleeve, as if to dry the other side of it.—R.B.

[2] Take three dishes, put clean water in one, foul water in another, and leave the third empty; blindfold a person and lead him to the hearth where the dishes are ranged; he (or she) dips the left hand; if by chance in the clean water, the future (husband or) wife will come to the bar of matrimony a maid; if in the foul, a widow; if in the empty dish, it foretells, with equal certainty, no marriage at all. It is repeated three times, and every time the arrangement of the dishes is altered.—R.B.

[3] 1715, when the Earl of Mar headed an insurrection.

[4] Sowens, with butter instead of milk to them, is always the Halloween Supper.—R.B.

To A Mouse
On turning her up in her Nest with the Plough, November 1785

Wee, sleekit, cow'rin, tim'rous beastie,
O, what a panic's in thy breastie!
Thou need na start awa sae hasty,
   Wi' bickering brattle!
I wad be laith to rin an' chase thee,
   Wi' murd'ring pattle!

I'm truly sorry man's dominion,
Has broken nature's social union,
An' justifies that ill opinion,
   Which makes thee startle
At me, thy poor, earth-born companion,
   An' fellow-mortal!

I doubt na, whyles, but thou may thieve;
What then? poor beastie, thou maun live!
A daimen icker in a thrave
   'S a sma' request;
I'll get a blessin' wi' the lave,
   An' never miss't!

Thy wee bit housie, too, in ruin!
It's silly wa's the win's are strewin!
An' naething, now, to big a new ane,
   O' foggage green!
An' bleak December's winds ensuin',
   Baith snell an' keen!

Thou saw the fields laid bare an' waste,
An' weary winter comin' fast,
An' cozie here, beneath the blast,
   Thou thought to dwell—
Till crash! the cruel coulter past
   Out thro' thy cell.

That wee bit heap o' leaves an' stibble,
Has cost thee monie a weary nibble!
Now thou's turn'd out, for a' thy trouble,
   But house or hald,
To thole the winter's sleety dribble,
   An' cranreuch cauld!

But, Mousie, thou art no thy lane,
In proving foresight may be vain:
The best-laid schemes o' mice an men
   Gang aft agley,
An' lea'e us nought but grief an' pain,
   For promis'd joy!

Still thou art blest, compar'd wi' me;
The present only toucheth thee:
But, Och! I backward cast my e'e,
      On prospects drear!
An' forward, tho' I canna see,
      I guess an' fear!

Epitaph On John Dove, Innkeeper

Here lies Johnie Pigeon;
What was his religion?
    Whae'er desires to ken,
To some other warl
Maun follow the carl,
    For here Johnie Pigeon had nane!

Strong ale was ablution,
Small beer persecution,
    A dram was *memento mori*;
But a full-flowing bowl
Was the saving his soul,
    And port was celestial glory.

Epitaph For James Smith, A Mauchline Wag

Lament him, Mauchline husbands a',
    He aften did assist ye;
For had ye staid hale weeks awa,
    Your wives they ne'er had miss'd ye.

Ye Mauchline bairns, as on ye pass
    To school in bands thegither,
O tread ye lightly on his grass—
    Perhaps he was your father!

Adam Armour's Prayer

Gude pity me, because I'm little!
For though I am an elf o' mettle,
An' can, like onie wabster's shuttle,
      Jink there or here;
Yet, scarce as lang's a gude kail-whittle,
      I'm unco queer.

An' now Thou kens our waefu' case;
For Geordie's jurr we're in disgrace,
Because we stang'd her through the place,
      An' hurt her spleuchan;
For whilk we daurna show our face
      Within the clachan.

An' now we're dern'd in dens and hollows,
And hunted, as was William Wallace,
Wi' constables—thae blackguard fallows,
       An' sodgers baith;
But Gude preserve us frae the gallows,
       That shamefu' death!

Auld grim black-bearded Geordie's sel'—
O shake him owre the mouth o' hell!
There let him hing, an' roar, an' yell
       Wi' hideous din,
And if he offers to rebel,
       Just heave him in.

When Death comes in wi' glimmerin blink,
An' tips auld drucken Nanse the wink,
May Sautan gie her doup a clink
       Within his yett,
An' fill her up wi' brimstone drink,
       Red, reeking, het.

At me tho' Jock and Jean are merry—
Some deil shall seize them in a hurry,
An' waft them in th' infernal wherry
       Straught through the lake,
An' gie their hides a noble curry
       Wi' oil of aik!

As for the 'jurr'—puir worthless body!
She's got mischief enough already;
Wi' stangéd hips, and buttocks bluidy
       She's suffer'd sair;
But, may she wintle in a woody,
       If she whore mair!

The Jolly Beggars, or Love and Liberty—A Cantata

Recitativo

When lyart leaves bestrew the yird,
Or, wavering like the bauckie-bird,[1]
   Bedim cauld Boreas' blast;
When hailstanes drive wi' bitter skyte,
And infant frosts begin to bite,
   In hoary cranreuch drest;
Ae night at e'en a merry core
   O' randie, gangrel bodies,
In Poosie-Nansie's held the splore,
   To drink their orra duddies;
      Wi' quaffing an' laughing,
        They ranted an' they sang,
      Wi' jumping an' thumping,
        The vera girdle rang.

[1] The old Scotch name for the Bat.—R.B.

First, neist the fire, in auld red rags,
Ane sat, weel brac'd wi' mealy bags,
   And knapsack a' in order;
His doxy lay within his arm;
Wi' usquebae an' blankets warm—
   She blinket on her sodger;
An' aye he gies the tozie drab
   The tither skelpin' kiss,
While she held up her greedy gab,
   Just like an aumous dish;
     Ilk smack still, did crack still,
      Just like a cadger's whip;
     Then staggering an' swaggering
      He roar'd this ditty up—

Air

Tune—*Soldier's Joy*

I am a son of Mars who have been in many wars,
   And show my cuts and scars wherever I come;
This here was for a wench, and that other in a trench,
   When welcoming the French at the sound of the drum.
       Lal de daudle, etc.

My prenticeship I past where my leader breath'd his last,
   When the bloody die was cast on the heights of Abram:[1]
And I servéd out my trade when the gallant game was play'd,
   And the Moro[2] low was laid at the sound of the drum.
       Lal de daudle, etc.

I lastly was with Curtis among the floating batt'ries,[3]
   And there I left for witness an arm and a limb;
Yet let my country need me, with Elliot[4] to head me,
   I'd clatter on my stumps at the sound of a drum.
       Lal de daudle, etc.

And now tho' I must beg, with a wooden arm and leg,
   And many a tatter'd rag hanging over my bum,
I'm as happy with my wallet, my bottle, and my callet,
   As when I used in scarlet to follow a drum.
       Lal de daudle, etc.

What tho' with hoary locks, I must stand the winter shocks,
   Beneath the woods and rocks oftentimes for a home,
When the t'other bag I sell, and the t'other bottle tell,
   I could meet a troop of hell, at the sound of a drum.
       Lal de daudle, etc.

[1] The battle ground in front of Quebec, where Wolfe victoriously fell in September 1759.
[2] El Moro was the castle that defended the harbour of Havana, Cuba, in 1762.
[3] At the Siege of Gibraltar in 1782.
[4] G. A. Elliot (Lord Heathfield), who defended Gibraltar during three years.

Recitativo

He ended; and the kebars sheuk,
    Aboon the chorus roar;
While frighted rattons backward leuk,
    An' seek the benmost bore:
A fairy fiddler frae the neuk,
    He skirl'd out, encore!
But up arose the martial chuck,
    An' laid the loud uproar.

Air
Tune—*Sodger Laddie*

I once was a maid, tho' I cannot tell when,
And still my delight is in proper young men;
Some one of a troop of dragoons was my daddie,
No wonder I'm fond of a sodger laddie,
        Sing, lal de lal, etc.

The first of my loves was a swaggering blade,
To rattle the thundering drum was his trade;
His leg was so tight, and his cheek was so ruddy,
Transported I was with my sodger laddie.
        Sing, lal de lal, etc.

But the godly old chaplain left him in the lurch;
The sword I forsook for the sake of the church:
He ventur'd the soul, and I riskéd the body,
'Twas then I proved false to my sodger laddie.
        Sing, lal de lal, etc.

Full soon I grew sick of my sanctified sot,
The regiment at large for a husband I got;
From the gilded spontoon to the fife I was ready,
I asked no more but a sodger laddie.
        Sing, lal de lal, etc.

But the peace it reduc'd me to beg in despair,
Till I met old boy in a Cunningham fair,
His rags regimental, they flutter'd so gaudy,
My heart it rejoic'd at a sodger laddie.
        Sing, lal de lal, etc.

And now I have liv'd—I know not how long,
And still I can join in a cup and a song;
But whilst with both hands I can hold the glass steady,
Here's to thee, my hero, my sodger laddie!
        Sing, lal de lal, etc.

Recitativo

Poor Merry-Andrew, in the neuk,
    Sat guzzling wi' a tinkler-hizzie;
They mind't na wha the chorus teuk,
    Between themselves they were sae busy:
At length, wi' drink an' courting dizzy,
    He stoiter'd up an' made a face—
Then turn'd an' laid a smack on Grizzie,
    Syne tun'd his pipes wi' grave grimace.

Air
Tune—*Auld Sir Symon*

Sir Wisdom's a fool when he's fou;
    Sir Knave is a fool in a session;
He's there but a 'prentice I trow,
    But I am a fool by profession.

My grannie she bought me a beuk,
    An' I held awa to the school;
I fear I my talent misteuk,
    But what will ye hae of a fool?

For drink I would venture my neck;
    A hizzie's the half of my craft;
But what could ye other expect
    Of ane that's avowedly daft?

I ance was tied up like a stirk,
    For civilly swearing and quaffin';
I ance was abus'd i' the kirk,
    For towsing a lass i' my daffin'.

Poor Andrew that tumbles for sport,
    Let naebody name wi' a jeer;
There's even, I'm tauld, i' the court
    A tumbler ca'd the Premier.

Observ'd ye yon reverend lad
    Mak faces to tickle the mob;
He rails at our mountebank squad—
    It's rivalship just i' the job.

And now my conclusion I'll tell,
    For faith I'm confoundedly dry:
The chiel that's a fool for himsel,
    Guid Lord! he's far dafter than I.

Recitativo

Then niest outspak a raucle carlin,
Wha kent fu' weel to cleek the sterling;

> For monie a pursie she had hooked,
> An' had in monie a well been douked;
> Her love had been a Highland laddie,
> But weary fa' the waefu' woodie!
> Wi' sighs and sobs she thus began
> To wail her braw John Highlandman:

Air

Tune—*O an ye were dead, Guidman*

A Highland lad my love was born,
The Lalland laws he held in scorn;
But he still was faithfu' to his clan,
My gallant, braw John Highlandman.

Chorus: Sing, hey my braw John Highlandman!
Sing, ho my braw John Highlandman!
There's not a lad in a' the lan'
Was match for my John Highlandman.

With his philibeg an' tartan plaid,
An' guid claymore down by his side,
The ladies' hearts he did trepan,
My gallant, braw John Highlandman.

We rangéd a' from Tweed to Spey,
An' liv'd like lords an' ladies gay;
For a Lalland face he fearéd none—
My gallant, braw John Highlandman.

They banish'd him beyond the sea.
But ere the bud was on the tree,
Adown my cheeks the pearls ran,
Embracing my John Highlandman.

But, och! they catch'd him at the last,
And bound him in a dungeon fast;
My curse upon them every one,
They've hang'd my braw John Highlandman!

And now a widow, I must mourn
The pleasures that will ne'er return:
The comfort but a hearty can,
When I think on John Highlandman.

Recitativo

> A pigmy scraper wi' his fiddle,
> Wha used at trysts an' fairs to driddle.
> Her strappin' limb and gausy middle
>   (He reach'd nae higher)
> Had hol'd his heartie like a riddle,
>   An' blawn't on fire.

Wi' hand on hainch, and upward e'e,
He croon'd his gamut, one, two, three,
Then in an arioso key,
   The wee Apollo
Set off wi' allegretto glee
   His giga solo:

Air
Tune—*Whistle owre the lave o't*

Let me ryke up to dight that tear,
An' go wi' me an' be my dear,
An' then your every care an' fear
 May whistle owre the lave o't.

Chorus: I am a fiddler to my trade,
An' a' the tunes that e'er I played,
The sweetest still to wife or maid,
 Was whistle owre the lave o't.

At kirns an' weddins we'se be there,
An' oh! sae nicely's we will fare;
We'll bowse about till Daddie Care
 Sing whistle owre the lave o't.

Sae merrily the banes we'll pyke,
An' sun oursel's about the dyke,
An' at our leisure, when ye like,
 We'll whistle owre the lave o't.

But bless me wi' your heav'n o' charms,
An' while I kittle hair on thairms,
Hunger, cauld, an' a' sic harms,
 May whistle owre the lave o't.

Recitativo

Her charms had struck a sturdy caird,
 As weel as poor gut-scraper;
He taks the fiddler by the beard,
 An' draws a roosty rapier—
He swoor, by a' was swearing worth,
 To speet him like a pliver,
Unless he wad from that time forth
 Relinquish her for ever.

Wi' ghastly e'e poor Tweedle-dee
 Upon his hunkers bended,
An' pray'd for grace wi' ruefu' face,
 An' sae the quarrel ended.
But tho' his little heart did grieve
 When round the tinkler prest her,
He feign'd to snirtle in his sleeve,
 When thus the caird address'd her:

Air

Tune—*Clout the Cauldron*

My bonnie lass, I work in brass,
    A tinkler is my station:
I've travell'd round all Christian ground
    In this my occupation;
I've taen the gold, an' been enrolled
    In many a noble squadron;
But vain they search'd, when off I march'd
    To go an' clout the cauldron.

Despise that shrimp, that wither'd imp,
    With a' his noise an' cap'rin;
An' tak a share with those that bear
    The budget and the apron!
And *by* that stowp! my faith an' houp,
    And *by* that dear Kilbaigie,[1]
If e'er ye want, or meet wi' scant,
    May I ne'er weet my craigie.

Recitativo

The caird prevail'd—th' unblushing fair
    In his embraces sunk;
Partly wi' love o'ercome sae sair,
    An' partly she was drunk:
Sir Violino, with an air
    That show'd a man o' spunk,
Wish'd unison between the pair,
    An' made the bottle clunk
                To their health that night.

But hurchin Cupid shot a shaft,
    That play'd a dame a shavie—
The fiddler rak'd her, fore and aft,
    Behint the chicken cavie.
Her lord, a wight o' Homer's craft,[2]
    Tho' limpin' wi' the spavie,
He hirpl'd up, an' lap like daft,
    An' shor'd them *Dainty Davie*.
                O' boot that night.

He was a care-defying blade
    As ever Bacchus listed!
Tho' Fortune sair upon him laid,
    His heart, she ever miss'd it.
He had no wish but—to be glad,
    Nor want but—when he thirsted;

[1] A peculiar sort of whisky so called, a great favorite with Poosie Nansie's clubs.—R.B. So named from Kilbaigie distillery in Clackmannan.
[2] Homer is allowed to be the oldest ballad-singer on record.—R.B.

He hated nought but—to be sad,
    An' thus the Muse suggested
        His sang that night:

Air

Tune—*For a' that, an' a' that*

I am a Bard of no regard,
    Wi' gentle folks an' a' that;
But Homer-like, the glowrin' byke,
    Frae town to town I draw that.

Chorus: For a' that, an' a' that,
    An' twice as muckle's a' that;
I've lost but ane, I've twa behin'—
    I've wife eneugh for a' that.

I never drank the Muses' stank,
    Castalia's burn, an' a' that;
But there it streams an' richly reams,
    My Helicon I ca' that.

Great love I bear to a' the fair,
    Their humble slave an' a' that;
But lordly will, I hold it still
    A mortal sin to thraw that.

In raptures sweet, this hour we meet,
    Wi' mutual love an' a' that;
But for how lang the flie may stang,
    Let inclination law that.

Their tricks an' craft hae put me daft,
    They've taen me in, an' a' that;
But clear your decks, and here's—'The Sex!'
    I like the jads for a' that.

Chorus: For a' that, an' a' that,
    An' twice as muckle's a' that;
My dearest bluid, to do them guid,
    They're welcome till't for a' that.

Recitativo

So sang the bard—and Nansie's wa's
Shook with a thunder of applause,
    Re-echo'd from each mouth!
They toom'd their pocks, they pawn'd their duds,
They scarcely left to co'er their fuds,
    To quench their lowin drouth.

Then owre again, the jovial thrang,
  The poet did request
To loose his pack an' wale a sang,
  A ballad o' the best;
    He rising, rejoicing,
      Between his twa Deborahs,
    Looks round him, an' found them
      Impatient for the chorus:

Air

Tune—*Jolly Mortals, fill your Glasses*

See the smoking bowl before us,
  Mark our jovial ragged ring!
Round and round take up the chorus,
  And in raptures let us sing—

Chorus: A fig for those by law protected!
  Liberty's a glorious feast!
Courts for cowards were erected,
  Churches built to please the priest.

What is title, what is treasure,
  What is reputation's care?
If we lead a life of pleasure,
  'Tis no matter how or where!

With the ready trick and fable,
  Round we wander all the day;
And at night in barn or stable,
  Hug our doxies on the hay.

Does the train-attended carriage
  Thro' the country lighter rove?
Does the sober bed of marriage
  Witness brighter scenes of love?

Life is all a variorum,
  We regard not how it goes;
Let them cant about decorum,
  Who have character to lose.

Here's to budgets, bags and wallets!
  Here's to all the wandering train!
Here's our ragged brats and callets,
  One and all cry out, Amen!

Chorus: A fig for those by law protected!
  Liberty's a glorious feast!
Courts for cowards were erected,
  Churches built to please the priest.

FOR A' THAT
Tune—*For a' that*
An Altered Version of the First Song in 'The Jolly Beggars'

Chorus: For a' that, an' a' that,
    And twice as meikle's a' that;
The bonnie lass that I loe best
    She'll be my ain for a' that.

Tho' women's minds, like winter winds,
    May shift, and turn, an' a' that,
The noblest breast adores them maist—
    A consequence I draw that.

Great love I bear to a' the fair,
    Their humble slave, an' a' that;
But lordly will, I hold it still
    A mortal sin to thraw that.

But there is ane aboon the lave,
    Has wit, and sense, an' a' that;
A bonnie lass, I like her best,
    And wha a crime dare ca' that?

In rapture sweet this hour we meet,
    Wi' mutual love an' a' that,
But for how lang the flie may stang,
    Let inclination law that.

Their tricks an' craft hae put me daft.
    They've taen me in, an' a' that;
But clear your decks, and here's—'The Sex!'
    I like the jads for a' that!

MERRY HAE I BEEN TEETHIN' A HECKLE
Tune—*The Bob of Dunblane*

O merry hae I been teethin' a heckle,
    An' merry hae I been shapin' a spoon;
O merry hae I been cloutin a kettle,
    An' kissin' my Katie when a' was done.
O a' the lang day I ca' at my hammer,
    An' a' the lang day I whistle and sing;
O a' the lang night I cuddle my kimmer,
    An' a' the lang night as happy's a king.

Bitter in dool I lickit my winnin's
    O' marrying Bess, to gie her a slave:
Blest be the hour she cool'd in her linens,
    And blythe be the bird that sings on her grave!
Come to my arms, my Katie, my Katie,
    An' come to my arms and kiss me again!
Drucken or sober, here's to thee, Katie!
    An' blest be the day I did it again.

THE COTTER'S SATURDAY NIGHT
Inscribed to R. Aiken, Esq., of Ayr

Let not Ambition mock their useful toil,
    Their homely joys, and destiny obscure;
Nor Grandeur hear, with a disdainful smile,
    The short and simple annals of the Poor.—Gray.

My lov'd, my honour'd, much respected friend!
    No mercenary bard his homage pays;
With honest pride, I scorn each selfish end,
    My dearest meed, a friend's esteem and praise:
To you I sing, in simple Scottish lays,
    The lowly train in life's sequester'd scene,
The native feelings strong, the guileless ways,
    What Aiken in a cottage would have been;
Ah! tho' his worth unknown, far happier there I ween!

November chill blaws loud wi' angry sugh;
    The short'ning winter day is near a close;
The miry beasts retreating frae the pleugh;
    The black'ning trains o' craws to their repose:
The toil-worn Cotter frae his labour goes—
    This night his weekly moil is at an end,
Collects his spades, his mattocks, and his hoes,
    Hoping the morn in ease and rest to spend,
And weary, o'er the moor, his course does hameward bend.

At length his lonely cot appears in view,
    Beneath the shelter of an aged tree;
Th' expectant wee-things, toddlin, stacher through
    To meet their dad, wi' flichterin noise and glee.
His wee-bit ingle, blinkin bonilie,
    His clean hearth-stane, his thrifty wifie's smile,
The lisping infant, prattling on his knee,
    Does a' his weary carking cares beguile,
And makes him quite forget his labour and his toil.

Belyve, the elder bairns come drapping in,
    At service out, amang the farmers roun';
Some ca' the pleugh, some herd, some tentie rin
    A cannie errand to a neebor town:
Their eldest hope, their Jenny, woman-grown,
    In youthfu' bloom—love sparkling in her e'e,
Comes hame, perhaps to show a braw new gown,
    Or deposite her sair-won penny-fee,
To help her parents dear, if they in hardship be.

With joy unfeign'd, brothers and sisters meet,
    And each for other's weelfare kindly spiers:
The social hours, swift-wing'd, unnotic'd fleet;
    Each tells the uncos that he sees or hears.

The parents partial eye their hopeful years;
    Anticipation forward points the view;
The mother, wi' her needle and her sheers,
    Gars auld claes look amaist as weel's the new;
The father mixes a' wi' admonition due.

Their master's and their mistress's command,
    The younkers a' are warned to obey;
And mind their labours wi' an eydent hand,
    And ne'er, tho' out o' sight, to jauk or play:
'And O! be sure to fear the Lord alway,
    And mind your duty, duly, morn and night!
Lest in temptation's path ye gang astray,
    Implore His counsel and assisting might:
They never sought in vain that sought the Lord aright.'

But hark! a rap comes gently to the door;
    Jenny, wha kens the meaning o' the same,
Tells how a neebor lad came o'er the moor,
    To do some errands, and convoy her hame.
The wily mother sees the conscious flame
    Sparkle in Jenny's e'e, and flush her cheek;
With heart-struck anxious care, enquires his name,
    While Jenny hafflins is afraid to speak;
Weel-pleased the mother hears, it's nae wild, worthless rake.

Wi' kindly welcome, Jenny brings him ben;
    A strappin' youth, he takes the mother's eye;
Blythe Jenny sees the visit's no ill taen;
    The father cracks of horses, pleughs and kye.
The youngster's artless heart o'erflows wi' joy,
    But blate an' laithfu', scarce can weel behave;
The mother, wi' a woman's wiles, can spy
    What makes the youth sae bashfu' and sae grave,
Weel-pleas'd to think her bairn's respected like the lave.

O happy love! where love like this is found:
    O heart-felt raptures! bliss beyond compare!
I've pacéd much this weary, mortal round,
    And sage experience bids me this declare—
'If Heaven a draught of heavenly pleasure spare,
    One cordial in this melancholy vale,
'Tis when a youthful, loving, modest pair,
    In other's arms, breathe out the tender tale,
Beneath the milk-white thorn that scents the ev'ning gale.'[1]

Is there, in human form, that bears a heart—
    A wretch! a villain! lost to love and truth!

[1] 'If anything on earth deserves the name of rapture or transport, it is the feeling of green eighteen in the company of the mistress of his heart, when she repays him with an equal return of affection.—*Commonplace Book*, April 1783.

That can, with studied, sly, ensnaring art,
    Betray sweet Jenny's unsuspecting youth?
Curse on his perjur'd arts! dissembling smooth!
    Are honour, virtue, conscience, all exil'd?
Is there no pity, no relenting ruth,
    Points to the parents fondling o'er their child?
Then paints the ruin'd maid, and their distraction wild!

But now the supper crowns their simple board,
    The halesome parritch, chief of Scotia's food;
The sowp their only hawkie does afford,
    That 'yont the hallan snugly chows her cood:
The dame brings forth, in complimental mood,
    To grace the lad, her weel-hain'd kebbuck, fell,
And aft he's prest, and aft he ca's it guid;
    The frugal wifie, garrulous, will tell
How 'twas a towmond auld, sin' lint was i' the bell.

The cheerfu' supper done, wi' serious face,
    They, round the ingle, form a circle wide;
The sire turns o'er, with patriarchal grace,
    The big ha'-Bible, ance his father's pride:
His bonnet rev'rently is laid aside,
    His lyart haffets wearing thin and bare;
Those strains that once did sweet in Zion glide,
    He wales a portion with judicious care;
And 'Let us worship God!' he says with solemn air.

They chant their artless notes in simple guise,
    They tune their hearts, by far the noblest aim:
Perhaps 'Dundee's' wild-warbling measures rise,
    Or plaintive 'Martyrs', worthy of the name;
Or noble 'Elgin' beets the heaven-ward flame,
    The sweetest far of Scotia's holy lays:
Compar'd with these, Italian trills are tame;
    The tickl'd ears no heart-felt raptures raise;
Nae unison hae they with our Creator's praise.

The priest-like father reads the sacred page,
    How Abram was the friend of God on high;
Or Moses bade eternal warfare wage,
    With Amalek's ungracious progeny;
Or how the royal bard did groaning lie
    Beneath the stroke of Heaven's avenging ire;
Or Job's pathetic plaint, and wailing cry;
    Or rapt Isaiah's wild, seraphic fire;
Or other holy seers that tune the sacred lyre.

Perhaps the Christian volume is the theme,
    How guiltless blood for guilty man was shed;
How He, who bore in Heaven the second name,
    Had not on earth whereon to lay His head:

How His first followers and servants sped;
    The precepts sage they wrote to many a land:
How he, who lone in Patmos banishéd,
    Saw in the sun a mighty angel stand,
And heard great Bab'lon's doom pronounc'd by Heaven's command.

Then kneeling down to Heaven's Eternal King,
    The saint, the father, and the husband prays:
Hope 'springs exulting on triumphant wing,'[1]
    That thus they all shall meet in future days:
There, ever bask in uncreated rays,
    No more to sigh, or shed the bitter tear,
Together hymning their Creator's praise,
    In such society, yet still more dear;
While circling Time moves round in an eternal sphere

Compar'd with this, how poor Religion's pride,
    In all the pomp of method, and of art,
When men display to congregations wide
    Devotion's ev'ry grace, except the heart!
The Power, incens'd, the pageant will desert,
    The pompous strain, the sacerdotal stole;
But haply, in some cottage far apart,
    May hear, well-pleas'd, the language of the soul;
And in His Book of Life the inmates poor enroll.

Then homeward all take off their sev'ral way;
    The youngling cottagers retire to rest;
The parent-pair their secret homage pay,
    And proffer up to Heaven the warm request,
That He who stills the raven's clam'rous nest,
    And decks the lily fair in flow'ry pride,
Would, in the way His Wisdom sees the best,
    For them and for their little ones provide;
But chiefly, in their hearts with grace divine preside.

From scenes like these, old Scotia's grandeur springs,
    That makes her lov'd at home, rever'd abroad:
Princes and lords are but the breath of kings,[2]
    'An honest man's the noblest work of God;'
And certes, in fair virtue's heavenly road,
    The cottage leaves the palace far behind;
What is a lordling's pomp? a cumbrous load,
    Disguising oft the wretch of human kind,
Studied in arts of hell, in wickedness refin'd!

O Scotia! my dear, my native soil!
    For whom my warmest wish to Heaven is sent,

---

[1] Pope's 'Windsor Forest'.—R.B.
[2] 'Princes and lords may flourish, or may fade;
A breath can make them, as a breath has made.'—Goldsmith's *Deserted Village*.

Long may thy hardy sons of rustic toil
    Be blest with health, and peace, and sweet content!
And O! may Heaven their simple lives prevent
    From luxury's contagion, weak and vile!
Then howe'er crowns and coronets be rent,
    A virtuous populace may rise the while,
And stand a wall of fire around their much lov'd isle.

O Thou! who pour'd the patriotic tide,
    That stream'd thro' great unhappy Wallace' heart,
Who dar'd to, nobly, stem tyrannic pride,
    Or nobly die, the second glorious part:
(The patriot's God, peculiarly thou art,
    His friend, inspirer, guardian, and reward!)
O never, never Scotia's realm desert,
    But still the patriot, and the patriot-bard
In bright succession raise, her ornament and guard!

ADDRESS TO THE DEIL

'O Prince! O chief of many thronéd Pow'rs
That led th' embattl'd Seraphim to war—'—Milton.

O Thou! whatever title suit thee—
Auld Hornie, Satan, Nick, or Clootie,
Wha in yon cavern grim an' sootie,
            Clos'd under hatches,
Spairges about the brunstane cootie,
            To scaud poor wretches!

Hear me, auld Hangie, for a wee,
An' let poor damnéd bodies be;
I'm sure sma' pleasure it can gie,
            Ev'n to a deil,
To skelp an' scaud poor dogs like me,
            An' hear us squeel!

Great is thy pow'r, an' great thy fame;
Far kenm'd an' noted is thy name;
An' tho' yon lowin' heuch's thy hame,
            Thou travels far;
An' faith! thou's neither lag nor lame,
            Nor blate, nor scaur.

Whyles, ranging like a roarin' lion,
For prey, a' holes and corners tryin';
Whyles, on the strong-wind'd tempest flyin',
            Tirlin' the kirks;
Whyles, in the human bosom pryin',
            Unseen thou lurks.

I've heard my rev'rend graunie say,
In lanely glens ye like to stray;

Or where auld ruin'd castles grey
        Nod to the moon,
Ye fright the nightly wand'rer's way,
        Wi' eldritch croon.

When twilight did my graunie summon,
To say her pray'rs, douse, honest woman!
Aft 'yont the dyke she's heard you bummin',
        Wi' eerie drone;
Or, rustlin', thro' the boortrees comin',
        Wi' heavy groan.

Ae dreary, windy, winter night,
The stars shot down wi' sklentin light,
Wi' you, mysel, I gat a fright,
        Ayont the lough;
Ye, like a rash-buss, stood in sight,
        Wi' wavin' sough.

The cudgel in my nieve did shake,
Each brist'ld hair stood like a stake,
When wi' an eldritch, stoor 'quaick, quaick',
        Amang the springs,
Awa ye squatter'd like a drake,
        On whistlin' wings.

Let warlocks grim, an' wither'd hags,
Tell how wi' you, on ragweed nags,
They skim the muirs an' dizzy crags,
        Wi' wicked speed;
And in kirkyards renew their leagues,
        Owre howket dead.

Thence countra wives, wi' toil and pain,
May plunge an' plunge the kirn in vain;
For oh! the yellow treasure's taen
        By witching skill;
An' dawtit, twal-pint hawkie's gane
        As yell's the bill.

Thence mystic knots mak great abuse
On young guidmen, fond, keen an' crouse,
When the best wark-lume i' the house,
        By cantrip wit,
Is instant made no worth a louse,
        Just at the bit.

When thowes dissolve the snawy hoord,
An' float the jinglin' icy boord,
Then water-kelpies haunt the foord,
        By your direction,

And 'nighted trav'llers are allur'd
        To their destruction.

And aft your moss-traversin Spunkies
Decoy the wight that late an' drunk is:
The bleezin, curst, mischievous monkies
        Delude his eyes,
Till in some miry slough he sunk is,
        Ne'er mair to rise.

When masons' mystic word an' grip
In storms an' tempests raise you up,
Some cock or cat your rage maun stop,
        Or, strange to tell!
The youngest brither ye wad whip
        Aff straught to hell.

Lang syne in Eden's bonnie yard,
When youthfu' lovers first were pair'd,
An' all the soul of love they shar'd,
        The raptur'd hour,
Sweet on the fragrant flow'ry swaird,
        In shady bow'r;[1]

Then you, ye auld, snick-drawing dog!
Ye cam to Paradise incog,
An' play'd on man a cursed brogue,
        (Black be your fa'!)
An' gied the infant warld a shog,
        'Maist ruin'd a'.

D'ye mind that day when in a bizz
Wi' reekit duds, an' reestit gizz,
Ye did present your smoutie phiz
        'Mang better folk,
An' sklented on the man of Uzz
        Your spitefu' joke?

An' how ye gat him i' your thrall,
An' brak him out o' house an hal',
While scabs and botches did him gall,
        Wi' bitter claw;
An' lows'd his ill-tongu'd wicked scaul',
        Was warst ava?

[1] The original verse ran:
'Lang syne, in Eden's happy scene
When strappin Adam's days were green,
And Eve was like my bonie Jean—
        My dearest part,
A dancin, sweet, young handsome quean,
        O' guileless heart.'
The change was made following a rupture with Jean Armour.

But a' your doings to rehearse,
Your wily snares an' fechtin fierce,
Sin' that day Michael[1] did you pierce,
      Down to this time,
Wad ding a Lallan tounge, or Erse,
      In prose or rhyme.

An' now, auld 'Cloots', I ken ye're thinkin,
A certain bardie's rantin', drinkin',
Some luckless hour will send him linkin'
      To your black pit;
But faith! he'll turn a corner jinkin',
      An' cheat you yet.

But fare-you-weel, auld Nickie-ben!
O wad ye tak a thought an' men'!
Ye aiblins might—I dinna ken—
      Still hae a stake—
I'm wae to think upo' yon den,
      Ev'n for your sake!

[1] *Vide* Milton, Book 6.—R.B.

SCOTCH DRINK

Gie him strong drink until he wink,
  That's sinking in despair;
An' liquor guid to fire his bluid,
  That's prest wi' grief an' care:
There let him bouse an' deep carouse,
  Wi' bumpers flowing o'er,
Till he forgets his loves or debts,
  An' minds his griefs no more.—Solomon's Proverbs, 31:6, 7

Let other poets raise a fracas
'Bout vines, an' wines, an' drucken Bacchus,
An' crabbit names an' stories wrack us,
      An' grate our lug:
I sing the juice Scotch bear can mak us,
      In glass or jug.

O thou, my Muse! guid auld Scotch drink!
Whether thro' wimplin worms thou jink,
Or, richly brown, ream owre the brink,
      In glorious faem,
Inspire me, till I lisp an' wink,
      To sing thy name!

Let husky wheat the haughs adorn,
An' aits set up their awnie horn,
An' pease an' beans, at e'en or morn,
      Perfume the plain:
Leeze me on thee, John Barleycorn,
      Thou king o' grain!

On thee aft Scotland chows her cood,
In souple scones, the wale o' food!
Or tumblin' in the boiling flood
      Wi' kail an' beef;
But when thou pours thy strong heart's blood,
      There thou shines chief.

Food fills the wame, an' keeps us leevin;
Tho' life's a gift no worth receivin',
When heavy-dragg'd wi' pine an' grievin';
      But oil'd by thee,
The wheels o' life gae down-hill, scrievin,
      Wi' rattlin' glee.

Thou clears the head o' doited Lear;
Thou cheers the heart o' drooping Care;
Thou strings the nerves o' Labour sair,
      At's weary toil;
Though even brightens dark Despair
      Wi' gloomy smile.

Aft, clad in massy siller weed,
Wi' gentles thou erects thy head;
Yet humbly kind in time o' need,
      The poor man's wine;
His weep drap parritch, or his bread,
      Thou kitchens fine.

Thou art the life o' public haunts;
But thee, what were our fairs and rants?
Ev'n godly meetings o' the saunts,
      By thee inspir'd,
When gaping they besiege the tents,
      Are doubly fir'd.[1]

That merry night we get the corn in,
O sweetly, then, thou reams the horn in!
Or reekin' on a New-year mornin'
      In cog or bicker,
An' just a wee drap sp'ritual burn in,
      An' gusty sucker!

When Vulcan gies his bellows breath,
An' ploughmen gather wi' their graith,
O rare! to see thee fizz an' freath
      I' th' luggit caup!
Then Burnewin comes on like death
      At every chap.

Nae mercy, then, for airn or steel;
The brawnie, banie, ploughman-chiel

[1] *See* 'The Holy Fair', page 141.

Brings hard owrehip, wi' sturdy wheel,
        The strong forehammer,
Till block an' studdie ring an' reel,
        Wi' dinsome clamour.

When skirling weanies see the light,
Thou maks the gossips clatter bright,
How fumblin' coofs their dearies slight,
        Wae worth the name!
Nae howdie gets a social night,
        Or plack frae them.

When neebors anger at a plea,
An' just as wud as wud can be,
How easy can the barley-brie
        Cement the quarrel!
It's aye the cheapest lawyer's fee
        To taste the barrel.

Alake! that e'er my Muse has reason
To wyte her countrymen wi' treason!
But monie daily weet their weason
        Wi' liquors nice,
An' hardly, in a winter season,
        E'er spier her price.

Wae worth that brandy, burnin' trash!
Fell source o' monie a pain an' brash!
Twins monie a poor, doylt, drucken hash
        O' half his days;
An' sends, beside, auld Scotland's cash
        To her warst faes.

Ye Scots wha wish auld Scotland well!
Ye chief, to you my tale I tell,
Poor, plackless devils like mysel!
        It sets you ill,
Wi' bitter, dearthfu' wines to mell,
        Or foreign gill.

May gravels round his blather wrench,
An' gouts torment him, inch by inch,
What twists his gruntle wi' a glunch
        O' sour disdain,
Out owre a glass o' whisky-punch
        Wi' honest men!

O Whisky! soul o' plays an' pranks!
Accept a bardie's humble thanks!
When wanting thee, what tuneless cranks
        Are my poor verses!
Thou comes—they rattle in their ranks,
        At ither's arses!

Thee, Ferintosh![1] O sadly lost!
Scotland lament frae coast to coast!
Now colic grips, an' barkin' hoast
      May kill us a';
For loyal Forbes' charter'd boast
      Is taen awa!

Thae curst horse-leeches o' th' Excise,
Wha mak the whisky stells their prize!
Haud up thy han', Deil! ance, twice, thrice!
      There, seize the blinkers!
An' bake them up in brunstane pies
      For poor damn'd drinkers.

Fortune! if thou'll but gie me still
Hale breeks, a scone, an' whisky gill,
An' rowth o' rhyme to rave at will,
      Tak a' the rest,
An' deal't about as thy blind skill
      Directs thee best.

---

[1] Whisky from a privileged distillery in Cromartyshire, belonging to Forbes of Culloden. The privilege was abolished by Parliament in 1785.

THE AULD FARMER'S NEW-YEAR MORNING SALUTATION
TO HIS AULD MARE, MAGGIE
On giving her the accustomed Ripp of Corn to hansel in the New Year

A Guid New-year I wish thee, Maggie!
Hae, there's a ripp to thy auld baggie:
Tho' thou's howe-backit now, an' knaggie,
      I've seen the day
Thou could hae gaen like onie staggie,
      Out-owre the lay.

Tho' now thou's dowie, stiff an' crazy,
An' thy auld hide as white's a daisie,
I've seen thee dappl't, sleek an' glaizie,
      A bonnie grey:
He should been tight that daur't to raize thee,
      Ance in a day.

Thou ance was i' the foremost rank,
A filly buirdly, steeve an' swank;
An' set weel down a shapely shank,
      As e'er tread yird;
An' could hae flown out-owre a stank,
      Like onie bird.

It's now some nine-an'-twenty year,
Sin' thou was my guid-father's mear;

He gied me thee, o' tocher clear,
      An' fifty mark;
Tho' it was sma', 'twas weel-won gear,
      An' thou was stark.

When first I gaed to woo my Jenny,
Ye then was trotting wi' your minnie:
Tho' ye was trickie, slee an' funnie,
      Ye ne'er was donsie;
But hamely, tawie, quiet an' cannie,
      An' unco sonsie.

That day, ye pranc'd wi' muckle pride,
When ye bure hame my bonnie bride:
An' sweet an' gracefu' she did ride,
      Wi' maiden air!
Kyle-Stewart[1] I could bragged wide
      For sic a pair.

Tho' now ye dow but hoyte and hobble,
An' wintle like a saumont coble,
That day, ye was a jinker noble,
      For heels an' win'!
An' ran them till they a' did wauble,
      Far, far, behin'!

When thou an' I were young an' skeigh,
An' stable-meals at fairs were dreigh,
How thou wad prance, an' snore, an' skreigh
      An' tak the road!
Town's-bodies ran an' stood abeigh,
      An' ca't thee mad.

When thou was corn't, an' I was mellow,
We took the road aye like a swallow:
At brooses thou had ne'er a fellow,
      For pith an' speed;
But ev'ry tail thou pay't them hollow,
      Whare'er thou gaed.

The sma', droop-rumpl't hunter cattle
Might aiblins waur't thee for a brattle;
But sax Scotch miles, thou try't their mettle,
      An' gart them whaizle:
Nae whip nor spur, but just a wattle
      O' saugh or hazel.

Thou was a noble fittie-lan',
As e'er in tug or tow was drawn!
Aft thee an' I, in aught hours' gaun,
      In guid March-weather,

[1] *See* note page 39.

Hae turn'd sax rood beside our han',
          For days thegither.

Thou never braing't, an' fetch't, an' fliskit;
But thy auld tail thou wad hae whiskit,
An' spread abreed thy weel-fill'd brisket,
          Wi' pith an' power,
Till sprittie knowes wad rair't an' riskit
          An' slypet owre.

When frosts lay lang, an' snaws were deep,
An' threaten'd labour back to keep,
I gied thy cog a wee-bit heap
          Aboon the timmer:
I kenn'd my Maggie wad na sleep,
          For that, or Simmer.

In cart or car thou never reestit;
The steyest brae thou wad hae fac't it;
Thou never lap, an' sten't, and breastit,
          Then stood to blaw;
But just thy step a wee thing hastit,
          Thou snoov't awa.

My 'pleugh'[1] is now thy bairn-time a',
Four gallant brutes as e'er did draw;
Forbye sax mae, I've sell't awa,
          That thou hast nurst:
They drew me thretteen pund an' twa,
          The vera warst.

Monie a sair daurk we twa hae wrought,
An' wi' the weary warl' fought!
An' monie an anxious day, I thought
          We wad be beat!
Yet here to crazy age we're brought,
          Wi' something yet.

An' think na', my auld trusty servan',
That now perhaps thou's less deservin',
An' thy auld days may end in starvin',
          For my last fow,
A heapit stimpart, I'll reserve ane
          Laid by for you.

We've worn to crazy years thegither;
We'll toyte about wi' ane anither;
Wi' tentie care I'll flit thy tether
          To some hain'd rig,
Whare ye may nobly rax your leather,
          Wi' sma' fatigue.

---

[1] A figure of speech here used for the plough team.

THE TWA DOGS
A Tale

'Twas in that place o' Scotland's isle,
That bears the name o' auld King Coil,[1]
Upon a bonnie day in June,
When wearin' thro' the afternoon,
Twa dogs, that were na thrang at hame,
Forgather'd ance upon a time.

    The first I'll name, they ca'd him Caesar,
Was keepit for His Honour's pleasure:
His hair, his size, his mouth, his lugs,
Show'd he was nane o' Scotland's dogs;
But whalpit some place far abroad,
Whare sailors gang to fish for cod.

    His lockéd, letter'd, braw brass collar
Show'd him the gentleman an' scholar;
But though he was o' high degree,
The fient a pride na pride had he,
But wad hae spent an hour caressin',
Ev'n wi' a tinkler-gipsy's messin':
At kirk or market, mill or smiddie,
Nae tawted tyke, tho' e'er sae duddie,
But he wad stan't, as glad to see him,
An' stroan't on stanes an' hillocks wi' him.

    The tither was a ploughman's collie—
A rhyming, ranting, raving billie,
Wha for his friend an' comrade had him,
And in his freaks had Luath[2] ca'd him,
After some dog in Highland Sang,[3]
Was made lang syne—Lord knows how lang.

    He was a gash an' faithfu' tyke,
As ever lap a sheugh or dyke.
His honest, sonsie, baws'nt face
Aye gat him friends in ilka place;
His breast was white, his touzie back
Weel clad wi' coat o' glossy black;
His gawsie tail, wi' upward curl,
Hung owre his hurdie's wi' a swirl.

    Nae doubt but they were fain o' ither,
And unco pack an' thick thegither;
Wi' social nose whyles snuff'd an' snowkit;
Whyles mice an' moudieworts they howkit;
Whyles scour'd awa in lang excursion,
An' worry'd ither in diversion;
Until wi' daffin' weary grown
Upon a knowe they set them down.
An' there began a lang digression.
About the 'lords o' the creation'.

---

[1] The district of King's Kyle in Ayrshire.
[2] Luath was the name of Burns' own dog.
[3] Luath, Cuchullin's dog in Ossian's 'Fingal'.—R.B.

Caesar

I've aften wonder'd, honest Luath,
What sort o' life poor dogs like you have;
An' when the gentry's life I saw,
What way poor bodies liv'd ava.
　Our laird gets in his rackéd rents,
His coals, his kane, an' a' his stents:
He rises when he likes himsel;
His flunkies answer at the bell;
He ca's his coach; he ca's his horse;
He draws a bonnie silken purse
As lang's my tail, where thro' the steeks,
The yellow letter'd Geordie keeks.
　Frae morn to e'en, it's nought but toiling
At baking, roasting, frying, boiling;
An' tho' the gentry first are stechin,
Yet ev'n the ha' folk fill their pechan
Wi' sauce, ragouts, an' sic like trashtrie,
That's little short o' downright wastrie.
Our whipper-in, wee, blasted wonner,
Poor, worthless elf, it eats a dinner,
Better than onie tenant-man
His Honour has in a' the lan':
An' what poor cot-folk pit their painch in,
I own it's past my comprehension.

Luath

Trowth, Caesar, whyles they're fash't eneugh:
A cotter howkin in a sheugh,
Wi' dirty stanes biggin a dyke,
Baring a quarry, an' sic like;
Himsel a wife, he thus sustains,
A smytrie o' wee duddie weans,
An' nought but his han'-daurk, to keep
Them right an' tight in thack an' rape.
　An' when they meet wi' sair disasters,
Like loss o' health or want o' masters,
Ye maist wad think, a wee touch langer,
An' they maun starve o' cauld an' hunger:
But how it comes, I never kent yet,
They're maistly wonderfu' contented;
An' buirdly chiels, an' clever hizzies,
Are bred in sic a way as this is.

Caesar

But then to see how ye're negleckit,
How huff'd, an' cuff'd, an' disrespeckit!
Lord man, our gentry care as little
For delvers, ditchers, an' sic cattle;
They gang as saucy by poor folk,
As I wad by a stinkin' brock.
　I've notic'd, on our laird's court-day—

An' monie a time my heart's been wae—
Poor tenant bodies, scant o'cash,
How they maun thole a factor's snash;
He'll stamp an' threaten, curse an' swear,
He'll apprehend them, poind their gear;
While they maun stan', wi' aspect humble,
An' hear it a', an' fear an' tremble!
    I see how folk live that hae riches;
But surely poor-folk maun be wretches!

Luath

    They're no sae wretched's ane wad think;
Tho' constantly on poortith's brink,
They're sae accustom'd wi' the sight,
The view o't gives them little fright.
    Then chance and fortune are sae guided,
They're aye in less or mair provided;
An' tho' fatigu'd wi' close employment,
A blink o' rest's a sweet enjoyment.
    The dearest comfort o' their lives,
Their grushie weans an' faithfu' wives;
The prattling things are just their pride,
That sweetens a' their fire side.
    An' whyles twalpennie worth o' nappy
Can mak the bodies unco happy;
They lay aside their private cares,
To mind the Kirk and State affairs;
They'll talk o' patronage an' priests,
Wi' kindling fury i' their breasts,
Or tell what new taxation's comin',
An' ferlie at the folk in Lon'on.
    As bleak-fac'd Hallowmass returns,
They get the jovial, rantin' kirns,
When rural life, of ev'ry station,
Unite in common recreation;
Love blinks, Wit slaps, an' social Mirth
Forgets there's Care upo' the earth.
    That merry day the year begins,
They bar the door on frosty win's;
The nappy reeks wi' mantling ream,
An' sheds a heart-inspiring steam;
The luntin pipe, an' sneeshin mill,
Are handed round wi' right guid will;
The cantie auld folks crackin' crouse,
The young anes rantin' thro' the house—
My heart has been sae fain to see them,
That I for joy hae barkit wi' them.
    Still it's owre true that ye hae said,
Sic game is now owre aften play'd;
There's monie a creditable stock
O' decent, honest, fawsont folk,

Are riven out baith root an' branch,
Some rascal's pridefu' greed to quench,
Wha thinks to knit himsel the faster
In favour wi' some gentle master,
Wha aiblins thrang a parliamentin,
For Britain's guid his saul indentin'—

Caesar

Haith, lad, ye little ken about it:
For Britain's guid! guid faith! I doubt it.
Say rather, gaun as Premiers lead him,
An' saying *aye* or *no*'s they bid him:
At operas an' plays parading,
Mortgaging, gambling, masquerading:
Or maybe, in a frolic daft,
To Hague or Calais takes a waft,
To mak a tour an' tak a whirl,
To learn *bon ton*, an' see the worl'.

There, at Vienna or Versailles,
He rives his father's auld entails;
Or by Madrid he takes the rout,
To thrum guitars an' fecht wi' nowt;
Or down Italian vista startles,
Whore-hunting amang groves o' myrtles:
Then bowses drumlie German-water,
To mak himsel look fair an' fatter,
An' clear the consequential sorrows,
Love-gifts of Carnival signoras.

For Britain's guid! for her destruction!
Wi' dissipation, feud, an' faction.

Luath

Hech, man! dear sirs! is that the gate
They waste sae monie a braw estate!
Are we sae foughten an' harass'd
For gear to gang that gate at last!

O would they stay aback frae courts,
An' please themsels wi' countra sports,
It wad for ev'ry ane be better,
The laird, the tenant, an' the cotter!
For thae frank, rantin', ramblin' billies,
Feint haet o' them's ill-hearted fellows;
Except for breakin' o' their timmer,
Or speakin' lightly o' their limmer,
Or shootin' of a hare or moorcock,
The ne'er-a-bit they're ill to poor folk,

But will ye tell me, Master Caesar,
Sure great folk's life's a life o' pleasure?
Nae cauld nor hunger e'er can steer them,
The very thought o't need na fear them.

Caesar

Lord, man, were ye but whyles whare I am,

The gentles, ye wad ne'er envy them!
  It's true, they need na starve or sweat,
Thro' winter's cauld, or Simmer's heat:
They've nae sair-wark to craze their banes,
An' fill auld age wi' grips an' granes:
But human bodies are sic fools,
For a' their colleges an' schools,
That when nae real ills perplex them,
They mak enow themsels to vex them;
An' aye the less they hae to sturt them,
In like proportion, less will hurt them.
  A country fellow at the pleugh,
His acre's till'd, he's right eneugh;
A country girl at her wheel,
Her dizzen's done, she's unco weel;
But gentlemen, an' ladies warst,
Wi' ev'n-down want o' wark are curst.
They loiter, lounging, lank an' lazy;
Tho' deil-haet ails them, yet uneasy;
Their days insipid, dull an' tasteless;
Their nights unquiet, lang an' restless.
  An' ev'n their sports, their balls an' races,
Their galloping through public places,
There's sic parade, sic pomp an' art,
The joy can scarcely reach the heart.
  The men cast out in party-matches,
Then sowther a' in deep debauches.
Ae night they're mad wi' drink an' whoring,
Niest day their life is past enduring.
  The ladies arm-in-arm in clusters,
As great an' gracious a' as sisters;
But hear their absent thoughts o' ither,
They're a' run-deils an' jads thegither.
Whyles, owre the wee bit cup an' platie,
They sip the scandal-potion pretty;
Or lee-lang nights, wi' crabbit leuks
Pore owre the devil's pictur'd beuks;
Stake on a chance a farmer's stackyard,
An' cheat like onie unhang'd blackguard.
  There's some exceptions, man an' woman;
But this is gentry's life in common.

  By this, the sun was out o' sight,
An' darker gloamin' brought the night:
The bum-clock humm'd wi' lazy drone,
The kye stood rowtin i' the loan;
When up they gat an' shook their lugs,
Rejoic'd they werena men but dogs;
An' each took aff his several way,
Resolv'd to meet some ither day.

THE AUTHOR'S EARNEST CRY AND PRAYER
To the Right Honourable and Honourable Scotch Representatives in the
House of Commons[1]

Dearest of distillation! last and best—
——How art thou lost!— Parody on Milton

Ye Irish lords, ye knights an' squires,[2]
Wha represent our brughs an' shires,
An' doucely manage our affairs
            In parliament,
To you a simple poet's pray'rs
            Are humbly sent.

Alas! my roupit Muse is hearse!
Your Honours' hearts wi' grief 'twad pierce,
To see her sittin' on her arse
            Low i' the dust,
And scriechin out prosaic verse,
            An' like to brust!

Tell them wha hae the chief direction,
Scotland an' me's in great affliction,
E'er sin' they laid that curst restriction
            On aquavitae;
An' rouse them up to strong conviction,
            An' move their pity.

Stand forth an' tell yon Premier youth[3]
The honest, open, naked truth:
Tell him o' mine an' Scotland's drouth,
            His servants humble:
The muckle deevil blaw you south
            If ye dissemble!

Does onie great man glunch an' gloom?
Speak out, an' never fash your thumb.
Let posts an' pensions sink or swoom
            Wi' them wha grant them;
If honestly they canna come,
            Far better want them.

In gath'rin votes you were na slack;
Now stand as tightly by your tack:
Ne'er claw your lug, an' fidge your back,
            An' hum an' haw;
But raise your arm, an' tell your crack
            Before them a'.

[1] This was written before the Act anent the Scotch distilleries, of session 1786, for which Scotland and the Author return their most grateful thanks.—R.B.
[2] Many of Scotland's MPs were poor Irish noblemen married to Scottish noblewomen.
[3] William Pitt the Younger.

Paint Scotland greetin' owre her thrissle;
Her mutchkin stowp as toom's a whissle;
An' damn'd excisemen in a bussle,
    Seizin' a stell,
Triumphant crushin't like a mussel,
    Or limpet shell!

Then on the tither hand present her—
A blackguard smuggler right behint her,
An' cheek-for-chow, a chuffie vintner
    Colleaguing join,
Picking her pouch as bare as Winter
    Of a' kind coin.

Is there, that bears the name o' Scot,
But feels his heart's bluid rising hot,
To see his poor auld mither's pot
    Thus dung in staves,
An' plunder'd o' her hindmost groat
    By gallows knaves?

Alas! I'm but a nameless wight,
Trode i' the mire out o' sight?
But could I like Montgomeries[1] fight,
    Or gab like Boswell,[2]
There's some sark-necks I wad draw tight,
    An' tie some hose well.

God bless your Honours! can ye see't,
The kind, auld cantie carlin greet,
An' no get warmly to your feet,
    An' gar them hear it,
An' tell them, wi'a patriot-heat,
    Ye winna bear it?

Some o' you nicely ken the laws,
To round the period an' pause,
An' with rhetoric clause on clause
    To mak harangues;
Then echo thro' Saint Stephen's wa's
    Auld Scotland's wrangs.

Dempster,[3] a true blue Scot I'se warran';
Thee, aith-detesting, chaste Kilkerran;[4]
An' that glib-gabbit Highland baron,
    The Laird o' Graham;[5]
An' ane, a chap that's damn'd auldfarran',
    Dundas his name:[6]

[1] The Montgomeries of Coilsfield.
[2] The biographer of Dr Johnson, James Boswell of Auchinleck.
[3] George Dempster of Dunnichen, MP.
[4] Sir Adam Ferguson of Kilkerran, MP.
[5] Marquis of Graham, afterwards Duke of Montrose.
[6] Right Hon. Henry Dundas, MP.

Erskine, a spunkie Norland billie;[1]
True Campbells, Frederick an' Ilay;[2]
An' Livistone, the bauld Sir Willie;[3]
    An' monie ithers,
Whom auld Demosthenes or Tully
    Might own for brithers.

See sodger Hugh,[4] my watchman stented,
If poets e'er are represented;
I ken if that your sword were wanted,
    Ye'd lend a hand;
But when there's ought to say anent it,
    Ye're at a stand.

Arouse, my boys! exert your mettle,
To get auld Scotland back her kettle!
Or faith! I'll wad my new pleugh-pettle,
    Ye'll see't or lang,
She'll teach you, wi' a reekin whittle,
    Anither sang.

This while she's been in crankous mood,
Her lost Militia[5] fir'd her bluid;
(Deil na they never mair do guid,
    Play'd her that pliskie!)
An' now she's like to rin red-wud
    About her whisky.

An' Lord! if ance they pit her till't,
Her tartan petticoat she'll kilt,
An' durk an' pistol at her belt,
    She'll tak the streets,
An' rin her whittle to the hilt,
    I' the first she meets!

For God-sake, sirs! then speak her fair,
An' straik her cannie wi' the hair,
An' to the muckle house repair,
    Wi' instant speed,
An' strive, wi' a' your wit an' lear,
    To get remead.

Yon ill-tongu'd tinkler, Charlie Fox,
May taunt you wi' his jeers and mocks;

[1] Thomas, afterward Lord Erskine.
[2] Lord Frederick Campbell, MP, second brother of the Duke of Argyll, and Ilay Campbell, Lord Advocate, afterwards Lord President of the Court of Session.
[3] Sir William Augustus Cunningham, Bt, of Livingston, sat as MP for the county of Linlithgow, where he had his estate, which he had to sell because of election debts.
[4] Colonel Hugh Montgomerie of Coilsfield, afterwards Earl of Eglinton. Burns suppressed this stanza in the first published edition because of the closing words alluding to this brave soldier's imperfect eloquence.
[5] The Scots Militia Bill was burdened with conditions which liberal Members would not accept, and it was opposed and lost.

But gie him't het, my hearty cocks!
      E'en cowe the cadie!
An' send him to his dicing box
      An' sportin' lady.

Tell you guid bluid o' auld Boconnock's,[1]
I'll be his debt twa mashlum bonnocks,[2]
An' drink his health in auld Nanse Tinnock's[3]
      Nine times a week,
If he some scheme, like tea an' winnocks,[4]
      Wad kindly seek.

Could he some commutation broach,
I'll pledge my aith in guid braid Scotch,
He need na fear their foul reproach
      Nor erudition,
Yon mixtie-maxtie, queer hotch-potch,
      The Coalition.[5]

Auld Scotland has a raucle tongue;
She's just a devil wi' a rung;
An' if she promise auld or young
      To tak their part,
Tho' by the neck she should be strung,
      She'll no desert.

And now, ye chosen Five-and-Forty,[6]
May still your mither's heart support ye;
Then, tho' a minister grow dorty,
      An' kick your place,
Ye'll snap your gingers, poor an' hearty,
      Before his face.

God bless your Honours, a' your days,
Wi' sowps o' kail and brats o' claise,
In spite o' a' the thievish kaes,
      That haunt St Jamie's!
Your humble poet sings an' prays,
      While Rab his name is.

Postscript

Let half-starv'd slaves in warmer skies
See future wines, rich-clust'ring, rise;
Their lot auld Scotland ne'er envies,
      But, blythe an' frisky,
She eyes her freeborn, martial boys
      Tak aff their whisky.

[1] William Pitt was a grandson of Robert Pitt of Boconnock in Cornwall.
[2] Bannocks or scones made of a mash of various kinds of grain.
[3] A worthy old hostess of the author's in Mauchline, where he sometimes studies politics over a glass of guid auld 'Scotch Drink'.—R.B.
[4] Some duty was taken off tea, and the loss made up by a window tax.
[5] The 1783 government of Fox and North.   [6] The Scottish MPs.

What tho' their Phoebus kinder warms,
While fragrance blooms and beauty charms!
When wretches range, in famish'd swarms,
       The scented groves;
Or hounded forth, dishonour arms
       In hungry droves!

Their gun's a burden on their shouther;
They downa bide the stink o' powther;
Their bauldest thought's a hank'ring swither
       To stan' or rin,
Till skelp—a shot—they're aff, a' throw'ther,
       To save their skin.

But bring a Scotchman frae his hill,
Clap in his cheek a Highland gill,
Say, such is royal George's will,
       An' there's the foe!
He has nae thought but how to kill
       Twa at a blow.

Nae cauld, faint-hearted doubtings tease him;
Death comes, wi' fearless eye he sees him;
Wi' bluidy hand a welcome gies him;
       An' when he fa's,
His latest draught o' breathin' lea'es him
       In faint huzzas.

Sages their solemn een may steek,
An' raise a philosophic reek,
An' physically causes seek,
       In clime an' season,
But tell me whisky's name in Greek,
       I'll tell the reason.

Scotland, my auld, respected mither!
Tho' whyles ye moistify your leather,
Till whare ye sit, on craps o' heather,
       Ye tine your dam;
Freedom an' whisky gang thegither!
       Take aff your dram!

THE ORDINATION

'For sense they little owe to frugal Heav'n—
To please the mob, they hide the little giv'n.'

Kilmarnock wabsters, fidge an' claw,
    An' pour your creeshie nations;
An' ye wha leather rax an' draw,
    Of a' denominations;
Swith to the Laigh Kirk, ane an' a',
    An' there tak up your stations;

Then aff to Begbie's[1] in a raw,
 An' pour divine libations
   For joy this day.

Curst Common-sense, that imp o' hell,
 Cam in wi' Maggie Lauder;[2]
But Oliphant[3] aft made her yell,
 An' Russell[4] sair misca'd her:
This day Mackinlay[5] taks the flail,
 An' he's the boy will blaud her!
He'll clap a shangan on her tail,
 An' set the bairns to daud her
   Wi' dirt this day.

Mak haste an' turn King David owre,
 And lilt wi' holy clangor;
O' double verse come gie us four,
 An' skirl up the Bangor:[6]
This day the kirk kicks up a stoure;
 Nae mair the knaves shall wrang her,
For Heresy is in her pow'r,
 And gloriously she'll whang her
   Wi' pith this day.

Come, let a proper text be read,
 An' touch it aff wi' vigour,
How graceless Ham[7] leugh at his dad,
 Which made Canaan a nigger;
Or Phineas[8] drove the murdering blade,
 Wi' whore-abhorring rigour;
Or Zipporah,[9] the scauldin jad,
 Was like a bluidy tiger
   I' th' inn that day.

There, try his mettle on the creed,
 An' bind him down wi' caution,
That stipend is a carnal weed
 He taks but for the fashion;
And gie him o'er the flock, to feed,
 And punish each transgression;
Especial, rams that cross the breed,
 Gie them sufficient threshin';
   Spare them nae day.

[1] Begbie's Inn, in a small court near the Laigh Kirk.
[2] Alluding to a scoffing ballad which was made on the admission of the late reverend and worthy Mr Lindsay to the 'Laigh Kirk'.—R.B.
[3] Rev. James Oliphant, minister of Chapel of Ease, Kilmarnock, from 1764 to 1774.
[4] Rev. John Russell of Kilmarnock, one of the 'Twa Herds'. He was successor to Oliphant.
[5] Rev. James Mackinlay, subject of the present poem, ordained 6 April 1786. As a preacher, he became 'a great favourite of the million'.
[6] A favourite psalm tune.   [7] Genesis 9:22.   [8] Numbers 25:8.   [9] Exodus 4:52.

Now, auld Kilmarnock, cock thy tail,
    An' toss thy horns fu' canty;
Nae mair thou'lt rowt out-owre the dale,
    Because thy pasture's scanty;
For lapfu's large o' gospel kail
    Shall fill thy crib in plenty,
An' runts o' grace the pick an' wale,
    No gi'en by way o' dainty,
            But ilka day.

Nae mair by Babel's streams we'll weep,
    To think upon our Zion;
And hing our fiddles up to sleep,
    Like baby-clouts a-dryin'!
Come, screw the pegs wi' tunefu' cheep,
    And o'er the thairms be tryin';
Oh, rare to see our elbucks wheep,
    And a' like lamb-tails flyin'
            Fu' fast this day.

Lang, Patronage, wi' rod o' airn,
    Has shor'd the Kirk's undoin';
As lately Fenwick, sair forfairn,
    Has proven to its ruin:[1]
Our patron, honest man! Glencairn,[2]
    He saw mischief was brewin';
An' like a godly, elect bairn,
    He's wal'd us out a true ane,
            And sound, this day.

Now Robertson[3] harangue nae mair,
    But steek your gab for ever;
Or try the wicked town of Ayr,
    For there they'll think you clever;
Or, nae reflection on your lear,
    Ye may commence a shaver;
Or to the Netherton[4] repair,
    An' turn a carpet weaver
            Aff-hand this day.

Mu'trie[5] and you were just a match,
    We never had sic twa drones;
Auld Hornie did the Laigh Kirk watch,
    Just like a winkin' baudrons,

---

[1] Rev. Wm. Boyd, a 'moderate', ordained pastor of Fenwick, 25 June 1782.
[2] The Earl of Glencairn, who exercised patronage in the appointment of ministers to the Laigh Kirk to the dismay of the people of Kilmarnock.
[3] Rev. John Robertson, colleague of Dr Mackinlay, ordained 1765, died 1798. He belonged to the 'Common-sense' order of preachers.
[4] A district of Kilmarnock, where carpet weaving was largely carried on.
[5] The Rev. John Multrie, a 'Moderate' whom Mackinlay succeeded.

And aye he catch'd the tither wretch,
   To fry them in his caudrons;
But now his Honour maun detach,
   Wi' a' his brimstone squadrons,
         Fast, fast this day.

See, see auld Orthodoxy's faes
   She's swingein' thro' the city!
Hark, how the nine-tail'd cat she plays!
   I vow it's unco pretty:
There, Learning, with his Greekish face,
   Grunts out some Latin ditty;
And Common-sense is gaun, she says,
   To mak to Jamie Beattie[1]
         Her plaint this day.

But there's Morality himsel,
   Embracing all opinions;
Hear, how he gies the tither yell,
   Between his twa companions!
See, how she peels the skin an' fell,
   As ane were peelin' onions!
Now there, they're packéd aff to hell,
   An' banish'd our dominions,
         Henceforth this day.

O happy day! rejoice, rejoice!
   Come bouse about the porter!
Morality's demure decoys
   Shall here nae mair find quarter:
Mackinlay, Russell, are the boys
   That heresy can torture;
They'll gie her on a rape a hoyse,
   And cowe her measure shorter
         By th' head some day.

Come, bring the tither mutchkin in,
   And here's—for a conclusion—
To ev'ry New-light[2] mother's son,
   From this time forth, Confusion!
If mair they deave us wi' their din,
   Or Patronage intrusion,
We'll light a spunk, and ev'ry skin,
   We'll rin them aff in fusion
         Like oil, some day.

[1] The poet and author of an 'Essay on Truth' who was reckoned to side with the moderate party in church matters.
[2] A cant phrase in the west of Scotland for those religious opinions which Dr Taylor of Norwich has defended so strenuously.—R.B.

To James Smith[1]

Friendship, mysterious cement of the soul!
Sweet'ner of Life, and solder of Society!
I owe thee much——— Blair.

Dear Smith, the slee'st, pawkie thief,
That e'er attempted stealth or rief!
Ye surely hae some warlock-brief
       Owre human hearts;
For ne'er a bosom yet was prief
       Against your arts.

For me, I swear by sun an' moon,
An' ev'ry star that blinks aboon,
Ye've cost me twenty pair o' shoon,
       Just gaun to see you;
An' ev'ry ither pair that's done,
       Mair taen I'm wi' you.

That auld, capricious carlin, Nature,
To mak amends for scrimpit stature,
She's turn'd you off, a human creature
       On her first plan,
And in her freaks, on ev'ry feature
       She's wrote the Man.

Just now I've taen the fit o' rhyme,
My barmie noddle's working prime,
My fancy yerkit up sublime,
       Wi' hasty summon;
Hae ye a leisure-moment's time
       To hear what's comin'?

Some rhyme a neebor's name to lash;
Some rhyme (vain thought!) for needfu' cash;
Some rhyme to court the countra clash,
       An' raise a din;
For me, an aim I never fash;
       I rhyme for fun.

The star that rules my luckless lot,
Has fated me the russet coat,
An' damn'd my fortune to the groat;
       But, in requit,
Has blest me with a random-shot
       O' countra wit.

This while my notion's taen a sklent,
To try my fate in guid, black prent;
But still the mair I'm that way bent,
       Something cries 'Hoolie!

[1] Merchant in Mauchline and one of the members of the Bachelor's Club.

I red you, honest man, tak tent!
        Ye'll shaw your folly;

'There's ither poets, much your betters,
Far seen in Greek, deep men o' letters,
Hae thought they had ensur'd their debtors,
        A' future ages;
Now moths deform, in shapeless tatters,
        Their unknown pages.'

Then farewell hopes of laurel-boughs,
To garland my poetic brows!
Henceforth I'll rove where busy ploughs
        Are whistlin' thrang,
An' teach the lanely heights an' howes
        My rustic sang.

I'll wander on wi' tentless heed,
How never-halting moments speed,
Till fate shall snap the brittle thread;
        Then, all unknown,
I'll lay me with th' inglorious dead,
        Forgot and gone!

But why o' death begin a tale?
Just now we're living sound an' hale;
Then top and maintop crowd the sail,
        Heave Care o'er-side!
And large, before Enjoyment's gale,
        Let's tak the tide.

This life, sae far's I understand,
Is a' enchanted fairyland,
Where Pleasure is the magic wand,
        That, wielded right,
Maks hours like minutes, hand in hand,
        Dance by fu' light.

The magic wand then let us wield;
For ance that five-an'-forty's speel'd,
See, crazy, weary, joyless eild,
        Wi' wrinkl'd face,
Comes hostin', hirplin' owre the field,
        Wi' creepin' pace.

When ance life's day draws near the gloamin',
Then fareweel vacant, careless roamin';
An' fareweel cheerfu' tankards foamin',
        An' social noise:
An' fareweel dear, deluding woman,
        The joy of joys!

O Life! how pleasant in thy morning,
Young Fancy's rays the hills adorning!
Cold-pausing Caution's lesson scorning,
   We frisk away,
Like school-boys, at th' expected warning,
   To joy an' play.

We wander there, we wander here,
We eye the rose upon the brier,
Unmindful that the thorn is near,
   Among the leaves;
And tho' the puny wound appear,
   Short while it grieves.

Some, lucky, find a flow'ry spot,
For which they never toil'd nor swat;
They drink the sweet and eat the fat,
   But care or pain;
And hap'ly eye the barren hut
   With high disdain.

With steady aim, some fortune chase;
Keen hope does ev'ry sinew brace;
Thro' fair, thro' foul, they urge the race,
   An' seize the prey:
Then cannie, in some cozie place,
   They close the day.

And others, like your humble servan',
Poor wights! nae rules nor roads observin',
To right or left eternal swervin',
   They zig-zag on;
Till, curst with age, obscure an' starvin',
   They aften groan.

Alas! what bitter toil an' straining—
But truce with peevish, poor complaining!
Is fortune's fickle *Luna* waning?
   E'n let her gang!
Beneath what light she has remaining,
   Let's sing our sang.

My pen I here fling to the door,
And kneel, ye Pow'rs! and warm implore,
'Tho' I should wander *Terra* o'er,
   In all her climes,
Grant me but this, I ask no more,
   Aye rowth o' rhymes.

'Gie dreeping roasts to countra lairds,
Till icicles hing frae their beards;

Gie fine braw claes to fine life-guards,
  And maids of honour;
An' yill an' whisky gie to cairds,
  Until they sconner.

'A title, Dempster[1] merits it;
A garter gie to Willie Pitt;
Gie wealth to some be-ledger'd cit,
  In cent per cent;
But give me real, sterling wit,
  And I'm content.

'While ye are pleas'd to keep me hale,
I'll sit down o'er my scanty meal,
Be 't water-brose or muslin-kail,
  Wi' cheerfu' face,
As lang's the Muses dinna fail
  To say the grace.'

An anxious e'e I never throws
Behint my lug, or by my nose;
I jouk beneath Misfortune's blows
  As weel 's I may;
Sworn foe to sorrow, care, and prose,
  I rhyme away.

O ye douce folk that live by rule,
Grave, tideless-blooded, calm an' cool,
Compar'd wi' you—O fool! fool! fool!
  How much unlike!
Your hearts are just a standing pool,
  Your lives, a dyke!

Nae hair-brain'd, sentimental traces
In your unletter'd, nameless faces!
In arioso trills and graces
  Ye never stray;
But *gravissimo*, solemn basses
  Ye hum away.

Ye are sae grave, nae doubt ye're wise;
Nae ferly tho' ye do despise
The hairum-scairum, ram-stam boys,
  The rattling squad:
I see ye upward cast your eyes—
  —Ye ken the road!

Whilst I—but I shall haud me there—
Wi' you I'll scarce gang onie where—

[1] George Dempster of Dunnichen, MP, a patriot referred to in 'The Author's Earnest Cry', page 113.

Then Jamie, I shall say nae mair,
        But quat my sang,
Content wi' you to mak a pair.
        Whare'er I gang.

THE VISION
Duan First[1]

The sun had clos'd the winter day,
The curlers quat their roarin' play,[2]
And hunger'd maukin taen her way,
        To kail-yards green,
While faithless snaws ilk step betray
        Whare she has been.

The thresher's weary flingin-tree,
The lee-lang day had tired me;
And when the day had clos'd his e'e,
        Far i' the west,
Ben i' the spence, right pensivelie,
        I gaed to rest.

There, lanely by the ingle-cheek,
I sat and ey'd the spewing reek,
That fill'd, wi' hoast-provoking smeek,
        The auld clay biggin;
An' heard the restless rattons squeak
        About the riggin.

All in this mottie, misty clime,
I backward mus'd on wasted time,
How I had spent my youthfu' prime,
        An' done nae thing,
But stringing blethers up in rhyme,
        For fools to sing.

Had I to guid advice but harket,
I might, by this, hae led a market,
Or strutted in a bank and clarket
        My cash-account;
While here, half-mad, half-fed, half-sarket.
        Is a' th' amount.

I started, mutt'ring, 'blockhead! coof!'
And heav'd on high my wauket loof,
To swear by a' yon starry roof,
        Or some rash aith,
That I henceforth wad be rhyme-proof
        Till my last breath—

[1] Duan, a term of Ossian's for the different divisions of a digressive poem. See his Cath-Loda, vol. 2 of M'Pherson's translation.—R.B.
[2] Not only from the hilarity of the game, but from the roaring sound of the curling stone along the hollow ice.

When click! the string the snick did draw;
An' jee! the door gaed to the wa';
An' by my ingle-lowe I saw,
        Now bleezin bright,
A tight, outlandish hizzie, braw,
        Come full in sight.

Ye need na doubt, I held my whisht;
The infant aith, half-form'd, was crusht
I glowr'd as eerie's I'd been dusht
        In some wild glen;
When sweet, like honest Worth, she blusht,
        An' steppéd ben.

Green, slender, leaf-clad holly-boughs
Were twisted, gracefu', round her brows;
I took her for some Scottish Muse,
        By that same token;
And come to stop those reckless vows,
        Would soon been broken.

A 'hair-brain'd, sentimental trace'
Was strongly markéd in her face;
A wildly witty, rustic grace
        Shone full upon her;
Her eye, ev'n turn'd on empty space,
        Beam'd keen with honour.

Down flow'd her robe, a tartan sheen,
Till half a leg was scrimply seen;
An' such a leg! my bonnie Jean
        Could only peer it;
Sae straught, sae taper, tight an' clean—
        Nane else came near it.

Her mantle large, of greenish hue,
My gazing wonder chiefly drew;
Deep lights and shades, bold-mingling, threw
        A lustre grand;
And seem'd, to my astonish'd view,
        A well-known land.

Here, rivers in the sea were lost;
There, mountains to the skies were tost:
Here, tumbling billows mark'd the coast,
        With surging foam;
There, distant shone Art's lofty boast,
        The lordly dome.

Here, Doon pour'd down his far-fetch'd floods;
There, well-fed Irwine stately thuds:

Auld hermit Ayr staw thro' his woods,
    On to the shore;
And many a lesser torrent scuds,
    With seeming roar.

Low, in a sandy valley spread,
An ancient borough rear'd her head;
Still, as in Scottish story read,
    She boasts a race
To ev'ry nobler virtue bred,
    And polish'd grace.[1]

By stately tow'r, or palace fair,
Or ruins pendent in the air,
Bold stems of heroes, here and there,
    I could discern;
Some seem'd to muse, some seem'd to dare,
    With feature stern.

My heart did glowing transport feel,
To see a race heroic[2] wheel,
And brandish round the deep-dyed steel,
    In sturdy blows;
While, back-recoiling, seem'd to reel
    Their suthron foes.

His Country's Saviour,[3] mark him well!
Bold Richardton's heroic swell;[4]
The chief, on Sark who glorious fell,[5]
    In high command;
And he whom ruthless fates expel
    His native land.

There, where a sceptr'd Pictish shade
Stalk'd round his ashes lowly laid,[6]
I mark'd a martial race, pourtray'd
    In colours strong:
Bold, soldier-featur'd, undismay'd,
    They strode along.

Thro' many a wild, romantic grove,[7]
Near many a hermit-fancied cove

[1] Here, in the first edition of Burns' works, *Duan First* came to a close; the additional seven stanzas following this were first printed in the Edinburgh edition, 1787, apparently in compliment to Mrs Dunlop and other influential friends of the author. Other stanzas, suppressed by Burns himself, are on page 131.

[2] The Wallaces.—R.B.   [3] William Wallace.—R.B.

[4] Adam Wallace of Richardton, cousin to the immortal preserver of Scottish independence.—R.B.

[5] Wallace, laird of Craigie, who was second in command under Douglas, Earl of Ormond, at the famous battle on the banks of Sark, fought in 1448. The glorious victory was principally owing to the judicious conduct and intrepid valour of the gallant laird of Craigie, who died of his wounds after the action.—R.B.

[6] Coilus, King of the Picts, from whom the district of Kyle is said to take its name, lies buried, as tradition says, near the family seat of the Montgomeries of Coilsfield, where his burial place is still shown.—R.B.

[7] Barskimming, the seat of the Lord Justice-Clerk.—R.B. (Sir Thomas Miller of Glenlee, afterwards President of the Court of Session.)

(Fit haunts for friendship or for love,
          In musing mood),
An agéd Judge, I saw him rove,
          Dispensing good.

With deep-struck, reverential awe,
The learned Sire and Son I saw:[1]
To Nature's God, and Nature's law,
          They gave their lore;
This, all its source and end to draw,
          That, to adore.

Brydon's brave ward[2] I well could spy,
Beneath old Scotia's smiling eye:
Who call'd on Fame, low standing by,
          To hand him on,
Where many a patriot-name on high,
          And hero shone.

Duan Second

With musing-deep, astonish'd stare,
I view'd the heavenly-seeming Fair;
A whisp'ring throb did witness bear
          Of kindred sweet,
When with an elder sister's air
          She did me greet.

'All hail! my own inspiréd bard!
In me thy native Muse regard!
Nor longer mourn thy fate is hard,
          Thus poorly low!
I come to give thee such reward,
          As we bestow!

'Know, the great genius of this land
Has many a light aerial band,
Who, all beneath his high command,
          Harmoniously,
As arts or arms they understand,
          Their labours ply.

'They Scotia's race among them share:
Some fire the sodger on to dare;
Some rouse the patriot up to bare
          Corruption's heart:
Some teach the bard—a darling care—
          The tuneful art.

---

[1] Catrine, the seat of the late Doctor and present Professor Stewart.—R.B.
[2] Colonel Fullarton.—R.B. He had travelled under the care of Patrick Brydone, author of a well-known publication, *Tour Through Sicily and Malta*.

''Mong swelling floods of reeking gore,
They, ardent, kindling spirits pour;
Or, 'mid the venal senate's roar,
        They, sightless, stand,
To mend the honest patriot-lore,
        And grace the hand.

'And when the bard, or hoary sage,
Charm or instruct the future age,
They bind the wild poetic rage
        In energy,
Or point the inconclusive page
        Full on the eye.[1]

'Hence, Fullarton, the brave and young;
Hence, Dempster's zeal-inspiréd tongue;[2]
Hence, sweet, harmonious Beattie sung
        His 'Minstrel lays';
Or tore, with noble ardour stung,
        The sceptic's bays.

'To lower orders are assign'd
The humbler ranks of humankind,
The rustic bard, the lab'ring hind,
        The artisan;
All choose, as various they're inclin'd,
        The various man.

'When yellow waves the heavy grain,
The threat'ning storm some strongly rein;
Some teach to meliorate the plain
        With tillage-skill;
And some instruct the shepherd-train,
        Blythe o'er the hill.

'Some hint the lover's harmless wile;
Some grace the maiden's artless smile;
Some soothe the lab'rer's weary toil
        For humble gains,
And make his cottage scenes beguile
        His cares and pains.

'Some, bounded to a district-space,
Explore at large man's infant race,
To mark the embryotic trace
        Of rustic bard;
And careful note each op'ning grace,
        A guide and guard.

'Of these am I—Coila my name;
And this district as mine I claim,

---

[1] This stanza was added in the second edition (1787).   [2] 'Truth-prevailing tongue' in first edition.

Where once the Campbells,[1] chiefs of fame,
    Held ruling pow'r:
I mark'd thy embryo-tuneful flame,
    Thy natal hour.

'With future hope I oft would gaze
Fond, on thy little early ways,
Thy rudely caroll'd, chiming phrase,
    In uncouth rhymes,
Fir'd at the simple, artless lays
    Of other times.

'I saw thee seek the sounding shore,
Delighted with the dashing roar;
Or when the North his fleecy store
    Drove thro' the sky,
I saw grim Nature's visage hoar
    Struck thy young eye.

'Or when the deep green-mantled earth
Warm cherish'd ev'ry floweret's birth,
And joy and music pouring forth
    In ev'ry grove,
I saw thee eye the gen'ral mirth
    With boundless love.

'When ripen'd fields and azure skies
Call'd forth the reapers' rustling noise,
I saw thee leave their ev'ning joys,
    And lonely stalk,
To vent thy bosom's swelling rise,
    In pensive walk.

'When youthful love, warm-blushing, strong,
Keen-shivering shot thy nerves along,
Those accents grateful to thy tongue,
    Th' adoréd Name,
I taught thee how to pour in song,
    To soothe thy flame.

'I saw thy pulse's maddening play,
Wild send thee Pleasure's devious way,
Misled by Fancy's meteor-ray,
    By passion driven;
But yet the light that led astray
    Was light from Heaven.

'I taught thy manners-painting strains,
The loves, the ways of simple swains,
Till now, o'er all my wide domains
    Thy fame extends;

[1] Mossgiel and its neighbourhood belonged to the Earl of Loudoun, family name Campbell.

> And some, the pride of Coila's plains,
> Become thy friends.

> 'Thou canst not learn, nor I can show,
> To paint with Thomson's landscape glow;
> Or wake the bosom-melting throe,
> With Shenstone's art;
> Or pour, with Gray, the moving flow,
> Warm on the heart.

> 'Yet all beneath th' unrivall'd rose,
> The lowly daisy sweetly blows;
> Tho' large the forest's monarch throws
> His army shade,
> Yet green the juicy hawthorn grows,
> Adown the glade.

> 'Then never murmur nor repine;
> Strive in thy humble sphere to shine;
> And trust me, not Potosi's mine,
> Nor king's regard,
> Can give a bliss o'ermatching thine,
> A rustic bard.

> 'To give my counsels all in one,
> Thy tuneful flame still careful fan:
> Preserve the dignity of Man,
> With soul erect;
> And trust the Universal Plan
> Will all protect.

> 'And wear thou *this*,'—she solemn said,
> And bound the holly round my head:
> The polish'd leaves and berries red
> Did rustling play;
> And, like a passing thought, she fled
> In light away.

Suppressed Stanzas Of 'The Vision'

To Mrs Stewart of Stair, Burns presented a manuscript copy of 'The Vision'. That copy has about twenty stanzas at the end of Duan First, which he cancelled when he came to print the piece in his Kilmarnock volume. Seven of these he restored in printing his second edition, as noted on page 127. The following are the verses that he left unpublished.

Following the 18th stanza:

With secret throes I mark'd that earth,
That cottage, witness of my birth;
And near I saw, bold issuing forth
In youthful pride,
A Lindsay race of noble worth,
Fam'd far and wide.

Where, hid behind a spreading wood,
An ancient Pict-built mansion stood,
I spied, among an angel brood,
A female pair;
Sweet shone their high maternal blood,
And father's air.[1]

[1] Sundrum.—R.B. Hamilton of Sundrum was married to a sister of Colonel Montgomerie of Coilsfield.

An ancient tower[1] to memory brought
How Dettingen's bold hero fought;
Still, far from sinking into nought,
    It owns a lord
Who far in western climates fought,
    With trusty sword.

Among the rest I well could spy
One gallant, graceful, martial boy,
The *soldier* sparkled in his eye,
    A diamond water.
I blest that noble badge with joy,
    That own'd me *frater*.[2]

After 20th stanza of the text:

Near by arose a mansion fine,[3]
The seat of many a muse divine;
Not rustic muses such as mine,
    With holly crown'd,
But th' ancient, tuneful, laurell'd Nine,
    From classic ground.

Hail! Nature's pang, more strong than death!
Warm Friendship's glow, like kindling wrath!
Love, dearer than the parting breath
    Of dying friend!
Not ev'n with life's wild devious path,
    Your force shall end!

I mourn'd the card that Fortune dealt,
To see where bonnie Whitefoords dwelt;[4]
But other prospects made me melt,
    That village near;[5]
There Nature, Friendship, Love, I felt,
    Fond-mingling, dear!

The Power that gave the soft alarms
In blooming Whitefoord's rosy charms,
Still threats the tiny, feather'd arms,
    The barbéd dart,
While lovely Wilhelmina warms
    The coldest heart.[6]

After 21st stanza of the text:

Where Lugar leaves his moorland plaid,[7]
Where lately Want was idly laid,
I marked busy, bustling Trade,
    In fervid flame,
Beneath a Patroness's aid,
    Of noble name.

Where Cessnock pours with gurgling sound;[9]
And Irwine, marking out the bound,
Enamour'd of the scenes around,
    Slow runs his race,
A name I doubly honour'd found,[10]
    With knightly grace.

Wild, countless hills I could survey,
And countless flocks as wild as they;
But other scenes did charms display,
    That better please,
Where polish'd manners dwell with Gray,
    In rural ease.[8]

Brydon's brave ward,[11] I saw him stand,
Fame humbly offering her hand,
And near, his kinsman's rustic band,[12]
    With one accord,
Lamenting their late blesséd land
    Must change its lord.

The owner of a pleasant spot,
Near sandy wilds, I last did note;[13]
A heart too warm, a pulse too hot
    At times, o'erran:
But large in ev'ry feature wrote,
    Appear'd the Man.

[1] Stair.—R.B.
[2] Captain James Montgomerie, Master of St James' Lodge, Tarbolton, to which the author has the honour to belong.—R.B.
[3] Auchinleck.—R.B. Home of James Boswell.
[4] Ballochmyle, an estate two miles from Mossgiel.
[5] Mauchline.
[6] A compliment to Miss Wilhelmina Alexander, sister of Claud Alexander of Ballochmyle, as successor, in that locality, to Miss Maria Whitefoord.
[7] Cumnock.—R.B.
[8] Mr Farquhar Gray.—R.B.
[9] Auchinskieth.—R.B.
[10] Caprington.—R.B.
[11] Colonel Fullerton.—R.B. Author of an *Account of the Agriculture of the County of Ayr*.
[12] Dr Fullerton.—R.B.
[13] Orangefield.—R.B.

The Rantin Dog, The Daddie O'T
Tune—*East nook o' Fife*

O wha my babie-clouts will buy?
O wha will tent me when I cry?
Wha will kiss me where I lie?
    The rantin dog, the daddie o't.

O wha will own he did the faut?
O wha will buy the groanin maut?
O wha will tell me how to ca't?
    The rantin dog, the daddie o't.

When I mount the creepie-chair,
Wha will sit beside me there?
Gie me Rob, I'll seek nae mair,
    The rantin' dog, the daddie o't.

Wha will crack to me my lane?
Wha will mak me fidgin' fain?
Wha will kiss me o'er again?
    The rantin dog, the daddie o't.

Here's His Health In Water
Tune—*The job of journey-work*

Altho' my back be at the wa',
    And tho' he be the fau'tor;
Altho' my back be at the wa',
    Yet, here's his health in water!
O wae gae by his wanton sides,
    Sae brawly 's he could flatter;
Till for his sake I'm slighted sair,
    An' dree the kintra clatter;
But tho' my back be at the wa',
    Yet here's his health in water!

He follow'd me baith out and in
    Thro' a' the nooks o' Killie;
He follow'd me baith out and in
    Wi' a stiff stanin' pillie.
But when he gat atween my legs,
    We made an unco splatter;
An' haith, I trow, I soupled it,
    Tho' bauldly he did blatter;
But now my back is at the wa',
    Yet here's his health in water.

Address To The Unco Guid
Or the Rigidly Righteous

My Son, these maxims make a rule,
    An' lump them aye thegither;
The Rigid Righteous is a fool,
    The Rigid Wise anither:
The cleanest corn that ere was dight
    May hae some pyles o' caff in;
So ne'er a fellow-creature slight
    For random fits o' daffin.—Solomon.—Eccles. Ch. 7, v. 16.

O ye wha are sae guid yoursel,
    Sae pious and sae holy,
Ye've nought to do but mark and tell
    Your neibours' fauts and folly!
Whase life is like a weel-gaun mill,
    Supplied wi' store o' water;
The heaped happer's ebbing still,
    An' still the clap plays clatter.

Hear me, ye venerable core,
    As counsel for poor mortals
That frequent pass douce Wisdom's door
    For glaikit Folly's portals;

I, for their thoughtless, careless sakes,
    Would here propone defences,
Their donsie tricks, their black mistakes,
    Their failings and mischances.

Ye see your state wi' theirs compared,
    And shudder at the niffer;
But cast a moment's fair regard,
    What maks the mighty differ;
Discount what scant occasion gave,
    That purity ye pride in;
And (what's aft mair than a' the lave),
    Your better art o' hiding.

Think, when your castigated pulse
    Gies now and then a wallop,
What ragings must his veins convulse,
    That still eternal gallop:
Wi' wind and tide fair i' your tail,
    Right on ye scud your sea-way;
But in the teeth o' baith to sail,
    It maks a unco leeway.

See Social Life and Glee sit down,
    All joyous and unthinking,
Till, quite transmugrified, they're grown
    Debauchery and Drinking:
O would they stay to calculate
    Th' eternal consequences;
Or your more dreaded hell to state,
    Damnation of expenses!

Ye high, exalted, virtuous dames,
    Tied up in godly laces,
Before ye gie poor Frailty names,
    Suppose a change o' cases;
A dear-lov'd lad, convenience snug,
    A treach'rous inclination—
But let me whisper i' your lug,
    Ye're aiblins nae temptation.

Then gently scan your brother man,
    Still gentler sister woman;
Tho' they may gang a kennin wrang,
    To step aside is human:
One point must still be greatly dark—
    The moving *Why* they do it;
And just as lamely can ye mark,
    How far perhaps they rue it.

Who made the heart, 'tis He alone
    Decidedly can try us;

He knows each chord, its various tone,
    Each spring, its various bias:
Then at the balance let's be mute,
    We never can adjust it;
What's done we partly may compute,
    But know not what's resisted.

THE INVENTORY
In Answer to a Mandate by the Surveyor of the Taxes[1]

Sir, as your mandate did request,
I send you here a faithfu' list,
O' gudes an' gear, an' a' my graith—
To which I'm clear to gi'e my aith.

    Imprimis, then, for carriage cattle,
I hae four brutes o' gallant mettle,
As ever drew afore a pettle:
My *lan'-afore's*[2] a guid auld has-been,
An' wight an' wilfu' a' his days been:
My *lan'-ahin's*[3] a weel gaun fillie,
That aft has borne me hame frae Killie.[4]
An' your auld borough monie a time
In days when riding was nae crime.
But ance, when in my wooing pride
I, like a blockhead, boost to ride,
The wilfu' creature sae I pat to—
Lord pardon a' my sins, an' that too!—
I play'd my fillie sic a shavie,
She's a' bedevil'd wi' the spavie.
My *furr-ahin's*[5] a wordy beast
As e'er in tug or tow was trac'd.
The fourth's a Highland Donald hastie,
A damn'd red-wud Kilburnie blastie;
Foreby a cowt, o' cowts the wale,
As ever ran afore a tail;
If he be spar'd to be a beast,
He'll draw me fifteen pund at least.
Wheel-carriages I ha'e but few,
Three carts—an' twa are feckly new—
An auld wheelbarrow, mair for token,
Ae leg an' baith the trams are broken;
I made a poker o' the spin'le,
An' my auld mither brunt the trin'le.
For men, I've three mischievous boys,

---

[1] In May 1785, to reduce the national debt, William Pitt added to the number of taxable articles, among them female servants. It became the duty of Mr Aiken, as tax surveyor for the district, to serve the usual notice on Burns, who made his return in these verses.

[2] Fore-horse on the left-hand of the plough.—R.B.
[3] Hindmost on the left-hand of the plough.—R.B.
[4] Kilmarnock.—R.B.
[5] Hindmost horse on the right-hand in the plough.—R.B.

Run-deils for rantin' an' for noise;
A gaudsman ane, a thrasher t'other:
Wee Davock hauds the nowt in fother.
I rule them as I ought, discreetly,
An' aften labour them completely,
An' aye on Sundays duly, nightly,
I on the Questions targe them tightly;
Till, faith! wee Davock's grown sae gleg,
Tho' scarcely langer than your leg,
He'll screed you aff Effectual Calling,
As fast as onie in the dwalling.
I've nane in female servant station,
(Lord keep me aye frae a' temptation!)
I hae nae wife—and that my bliss is—
An' ye have laid nae tax on misses;
An' then, if kirk folks dinna clutch me,
I ken the deevils dare na touch me.
Wi' weans I'm mair than weel contented,
Heav'n sent me ane mae than I wanted!
My sonsie, smirking, dear-bought Bess,
She stares the daddy in her face,
Enough of ought ye like but grace;
But her, my bonnie, sweet wee lady,
I've paid enough for her already;
An' gin ye tax her or her mither,
By the Lord, ye'se get them a' thegither!

And now, remember, Mr Aiken,
Nae kind o' licence out I'm takin';
Frae this time forth, I do declare,
I'se ne'er ride horse nor hizzie mair;
Thro' dirt and dub for life I'll paidle,
Ere I sae dear pay for a saddle;
My travel a' on foot I'll shank it,
I've sturdy bearers, Gude be thankit!
The Kirk an' you may tak you that,
It puts but little in your pat;
Sae dinna put me in your beuk,
Nor for my ten white shillings leuk.

This list, wi' my ain hand I wrote it,
The day and date as under noted;
Then know all ye whom it concerns,
Subscripsi huic,
                                    ROBERT BURNS.
Mossgiel, February 22, 1786.

EPITAPH

Lo worms enjoy the seat of bliss
Where Lords and Lairds afore did kiss.

To John Kennedy,[1] Dumfries House

Mossgiel, 3rd March, 1786
Now, Kennedy, if foot or horse
E'er bring you in by Mauchline corse,
Lord, man, there's lasses there wad force
    A hermit's fancy;
An' down the gate, in faith, they're worse,
    An' mair unchancy.

But as I'm sayin, please step to Dow's
An' taste sic gear as Johnnie brews,
Till some bit callan bring me news
    That ye are there;
An' if we dinna hae a bouze,
    I'se ne'er drink mair.

It's no' I like to sit an' swallow,
Then like a swine to puke an' wallow;
But gie me just a true good fallow,
    Wi' right ingine,
And spunkie ance to mak us mellow,
    An' then we'll shine.

Now if ye're ane o' warl's folk,
Wha rate the wearer by the cloak,
An' sklent on poverty their joke,
    Wi' bitter sneer,
Wi' you nae friendship I will troke,
    Nor cheap nor dear.

But if, as I'm informéd weel,
Ye hate as ill's the very deil
The flinty heart that canna feel—
    Come, sir, here's to you!
Hae, there's my haun', I wiss you weel,
    An' gude be wi' you.

[1] Factor to the Earl of Dumfries and later the Earl of Breadalbane.

To Mr McAdam Of Craigen-Gillan
In Answer to an Obliging Letter he sent in the
Commencement of my Poetic Career.

Sir, o'er a gill I gat your card,
    I trow it made me proud;
'See wha taks notice o' the bard!'
    I lap and cried fu' loud.

Now deil-ma-care about their jaw,
    The senseless, gawky million;
I'll cock my nose abune them a',
    I'm roos'd by Craigen-Gillan!

'Twas noble, sir—'twas like yoursel,
    To grant your high protection:
A great man's smile ye ken fu' well
    Is aye a blest infection.

Tho', by his banes, wha in a tub
    Match'd Macedonian Sandy![1]
On my ain legs, thro' dirt and dub,
    I independent stand aye.

And when those legs to gude, warm kail,
    Wi' welcome canna bear me,
A lee dyke-side, a sybow-tail,
    An' barley-scone shall cheer me.

Heaven spare you lang to kiss the breath
    O' monie flow'ry simmers!
An' bless your bonnie lasses baith,
    I'm tauld they're lo'esome kimmers!

An' God bless young Dunaskin's laird—,
    The blossom of our gentry!
An' may he wear an auld man's beard,
    A credit to his country.

[1] Diogenes.

To A Louse
On seeing One on a Lady's Bonnet at Church

Ha! whaur ye gaun, ye crowlin ferlie?
Your impudence protects you sairly:
I canna say but ye strunt rarely,
    Owre gauze and lace;
Tho', faith, I fear ye dine but sparely
    On sic a place.

Ye ugly, creepin, blastit wonner,
Detested, shunn'd, by saunt an' sinner,
How daur ye set your fit upon her,
    Sae fine a lady?
Gae somewhere else and seek your dinner
    On some poor body.

Swith, in some beggar's haffet squattle;
There ye may creep, and sprawl, and sprattle,
Wi' ither kindred, jumping cattle,
    In shoals and nations;
Whaur horn nor bane ne'er daur unsettle
    Your thick plantations.

Now haud you there, ye're out o' sight,
Below the fatt'rels, snug and tight;

Na, faith ye yet! ye'll no be right,
　　　　Till ye've got on it,
The verra tapmost, tow'rin' height
　　　　O' Miss's bonnet.

My sooth! right bauld ye set your nose out,
As plump an' grey as ony groset:
O for some rank, mercurial rozet,
　　　　Or fell, red smeddum,
I'd gie you sic a hearty dose o't,
　　　　Wad dress your droddum!

I wad na been surpris'd to spy
You on an auld wife's flainen toy;
Or aiblins some bit dubbie boy,
　　　　On's wyliecoat;
But Miss's fine Lunardi![1] fye!
　　　　How daur ye do't?

O Jeany, dinna toss your head,
An' set your beauties a' abread!
Ye little ken what cursed speed
　　　　The blastie's makin:
Thae winks an' finger-ends, I dread,
　　　　Are notice takin!

O wad some Power the giftie gie us
To see oursels as ithers see us!
It wad frae monie a blunder free us,
　　　　An' foolish notion:
What airs in dress an' gait wad lea'e us,
　　　　An' ev'n devotion!

[1] Balloon-shaped bonnet. Vincent Lunardi, on 15 September 1784, ascended from London in an air balloon—the earliest attempt in Britain; and on 5 October 1785 he did the same feat from Heriot's Green, Edinburgh.

INSCRIBED ON A WORK OF HANNAH MORE'S
Presented to the Author by a Lady.

Thou flattering mark of friendship kind,
Still may thy pages call to mind
　　　　The dear, the beauteous donor;
Though sweetly female every part,
Yet such a head, and more the heart,
　　　　Does both the sexes honour:
She show'd her taste refined and just,
　　　　When she selected thee;
Yet deviating, own I must,
　　　　For so approving me:
　　　　　　But kind still, I'll mind still,
　　　　　　　　The *giver* in the gift;
　　　　　　I'll bless her, an' wiss her
　　　　　　　　A friend aboon the lift.

ON MISS WILHELMINA ALEXANDER[1]—SONG, OR THE LASS OF BALLOCHMYLE
Tune—*Ettrick banks*

'Twas even—the dewy fields were green,
    On every blade the pearls hang,
The zephyr wanton'd round the bean,
    And bore its fragrant sweets alang;
In every glen the mavis sang,
    All Nature list'ning seem'd the while;
Except where greenwood echoes rang
    Amang the braes o' Ballochmyle.

With careless step I onward stray'd,
    My heart rejoic'd in Nature's joy,
When, musing in a lonely glade,
    A maiden fair I chanc'd to spy.
Her look was like the morning's eye,
    Her air like Nature's vernal smile,
Perfection whisper'd, passing by:
    'Behold the Lass o' Ballochmyle!'

Fair is the morn in flowery May,
    And sweet is night in autumn mild,
When roving through the garden gay
    Or wand'ring in the lonely wild;
But woman, Nature's darling child,
    There all her charms she does compile,
And all her other works are foil'd
    By the bonnie Lass o' Ballochmyle.

O had she been a country maid,
    And I the happy country swain,
Though shelt'red in the lowest shed
    That ever rose on Scotia's plain:
Through weary winter's wind and rain
    With joy, with rapture I would toil,
And nightly to my bosom strain
    The bonnie Lass o' Ballochmyle.

Then Pride might climb the slipp'ry steep
    Where fame and honours lofty shine;
And thirst of gold might tempt the deep
    Or downward seek the Indian mine.
Give me the cot below the pine,
    To tend the flocks or till the soil,
And every day have joys divine
    With the bonnie Lass o' Ballochmyle.

---

[1] Wilhelmina Alexander of Ballochmyle (*see also* notes, page 132). Burns sent the song to her with a letter, seeking permission to publish it in the new edition of his poems about to be issued in Edinburgh. She took not notice of his request. In later years, however, she was proud to exhibit both the song and the letter.

The Holy Fair[1]

A robe of seeming truth and trust
    Hid crafty Observation;
And secret hung, with poison'd crust,
    The dirk of Defamation:
A mask that like the gorget show'd,
    Dye-varying on the pigeon;
And for a mantle large and broad,
    He wrapt him in *Religion*.—Hypocrisy à-la-Mode

Upon a simmer Sunday morn,
    When Nature's face is fair,
I walked forth to view the corn,
    An' snuff the caller air.
The rising sun owre Galston Muirs
    Wi' glorious light was glintin';
The hares were hirplin' down the furrs,
The lav'rocks they were chantin'
        Fu' sweet that day.

As lightsomely I glowr'd abroad,
    To see a scene sae gay,
Three hizzies, early at the road,
    Cam skelpin' up the way.
Twa had manteeles o' dolefu' black,
    But ane wi' lyart lining;
The third, that gaed a wee a-back,
    Was in the fashion shining
        Fu' gay that day.

The twa appear'd like sisters twin,
    In feature, form an' claes;
Their visage wither'd, lang an' thin,
    An' sour as ony slaes:
The third cam up, hap-stap-an'-loup,
    As light as ony lambie,
An' wi'a curchie low did stoop,
    As soon as e'er she saw me,
        Fu' kind that day.

Wi' bonnet aff, quoth I, 'Sweet lass,
    I think ye seem to ken me;
I'm sure I've seen that bonnie face
    But yet I canna name ye.'
Quo' she, an' laughin' as she spak,
    An' taks me by the han's,
'Ye, for my sake, hae gien the feck
    Of a' the ten comman's
        A screed some day.

'My name is Fun—your cronie dear,
    The nearest friend ye hae;

[1] 'Holy Fair' is a common phrase in the west of Scotland for a sacramental occasion.—R.B.

An' this is Superstition here,
    An' that's Hypocrisy.
I'm gaun to Mauchline Holy Fair,
    To spend an hour in daffin:
Gin ye'll go there, yon runkl'd pair,
    We will get famous laughin'
        At them this day.'

Quoth I, 'Wi' a' my heart, I'll do't;
    I'll get my Sunday's sark on,
An' meet you on the holy spot;
    Faith, we'se hae fine remarkin!'
Then I gaed hame at crowdie-time,
    An' soon I made me ready;
For roads were clad, frae side to side,
    Wi' monie a wearie body
        In droves that day.

Here farmers gash, in ridin graith,
    Gaed hoddin by their cotters;
There swankies young, in braw braid-claith,
    Are springing owre the gutters.
The lasses, skelpin barefit, thrang,
    In silks an' scarlets glitter;
Wi' sweet-milk cheese, in monie a whang,
    An' farls, bak'd wi' butter,
        Fu' crump that day.

When by the plate we set our nose,
    Weel heapéd up wi' ha'pence,
A greedy glowr black-bonnet throws,
    An' we maun draw our tippence.
Then in we go to see the show:
    On ev'ry side they're gath'rin';
Some carrying dails, some chairs an' stools,
    An' some are busy bleth'rin'
        Right loud that day.

Here stands a shed to fend the show'rs,
    An' screen our countra gentry;
There 'Racer Jess',[1] an' twa-three whores,
    Are blinkin at the entry.
Here sits a raw o' tittlin jads,
    Wi' heaving breast an' bare neck;
An' there a batch o' wabster lads,
    Blackguarding frae Kilmarnock,
        For fun this day.

---

[1] February 1813, died at Mauchline, Janet Gibson—the 'Racer Jess' of Burns' 'Holy Fair', remarkable for her pedestrian feats. She was a daughter of 'Poosie Nansie', who figures in 'The Jolly Beggars'.—*Newspaper Obituary*

Here, some are thinkin' on their sins,
    An' some upo' their claes;
Ane curses feet that fyl'd his shins,
    Anither sighs an' prays:
On this hand sits a chosen swatch,
    Wi' screwed-up, grace-proud faces;
On that, a set o' chaps, at watch,
    Thrang winkin' on the lasses
              To chairs that day.

O happy is that man, an' blest!
    Nae wonder that it pride him!
Whase ain dear lass, that he likes best,
    Comes clinkin' down beside him!
Wi' arms repos'd on the chair back,
    He sweetly does compose him;
Which, by degrees, slips round her neck,
    An's loof upon her bosom,
              Unkend that day.

Now a' the congregation o'er
    Is silent expectation;
For Moodie speels the holy door,[1]
    Wi' tidings o' damnation:
Should Hornie, as in ancient days,
    'Mang sons o' God present him,
The vera sight o' Moodie's face,
    To 's ain het hame had sent him
              Wi' fright that day.

Hear how he clears the points o' faith
    Wi' rattlin' and wi' thumpin'!
Now meekly calm, now wild in wrath,
    He's stampin', an' he's jumpin'!
His lengthen'd chin, his turn'd-up snout,
    His eldritch squeel an' gestures,
O how they fire the heart devout,
    Like cantharidian plaisters
              On sic a day!

But hark! the tent has chang'd its voice,
    There's peace an' rest nae langer;
For a' the real judges rise,
    They canna sit for anger.
Smith[2] opens out his cauld harangues,
    On practice and on morals;
An' aff the godly pour in thrangs,
    To gie the jars an' barrels
              A lift that day.

[1] Rev. Alexander Moodie of Riccarton.   [2] Rev. George (subsequently Dr) Smith of Galston.

What signifies his barren shine,
    Of moral powers an' reason?
His English style, and gesture fine,
    Are a' clean out o' season.
Like Socrates or Antonine,
    Or some auld pagan heathen,
The *moral man* he does define,
    But ne'er a word o' *faith* in
            That's right that day.

In guid time comes an antidote
    Against sic poison'd nostrum;
For Peebles, frae the water-fit,[1]
    Ascends the holy rostrum:
See, up he's got the word o' God,
    An' meek an' mim has view'd it,
While 'Common-sense' has taen the road,
    An' aff, an' up the Cowgate[2]
            Fast, fast that day.

Wee Miller[3] neist the guard relieves,
    An' Orthodoxy raibles,
Tho' in his heart he weel believes,
    An' thinks it auld wives' fables:
But faith! the birkie wants a manse,
    So, cannilie he hums them;
Altho' his carnal wit an' sense
    Like hafflins-wise o'ercomes him
           At times that day.

Now, butt an' ben, the change-house fills,
    Wi' yill-caup commentators;
Here's cryin' out for bakes and gills,
    An' there the pint-stowp clatters;
While thick an' thrang, an' loud an' lang,
    Wi' logic an' wi' scripture,
They raise a din, that in the end
    Is like to breed a rupture
           O' wrath that day.

Leeze me on drink! it gies us mair
    Than either school or college;
It kindles wit, it waukens lear,
    It pangs us fou o' knowledge:
Be't whisky-gill or penny-wheep,
    Or ony stronger potion,
It never fails, on drinkin' deep,
    To kittle up our notion,
           By night or day.

[1] Rev. Wm Peebles of 'The Water-fit', Newton-upon-Ayr.
[2] A street so called which faces the tent in Mauchline.—R.B.
[3] Rev. Alex. Miller, afterward of Kilmaurs, supposed to be at heart a 'moderate'.

The lads an' lasses, blythely bent
  To mind baith saul an' body,
Sit round the table, weel content,
  An' steer about the toddy:
On this ane's dress, an' that ane's leuk,
  They're makin' observations;
While some are cozie i' the neuk,
  An' forming assignations
     To meet some day.

But now the Lord's ain trumpet touts,
  Till a' the hills are rairin,
And echoes back return the shouts;
  Black Russell is na sparin:[1]
His piercin words, like Highlan' swords,
  Divide the joints an' marrow;
His talk o' Hell, whare devils dwell,
  Our vera 'sauls does harrow'[2]
     Wi' fright that day!

A vast, unbottom'd, boundless pit,
  Fill'd fou o' lowin brunstane,
Whase raging flame, an' scorching heat,
  Wad melt the hardest whun-stane!
The half-asleep start up wi' fear,
  An' think they hear it roarin';
When presently it does appear,
  'Twas but some neebor snorin'
     Asleep that day.

'Twad be owre lang a tale to tell,
  How monie stories past,
An' how they crouded to the yill,
  When they were a' dismist:
How drink gaed round, in cogs an' caups,
  Amang the furms an' benches;
An' cheese an' bread, frae women's laps,
  Was dealt about in lunches
     An' dawds that day.

In comes a gawsie, gash guidwife,
  An' sits down by the fire,
Syne draws her kebbuck an' her knife;
  The lasses they are shyer.
The auld guidmen, about the grace
  Frae side to side they bother;
Till some ane by his bonnet lays,
  An' gies them't like a tether,
     Fu' lang that day.

---

[1] Rev. John Russell, one of 'The Twa Herds' (*see* page 43).   [2] Shakespeare's Hamlet.—R.B.

Waesucks! for him that gets nae lass,
    Or lasses that hae naething!
Sma' need has he to say a grace,
    Or melvie his braw claithing!
O wives, be mindfu' ance yoursel
    How bonnie lads ye wanted;
An' dinna, for a kebbuck-heel,
    Let lasses be affronted
        On sic a day!

Now 'Clinkumbell', wi' rattlin' tow,
    Begins to jow an' croon;
Some swagger hame, the best they dow,
    Some wait the afternoon.
At slaps the billies halt a blink,
    Till lasses strip their shoon:
Wi' faith an' hope, an' love an' drink,
    They're a' in famous tune
        For crack that day.

How monie hearts this day converts
    O' sinners and o' lasses!
Their hearts o' stane, gin night, are gane
    As saft as ony flesh is:
There's some are fou o' love divine;
    There's some are fou o' brandy;
An' monie jobs that day begin,
    May end in houghmagandie
        Some ither day.

Song Composed In Spring
Tune—*Jockey's grey breeks*

Chorus: And maun I still on Menie[1] doat,
    And bear the scorn that's in her e'e?
For it's jet, jet black, an' it's like a hawk,
    An' it winna let a body be.

Again rejoicing Nature sees
    Her robe assume its vernal hues:
Her leafy locks wave in the breeze,
    All freshly steep'd in morning dews.

In vain to me the cowslips blaw,
    In vain to me the vi'lets spring;
In vain to me in glen or shaw,
    The mavis and the lintwhite sing.

The merry ploughboy cheers his team,
    Wi' joy the tentie seedsman stalks,

[1] Menie is the common abbreviation of Marianne.—R.B.

But life to me's a weary dream,
    A dream of ane that never wauks.

The wanton coot the water skims,
    Amang the reeds the ducklings cry,
The stately swan majestic swims,
    And ev'ry thing is blest but I.

The sheep-herd steeks his faulding slap,
    And owre the moorlands whistles shill:
Wi' wild, unequal, wand'ring step,
    I meet him on the dewy hill.

And when the lark, 'tween light and dark,
    Blythe waukens by the daisy's side,
And mounts and sings on flittering wings,
    A woe-worn ghaist I hameward glide.

Come winter, with thine angry howl,
    And raging, bend the naked tree;
Thy gloom will soothe my cheerless soul,
    When nature all is sad like me!

TO A MOUNTAIN DAISY
On turning One down with the Plough, in April 1786

Wee, modest crimson-tippéd flow'r,
Thou's met me in an evil hour;
For I maun crush amang the stoure
        Thy slender stem:
To spare thee now is past my pow'r,
        Thou bonnie gem.

Alas! it's no thy neebor sweet,
The bonnie lark, companion meet!
Bending thee 'mang the dewy weet,
        Wi' spreckl'd breast,
When upward-springing, blythe, to greet
        The purpling east.

Cauld blew the bitter-biting north
Upon thy early, humble birth;
Yet cheerfully thou glinted forth
        Amid the storm,
Scarce rear'd above the parent-earth
        Thy tender form.

The flaunting flow'rs our gardens yield,
High shelt'ring woods and wa's maun shield;
But thou, beneath the random bield
        O' clod or stane,
Adorns the histie stibble-field,
        Unseen, alane.

There, in thy scanty mantle clad,
Thy snawie bosom sun-ward spread,
Thou lifts thy unassuming head
      In humble guise;
But now the share uptears thy bed,
      And low thou lies!

Such is the fate of artless maid,
Sweet flow'ret of the rural shade!
By love's simplicity betray'd,
      And guileless trust;
Till she, like thee, all soil'd, is laid
      Low i' the dust.

Such is the fate of simple bard,
On life's rough ocean luckless starr'd!
Unskilful he to note the card
      Of prudent lore,
Till billows rage, and gales blow hard,
      And whelm him o'er!

Such fate to suffering worth is giv'n,
Who long with wants and woes has striv'n,
By human pride or cunning driv'n
      To mis'ry's brink;
Till wrench'd of ev'ry stay but Heav'n,
      He, ruin'd, sink!

Ev'n thou who mourn'st the Daisy's fate,
That fate is thine—no distant date;
Stern Ruin's plough-share drives, elate,
      Full on thy bloom,
Till crush'd beneath the furrow's weight,
      Shall be thy doom!

To Ruin

All hail! inexorable lord!
At whose destruction-breathing word,
    The mightiest empires fall!
Thy cruel, woe-delighted train,
The ministers of grief and pain,
    A sullen welcome, all!
With stern-resolv'd despairing eye,
    I see each aiméd dart;
For one has cut my dearest tie
    And quivers in my heart.
      Then low'ring, and pouring,
        The storm no more I dread;
      Tho' thick'ning, and black'ning,
        Round my devoted head.

And thou grim Pow'r, by life abhorr'd,
While life a pleasure can afford,
    Oh! hear a wretch's pray'r!
Nor more I shrink appall'd, afraid;
I court, I beg thy friendly aid,
    To close this scene of care!
When shall my soul, in silent peace,
    Resign life's joyless day?
My weary heart its throbbing cease,
    Cold mould'ring in the clay?
      No fear more, no tear more,
        To stain my lifeless face,
      Enclaspéd, and graspéd,
        Within thy cold embrace!

THE LAMENT
Occasioned by the Unfortunate Issue of a Friend's Amour

Alas! how oft does goodness wound itself,
And sweet affection prove the spring of woe!—Home

O thou pale Orb that silent shines
    While care-untroubled mortals sleep!
Thou seest a wretch who inly pines.
    And wanders here to wail and weep!
With woe I nightly vigils keep,
    Beneath thy wan, unwarming beam;
And mourn, in lamentation deep,
    How life and love are all a dream!

I joyless view thy rays adorn
    The faintly markéd, distant hill;
I joyless view thy trembling horn,
    Reflected in the gurgling rill.
My fondly fluttering heart, be still!
    Thou busy pow'r, remembrance, cease!
Ah! must the agonising thrill
    For ever bar returning peace!

No idly feign'd, poetic pains,
    My sad, lovelorn lamentings claim:
No shepherd's pipe—Arcadian strains;
    No fabled tortures, quaint and tame.
The plighted faith, the mutual flame,
    The oft-attested Powers above,
The promis'd father's tender name;
    These were the pledges of my love!

Encircled in her clasping arms,
    How have the raptur'd moments flown!
How have I wish'd for Fortune's charms,
    For her dear sake, and her's alone!

And, must I think it! is she gone,
    My secret heart's exulting boast?
And does she heedless hear my groan?
    And is she ever, ever lost?

Oh! can she bear so base a heart,
    So lost to honour, lost to truth,
As from the fondest lover part,
    The plighted husband of her youth?
Alas! life's path may be unsmooth!
    Her way may lie thro' rough distress!
Then, who her pangs and pains will soothe,
    Her sorrows share, and make them less?

Ye wingéd hours that o'er us pass'd,
    Enraptur'd more, the more enjoy'd,
Your dear remembrance in my breast,
    My fondly treasur'd thoughts employ'd.
That breast, how dreary now, and void,
    For her too scanty once of room!
Ev'n ev'ry ray of hope destroy'd,
    And not a wish to gild the gloom!

The morn that warns th' approaching day,
    Awakes me up to toil and woe:
I see the hours, in long array,
    That I must suffer, lingering, slow.
Full many a pang, and many a throe,
    Keen recollection's direful train,
Must wring my soul, ere Phoebus, low,
    Shall kiss the distant western main.

And when my nightly couch I try,
    Sore harass'd out with care and grief,
My toil-beat nerves, and tear-worn eye,
    Keep watchings with the nightly thief:
Or if I slumber, fancy, chief,
    Reigns, haggard-wild, in sore afright:
Ev'n day, all-bitter, brings relief
    From such a horror-breathing night.

O thou bright queen, who, o'er th' expanse,
    Now highest reign'st, with boundless sway!
Oft has thy silent-marking glance
    Observ'd us, fondly wand'ring, stray!
The time, unheeded, sped away,
    While love's luxurious pulse beat high,
Beneath thy silver-gleaming ray,
    To mark the mutual-kindling eye.

Oh! scenes in strong remembrance set!
    Scenes, never, never to return!

Scenes, if in stupor I forget,
    Again I feel, again I burn!
From ev'ry joy and pleasure torn,
    Life's weary vale I'll wander thro';
And hopeless, comfortless, I'll mourn
    A faithless woman's broken vow!

DESPONDENCY—AN ODE

Oppress'd with grief, oppress'd with care,
A burden more than I can bear,
    I set me down and sigh:
O life! thou art a galling load,
Along a rough, a weary road,
    To wretches such as I!
Dim backward as I cast my view,
    What sick'ning scenes appear!
What sorrows yet may pierce me through,
    Too justly I may fear!
      Still caring, despairing,
        Must be my bitter doom;
      My woes here, shall close ne'er
        But with the closing tomb!

Happy! ye sons of busy life,
Who, equal to the bustling strife,
    No other view regard!
Ev'n when the wishéd end's denied,
Yet while the busy means are plied,
    They bring their own reward:
Whilst I, a hope-abandon'd wight,
    Unfitted with an aim,
Meet ev'ry sad-returning night,
    And joyless morn the same!
      You, bustling, and justling,
        Forget each grief and pain;
      I, listless, yet restless,
        Find ev'ry prospect vain.

How blest the solitary's lot,
Who, all-forgetting, all forgot,
    Within his humble cell,
The cavern wild with tangling roots,
Sits o'er his newly gather'd fruits,
    Beside his crystal well!
Or haply, to his ev'ning thought,
    By unfrequented stream,
The ways of men are distant brought,
    A faint-collected dream:
      While praising, and raising
        His thoughts to Heav'n on high,
      As wand'ring, meand'ring,
        He views the solemn sky.

Than I, no lonely hermit plac'd
Where never human footstep trac'd,
    Less fit to play the part,
The lucky moment to improve,
And just to stop, and just to move,
    With self-respecting art:
But ah! those pleasures, loves and joys,
    Which I too keenly taste,
The solitary can despise,
    Can want, and yet be blest!
        He needs not, he heeds not,
            Or human love or hate;
        Whilst I here, must cry here
            At perfidy ingrate!

O, enviable, early days,
When dancing thoughtless pleasure's maze,
    To care, to guilt unknown!
How ill exchang'd for riper times,
To feel the follies, or the crimes,
    Of others, or my own!
Ye tiny elves that guiltless sport,
    Like linnets in the bush,
Ye little know the ills ye court,
    When manhood is your wish!
        The losses, the crosses,
            That active man engage;
        The fears all, the tears all,
            Of dim declining age!

To Gavin Hamilton, Esq., Mauchline,
Recommending a Boy.

Mossgaville, May 3, 1786.
I hold it, sir, my bounden duty
To warn you how that Master Tootie,
    Alias, Laird M'Gaun,
Was here to hire yon lad away
'Bout whom ye spak the tither day,
    An' wad hae don't aff han':
But lest he learn the callan tricks,
    As, faith, I muckle doubt him,
Like scrapin' out auld Crummie's nicks,
    An' tellin lies about them;
        As lief then, I'd have then
            Your clerkship he should sair,
        If sae be, ye may be
            Not fitted other where.

Altho' I say't, he's gleg enough,
An' 'bout a house that's rude an' rough,
    The boy might learn to swear;

But then wi' you he'll be sae taught,
An' get sic fair example straught,
 I hae na ony fear.
Ye'll catechise him every quirk,
 An' shore him weel wi' hell;
An' gar him follow to the kirk—
 —Ay when ye gang yoursel.
  If ye, then, maun be then,
   Frae hame this comin' Friday,
  Then please, sir, to lea'e, sir,
   The orders wi' your lady.

My word of honour I hae gi'en,
In Paisley John's, that night at e'en,
 To meet the warld's worm;
To try to get the twa to gree,
An' name the airles an' the fee,
 In legal mode an' form:
I ken he weel a snick can draw,
 When simple bodies let him:
An' if a Devil be at a',
 In faith he's sure to get him.
  To phrase you, an' praise you,.
   Ye ken your Laureat scorns:
  The pray'r still, you share still
   Of grateful Minstrel Burns.

Versified Reply To An Invitation

Sir,
Yours this moment I unseal,
 And faith I'm gay and hearty!
To tell the truth and shame the deil,
 I am as fou as Bartie:
But Foorsday, sir, my promise leal,
 Expect me o' your partie,
If on a beastie I can speel,
 Or hurl in a cartie.
  Yours, Robert Burns
Mauchlin, Monday night, 10 o'clock

Will Ye Go To The Indies, My Mary?
Tune—*Will ye go to the ewe-bughts, Marion?*

Will ye go to the Indies, my Mary,
 And leave auld Scotia's shore?
Will ye go to the Indies, my Mary,
 Across th' Atlantic roar?

O sweet grows the lime and the orange,
 And the apple on the pine;

But a' the charms o' the Indies
    Can never equal thine.

I hae sworn by the Heavens to my Mary,
    I hae sworn by the Heavens to be true;
And sae may the Heavens forget me,
    When I forget my vow!

O plight me your faith, my Mary,
    And plight me your lily-white hand;
O plight me your faith, my Mary,
    Before I leave Scotia's strand.

We hae plighted our troth, my Mary,
    In mutual affection to join;
And curst be the cause that shall part us!
    The hour and the moment o' time!

My Highland Lassie, O
Tune—*The deuks dang o'er my daddy*

Chorus: Within the glen sae bushy, O,
    Aboon the plain sae rashy, O,
I set me down wi' right guid will,
    To sing my Highland lassie, O.

Nae gentle dames, tho' ne'er sae fair,
Shall ever be my muse's care:
Their titles a' are empty show;
Gie me my Highland lassie, O.

O were yon hills and valleys mine,
Yon palace and yon gardens fine!
The world then the love should know
I bear my Highland Lassie, O.

But fickle fortune frowns on me,
And I maun cross the raging sea;
But while my crimson currents flow,
I'll love my Highland lassie, O.

Altho' thro' foreign climes I range,
I know her heart will never change,
For her bosom burns with honour's glow,
My faithful Highland lassie, O.

For her I'll dare the billow's roar,
For her I'll trace a distant shore,
That Indian wealth may lustre throw
Around my Highland lassie, O.

She has my heart, she has my hand,
By secret troth and honour's band!
Till the mortal stroke shall lay me low,
I'm thine, my Highland lassie, O.

Farewell the glen sae bushy, O!
    Farewell the plain sae rashy, O!
To other lands I now must go,
    To sing my Highland lassie, O.

Epistle To A Young Friend
May —— 1786

I lang hae thought, my youthfu' friend,[1]
    A something to have sent you,
Tho' it should serve nae ither end
    Than just a kind memento;
But how the subject theme may gang,
    Let time and chance determine;
Perhaps it may turn out a sang:
    Perhaps, turn out a sermon.

[1] Andrew Aiken, son of Robert Aiken, writer in Ayr.

Ye'll try the world soon, my lad;
　　And, Andrew dear, believe me,
Ye'll find mankind an unco squad,
　　And muckle they may grieve ye:
For care and trouble set your thought,
　　Ev'n when your end's attained;
And a' your views may come to nought,
　　Where ev'ry nerve is strained.

I'll no say men are villains a';
　　The real, harden'd wicked,
Wha hae nae check but human law,
　　Are to a few restricked;
But, Och! mankind are unco weak,
　　An' little to be trusted;
If *self* the wavering balance shake,
　　It's rarely right adjusted!

Yet they wha fa' in fortune's strife,
　　Their fate we shouldna censure;
For still, th' important end of life
　　They equally may answer:
A man may hae an honest heart,
　　Tho' poortith hourly stare him;
A man may tak a neebor's part,
　　Yet hae nae cash to spare him.

Aye free, aff-han', your story tell,
　　When wi' a bosom crony;
But still keep something to yoursel
　　Ye scarcely tell to ony.
Conceal yoursel as weel's ye can
　　Frae critical dissection;
But keek thro' ev'ry other man,
　　Wi' sharpen'd, sly inspection.

The sacred lowe o' weel-plac'd love,
　　Luxuriantly indulge it;
But never tempt th' illicit rove,
　　Tho' naething should divulge it:
I waive the quantum o' the sin,
　　The hazard of concealing;
But, Och! it hardens a' within,
　　And petrifies the feeling!

To catch Dame Fortune's golden smile,
　　Assiduous wait upon her;
And gather gear by ev'ry wile
　　That's justified by honour;
Not for to hide it in a hedge,
　　Nor for a train-attendant;
But for the glorious privilege
　　Of being independent.

The fear o' hell's a hangman's whip,
    To haud the wretch in order;
But where ye feel your honour grip,
    Let that aye be your border;
Its slightest touches, instant pause—
    Debar a' side-pretences;
And resolutely keep its laws,
    Uncaring consequences.

The great Creator to revere,
    Must sure become the creature;
But still the preaching cant forbear,
    And ev'n the rigid feature:
Yet ne'er with wits profane to range,
    Be complaisance extended;
An atheist-laugh's a poor exchange
    For Deity offended!

When ranting round in pleasure's ring,
    Religion may be blinded;
Or if she gie a random sting,
    It may be little minded;
But when on life we're tempest driv'n,
    A conscience but a canker—
A correspondence fix'd wi' Heav'n,
    Is sure a noble anchor!

Adieu, dear, amiable youth!
    Your heart can ne'er be wanting!
May prudence, fortitude and truth,
    Erect your brow undaunting!
In ploughman phrase, 'God send you speed,'
    Still daily to grow wiser;
And may ye better reck the rede,
    Then ever did th' adviser!

ADDRESS OF BEELZEBUB
To the President of the Highland Society

To the Right Honourable the Earl of Breadalbane, President of the Right Honourable the Highland Society, which met, on the 23rd of May last, at the Shakespeare, Covent Garden, to concert ways and means to frustrate the designs of five hundred Highlanders, who, as the Society were informed by Mr M'Kenzie of Applecross, were so audacious as to attempt an escape from their lawful lords and masters whose property they are by emigrating from the lands of Mr Macdonald of Glengary to the wilds of Canada, in search of that fantastic thing—LIBERTY.

Long life, my Lord, an' health be yours,
Unskaithed by hunger'd Highland boors;
Lord, grant me nae duddie, desperate beggar,
Wi' dirk, claymore, and rusty trigger,
May twin auld Scotland o' a life
She likes—as butchers like a knife.

Faith, you and Applecross were right
To keep the Highland hounds in sight:
I doubt na, they wad bid nae better,
Than let them ance out owre the water;
Then up amang thae lakes and seas,
They'll mak what rules and laws they please:
Some daring Hancocke, or a Franklin,
May set their Highland bluid a-ranklin;
Some Washington again may head them,
Or some Montgomery, fearless, lead them,
Till God knows what may be effected,
When by such heads and hearts directed;
Poor dunghill sons of dirt and mire
May to Patrician rights aspire!
Nae sage North, now, nor sager Sackville,
To watch and premier o'er the pack vile!
An' whare will ye get Howes and Clintons
To bring them to a right repentance?—
To cowe the rebel generation,
An' save the honour o' the nation?
They, an' be damn'd! what right hae they
To meat, or sleep, or light o' day?—
Far less to riches, pow'r, or freedom,
But what your lordship likes to gie them!

But hear, my lord! Glengarry, hear!
Your hand's owre light to them, I fear;
Your factors, grieves, trustees, and bailies,
I canna say but they do gaylies;
They lay aside a' tender mercies,
An' tirl the hallions to the birses;
Yet while they're only poin'd and herriet,
They'll keep their stubborn Highland spirit;
But smash them! crash them a' to spails!
An' rot the dyvors i' the jails!
The young dogs—swinge them to the labour—
Let wark an' hunger mak them sober!
The hizzies, if they're oughtlins fawsont,
Let them in Drury Lane be lesson'd!
An' if the wives an' dirty brats
Come thiggin at your doors an' yetts,
Flaffin wi' duds, an' grey wi' beas',
Frightin' awa' your deucks an' geese—
Get out a horsewhip or a jowler—
The langest thong, the fiercest growler—
An' gar the tatter'd gypsies pack,
Wi' a' their bastards on their back!

Go on, my lord! I lang to meet you,
An' in my house at hame to greet you;
Wi' common lords ye shanna mingle,

The benmost neuk beside the ingle,
At my right hand assign'd your seat,
'Tween Herod's hip an' Polycrate;
Or if ye on your station tarrow,
Between Almagro an' Pizarro,
A seat, I'm sure ye're well deservin't;
An' till ye come—your humble servant,
Hell, 1st June, *Anno Mundi*, 5790   Beelzebub

A Dream

On reading, in the public papers, the Laureate's Ode, with the other parade of June 4th, 1786, the Author was no sooner dropt asleep, than he imagined himself transported to the Birth-day Levee; and, in his dreaming fancy, made the following Address:

Thoughts, words, and deeds, the Statute blames with reason;
But surely *Dreams* were ne'er indicted Treason.

Guid mornin' to your Majesty!
    May Heaven augment your blisses
On ev'ry new birth-day ye see,
    A humble poet wishes!
My bardship here, at your Levee,
    On sic a day as this is,
Is sure an uncouth sight to see,
    Amang thae birth-day dresses
            Sae fine this day.

I see ye're complimented thrang,
    By mony a lord an' lady;
'God save the King' 's a cuckoo sang
    That's unco easy said aye:
The poets, too, a venal gang,
    Wi' rhymes weel-turn'd an' ready,
Wad gar you trow ye ne'er do wrang,
    But aye unerring steady,
            On sic a day.

For me! before a monarch's face
    Ev'n there I winna flatter;
For neither pension, post, nor place,
    Am I your humble debtor:
So, nae reflection on Your Grace,
    Your Kingship to bespatter;
There's monie waur been o' the race,
    And aiblins ane been better
            Than you this day.

'Tis very true, my sovereign King,
    My skill may weel be doubted;
But facts are chiels that winna ding,
    An' downa be disputed:

Your royal nest, beneath your wing,
　　Is e'en right reft an' clouted,
And now the third part o' the string,
　　An' less, will gang aboot it
　　　　　　Than did ae day.[1]

Far be 't frae me that I aspire
　　To blame your legislation,
Or say, ye wisdom want, or fire,
　　To rule this mighty nation:
But faith! I muckle doubt, my sire,
　　Ye've trusted 'ministration
To chaps, wha, in barn or byre,
　　Wad better fill'd their station
　　　　　　Than courts yon day.

And now ye've gien auld Britain peace,
　　Her broken shins to plaister;
Your sair taxation does her fleece,
　　Till she has scarce a tester:
For me, thank God, my life's a lease,
　　Nae bargain wearing faster,
Or, faith! I fear, that, wi' the geese,
　　I shortly boost to pasture
　　　　　　I' the craft some day.

I'm no mistrusting Willie Pitt,
　　When taxes he enlarges,
(An' Will's a true guid fallow's get,
　　A name not envy spairges),
That he intends to pay your debt,
　　An' lessen a' your charges;
But, God-sake! let nae saving fit
　　Abridge your bonnie barges
　　　　　　An' boats this day.[2]

Adieu, my Liege; may freedom geck
　　Beneath your high protection;
An' may ye rax Corruption's neck,
　　And gie her for dissection!
But since I'm here, I'll no neglect,
　　In loyal, true affection,
To pay your Queen, with due respect,
　　My fealty an' subjection
　　　　　　This great birth-day.

Hail, Majesty most Excellent!
　　While nobles strive to please ye,

---

[1] A reference to the loss of the North American colonies.
[2] In the spring of 1786, some discussion arose in parliament about a proposal to give up sixty-four gun ships, when the navy supplies were being considered.

Will ye accept a compliment,
    A simple poet gies ye?
Thae bonnie bairntime, Heav'n has lent,
    Still higher may they heeze ye
In bliss, till fate some day is sent
    For ever to release ye
        Frae care that day.

For you, young Potentate o' Wales,
    I tell your Highness fairly,
Down Pleasure's stream, wi' swelling sails,
    I'm tauld ye're driving rarely;
But some day ye may gnaw your nails,
    An' curse your folly sairly,
That e'er ye brak Diana's pales,
    Or rattl'd dice wi' Charlie[1]
        By night or day.

Yet aft a ragged cowte's been known,
    To mak a noble aiver;
So, ye may doucely fill the throne,
    For a' their clish-ma-claver:
There, him[2] at Agincourt wha shone,
    Few better were or braver;
And yet, wi' funny, queer Sir John,[3]
    He was an unco shaver
        For monie a day.

For you, right rev'rend Osnaburg,[4]
    Nane sets the lawn-sleeve sweeter,
Altho' a ribbon at your lug
    Wad been a dress completer:
As ye disown yon paughty dog,
    That bears the keys of Peter,
Then swith! an' get a wife to hug,
    Or trowth, ye'll stain the mitre
        Some luckless day!

Young, royal 'tarry-breeks', I learn,
    Ye've lately come athwart her—
A glorious galley,[5] stem and stern,
    Weel rigg'd for Venus barter;
But first hang out, that she'll discern,
    Your hymeneal charter;
Then heave aboard your grapple airn,
    An' large upon her quarter,
        Come full that day.

[1] The Prince of Wales was then of the Whig, or Fox, Party.
[2] King Henry V.—R.B.
[3] Sir John Falstaff, *vid*. Shakespeare.—R.B.
[4] Frederick, first a bishop, and afterwards Duke of York.
[5] Alluding to the newspaper account of a certain Royal sailor's amour.—R.B. This was Prince William Henry,
    afterwards King William IV, third son of George III, who in his youth married Mrs Jordan, the actress.

Ye, lastly, bonnie blossoms a',
    Ye royal lasses dainty,
Heav'n mak you guid as weel as braw,
    An' gie you lads a-plenty!
But sneer na British boys awa!
    For kings are unco scant aye,
An' German gentles are but sma',
    They're better just than want aye
            On onie day.

Gad bless you a'! consider now,
    Ye're unco muckle dautit;
But ere the course o' life be through,
    It may be bitter sautit:
An' I hae seen their coggie fou,
    That yet hae tarrow't at it,
But or the day was done, I trow,
    The laggen they hae clautit
            Fu' clean that day.

A DEDICATION
To Gavin Hamilton, Esq.

Expect na, Sir, in this narration,
A fleechin, fleth'rin Dedication,
To roose you up, an' ca' you guid,
An' sprung o' great an' noble bluid;
Because ye're surnam'd like His Grace—
Perhaps related to the race:
Then, when I'm tir'd—and sae are ye,
Wi' monie a fulsome, sinfu' lie,
Set up a face, how I stop short,
For fear your modesty be hurt.

    This may do—maun do, Sir, wi' them wha
Maun please the great folk for a wamefou;
For me! sae laigh I need na bow,
For, Lord be thankit, I can plough;
And when I downa yoke a naig,
Then, Lord be thankit, I can beg;
Sae I shall say—an' that's nae flatt'rin—
It's just sic poet an' sic patron.

    The Poet, some guid angel help him,
Or else, I fear, some ill ane skelp him!
He may do weel for a' he's done yet,
But only—he's no just begun yet.

    The Patron (Sir, ye maun forgie me,
I winna lie, come what will o' me),
On ev'ry hand it will allow'd be,
He's just—nae better than he should be.

I readily and freely grant,
He downa see a poor man want;
What's no his ain, he winna tak it;
What ance he says, he winna break it;
Ought he can lend he'll no refus't,
Till aft his guidness is abus'd;
And rascals whyles that do him wrang,
Ev'n that, he does na mind it lang:
As master, landlord, husband, father,
He does na fail his part in either.

But then, nae thanks to him for a' that;
Nae godly symptom ye can ca' that;
It's naething but a milder feature
Of our poor, sinfu' corrupt nature:
Ye'll get the best o' moral works,
'Mang black Gentoos, and pagan Turks,
Or hunters wild on Ponotaxi,
Wha never heard of orthodoxy.
That he's the poor man's friend in need,
The gentleman in word and deed,
It's no through terror of damnation;
It's just a carnal inclination.

Morality, thou deadly bane,
Thy tens o' thousands thou hast slain!
Vain is his hope, whase stay an' trust is
In moral mercy, truth and justice!

No—stretch a point to catch a plack;
Abuse a brother to his back;
Steal through the winnock frae a whore,
But point the rake that taks the door;
Be to the poor like onie whunstane,
And haud their noses to the grunstane;
Ply ev'ry art o' legal thieving;
No matter—stick to sound believing.

Learn three-mile pray'rs, an' half-mile graces,
Wi' weel-spread looves, an' lang, wry faces;
Grunt up a solemn, lengthen'd groan,
And damn a' parties but your own;
I'll warrant then, ye're nae deceiver,
A steady, sturdy, staunch believer.

O ye wha leave the springs o' Calvin,
For gumlie dubs of your ain delvin!
Ye sons of Heresy and Error,
Ye'll some day squeel in quaking terror!
When Vengeance draws the sword in wrath,
And in the fire throws the sheath;

When Ruin, with his sweeping besom,
Just frets till Heav'n commission gies him;
While o'er the harp pale Misery moans,
And strikes the ever-deep'ning tones,
Still louder shrieks, and heavier groans!

Your pardon, sir, for this digression:
I maist forgat my Dedication;
But when divinity comes 'cross me,
My readers still are sure to lose me.

So, sir, you see 'twas nae daft vapour;
But I maturely thought it proper,
When a' my works I did review,
To dedicate them, Sir, to you:
Because (ye need na tak it ill)
I thought them something like yoursel.

Then patronise them wi' your favour,
And your petitioner shall ever—
I had amaist said, ever pray,
But that's a word I need na say;
For prayin, I hae little skill o't,
I'm baith dead-sweer, an' wretched ill o't;
But I'se repeat each poor man's pray'r,
That kens or hears about you, Sir—

'May ne'er Misfortune's gowling bark,
Howl thro' the dwelling o' the clerk!
May ne'er his gen'rous, honest heart,
For that same gen'rous spirit smart!
May Kennedy's[1] far-honour'd name
Lang beet his hymeneal flame,
Till Hamiltons, at least a dizzen,
Are frae their nuptial labours risen:
Five bonnie lasses round their table,
And sev'n braw fellows, stout an' able,
To serve their king an' country weel,
By word, or pen, or pointed steel!
May health and peace, with mutual rays,
Shine on the ev'ning o' his days;
Till his wee, curlie John's ier-oe,
When ebbing life nae mair shall flow,
The last, sad, mournful rites bestow!'

I will not wind a lang conclusion,
With complimentary effusion;
But, whilst your wishes and endeavours
Are blest with Fortune's smiles and favours,
I am, Dear Sir, with zeal most fervent,
Your much indebted, humble servant.

[1] Kennedy was the surname of Hamilton's wife's family.

But if, which Pow'rs above prevent,
That iron-hearted carl, Want,
Attended, in his grim advances,
By sad mistakes, and black mischances,
While hopes, and joys, and pleasures fly him,
Make you as poor a dog as I am,
Your humble servant then no more;
For who would humbly serve the poor?
But by a poor man's hopes in Heav'n!
While recollection's pow'r is giv'n,
If, in the vale of humble life,
The victim sad of Fortune's strife,
I, through the tender-gushing tear,
Should recognise my master dear;
If friendless, low, we meet together,
Then, Sir, your hand—my Friend and Brother!

To Dr Mackenzie, Mauchline

Friday first's the day appointed
By our Right Worshipful anointed,
    To hold our grand procession;
To get a blade o' Johnnie's morals,
And taste a swatch o' Manson's barrels
    I' the way of our profession.
The Master and the Brotherhood
    Would a' be glad to see you;
For me I would be mair than proud
    To share the mercies wi' you.
        If Death, then, wi' skaith, then,
            Some mortal heart is hechtin,
        Inform him, and storm him,
            That Saturday you'll fecht him.

The Farewell To The Brethren
Of St James' Lodge, Tarbolton.
Tune—*Guidnight, and joy be wi' you a'*

Adieu! a heart-warm fond adieu;
    Dear brothers of the *mystic tie*!
Ye favoured, *enlighten'd* Few,
    Companions of my social joy!
Tho' I to foreign lands must hie,
    Pursuing Fortune's slidd'ry ba',
With melting heart, and brimful eye,
    I'll mind you still, tho' far awa.

Oft have I met your social band,
    And spent the cheerful, festive night;
Oft, honour'd with supreme command,
    Presided o'er the *Sons of light*:

And by that *hieroglyphic* bright,
    Which none but *Craftsmen* ever saw!
Strong Mem'ry on my heart shall write
    Those happy scenes when far awa!

May Freedom, Harmony and Love,
    Unite you in the *grand Design*,
Beneath th' Omniscient Eye above,
    The glorious *Architect* Divine!
That you may keep th' *unerring line*,
    Still rising by the *plummet's law*,
Till *Order* bright completely shine,
    Shall be my pray'r when far awa.

And *you*, farewell! whose merits claim,
    Justly that *highest badge* to wear!
Heav'n bless your honour'd noble name,
    To *Masonry* and *Scotia* dear!
A last request permit me here,—
    When yearly ye assemble a',
One *round*, I ask it with a *tear*,
    To him, *the Bard that's far awa.*

On A Scotch Bard Gone To The West Indies

A' ye wha live by sowps o' drink,
A' ye wha live by crambo-clink,
A' ye wha live and never think,
        Come, mourn wi' me!
Our billie 's gi'en us a' a jink,
      An' owre the sea!

Lament him, a' ye rantin' core,
Wha dearly like a random splore;
Nae mair he'll join the merry roar,
      In social key;
For now he's taen anither shore.
      An' owre the sea!

The bonnie lasses weel may wiss him,
And in their dear petitions place him:
The widows, wives, an' a' may bless him,
      Wi' tearfu' e'e;
For weel I wat they'll sairly miss him
      That's owre the sea!

O Fortune, they hae room to grumble!
Hadst thou taen aff some drowsy bummle,
Wha can do nought but fyke an' fumble,
      'Twad been nae plea;
But he was gleg as onie wumble,
      That's owre the sea!

Auld, cantie Kyle may weepers wear,
An' stain them wi' the saut, saut tear;
'Twill mak her poor auld heart, I fear,
    In flinders flee:
He was her Laureat monie a year,
    That's owre the sea!

He saw Misfortune's cauld nor-west
Lang mustering up a bitter blast;
A jillet brak his heart at last,
    Ill may she be!
So, took a berth afore the mast,
    An' owre the sea.

To tremble under Fortune's cummock,
On a scarce a bellyfu' o' drummock,
Wi' his proud, independent stomach,
    Could ill agree;
So, row't his hurdies in a hammock,
    An' owre the sea.

He ne'er was gi'en to great misguidin,
Yet coin his pouches wad na bide in;
Wi' him it ne'er was under hiding;
    He dealt it free:
The Muse was a' that he took pride in,
    That's owre the sea.

Jamaica bodies, use him weel,
An' hap him in cozie biel:
Ye'll find him aye a dainty chiel,
    An' fou o' glee:
He wad na wrang'd the vera deil,
    That's owre the sea.

Farewell, my rhyme-composing billie!
Your native soil was right ill-willie;
But may ye flourish like a lily,
    Now bonilie!
I'll toast you in my hindmost gillie,
    Tho' owre the sea!

FAREWELL TO ELIZA
Tune—*Gilderoy*

From thee, Eliza, I must go,
    And from my native shore;
The cruel fates between us throw
    A boundless ocean's roar:
But boundless oceans, roaring wide,
    Between my love and me,
They never, never can divide
    My heart and soul from thee.

Farewell, farewell, Eliza dear,
    The maid that I adore!
A boding voice is in mine ear,
    We part to meet no more!
But the latest throb that leaves my heart,
    While Death stands victor by,
That throb, Eliza, is thy part,
    And thine that latest sigh!

A Bard's Epitaph

Is there a whim-inspiréd fool,
Owre fast for thought, owre hot for rule,
Owre blate to seek, owre proud to snool,
      Let him draw near;
And owre this grassy heap sing dool,
      And drap a tear.

Is there a bard of rustic song,
Who, noteless, steals the crowds among,
That weekly this area throng,
      O, pass not by!
But, with a frater-feeling strong,
      Here, heave a sigh.

Is there a man, whose judgment clear
Can others teach the course to steer,
Yet runs, himself, life's mad career,
      Wild as the wave,
Here pause—and thro' the starting tear,
      Survey this grave.

The poor inhabitant below
Was quick to learn the wise to know,
And keenly felt the friendly glow,
      And softer flame;
But thoughtless follies laid him low,
      And stain'd his name!

Reader, attend! whether thy soul
Soars fancy's flights beyond the pole,
Or darkling grubs this earthly hole,
      In low pursuit:
Know, prudent, cautious, self-control
      Is wisdom's root.

For Robert Aiken, Esq.

Know thou, O stranger to the fame
Of this much lov'd, much honour'd name!
(For none that knew him need be told)
A warmer heart Death ne'er made cold.

For Gavin Hamilton, Esq.

The poor man weeps—here Gavin sleeps,
   Whom canting wretches blam'd;
But with such as he, where'er he be,
   May I be sav'd or damn'd!

On 'Wee Johnie'

Hic jacet wee Johnie

Whoe'er thou art, O reader, know
    That Death has murder'd Johnie;
An' here his *body* lies fu' low—
    For *saul* he ne'er had ony.

A Tale

'Twas where the birch and sounding thong are plyed,
The noisy domicile of Pedant-pride;
Where Ignorance her darkening vapour throws,
And Cruelty directs the thickening blows;
Upon a time, Sir Abece the great,
In all his pedagogic powers elate,
His awful Chair of state resolves to mount,
And call the trembling Vowels to account.

    First enter'd A; a grave, broad, solemn wight,
But ah! deform'd, dishonest to the sight!
His twisted head look'd backward on his way,
And flagrant from the scourge he grunted, AI!
A maiden fair I chanc'd to spy:

    Reluctant, E stalk'd in; with piteous race
The jostling tears ran down his honest face!
That name, that well-worn name, and all his own,
Pale he surrenders at the tyrant's throne!
    The Pedant stifles keen the Roman sound
Not all his mongrel dipthongs can compound;
And next the title following close behind,
He to th nameless, ghastly wretch assign'd.

    The cob-webb'd, Gothic dome resounded, Y!
In sullen vengeance, I, disdain'd reply;
The Pedant swung his felon cudgel round,
And knock'd the groaning Vowel to the ground!

    In rueful apprehension enter'd O,
The wailing minstrel of despairing woe;
Th' Inquisitor of Spain the most expert
Might there have learnt new mysteries of his art:
So grim, deform'd, with horrors, entering U,
His dearest friend and brother scarcely knew!

    As trembling U stood staring all aghast,
The Pedant in his left hand clutch'd him fast;
In helpless infant's tears he dipp'd his right,
Baptis'd him EU, and kick'd him from his sight.

Now Health Forsakes—A Fragment

Now health forsakes that angel face,
    Nae mair my Dearie smiles;

Pale sickness withers ilka grace,
  And a' my hopes beguiles:
The cruel Powers reject the prayer
  I hourly mak for thee;
Ye Heavens how great is my despair,
  How can I see him die!

FAREWELL LINES TO MR JOHN KENNEDY

Farewell, dear friend! may guid luck hit you!
And 'mang her favourites admit you:
If e'er Detraction shore to smit you
      May nane believe him!
And ony deil that thinks to get you,
      Good Lord, deceive him!

LINES TO AN OLD SWEETHEART
Written on the Blank Leaf of a Copy of the Kilmarnock Edition of the Author's Poems

Once fondly lov'd, and still remember'd dear,
  Sweet early object of my youthful vows,
Accept this mark of friendship, warm, sincere—
  Friendship! 'tis all cold duty now allows.
And when you read the simple artless rhymes,
  One friendly sigh for him—he asks no more—
Who distant burns in flaming torrid climes,
  Or haply lies beneath th' Atlantic roar.

LINES WRITTEN ON A BANKNOTE

Wae worth thy pow'r, thou curséd leaf!
Fell source o' a' my woe and grief!
For lack o' thee I've lost my lass,
For lack o' thee I scrimp my glass:
I see the children of affliction,
Unaided through thy curs'd restriction;
I've seen th' oppressor's cruel smile,
Amid his hapless victim's spoil,
And for thy potence vainly wished,
To crush the villain in the dust!
For lack o' thee, I leave this much lov'd shore,
  Never, perhaps, to greet old Scotland more.
    Kyle   R.B.

STANZAS ON NAETHING
Extempore Epistle to Gavin Hamilton, Esq.

To you, Sir, this summons I've sent,
  Pray, whip till the pownie is freathing;
But if you demand what I want,
  I honestly answer you—naething.

Ne'er scorn a poor Poet like me,
　　For idly just living and breathing,
While people of every degree
　　Are busy employed about—naething.

Poor Centum-per-centum may fast,
　　And grumble his hurdies their claithing,
He'll find, when the balance is cast,
　　He's gane to the devil for—naething.

The courtier cringes and bows,
　　Ambition has likewise its plaything;
A coronet beams on his brows;
　　And what is a coronet?—naething.

Some quarrel the Presbyter gown,
　　Some quarrel Episcopal graithing;
But every good fellow will own
　　Their quarrel is a' about—naething.

The lover may sparkle and glow,
　　Approaching his bonnie bit gay thing:
But marriage will soon let him know
　　He's gotten—a buskit-up naething.

The Poet may jingle and rhyme,
　　In hopes of a laureate wreathing,
And when he has wasted his time,
　　He's kindly rewarded wi'—naething.

The thundering bully may rage,
　　And swagger and swear like a heathen;
But collar him fast, I'll engage,
　　You'll find that his courage is—naething.

Last night wi' a feminine whig—
　　A Poet she couldna put faith in;
But soon we grew lovingly big,
　　I taught her, her terrors were—naething.

Her whigship was wonderful pleased,
　　But charmingly tickled wi' ae thing,
Her fingers I lovingly squeezed,
　　And kissed her, and promised her—naething.

The priest anathémas may threat—
　　Predicament, sir, that we're baith in;
But when honour's reveillé is beat,
　　The holy artillery's—naething.

And now I must mount on the wave—
　My voyage perhaps there is death in;
But what is a watery grave?
　The drowning a Poet is—naething.

And now, as grim death's in my thought,
　To you, Sir, I make this bequeathing;
My service as long as ye've ought,
　And my friendship, by God, when ye've naething.

THE FAREWELL

The valiant, in himself, what can he suffer?
Or what does he regard his single woes?
But when, alas! he multiplies himself,
To dearer selves, to the lov'd tender fair,
To those whose bliss, whose beings hang upon him,
To helpless children! then, O then! he feels
The point of misery fest'ring in his heart,
And weakly weeps his fortune like a coward:
Such, such am I!—undone!— Thomson's *Edward and Eleanora*

Farewell, old Scotia's bleak domains,
Far dearer than the torrid plains,
　Where rich ananas blow!
Farewell, a mother's blessing dear!
A brother's sigh! a sister's tear!
　My Jean's heart-rending throe!
Farewell, my Bess! tho' thou'rt bereft
　Of my paternal care,
A faithful brother I have left,
　My part in him thou'lt share!
　　Adieu, too, to you too,
　　　My Smith, my bosom frien';
　　When kindly you mind me,
　　　O then befriend my Jean!

What bursting anguish tears my heart;
From thee, my Jeany, must I part!
　Thou, weeping, answ'rest 'No!'
Alas! misfortune stares my face,
And points to ruin and disgrace,
　I for thy sake must go!
Thee, Hamilton, and Aiken dear,
　A grateful, warm adieu:
I, with a much indebted tear,
　Shall still remember you!
　　All hail then, the gale then,
　　　Wafts me from thee, dear shore!
　　It rustles, and whistles
　　　I'll never see thee more!

THE CALF

To the Rev. James Steven, on his Text, Malachi, Chapter 4, verse 2:
'And ye shall go forth, and grow up, as Calves of the stall'

Right, Sir! your text I'll prove it true,
    Tho' heretics may laugh;
For instance, there's yourself just now,
    God knows, an unco calf!

And should some patron be so kind,
    As bless you wi' a kirk,
I doubt na, Sir, but then we'll find,
    Ye're still as great a stirk.

But, if the lover's raptur'd hour
    Shall ever be your lot,
Forbid it, ev'ry heavenly Power,
    You e'er should be a stot!

Tho' when some kind connubial dear
    Your but-and-ben adorns,
The like has been that you may wear
    A noble head of horns.

And, in your lug, most reverend James,
    To hear you roar and rowte,
Few men o' sense will doubt your claims
    To rank amang the nowte.

And when ye're number'd wi' the dead,
    Below a grassy hillock,
Wi' justice they may mark your head—
    'Here lies a famous bullock!'

NATURE'S LAW—A POEM

A Poem Humbly inscribed to Gavin Hamilton, Esq.

'Great Nature spoke: observant man obey'd.'—Pope

Let other heroes boast their scars,
    The marks of sturt and strife;
And other poets sing of wars,
    The plagues of human life;
Shame fa' the fun, wi' sword and gun
    To slap mankind like lumber!
I sing his name and nobler fame,
    Wha multiplies our number.

Great Nature spoke, with air benign,
    'Go on, ye human race!
This lower world I you resign;
    Be fruitful and increase.
The liquid fire of strong desire
    I've pour'd it in each bosom;
Here, on this hand, does Mankind stand,
    And there is Beauty's blossom!'

The hero of these artless strains,
    A lowly bard was he,
Who sung his rhymes in Coila's plains,
    With meikle mirth an' glee;
Kind Nature's care had given his share
    Large, of the flaming current:
And, all devout, he never sought
    To stem the sacred torrent.

He felt the powerful, high behest
    Thrill, vital, thro' and thro';

And sought a correspondent breast,
    To give obedience due:
Propitious Powers screen'd the young flow'rs,
    From mildews of abortion;
And low! the bard—a great reward—
    Has got a double portion!

Auld, cantie Coil may count the day,
    As annual it returns,
The third of Libra's equal sway,
    That gave another Burns
With future rhymes, in other times,
    To emulate his sire—
To sing auld Coil in nobler style,
    With more poetic fire.

Ye Powers of peace, and peaceful song,
    Look down with gracious eyes;
And bless auld Coila, large and long,
    With multiplying joys;
Lang may she stand to prop the land,
    The flow'r of ancient nations;
And Burnses spring, her fame to sing,
    To endless generations!

On Willie Chalmers

'Mr Chalmers, a gentleman in Ayrshire, a particular friend of mine, asked me to write a poetic epistle to a young lady, his Dulcinea. I had seen her, but was scarcely acquainted with her, and wrote as follows'

Wi' braw new branks in mickle pride,
    And eke a braw new brechan,
My Pegasus I'm got astride,
    And up Parnassus pechin;
Whyles o'er a bush wi' downward crush,
    The doited beastie stammers;
Then up he gets, and off he sets,
    For sake o' Willie Chalmers.

I doubt na, lass, that weel kend name
    May cost a pair o' blushes;
I am nae stranger to your fame,
    Nor his warm urgéd wishes.
Your bonnie face sae mild and sweet,
    His honest heart enamours;
And faith ye'll no' be lost a whit,
    Tho' wair'd on Willie Chalmers.

Auld Truth hersel' might swear ye're fair,
    And Honour safely back her,
And Modesty assume your air,
    And ne'er a ane mistak her;

And sic twa love-inspiring een
    Might fire even holy palmers:
Nae wonder then they've fatal been
    To honest Willie Chalmers.

I doubt na Fortune may you shore
    Some mim-mou'd pouther'd priestie,
Fu' lifted up wi' Hebrew lore,
    And band upon his breastie;
But oh! what signifies to you
    His lexicons and grammars;
The feeling heart's the royal blue,
    And that's wi' Willie Chalmers.

Some gapin', glowrin' countra laird
    May warsle for your favour;
May claw his lug, and straik his beard,
    And hoast up some palaver:
My bonnie maid, before ye wed
    Sic clumsy-witted hammers,
Seek heaven for help, and barefit skelp
    Awa wi' Willie Chalmers.

Forgive the Bard! my fond regard
    For ane that shares my bosom,
Inspires my Muse to gie 'm his dues
    For deil a hair I roose him!
May powers aboon unite you soon,
    And fructify your amours,
And every year come in mair dear
    To you and Willie Chalmers.

ANSWER TO A TRIMMING EPISTLE RECEIVED FROM A TAILOR

What ails ye now, ye lousie bitch,
To thresh my back at sic a pitch?
Losh, man! hae mercy wi' your natch,
        Your bodkin's bauld;
I didna suffer half sae much
        Frae Daddie Auld.

What tho' at times when I grow crouse,
I gie their wames a random pouse,
Is that enough for you to souse
        Your servant sae?
Gae mind your seam, ye prick-the-louse,
        An' jag-the-flae!

King David, o' poetic brief,
Wrocht 'mang the lasses sic mischief
As fill'd his after-life wi' grief
        An' bloody rants,

An' yet he's rank'd amang the chief
   O' lang-syne saunts.

And maybe, Tam, for a' my cants,
My wicked rhymes, an' drucken rants,
I'll gie auld cloven's Clootie's haunts
   An unco slip yet,
An' snugly sit amang the saunts,
   At Davie's hip yet!

But, fegs! the session says I maun
Gae fa' upo' anither plan,
Than garrin lasses coup the cran,
   Clean heels owre body,
And sairly thole their mither's ban
   Afore the howdy.

This leads me on to tell for sport,
How I did wi' the Session sort—
Auld Clinkum, at the inner port,
   Cried three times, 'Robin!
Come hither, lad, and answer for't—
   Ye're blam'd for jobbin'!'

Wi' pinch I put a Sunday's face on,
An' snoov'd awa before the Session—
I made an open, fair confession—
   I scorn't to lee,
An' syne Mess John, beyond expression,
   Fell foul o' me.

A furnicator-loun he call'd me,
An' said my faut frae bliss expell'd me;
I own'd the tale was true he tell'd me,
   'But, what the matter?'
Quo' I, 'I fear unless ye geld me,
   I'll ne'er be better!'

'Geld you!' quo' he, 'and whatfor no'?
If that your right hand, leg or toe
Should ever prove your sp'ritual foe,
   You should remember
To cut it aff—an' whatfor no'?
   Your dearest member!'

'Na, na,' quo' I, 'I'm no' for that,
Gelding's nae better than 'tis ca't;
I'd rather suffer for my faut
   A hearty flewit,
As sair owre hip as ye can draw't,
   Tho' I should rue it!

'Or, gin ye like to end the bother,
To please us a'—I've just ae ither—
When next wi' yon lass I forgather,
    Whate'er betide it,
I'll frankly gie her 't a' thegither,
    An' let her guide it.'

But, sir, this pleas'd them warst ava,
An' therefore, Tam, when that I saw,
I said 'Gude night,' an' cam' awa',
    An' left the Session;
I saw they were resolvéd a'
    On my oppression.

THE BRIGS OF AYR
A Poem
Inscribed to John Ballantine, Esq.,[1] Ayr

The simple Bard, rough at the rustic plough,
Learning his tuneful trade from ev'ry bough;
The chanting linnet, or the mellow thrush,
Hailing the setting sun, sweet, in the green thorn bush;
The soaring lark, the perching red-breast shrill,
Or deep-ton'd plovers grey, wild-whistling o'er the hill;
Shall he, nurst in the peasant's lowly shed,
To hardy independence bravely bred,
By early poverty to hardship steel'd,
And train'd to arms in stern Misfortune's field,
Shall he be guilty of their hireling crimes,
The servile, mercenary Swiss of rhymes?
Or labour hard the panegyric close,
With all the venal soul of dedicating Prose?
No! though his artless strains he rudely sings,
And throws his hand uncouthly o'er the strings,
He glows with all the spirit of the Bard,
Fame, honest fame, his great, his dear reward.
Still, if some patron's gen'rous care he trace,
Skill'd in the secret, to bestow with grace;
When Ballantine befriends his humble name,
And hands the rustic stranger up to fame,
With heartfelt throes his grateful bosom swells,
The godlike bliss, to give, alone excels.

    'Twas when the stacks get on their winter-hap,
And thack and rape secure the toil-won crap;
Potatoe-bings are snugged up frae skaith
O' coming Winter's biting, frosty breath;
The bees, rejoicing o'er their summer toils,
Unnumber'd buds an' flow'rs' delicious spoils,

---

[1] Banker in Ayr, Dean of Guild and later provost of Ayr, one of the promoters of the building of the new bridge, begun in May 1786 and completed in November 1788.

Seal'd up with frugal care in massive waxen piles,
Are doom'd by Man, that tyrant o'er the weak,
The death o' devils, smoor'd wi' brimstone reek:
The thund'ring guns are heard on ev'ry side,
The wounded coveys, reeling, scatter wide;
The feather'd field-mates, bound by Nature's tie,
Sires, mothers, children, in one carnage lie:
(What warm, poetic heart but inly bleeds,
And execrates man's savage, ruthless deeds!)
Nae mair the flow'r in field or meadow springs,
Nae mair the grove with airy concert rings,
Except perhaps the Robin's whistling glee,
Proud o' the height o' some bit half-lang tree:
The hoary morns precede the sunny days,
Mild, calm, serene, wide-spreads the noontide blaze,
While thick the gossamour waves wanton in the rays.

'Twas in that season, when a simple Bard,
Unknown and poor, simplicity's reward,
Ae night, within the ancient brugh of Ayr,
By whim inspir'd, or haply prest wi' care,
He left his bed, and took his wayward route,
And down by *Simpson's*[1] wheel'd the left about:
(Whether impell'd by all-directing Fate,
To witness what I after shall narrate;
Or whether, rapt in meditation high,
He wander'd out, he knew not where or why:)
The drowsy Dungeon-clock[2] had number'd two,
and Wallace Tower[2] had sworn the fact was true:
The tide-swoln firth, with sullen-sounding roar,
Through the still night dash'd hoarse along the shore:
All else was hush'd as Nature's closed e'e;
The silent moon shone high o'er tow'r and tree;
The chilly frost, beneath the silver beam,
Crept, gently crusting, o'er the glittering stream—

When, lo! on either hand the list'ning Bard,
The clanging sugh of whistling wings is heard;
Two dusky forms dart through the midnight air;
Swift as the gos[3] drives on the wheeling hare;
Ane on th' Auld Brig his airy shape uprears,
The ither flutters o'er the rising piers:
Our warlock Rhymer instantly descried
The Sprites that owre the Brigs of Ayr preside.
(That Bards are second-sighted is nae joke,
And ken the lingo of the sp'ritual folk;
Fays, Spunkies, Kelpies, a', they can explain them,
And ev'n the vera deils they brawly ken them).
Auld Brig appear'd of ancient Pictish race,

---

[1] A noted tavern at the Auld Brig end.—R.B.   [3] The Gos-hawk, or Falcon.—R.B.
[2] The two steeples.—R.B.

The very wrinkles Gothic in his face:
He seem'd as he wi' Time had warstl'd lang,
Yet, teughly doure, he bade an unco bang.
New Brig was buskit in a braw new coat,
That he, at Lon'on, frae ane Adams got;
In 's hand five taper staves as smooth 's a bead,
Wi' virls and whirlygigums at the head.
The Goth was stalking round with anxious search,
Spying the time-worn flaws in every arch;
It chanc'd his new-come neebor took his e'e,
And e'en a vexed and angry heart had he!
Wi' thieveless sneer to see his modish mien,
He, down the water, gies him this guid-e'en—

Auld Brig

'I doubt na, frien', ye'll think ye're nae sheepshank,
Ance ye were streekit owre frae bank to bank!
But gin ye be a brig as auld as me,
Tho' faith, that date, I doubt, ye'll never see;
There'll be, if that day come, I'll wad a boddle,
Some fewer whigmaleeries in your noddle.'

New Brig

'Auld Vandal! ye but show your little mense,
Just much about it wi' your scanty sense;
Will your poor, narrow foot-path of a street,
Where twa wheel-barrows tremble when they meet,
Your ruin'd, formless bulk o' stane and lime,
Compare wi' bonnie brigs o' modern time?
There's men of taste wou'd tak the Ducat stream,[1]
Tho' they should cast the vera sark and swim,
Ere they would grate their feelings wi' the view
Of sic an ugly, Gothic hulk as you.'

Auld Brig

'Conceited gowk! puff'd up wi' windy pride!
This mony a year I've stood the flood an' tide;
And tho' wi' crazy eild I'm sair forfairn,
I'll be a brig when ye're a shapeless cairn!
As yet ye little ken about the matter,
But twa-three winters will inform ye better.
When heavy, dark, continued, a'-day rains,
Wi' deepening deluges o'erflow the plains;
When from the hills where springs the brawling Coil,
Or stately Lugar's mossy fountains boil;
Or where the Greenock winds his moorland course.
Or haunted Garpal[2] draws his feeble source,
Arous'd by blustering winds an' spotting thowes,
In mony a torrent down the snaw-broo rowes;

---

[1] A noted ford, just above the Auld Brig.—R.B.
[2] The banks of Garpal Water is one of the few places in the West of Scotland where those fancy scaring beings, known by the name of Ghaists still continue pertinaciously to inhabit.—R.B.

While crashing ice, borne on the rolling spate,
Sweeps dams, an' mills, an' brigs, a' to the gate;
And from Glenbuck,[1] down to the Ratton-key,[2]
Auld Ayr is just one lengthen'd, tumbling sea!
Then down ye'll hurl, deil nor ye never rise!
And dash the gumlie jaups up to the pouring skies.
A lesson sadly teaching, to your cost,
That Architecture's noble art is lost!'

New Brig
'Fine architecture, trowth, I needs must say't o't,
The Lord be thankit that we've tint the gate o't!
Gaunt, ghastly, ghaist-alluring edifices,
Hanging with threat'ning jut like precipices;
O'er-arching, mouldy, gloom-inspiring coves,
Supporting roofs, fantastic, stony groves;
Windows and doors in nameless sculptures drest,
With order, symmetry, or taste unblest;
Forms like some bedlam Statuary's dream,
The craz'd creations of misguided whim;
Forms might be worshipp'd on the bended knee,
And still the second dread command be free,
Their likeness is not found on earth, in air, or sea.
Mansions that would disgrace the building taste
Of any mason reptile, bird, or beast:
Fit only for a doited monkish race,
Or frosty maids forsworn the dear embrace,
Or cuifs of later times, wha held the notion,
That sullen gloom was sterling, true devotion:
Fancies that our guid Brugh denies protection,
And soon may they expire, unblest wi' resurrection!'

Auld Brig
'O ye, my dear-remember'd, ancient yealings,
Were ye but here to share my wounded feelings!
Ye worthy Proveses, an' mony a Bailie,
Wha in the paths o' righteousness did toil aye;
Ye dainty Deacons, an' ye douce Conveners,
To whom our moderns are but causey-cleaners;
Ye godly Councils, wha hae blest this town;
Ye godly Brethren o' the sacred gown,
Wha meekly gie your hurdies to the smiters;
And (what would now be strange) ye godly Writers:
A' ye douce folk I've borne aboon the broo,
Were ye but here, what would ye say or do?
How would your spirits groan in deep vexation,
To see each melancholy alteration;
And, agonising, curse the time and place
When ye begat the base degen'rate race!
Nae langer rev'rend men, their country's glory,

---

[1] The source of the River Ayr.—R.B.   [2] A small landing place above the large quay.—R.B.

In plain braid Scots hold forth a plain braid story:
Nae langer thrifty citizens, an' douce,
Meet owre a pint, or in the Council-house;
But staumrel, corky-headed, graceless Gentry,
The herryment and ruin of the country;
Men, three-parts made by tailors and by barbers,
Wha waste your weel-hain'd gear on damn'd new brigs and harbours!'

New Brig

'Now haud you there! for faith ye've said enough,
And muckle mair than ye can mak to through.
As for your Priesthood, I shall say but little,
Corbies and *Clergy* are a shot right kittle:
But, under favour o' your langer beard,
Abuse o' Magistrates might weel be spar'd;
To liken them to your auld-warld squad,
I must needs say, comparisons are odd.
In Ayr, wag-wits nae mair can have a handle
To mouth 'A Citizen,' a term o' scandal;
Nae mair the Council waddles down the street,
In all the pomp of ignorant conceit;
Men wha grew wise priggin owre hops an' raisins,
Or gather'd lib'ral views in Bonds and Seisins:
If haply Knowledge, on a random tramp,
Had shor'd them with a glimmer of his lamp,
And would to Common-sense for once betray'd them,
Plain, dull Stupidity stept kindly in to aid them.'

What farther clishmaclaver might been said,
What bloody wars, if Sprites had blood to shed,
No man can tell; but, all before their sight,
A fairy train appear'd in order bright:
Adown the glittering stream they featly danc'd;
Bright to the moon their various dresses glanc'd:
They footed o'er the wat'ry glass so neat,
The infant ice scarce bent beneath their feet:
While arts of Minstrelsy among them rung,
And soul-ennobling Bards heroic ditties sung.

O had M'Lauchlan,[1] thairm-inspiring sage,
Been there to hear this heavenly band engage,
When thro' his dear strathspeys they bore with Highland rage;
Or when they struck old Scotia's melting airs,
The lover's raptured joys or bleeding cares;
How would his Highland lug been nobler fir'd,
And ev'n his matchless hand with finer touch inspir'd!
No guess could tell what instrument appear'd,
But all the soul of Music's self was heard;
Harmonious concert rung in every part,
While simple melody pour'd moving on the heart.

[1] A well-known performer of Scottish music on the violin.—R.B.

The Genius of the Stream in front appears,
A venerable Chief advanc'd in years;
His hoary head with water-lilies crown'd,
His manly leg with garter tangle bound.
Next came the loveliest pair in all the ring,
Sweet female Beauty hand in hand with Spring;
Then, crown'd with flow'ry hay, came Rural Joy,
And Summer, with his fervid-beaming eye:
All-cheering Plenty, with her flowing horn,
Led yellow Autumn wreath'd with nodding corn;
Then Winter's time-bleach'd locks did hoary show,
By Hospitality with cloudless brow.
Next followed Courage with his martial stride,
From where the Feal wild-woody coverts hide;[1]
Benevolence, with mild, benignant air,
A female form, came from the tow'rs of Stair;[2]
Learning and Worth in equal measures trode,
From simple Catrine, their long-lov'd abode:[3]
Last, white-rob'd Peace, crown'd with a hazel wreath,
To rustic Agriculture did bequeath
The broken, iron instruments of death:
At sight of whom our Sprites forgat their kindling wrath.

[1] A compliment to the warlike Montgomeries of Coilsfield. The Feal or Faile Water flows through the grounds behind the mansion and joins the Ayr at Fealford.
[2] A compliment to Mrs Stewart of Stair. [3] A compliment to Professor Dugald Stewart of Catrine House.

PRAYER—O THOU DREAD POWER
Lying at a Reverend Friend's[1] House One Night, the Author left the Following Verses in the Room where he slept

O Thou dread Power, who reign'st above!
    I know Thou wilt me hear,
When for this scene of peace and love,
    I make this pray'r sincere.

The hoary Sire—the mortal stroke,
    Long, long be pleas'd to spare;
To bless this little filial flock,
    And show what good men are.

She, who her lovely offspring eyes
    With tender hopes and fears,
O bless her with a mother's joys,
    But spare a mother's tears!

Their hope, their stay, their darling youth,
    In manhood's dawning blush;
Bless him, Thou God of love and truth,
    Up to a parent's wish.

[1] Dr Lawrie, minister of Loudon.

The beauteous, seraph sister-band,
    With earnest tears I pray,
Thou know'st the snares on ev'ry hand,
    Guide Thou their steps alway.

When, soon or late, they reach that coast,
    O'er Life's rough ocean driven,
May they rejoice, no wand'rer lost,
    A family in Heaven!

IRVINE'S BAIRNS[1]

The night was still, and o'er the hill
    The moon shone on the castle wa';
The mavis sang, while dew-drops hang
    Around her on the castle wa';
Sae merrily they danced the ring
    Frae eenin' till the cock did craw;
And aye the o'erword o' the spring
    Was Irvine's bairns are bonnie a'.

[1] Inspired by the view from Dr Lawrie's manse, overlooking the old castle of Newmilns and Irvine Water, and the company of Dr Lawrie's children.

FAREWELL SONG TO THE BANKS OF AYR
Tune—*Roslin Castle*
'I composed this song as I conveyed my chest so far on my road to Greenock, where I was to embark in a few days for Jamaica. I meant it as my farewell dirge to my native land.'—R.B.

The gloomy night is gath'ring fast,
Loud roars the wild, inconstant blast,
Yon murky cloud is foul with rain,
I see it driving o'er the plain;
The hunter now has left the moor,
The scatt'red coveys meet secure,
While here I wander, pressed with care,
Along the lonely banks of Ayr.

The Autumn mourns her rip'ning corn
By early Winter's ravage torn;
Across her placid, azure sky,
She sees the scowling tempest fly:
Chill runs my blood to hear it rave,
I think upon the stormy wave,
Where many a danger I must dare,
Far from the bonnie banks of Ayr.

'Tis not the surging billow's roar,
'Tis not that fatal, deadly shore;
Tho' death in ev'ry shape appear,
The wretched have no more to fear:

But round my heart the ties are bound,
That heart transpierc'd with many a wound;
These bleed afresh, those ties I tear,
To leave the bonnie banks of Ayr.

Farewell, old Coila's hills and dales,
Her heathy moors and winding vales;
The scenes where wretched Fancy roves,
Pursuing past, unhappy loves!
Farewell, my friends! farewell, my foes!
My peace with these, my love with those—
The bursting tears my heart declare—
Farewell, the bonnie banks of Ayr!

Address To The Toothache

My curse upon your venom'd stang,
That shoots my tortur'd gums alang,
And through my lug gies mony a twang,
   Wi' gnawing vengeance,
Tearing my nerves wi' bitter pang,
   Like racking engines!

When fevers burn, or ague freezes,
Rheumatics gnaw, or cholic squeezes,
Our neighbour's sympathy can ease us,
   Wi' pitying moan;
But thee—thou hell o' a' diseases—
   Aye mocks our groan.

Adown my beard the slavers trickle!
I throw the wee stools o'er the mickle,
As round the fire the giglets keckle,
   To see me loup,
While raving mad, I wish a heckle
   Were in their doup!

O' a' the numerous human dools,
Ill hairsts, daft bargains, cutty stools,
Or worthy friends rak'd i' the mools—
   Sad sight to see!
The tricks o' knaves, or fash o'fools—
   Thou bear'st the gree.

Where'er that place be priests ca' hell,
Where a' the tones o' misery yell,
An' rankéd plagues their numbers tell,
   In dreadfu' raw,
Thou, Toothache, surely bear'st the bell,
   Amang them a'!

O thou grim, mischief-making chiel,
That gars the notes o' discord squeel,
Till daft mankind aft dance a reel
      In gore, a shoe-thick—
Gie a' the faes o' SCOTLAND's weal
      A townmond's toothache!

ON DINING WITH LORD DAER[1]

This wot ye all whom it concerns,
I, Rhymer Robin, alias Burns,
      October twenty-third—
A ne'er-to-be-forgotten day—
Sae far I sprackl'd up the brae,
      I dinner'd wi' a Lord.

I've been at drucken writers' feasts,
Nay, been bitch-fou 'mang godly priests—
      Wi' rev'rence be it spoken!
I've even join'd the honour'd jorum,
When mighty Squireships of the quorum,
      Their hydra-drouth did sloken!

But wi' a Lord!—stand out my shin,
A Lord—a Peer—an Earl's son!
      Up higher yet my bonnet!
An' sic a Lord!—lang Scoth ells twa,
Our Peerage he o'erlooks them a',
      As I look o'er my sonnet.

But O for Hogarth's magic pow'r
To show Sir Bardy's willyart glow'r!—
      And how he star'd and stammer'd,
When goavin, as if led wi' branks,
An' stumpin on his ploughman shanks,
      He in the parlour hammer'd.

I sidling shelter'd in a nook,
An' at his lordship steal't a look,
      Like some portentous omen!
Except good sense and social glee,
An'—what surpris'd me—modesty,
      I markéd nought uncommon.

I watch'd the symptoms o' the Great,
The gentle pride, the lordly state,
      The arrogant assuming;
The fient a pride—nae pride had he,
Nor sauce, nor state that I could see,
      Mair than an honest ploughman!

---

[1] At the house of Professor Dugald Stewart. Lord Daer was the son and heir apparent of the fourth Earl of Selkirk. In 1786 he had just returned from France, where he had mixed with some distinguished men and contracted very liberal opinions.

Then from his Lordship I shall learn,
Henceforth to meet with unconcern
      One rank as well's another;
Nae honest, worthy man need care
To meet with noble youthful Daer,
      For he but meets a brother.

Masonic Song
Tune—*Shawnboy*

Ye sons of old Killie, assembled by Willie,
    To follow the noble vocation;
Your thrifty old mother has scarce such another
    To sit in that honouréd station.
I've little to say, but only to pray,
    As praying's the ton of your fashion;
A prayer from the Muse you well may excuse—
    'Tis seldom her favourite passion.

Ye powers who preside o'er the wind and the tide,
    Who markéd each element's border;
Who forméd this frame with beneficent aim,
    Whose sovereign statute is order!
Within this dear mansion, may wayward Contention
    Or witheréd Envy ne'er enter;
May secrecy round be the mystical bound,
    And brotherly Love be the centre!

Tam Samson's Elegy

'When this worthy old *sportsman* went out, last muirfowl season, he supposed it was to be, in Ossian's phrase, 'the last of his fields,' and expressed an ardent wish to die and be buried in the muirs. On this hint the author composed his elegy and epitaph.'—R.B.

An honest man's the noblest work of God—Pope.

Has auld Kilmarnock seen the Deil?
Or great McKinlay[1] thrawn his heel?
Or Robertson[2] again grown weel,
      To preach an' read?
'Na' waur than a'! cries ilka chiel,
      'Tam Samson's dead!'

Kilmarnock lang may grunt an' grane,
An' sigh, an' sab, an' greet her lane,
An' cleed her bairns, man, wife, an' wean,
      In mourning weed;
To Death she's dearly pay'd the kane,
      Tam Samson's dead!

[1] A certain preacher, a great favourite with the million. *Vide* 'The Ordination' stanza ii.—R.B.
[2] Another preacher, an equal favourite with the *few*, who was at that time ailing. For him see also 'The Ordination,' stanza ix.—R.B.

The Brethren, o' the mystic level
May hing their head in woefu' bevel,
While by their nose the tears will revel,
      Like ony bead;
Death's gien the Lodge an unco devel,
      Tam Samson's dead!

When Winter muffles up his cloak,
And binds the mire[1] like a rock;
When to the loughs the curlers flock,
      Wi' gleesome speed,
Wha will they station at the 'cock'?[1]
      Tam Samson's dead!

He was the king o' a' the core,
To guard, or draw, or wick a bore,[1]
Or up the rink[1] like Jehu roar,
      In time o' need;
But now he lags on Death's hog-score,[1]
      Tam Samson's dead!

Now safe the stately sawmont sail,
And trouts bedropp'd wi' crimson hail,
And eels, weel kend for souple tail,
      And geds for greed,
Since, dark in Death's fish-creel, we wail
      Tam Samson's dead!

Rejoice, ye birring paitricks a';
Ye cootie muircocks, crousely craw;
Ye maukins, cock your fud fu' braw
      Withoutten dread;
Your mortal fae is now awa,
      Tam Samson's dead!

That woefu' morn be ever mourn'd,
Saw him in shooting graith adorn'd,
While pointers round impatient burn'd,
      Frae couples free'd;
But och! he gaed and ne'er return'd!
      Tam Samson's dead!

In vain auld age his body batters,
In vain the gout his ankles fetters,
In vain the burns cam down like waters,
      An acre-braid!
Now ev'ry auld wife, greetin, clatters
      'Tam Samson's dead!'

Owre monie a weary hag he limpit,
An' aye the tither shot he thumpit,

---

[1] These are all technical terms in the game of curling.

Till coward Death behind him jumpit,
>Wi' deadly feide;
Now he proclaims, wi' tout o' trumpet,
>'Tam Samson's dead!'

When at his heart he felt the dagger,
He reel'd his wonted bottle-swagger,
But yet he drew the mortal trigger,
>Wi' weel-aim'd heed;
'Lord, five!' he cry'd, an' owre did stagger;
>Tam Samson's dead!

Ilk hoary hunter mourn'd a brither;
Ilk sportsman-youth bemoan'd a father;
Yon auld grey stane, amang the heather,
>Marks out his head;
Whare Burns has wrote, in rhyming blether,
>'Tam Samson's dead!'

There, low he lies in lasting rest;
Perhaps upon his mould'ring breast
Some spitefu' muirfowl bigs her nest,
>To hatch and breed:
Alas! nae mair he'll them molest—
>Tam Samson's dead!

When August winds the heather wave,
And sportsmen wander by yon grave,
Three volleys let his memory crave,
>O' pouther an' lead,
Till Echo answer frae her cave,
>'Tam Samson's dead!'

Heav'n rest his saul, whare'er he be!
Is th' wish o' mony mae than me:
He had twa fauts, or maybe three,
>Yet what remead?
Ae social, honest man want we:
>Tam Samson's dead!

The Epitaph

Tam Samson's weel-worn clay here lies,
>Ye canting zealots, spare him!
If honest worth in Heaven rise,
>Ye'll mend or ye win near him.

Per Contra

Go, Fame, an' canter like a filly
Thro' a' the streets an' neuks o' Killie;[1]
Tell ev'ry social honest billie
>To cease his grievin';
For yet, unskaithed by Death's gleg gullie,
>Tam Samson's leevin'!

---

[1] Killie is a phrase the country-folks sometimes use for the name of a certain town in the west [Kilmarnock]—R.B.

EPIGRAM ON ROUGH ROADS

I'm now arrived—thanks to the gods!—
    Thro' pathways rough and muddy,
A certain sign that making roads
    Is no this people's study:
Altho' I'm not wi' Scripture cram'd,
    I'm sure the Bible says
That heedless sinners shall be damn'd
    Unless they mend their *ways*.

EPISTLE TO MAJOR LOGAN

Hail, thairm-inspirin', rattlin' Willie!
Though fortune's road be rough an' hilly
To every fiddling, rhyming billie,
        We never heed,
But take it like the unback'd filly,
        Proud o' her speed.

When idly goavin', whyles we saunter,
Yirr! fancy barks, awa we canter,
Up hill, down brae, till some mischanter,
        Some black bog-hole,
Arrests us, then the scathe an' banter
        We're forced to thole.

Hale be your heart! hale be your fiddle!
Lang may your elbuck jink and diddle,
To cheer you through the weary widdle
        O' this wild warl'.
Until you on a crummock driddle,
        A grey-hair'd carl.

Come wealth, come poortith, late or soon,
Heaven send your heart-strings aye in tune,
And screw your temper-pins aboon—
        A fifth or mair—
The melancholious, lazy croon
        O' cankrie care.

May still your life from day to day,
Nae *lente largo* in the play,
But *allegretto forté* gay,
        Harmonious flow,
A sweeping, kindling, bauld strathspey—
        Encore! Bravo!

A blessing on the cheery gang
Wha dearly like a jig or sang,
An' never think o' right an' wrang
        By square an' rule,

But, as the clegs o' feeling stang,
    Are wise or fool!

My hand-waled curse keep hard in chase
The harpy, hoodock, purse-proud race,
Wha count on poortith as disgrace—
    Their tuneless hearts!
May fireside discords jar a bass
    To a' their parts!

But come, your hand, my careless brither,
I' th' ither warl'—if there's anither,
An' that there is, I've little swither
    About the matter—
We, cheek for chow shall jog thegither,
    I'se ne'er bid better.

We've faults and failings—granted clearly,
We're frail backsliding mortals merely;
Eve's bonnie squad, priests wyte them sheerly
    For our grand fa';
But still, but still, I like them dearly—
    God bless them a'!

Ochone for poor Castalian drinkers,
When they fa' foul o' earthly jinkers!
The witching, curs'd, delicious blinkers
    Hae put me hyte,
And gart me weet my waukrife winkers,
    Wi' girnin' spite.

By by yon moon!—and that's high swearin'—
An' every star within my hearin'!
An' by her een wha was a dear ane!
    I'll ne'er forget;
I hope to gie the jads a clearin'
    In fair play yet.

My loss I mourn, but not repent it;
I'll seek my pursie whare I tint it;
Ance to the Indies I were wonted,
    Some cantraip hour
By some sweet elf I'll yet be dinted—
    Then *vive l'amour*!

Faites mes baissemains respectueuse,
To sentimental sister Susie,
And honest Lucky; no' to roose you,
    Ye may be proud,
That sic a couple Fate allows ye
    To grace your blood.

Nae mair at present can I measure,
An' trowth my rhymin' ware's nae treasure;
But when in Ayr, some half-hour's leisure,
  Be't light, be't dark,
Sir Bard will do himself the pleasure
  To call at Park.
Mossgiel, 30th October 1786. Robert Burns

Rusticity's Ungainly Form

Rusticity's ungainly form
  May cloud the highest mind;
But when the heart is nobly warm,
  The good excuse will find:
Propriety's cold, cautious rules
  Warm Fervour may o'erlook:
But spare poor Sensibility
  Th' ungentle, harsh rebuke.

A Winter Night

Poor naked wretches, wheresoe'er you are,
That bide the pelting of this pitiless storm!
How shall your houseless heads, and unfed sides,
Your loop'd and window'd raggedness, defend you
From seasons such as these? Shakespeare.

When biting Boreas, fell and doure,
Sharp shivers thro' the leafless bow'r;
When Phoebus gies a short-liv'd glow'r,
  Far south the lift,
Dim-dark'ning thro' the flaky show'r,
  Or whirling drift:

Ae night the storm the steeples rocked,
Poor Labour sweet in sleep was locked,
While burns, wi' snawy wreaths up-choked,
  Wild-eddying swirl,
Or thro' the mining outlet bocked,
  Down headlong hurl:

List'ning the doors an' winnocks rattle,
I thought me on the ourie cattle,
Or silly sheep, wha bide this brattle
  O' winter war,
And thro' the drift, deep-lairing, sprattle
  Beneath a scar.

Ilk happing bird, wee, helpless thing!
That, in the merry months o' spring,
Delighted me to hear thee sing,
  What comes o' thee?

Whare wilt thou cow'r thy chittering wing,
      An' close thy e'e?

Ev'n you, on murdering errands toil'd,
Lone from your savage homes exil'd,
The blood-stain'd roost, and sheep-cote spoil'd
      My heart forgets,
While pityless the tempest wild
      Sore on you beats!

Now Phoebe, in her midnight reign,
Dark-muff'd, view'd the dreary plain;
Still crowding thoughts, a pensive train,
      Rose in my soul,
When on my ear this plantive strain,
      Slow, solemn, stole—

  'Blow, blow, ye Winds, with heavier gust!
And freeze, thou bitter-biting Frost!
Descend, ye chilly, smothering Snows!
Not all your rage, as now united, shows
    More hard unkindness unrelenting,
    Vengeful malice unrepenting,
Than heaven-illumin'd Man on brother Man bestows!

  'See stern Oppression's iron grip,
    Or mad Ambition's gory hand,
Sending, like blood-hounds from the slip,
    Woe, Want, and Murder o'er a land!
Ev'n in the peaceful rural vale,
Truth, weeping, tells the mournful tale,
How pamper'd Luxury, Flatt'ry by her side,
  The parasite empoisoning her ear,
  With all the servile wretches in the rear,
Looks o'er proud Property, extended wide;
  And eyes the simple, rustic Hind,
    Whose toil upholds the glitt'ring show,
  A creature of another kind,
  Some coarser substance, unrefin'd,
Plac'd for her lordly use thus far, thus vile, below!

  'Where, where is Love's fond, tender throe,
With lordly Honour's lofty brow,
    The pow'rs you proudly own?
Is there, beneath Love's noble name,
Can harbour, dark, the selfish aim,
    To bless himself alone?
Mark maiden-innocence a prey
To love-pretending snares:
This boasted Honour turns away,
Shunning soft Pity's rising sway,

Regardless of the tears and unavailing pray'rs!
   Perhaps this hour, in Misery's squalid nest,
   She strains your infant to her joyless breast,
And with a mother's fears shrinks at the rocking blast!

   'Oh ye! who, sunk in beds of down,
     Feel not a want but what yourselves create,
     Think, for a moment, on his wretched fate,
   Whom friends and fortune quite disown!
Ill-satisfy'd, keen Nature's clam'rous call,
   Stretch'd on his straw he lays himself to sleep,
While through the ragged roof and chinky wall,
     Chill, o'er his slumbers, piles the drifty heap!
     Think on the Dungeon's grim confine,
     Where Guilt and poor Misfortune pine!
     Guilt, erring Man, relenting view,
     But shall thy legal rage pursue
     The Wretch, already crushéd low
     By cruel Fortune's undeservéd blow?
Affliction's sons are brothers in distress;
A brother to relieve, how exquisite the bliss!'

   I heard nae mair, for Chanticleer
     Shook off the pouthery snaw,
   And hail'd the morning with a cheer,
     A cottage-rousing craw.

   But deep this truth impress'd my mind—
     Thro' all His works abroad,
   The heart benevolent and kind
     The most resembles God.

Yon Wild Mossy Mountains

Yon wild mossy mountains sae lofty and wide,
That nurse in their bosom the youth o' the Clyde,
Where the grouse lead their coveys thro' the heather to feed,
And the shepherd tends his flock as he plays on his reed.

Not Gowrie's rich valley, nor Forth's sunny shores,
To me hae the charms o' yon wild, mossy moors;
For there, by a lanely, sequesteréd stream,
Besides a sweet lassie, my thought and my dream.

Amang thae wild mountains shall still be my path,
Ilk stream foaming down its ain green, narrow strath,
For there, wi' my lassie, the day lang I rove,
While o'er us unheeded flie the swift hours o'love.

She is not the fairest, altho' she is fair,
O' nice education but sma' is her share;

Her parentage humble as humble can be;
But I lo'e the dear lassie because she lo'es me.

To beauty what man but maun yield him a prize,
In her armour of glances, and blushes, and sighs?
And when wit and refinement hae polish'd her darts,
They dazzle our een, as they flie to our hearts.

But kindness, sweet kindness, in the fond-sparkling e'e,
Has lustre outshining the diamond to me;
And the heart beating love as I'm clasp'd in her arms,
O, these are my lassie's all-conquering charms!

Address To Edinburgh

Edina! Scotia's darling seat!
    All hail thy palaces and tow'rs,
Where once beneath a Monarch's feet,
    Sat Legislation's sov'reign pow'rs!
From marking wildly scatt'red flow'rs,
    As on the banks of Ayr I stray'd,
And singing, lone, the lingering hours,
    I shelter in they honour'd shade.

Here Wealth still swells the golden tide,
    As busy Trade his labours plies;
There Architecture's noble pride
    Bids elegance and splendour rise;
Here Justice, from her native skies,
    High wields her balance and her rod;
There Learning, with his eagle eyes,
    Seeks Science in her coy abode.

Thy sons, Edina, social, kind,
    With open arms the stranger hail;
Their views enlarg'd, their lib'ral mind,
    Above the narrow, rural vale:
Attentive still to Sorrow's wail,
    Or modest Merit's silent claim;
And never may their sources fail!
    And never Envy blot their name!

Thy daughters bright thy walks adorn,
    Gay as the gilded summer sky,
Sweet as the dewy, milk-white thorn,
    Dear as the raptur'd thrill of joy!
Fair Burnet[1] strikes th' adoring eye,
    Heaven's beauties on my fancy shine;
I see the Sire of Love on high,
    And own His work indeed divine!

---

[1] 'Heavenly Miss Burnet, daughter to Lord Monboddo, at whose house I have had the honour to be more than once. There has not been anything nearly like her in all the combinations of beauty, grace, and goodness the Creator has formed, since Milton's Eve on the first day of her existence.'—R.B.

There, watching high the least alarms,
    Thy rough, rude fortress gleams afar;
Like some bold vet'ran, grey in arms,
    And mark'd with many a seamy scar:
The pond'rous wall and massy bar,
    Grim-rising o'er the rugged rock,
Have oft withstood assailing war,
    And oft repell'd th' invader's shock.

With awe-struck thought, and pitying tears,
    I view that noble, stately Dome,
Where Scotia's kings of other years,
    Fam'd heroes! had their royal home:
Alas, how chang'd the times to come!
    Their royal name low in the dust!
Their hapless race wild-wand'ring roam!
    Tho' rigid Law cries out ''twas just!'

Wild beats my heart to trace your steps,
    Whose ancestors, in days of yore,
Thro' hostile ranks and ruin'd gaps
    Old Scotia's bloody lion bore:
Ev'n *I* who sing in rustic lore,
    Haply my sires have left their shed,
And fac'd grim Danger's loudest roar,
    Bold-following where your fathers led!

Edina! Scotia's darling seat!
    All hail thy palaces and tow'rs;
Where once, beneath a Monarch's feet,
    Sat Legislation's sovereign pow'rs:
From marking wildly scatt'red flow'rs,
    As on the banks of Ayr I stray'd,
And singing, lone, the ling'ring hours,
    I shelter in thy honour'd shade.

ADDRESS TO A HAGGIS

Fair fa' your honest, sonsie face,
Great chieftain o' the pudding-race!
Aboon them a' yet tak your place,
            Painch, tripe, or thairm:
Weel are ye wordy o' a grace
            As lang's my arm.

The groaning trencher there ye fill,
Your hurdies like a distant hill,
Your pin wad help to mend a mill
            In time o' need,
While thro' your pores the dews distil
            Like amber bead.

His knife see rustic Labour dight,
An' cut you up wi' ready sleight,
Trenching your gushing entrails bright,
        Like onie ditch;
And then, O what a glorious sight,
        Warm-reekin', rich!

Then, horn for horn, they stretch an' strive,
Deil tak the hindmost! on they drive,
Till a' their weel-swall'd kytes belyve
        Are bent like drums;
Then auld Guidman, maist like to rive,
        'Bethankit!' hums.

Is there that owre his French *ragout*
Or *olio* that wad staw a sow,
Or *fricassee* wad make her spew
        Wi' perfect sconner,
Looks down wi' sneering, scornfu' view
        On sic a dinner?

Poor devil! see him owre his trash,
As feckles as a wither'd rash,
His spindle shank a guid whip-lash,
        His nieve a nit;
Thro' bloody flood or field to dash,
        O how unfit!

But mark the Rustic, haggis-fed,
The trembling earth resounds his tread,
Clap in his walie nieve a blade,
        He'll mak it whissle;
An' legs an' arms, an' hands will sned,
        Like taps o' thrissle.

Ye Pow'rs wha mak mankind your care,
And dish them out their bill o' fare,
Auld Scotland wants nae skinking ware
        That jaups in luggies;
But, if ye wish her gratefu' prayer,
        Gie her a haggis!

TO MISS LOGAN

With Beattie's Poems, for a New-Year's Gift, 1 January 1787

Again the silent wheels of time
    Their annual round have driv'n,
And you, tho' scarce in maiden prime,
    Are so much nearer Heav'n.

No gifts have I from Indian coasts
    The infant year to hail;

I send you more than India boasts,
    In Edwin's simple tale.

Our sex with guile, and faithless love
    Is charg'd, perhaps too true;
But may, dear maid, each lover prove
    An Edwin still to you.

RATTLIN', ROARIN' WILLIE[1]

O rattlin', roarin' Willie,
    O he held to the fair,
An' for to sell his fiddle,
    And buy some other ware;
But parting wi' his fiddle,
    The saut tear blint his ee;
And, rattlin', roarin' Willie,
    You're welcome hame to me!

'O Willie, come sell your fiddle,
    O sell your fiddle sae fine;
O Willie, come sell your fiddle,
    And buy a pint o' wine.'
'If I should sell my fiddle,
    The warld would think I was mad;
For mony a rantin' day
    My fiddle an' I hae had.'

As I cam by Crochallan,
    I cannily keekit ben;
Rattlin', roarin' Willie
    Was sittin at yon boord-en'—
Sittin at yon boord-en',
    And amang gude companie;
Rattlin', roarin' Willie,
    You're welcome hame to me!

[1] William Dunbar, W. S., Edinburgh, and Colonel of the Crochallan corps, a club of wits who took that title at the time of raising the fencibles regiments.

BONNIE DUNDEE
Tune—Adew Dundee

'O whar gat ye that hauver-meal bannock?'
    'O silly blind boy, O dinna ye see;
I gat it frae a young brisk sodger laddie,
    Between Saint Johnston and Bonnie Dundee.
O gin I saw the laddie that gae me't!
    Aft has he doudl'd me up on his knee:
May Heaven protect by bonnie Scots laddie,
    And send him safe hame to his babie and me!

'My blessin's upon thy sweet wee lippie!
    My blessin's upon thy e'e-brie!
Thy smiles are sae like my blythe sodger laddie,
    Thou's aye the dearer, and dearer to me!
But I'll big a bow'r on yon bonnie banks,
    Whare Tay rins wimplin' by sae clear;
An' I'll cleed thee in the tartan sae fine,
    And mak thee a man like thy daddie dear.

EXTEMPORE IN THE COURT OF SESSION
Tune—*Gilliecrankie*

LORD ADVOCATE
He clench'd his pamphlet in his fist,
    He quoted and he hinted,
Till, in a declamation-mist,
    His argument he tint it:
He gaped for't, he graped for't,
    He fand it was awa, man;
But what his common sense came short,
    He eked out wi' law, man.

MR ERSKINE
Collected, Harry stood awee,
    Then open'd out his arm, man;
His Lordship sat, wi' ruefu' e'e,
    And ey'd the gathering storm, man:
Like wind-driv'n hail, it did assail,
    Or torrents owre a linn, man;
The Bench sae wise, lift up their eyes,
    Half-wauken'd wi' the din, man.

INSCRIPTION ON THE TOMB OF FERGUSSON THE POET[1]

No sculptur'd marble here, nor pompous lay,
    'No storied urn nor animated bust,'[2]
This simple stone directs pale Scotia's way,
    To pour her sorrows o'er the Poet's dust.

She mourns, sweet tuneful youth, thy hapless fate;
    Tho' all the powers of song thy fancy fired,
Yet Luxury and Wealth lay by in state,
    And, thankless, starv'd what they so much admired.

This humble tribute, with a tear, now gives
    A brother Bard—he can no more bestow:
But dear to fame thy Song immortal lives,
    A nobler monument than Art can show.

[1] The stone was erected at Burns' expense in February-March 1789 to mark the grave of his 'elder brother in misfortune' in the Canongate Churchyard, Edinburgh.   [2] Gray's Elegy.

LINES UNDER THE PORTRAIT OF FERGUSSON

Curse on ungrateful man, that can be pleased,
And yet can starve the author of the pleasure!
O thou, my elder brother in misfortune,
By far my elder brother in the muses,
With tears I pity thy unhappy fate!
Why is the bard unpitied by the world,
Yet has so keen a relish of its pleasures?

Epistle To Mrs Scott
Guidwife of Wauchope House, Roxburghshire.

Guidwife,
I mind it weel in early date,
When I was beardless, young, and blate,
 An' first could thresh the barn,
Or haud a yokin' at the pleugh;
An' tho' forfoughten sair eneugh,
 Yet unco proud to learn:
When first amang the yellow corn
 A man I reckon'd was,
An' wi' the lave ilk merry morn
 Could rank my rig and lass,
  Still shearing, and clearing
   The tither stookéd raw,
  Wi' claivers, an' haivers,
   Wearing the day awa.

E'en then, a wish, I mind its pow'r—
A wish that to my latest hour
 Shall strongly heave my breast—
That I, for poor auld Scotland's sake,
Some usefu' plan or book could make,
 Or sing a sang at least!
The rough burr-thistle, spreading wide
 Amang the bearded bear—
I turn'd my weeder-clips aside,
 An' spar'd the symbol dear!
  No nation, no station,
   My envy e'er could raise;
  A Scot still, but blot still,
   I knew nae higher praise.

But still the elements o' sang,
In formless jumble, right an' wrang,
 Wild floated in my brain;
'Till on that hairst I said before,
My partner in the merry core,
 She rous'd the forming strain:
I see her yet, the sonsie quean,
 That lighted up my jingle,
Her witching smile, her pawky een
 That gart my heart-strings tingle;
  I firéd, inspiréd,
   At every kindling keek,
  But bashing, and dashing,
   I feeréd aye to speak.

Health to the sex! ilk gude chiel says,
Wi' merry dance in winter days,
 An' we to share in common;

The gust o' joy, the balm of woe,
The saul o' life, the heav'n below,
    Is rapture-giving woman!
Ye surly sumphs, who hate the name!
    Be mindfu' o' your mither;
She, honest woman, may think shame
    That ye're connected with her:
        Ye're wae men, ye're nae men
            That slight the lovely dears;
      To shame ye—disclaim ye,
          Ilk honest birkie swears!

For you, no' bred to barn and byre,
Wha sweetly tune the Scottish lyre,
    Thanks to you for your line!
The marled plaid ye kindly spare,
By me should gratefully be ware;
    'Twad please me to the nine!
I'd be mair vauntie o' my hap,
    Douce hingin' owre my curple,
Than ony ermine ever lap,
    Or proud imperial purple.
      Farewell then, lang hale then,
        An' plenty be your fa';
    May losses and crosses
        Ne'er at your hallan ca'!
March, 1787   R. BURNS

VERSES INTENDED TO BE WRITTEN BELOW A NOBLE EARL'S PICTURE[1]

Whose is that noble, dauntless brow?
    And whose that eye of fire?
And whose that generous princely mien,
    Even rooted foes admire?

Stranger! to justly show that brow,
    And mark that eye of fire,
Would take *His* hand, whose vernal tints
    His other works admire.

Bright as a cloudless summer sun,
    With stately port he moves;
His guardian Seraph eyes with awe
    The noble ward he loves.

Among the illustrious Scottish sons
    That chief thou may'st discern,
Mark Scotia's fond-returning eye—
    It dwells upon Glencairn.

[1] James, fourteenth Earl of Glencairn, friend of Burns and his patron, died in January 1791 at Falmouth on his way back from a voyage to Lisbon where he had gone in a vain search for health. He was forty-two. Burns put on mourning for him and called one of his sons James Glencairn. *See also* page 299.

PROLOGUE SPOKEN BY MR WOODS
On his Benefit Night, Monday 16 April 1787

When, by a generous Public's kind acclaim,
That dearest meed is granted—honest fame;
When here your favour is the actor's lot,
Nor even the man in private life forgot;
What breast so dead to heav'nly Virtue's glow,
But heaves impassioned with the grateful throe?

Poor is the task to please a barbarous throng,
It needs no Siddons' powers in Southern's song;
But here an ancient nation, famed afar,
For genius, learning high, as great in war—
Hail, CALEDONIA, name for ever dear!
Before whose sons I'm honour'd to appear!
Where every science—every nobler art—
That can inform the mind, or mend the heart,
Is known; as grateful nations oft have found,
Far as the rude barbarian marks the bound.
Philosophy,[1] no idle pedant dream,
Here holds her search by heaven-taught Reason's beam;
Here History[2] paints with elegance and force
The tide of Empire's fluctuating course;
Here Douglas[3] forms wild Shakespeare into plan,
And Harley[4] rouses all the God in man.
When well-form'd taste and sparkling wit unite
With manly lore or female beauty bright,
(Beauty, where faultless symmetry and grace
Can only charm us in the second place),
Witness my heart, how oft with panting fear,
As on this night, I've met these judges here!
But still the hope Experience taught to live,
Equal to judge—you're candid to forgive.
No hundred-headed riot here we meet,
With Decency and Law beneath his feet;
Nor Insolence assumes fair Freedom's name:
Like CALEDONIANS, you applaud or blame.

O Thou, dread Power! whose empire-giving hand
Has oft been stretch'd to shield the honour'd land!
Strong may she glow with all her ancient fire!
May every son be worthy of his sire!
Firm may she rise, with generous disdain
At Tyranny's, or direr Pleasure's chain!
Still, self-dependent in her native shore,
Bold may she brave grim Danger's loudest roar,
Till Fate the curtain drop on worlds to be no more.

---

[1] Professor Reid at St Andrews and Dugald Stewart at Edinburgh.
[2] Robertson and Hume the historians.
[3] Home's *Tragedy of Douglas*.
[4] The *Man of Feeling* by Henry Mackenzie.

THE BONNIE MOOR-HEN

Chorus: I rede you beware at the hunting, young men;
I rede you beware at the hunting, young men;
Tak some on the wing, and some as they spring,
But cannily steal on a bonnie moor-hen.

The heather was blooming, the meadows were mawn,
Our lads gaed a-hunting, ae day at the dawn,
O'er moors and o'er mosses and mony a glen,
At length they discover'd a bonnie moor-hen.

Sweet-brushing the dew from the brown heather bells
Her colours betray'd her on yon mossy fells;
Her plumage outlustred the pride o' the spring,
And O! as she wanton'd gay on the wing.

Auld Phoebus himsel, as he peep'd o'er the hill,
In spite, at her plumage he tried his skill:
He levell'd his rays where she bask'd on the brae—
His rays were outshone, and but mark'd where she lay.

They hunted the valley, they hunted the hill,
The best of our lads wi' the best o' their skill;
But still as the fairest she sat in their sight,
Then, whirr! she was over, a mile at a flight.

MY LORD A-HUNTING
Tune—*I rede you beware at the hunting*

Chorus: My lady's gown, there's gairs upon 't,
And gowden flowers sae rare upon 't;
But Jenny's jimps and jirkinet,
My lord thinks meikle mair upon 't.

My lord a-hunting he is gane,
But hounds or hawks wi' him are nane;
By Colin's cottage lies his game,
If Colin's Jenny be at hame.

My lady's white, my lady's red,
And kith and kin o' Cassillis' blude;
But her ten-pund lands o' tocher gude
Were a' the charms his lordship lo'ed.

Out o'er yon muir, out o'er yon moss,
Whare gor-cocks thro' the heather pass,
There wons auld Colin's bonnie lass,
A lily in a wilderness.

Sae sweetly move her genty limbs,
Like music notes o' lovers' hymns:

The diamond-dew in her een sae blue,
Where laughing love sae wanton swims.

My lady's dink, my lady's drest,
The flower and fancy o' the west;
But the lassie than a man lo'es best,
O that's the lass to mak him blest.

IMPROMPTU AT ROSLIN INN

My blessings on ye, honest wife!
   I ne'er was here before;
Ye've gi'en us walth for horn and knife,
   Nae heart could wish for more:
Heaven keep you free frae care and strife,
   Till far ayont fourscore;
And while I toddle on thro' life,
   I'll ne'er gae by your door.

EPIGRAM ADDRESSED TO AN ARTIST

Dear————, I'll gie ye some advice,
   You'll tak it no uncivil:
You shouldna paint at angels mair,
   But try and paint the devil.

To paint an angel's kittle wark,
   Wi' auld Nick there's less danger;
You'll easy draw a lang-kent face,
   But no sae weel a stranger.

THE BOOKWORMS

Through and through the inspiréd leaves,
   Ye maggots, make your windings;
But O respect his lordship's taste,
   And spare his golden bindings.

ON ELPHINSTONE'S TRANSLATION OF MARTIAL'S EPIGRAMS

O Thou whom Poesy abhors!
Whom Prose has turnéd out of doors,
Heard'st thou that groan? proceed no further!
'Twas laurel'd Martial calling murther!

A BOTTLE AND A FRIEND

Chorus: There's nane that's blest of human kind,
But the cheerful and the gay, man,
   Fal, la, la, etc.

Here's a bottle and an honest friend!
   What wad ye wish for mair, man?
Wha kens, before his life may end,
   What his share may be o' care, man?
Then catch the moments as they fly,
   And use them as ye ought, man:
Believe me, happiness is shy,
   And comes not aye when sought, man.

LINES WRITTEN UNDER MISS BURNS'[1] PICTURE

Cease, ye prudes, your envious railing,
    Lovely Burns has charms—*confess*;
True it is, she had one failing,
    Had a woman ever less?

[1] Margaret Burns, from Durham, who gained a certain notoriety in Edinburgh.

EPITAPH FOR WILLIAM NICOL[1] OF THE HIGH SCHOOL, EDINBURGH

Ye maggots, feed on Nicol's brain,
    For few sic feasts you've gotten;
And fix your claws in Nicol's heart,
    For deil a bit o't's rotten.

[1] *See* 'Willie Brew'd A Peck O' Maut', page 265.

EPITAPH FOR MR WILLIAM MICHIE
Schoolmaster of Cleish Parish, Fifeshire.

Here lie Willie Michie's banes;
    O Satan! when ye tak him,
Gie him the schulin o' your weans,
    For clever deils he'll mak them!

HEY, CA' THRO'

Chorus: Hey, ca' thro', ca' thro',
    For we hae mickle ado;
Hey, ca' thro', ca' thro',
    For we hae mickle ado;

We hae tales to tell,
    An' we hae sangs to sing;
We hae pennies tae spend,
    An' we hae pints to bring.

Up wi' the carls o' Dysart,
    And the lads o' Buckhaven,
And the kimmers o' Largo,
    And the lasses o' Leven.

We'll live a' our days,
    And them that comes behin',
Let them do the like,
    An' spend the gear they win.

ADDRESS TO WILLIAM TYTLER, ESQ.,[1] OF WOODHOUSELEE
With an Impression of the Author's Portrait.

Reveréd defender of beauteous Stuart,
    Of Stuart, a name once respected—
A name which to love was the mark of a true heart,
    But now 'tis despis'd and neglected.

Tho' something like moisture conglobes in my eye,
    Let no one misdeem me disloyal;
A poor friendless wand'rer may well claim a sigh,
    Still more if that wand'rer were royal.

My fathers that name have rever'd on a throne;
    My fathers have diéd to right it;

[1] Author of *An Enquiry into the Evidence against Mary, Queen of Scots*, 1759.

Those fathers would spurn their degenerate son,
  That name should he scoffingly slight it.

Still in prayers for King George I most heartily join,
  The Queen, and the rest of the gentry;
Be they wise, be they foolish, is nothing of mine;
  Their title's avow'd by my country.

But why of that epocha make such a fuss,
  That gave us the Hanover stem?
If bringing them over was lucky for us,
  I'm sure 'twas as lucky for them.

But, loyalty, truce! we're on dangerous ground,
  Who knows how the fashions may alter?
The doctrine, today, that is loyalty sound,
  Tomorrow may bring us a halter!

I send you a trifle, a head of a bard,
  A trifle scarce worthy your care;
But accept it, good Sir, as a mark of regard,
  Sincere as a saint's dying prayer.

Now life's chilly evening dim shades on your eye,
  And ushers the long dreary night;
But you, like the star that athwart gilds the sky,
  Your course to the latest is bright.

To Miss Ainslie In Church
While looking up the Text during Sermon

  Fair maid, you need not take the hint,
    Nor idle texts pursue;
  'Twas guilty *sinners* that he meant,
    Not *angels* such as you.

Lament For The Absence Of William Creech, Publisher

  Auld chuckie Reekie's[1] sair distrest,
  Down droops her ance weel-burnish'd crest,
  Nae joy her bonnie buskit nest
      Can yield ava,
  Her darling bird that she lo'es best—
      Willie's awa!

  O Willie was a witty wight,
  And had o' things an unco slight,
  Auld Reekie aye he keepit tight,
      And trig an' braw;

---

[1] The epithet 'Auld Reekie' is said to have been first applied to Edinburgh by King James VI, on viewing it from the Fife coast at early morning while the citizens were lighting their fires. The term 'chuckie', added by Burns, suggests the figure of the maternal hen and chickens.

But now they'll busk her like a fright—
    Willie's awa!

The stiffest o' them a' he bow'd,
The bauldest o' them a' he cow'd;
They durst nae mair than he allow'd,
    That was a law:
We've lost a birkie weel worth gowd;
    Willie's awa!

Now gawkies, tawpies, gowks and fools,
Frae colleges and boarding schools,
May sprout like simmer puddock-stools
    In glen or shaw;
He wha could brush them down to mools—
    Willie's awa!

The brethren o' the Commerce-chaumer[1]
May mourn their loss wi' doolfu' clamour;
He was a dictionar and grammar
    Among them a';
I fear they'll now mak mony a stammer;
    Willie's awa!

Nae mair we see his levee door
Philosophers and poets pour,[2]
And toothy critics by the score,
    In bloody raw!
The adjutant o' a' the core—
    Willie's awa!

Now worthy Gregory's Latin face,
Tytler's and Greenfield's modest grace;
Mackenzie, Stewart, such a brace
    As Rome ne'er saw;
They a' maun meet some ither place,
    Willie's awa!

Poor Burns—ev'n 'Scotch Drink' canna quicken,
He cheeps like some bewilder'd chicken
Scar'd frae its minnie and the cleckin,
    By hoodie-craw;
Grieg's gien his heart an unco kickin'—
    Willie's awa!

Now ev'ry sour-mou'd girnin' blellum,
And Calvin's folk, are fit to fell him;
And self-conceited critic skellum
    His quill may draw;

[1] The Chamber of Commerce, Edinburgh, of which Creech was Secretary.
[2] Many literary gentlemen were accustomed to meet at Creech's house at breakfast. Burns often met them there when he called, hence the name 'levee'.

He wha could brawlie ward their bellum,
    Willie's awa!

Up wimpling stately Tweed I've sped,
And Eden scenes on crystal Jed,
And Ettrick banks now roaring red,
    While tempests blaw;
But every joy and pleasure's fled—
    Willie's awa!

May I be slander's common speech—
A text for infamy to preach;
And, lastly, streekit out to bleach
    In winter snaw,
When I forget thee, WILLIE CREECH,
    Tho' far awa!

May never wicked Fortune touzle him!
May never wicked men bamboozle him!
Until a pow as auld's Methusalem
    He canty claw!
Then to the blessed new Jerusalem,
    Fleet wing awa!

To Mr Renton Of Lamerton

Your billet, sir, I grant receipt;
Wi' you I'll canter ony gate,
Tho' 'twere a trip to yon blue warl',
Whare birkies march on burning marl:
Then, sir, God willing, I'll attend ye,
And to his goodness I commend ye.
                R. Burns

Epigram At Inverary

Whoe'er he be that sojourns here,
    I pity much his case,
Unless he comes to wait upon
    The Lord *their* God—his Grace.

There's naething here but Highland pride,
    And Highland scab and hunger;
If Providence has sent me here,
    'Twas surely in an anger.

Epigram to Miss Jean Scott

O had each Scot of ancient times
    Been, Jeanie Scott, as thou art,
The bravest heart on English ground
    Had yielded like a coward.

ON READING IN A NEWSPAPER THE DEATH OF JOHN MACLEOD, ESQ.
Brother to a Young Lady, a Particular Friend of the Author's

Sad thy tale, thou idle page,
    And rueful thy alarms:
Death tears the brother of her love
    From Isabella's arms.

Sweetly deckt with pearly dew
    The morning rose may blow;
But cold successive noontide blasts
    May lay its beauties low.

Fair on Isabella's morn
    The sun propitious smil'd;
But, long ere noon, succeeding clouds
    Succeeding hopes beguil'd.

Fate oft tears the bosom chords
    That Nature finest strung:
So Isabella's heart was form'd,
    And so that heart was wrung.

Dread Omnipotence, alone,
    Can heal the wound he gave;
Can point the brimful grief-worn eyes
    To scenes beyond the grave.

Virtue's blossoms there shall blow,
    And fear no withering blast;
There Isabella's spotless worth
    Shall happy be at last.

ON THE DEATH OF SIR JAMES HUNTER BLAIR[1]

The lamp of day, with ill-presaging glare,
    Dim, cloudy, sank beneath the western wave;
Th' inconstant blast howl'd thro' the darkening air,
    And hollow whistled in the rocky cave.

Lone as I wander'd by each cliff and dell,
    Once the lov'd haunts of Scotia's royal train;[2]
Or mus'd where limpid streams, once hallow'd well,[3]
    Or mould'ring ruins mark the sacred fane.[4]

Th' increasing blast roar'd round the beetling rocks,
    The clouds swift-wing'd flew o'er the starry sky,
The groaning trees untimely shed their locks,
    And shooting meteors caught the startled eye.

The paly moon rose in the livid east.
    And 'mong the cliffs disclos'd a stately form
In weeds of woe, that frantic beat her breast,
    And mix'd her wailings with the raving storm

Wild to my heart the filial pulses glow—
    'Twas Caledonia's trophied shield I view'd:
Her form majestic droop'd in pensive woe,
    The lightning of her eye in tears imbued.

Revers'd that spear, redoubtable in war,
    Reclined that banner, erst in fields unfurl'd,
That like a deathful meteor gleam'd afar,
    And brav'd the mighty monarchs of the world.

---

[1] Sir James Hunter Blair was Lord Provost of Edinburgh from October 1784 to October 1786 and 'old Provost' in 1786–87. He died on 1 July 1787.
[2] The King's Park at Holyrood House.—R.B.   [3] Saint Anthony's well.—R.B.   [4] St Anthony's Chapel.—R.B.

'My patriot son fills an untimely grave!'
    With accents wild and lifted arms she cried;
'Low lies the hand that oft was stretch'd to save,
    Low lies the heart that swell'd with honest pride.

'A weeping country joins a widow's tear;
    The helpless poor mix with the orphan's cry,
The drooping arts surround their patron's bier,
    And grateful science heaves the heartfelt sigh!

'I saw my sons resume their ancient fire,
    I saw fair Freedom's blossoms richly blow;
But ah! how hope is born but to expire!
    Relentless fate has laid their guardian low.

'My patriot falls; but shall he lie unsung,
    While empty greatness saves a worthless name?
No: every muse shall join her tuneful tongue,
    And future ages hear his growing fame.

'And I will join a mother's tender cares,
    Thro' future times to make his virtues last;
That distant years may boast of other Blairs!'—
    She said, and vanish'd with the sweeping blast.

To Miss Ferrier
Enclosing the Elegy on Sir J. H. Blair

Nae heathen name shall I prefix,
    Frae Pindus or Parnassus;
Auld Reekie dings them a' to sticks,
    For rhyme-inspiring lasses.

Jove's tunefu' dochters three times three
    Made Homer deep their debtor;
But, gi'en the body half an e'e,
    Nine Ferriers wad done better!

Last day my mind was in a bog,
    Down George's Street I stoited;
A creeping cauld prosaic fog
    My very sense doited.

Do what I dought to set her free,
    My saul lay in the mire;
Ye turned a neuk—I saw your e'e—
    She took the wing like fire!

The mournfu' sang I here enclose,
    In gratitude I send you,
And pray, in rhyme as weel as prose,
    A' gude things may attend you!

IMPROMPTU ON CARRON IRON WORKS

We cam na here to view your warks,
    In hopes to be mair wise,
But only, lest we gang to hell,
    It may be nae surprise:
But when we tirl'd at your door,[1]
    Your porter dought na hear us;
Sae may, shou'd we to Hell's yetts come,
    Your billy Satan sair us!

WRITTEN BY SOMEBODY ON THE WINDOW
Of an Inn at Stirling, on seeing the Royal Palace in Ruins

Here Stuarts once in glory reign'd,
And laws for Scotland's weal ordain'd;
But now unroof'd their palace stands,
Their sceptre's fall'n to other hands;
Fallen indeed, and to the earth,
Whence grovelling reptiles take their birth.
The injur'd Stewart line is gone,
A race outlandish fills their throne—
An idiot race, to honour lost;
Who know them best despise them most!

THE POET'S REPLY TO THE THREAT OF A CENSORIOUS CRITIC
'My imprudent lines were answered, very petulantly, by *somebody*, I believe, a Rev. Mr
Hamilton. In a MS., where I met the answer, I wrote below':

With Esop's lion, Burns says: Sore I feel
Each other blow, but damn that ass's heel!

THE LIBELLER'S SELF-REPROOF

Rash mortal, and slanderous poet, thy name
Shall no longer appear in the records of fame;
Dost not know that old Mansfield, who writes like the Bible,
Says—the more 'tis a truth, sir, the more 'tis a libel!

VERSES WRITTEN WITH A PENCIL
Over the Chimney-piece in the Parlour of the Inn at Kenmore

Admiring Nature in her wildest grace,
These northern scenes with weary feet I trace;
O'er many a winding dale and painful steep,
Th' abodes of coveyed grouse and timid sheep,
My savage journey, curious, I pursue,
Till fam'd Breadalbane opens to my view.—
The meeting cliffs each deep-sunk glen divides,
The woods, wild scatter'd, clothe their ample sides;
Th' outstretching lake, embosomed 'mong the hills,

The eye with wonder and amazement fills;
The Tay, meand'ring sweet in infant pride,
The palace rising on his verdant side;
The lawns, wood-fring'd in Nature's native taste;
The hillocks, dropt in Nature's careless haste;
The arches, striding o'er the new-born stream;
The village, glittering in the noontide beam—

Poetic ardours in my bosom swell,
Lone wand'ring by the hermit's mossy cell:
The sweeping theatre of hanging woods;
The incessant roar of headlong tumbling floods—

Here Poesy might wake her heaven-taught lyre,
And look through Nature with creative fire;
Here, to the wrongs of Fate half reconcil'd,
Misfortunes lightened steps might wander wild;
And Disappointment, in these lonely bounds,
Find balm to soothe her bitter, rankling wounds:
Here heart-struck Grief might heavenward stretch her scan,
And injured Worth forget and pardon man.

THE BIRKS OF ABERFELDY
Tune—*Birks of Abergeldie*

Chorus: Bonnie lassie, will ye go,
Will ye go, will ye go,
Bonnie lassie, will ye go
    To the birks of Aberfeldy?

Now Simmer blinks on flow'ry braes,
And o'er the crystal streamlets plays;
Come let us spend the lightsome days,
    In the birks of Aberfeldy.

The little birdies blythely sing,
While o'er their heads the hazels hing,
Or lightly flit on wanton wing,
    In the birks of Aberfeldy.

The braes ascend like lofty wa's,
The foaming stream deep-roaring fa's,
O'erhung wi' fragrant spreading shaws,
    The birks of Aberfeldy.

The hoary cliffs are crown'd wi' flowers,
White o'er the linns the burnie pours,
And rising, weets wi' misty showers
    The birks of Aberfeldy.

Let Fortune's gifts at random flee,
They ne'er shall draw a wish frae me;
Supremely blest wi' love and thee,
    In the birks of Aberfeldy.

THE HUMBLE PETITION OF BRUAR WATER[1]
To the Noble Duke of Athole.

My Lord, I know your noble ear
    Woe ne'er assails in vain;
Embolden'd thus, I beg you'll hear
    Your humble slave complain,

---

[1] Bruar Falls, in Athole, are exceedingly picturesque and beautiful, but their effect is much impaired by the want of trees and shrubs.—R.B.

How saucy Phoebus' scorching beams,
　　In flaming summer-pride,
Dry-withering, waste my foamy streams,
　　And drink my crystal tide.

The lightly jumping, glowrin' trouts,
　　That thro' my waters play,
If, in their random, wanton spouts,
　　They near the margin stray;
If, hapless chance! they linger lang,
　　I'm scorching up so shallow,
They're left the whitening stanes amang,
　　In gasping death to wallow.

Last day I grat wi' spite and teen,
　　As poet Burns came by,
That, to a bard, I should be seen
　　Wi' half my channel dry;
A panegyric rhyme, I ween,
　　Even as I was, he shor'd me;
But, had I in my glory been,
　　He, kneeling, wad ador'd me.

Here, foaming down the skelvy rocks,
　　In twisting strength I rin;
There, high my boiling torrent smokes,
　　Wild-roaring o'er a linn:
Enjoying each large spring and well,
　　As Nature gave them me,
I am, altho' I say't mysel,
　　Worth gaun a mile to see.

Would then my noble master please
　　To grant my highest wishes,
He'll shade my banks wi' tow'ring trees,
　　And bonnie spreading bushes.
Delighted doubly then, my Lord,
　　You'll wander on my banks,
And listen mony a grateful bird
　　Return you tuneful thanks.

The sober laverock, warbling wild,
　　Shall to the skies aspire;
The gowdspink, Music's gayest child,
　　Shall sweetly join the choir:
The blackbird strong, the lintwhite clear,
　　The mavis mild and mellow;
The robin pensive Autumn cheer,
　　In all her locks of yellow.

This, too, a covert shall ensure,
　　To shield them from the storm;
And coward maukin sleep secure,
　　Low in her grassy form:

Here shall the shepherd make his seat,
    To weave his crown of flowers;
Or find a sheltering, safe retreat,
    From prone-descending showers.

And here by sweet endearing stealth,
    Shall meet the loving pair,
Despising worlds, with all their wealth,
    As empty idle care:
The flowers shall vie in all their charms
    The hour of heaven to grace,
And birks extend their fragrant arms
    To screen the dear embrace.

Here haply too, at vernal dawn,
    Some musing bard may stray,
And eye the smoking, dewy lawn,
    And misty mountain grey;
Or, by the reaper's nightly beam,
    Mild-chequering thro' the trees,
Rave to my darkly dashing stream,
    Hoarse-swelling on the breeze.

Let lofty firs, and ashes cool,
    My lowly banks o'erspread,
And view, deep-bending in the pool,
    Their shadows' wat'ry bed:
Let fragrant birks, in woodbines drest,
    My craggy cliffs adorn;
And, for the little songster's nest,
    The close embowering thorn.

So may old Scotia's darling hope,
    Your little angel band,
Spring, like their fathers, up to prop
    Their honour'd native land!
So may, thro' Albion's farthest ken,
    To social-flowing glasses,
The grace be—'Athole's honest men,
    And Athole's bonnie lasses!'

LINES ON THE FALL OF FYERS NEAR LOCH NESS
Written with a Pencil on the Spot

Among the heathy hills and ragged woods
The roaring Fyers pours his mossy floods;
Till full he dashes on the rocky mounds,
Where, thro' a shapeless breach, his stream resounds.
As high in air the bursting torrents flow,
As deep recoiling surges foam below,
Prone down the rock the whitening sheet descends,

And viewless Echo's ear, astonish'd, rends.
Dim-seen, through rising mists and ceaseless showers,
The hoary cavern, wide surrounding, lowers:
Still thro' the gap the struggling river toils,
And still, below, the horrid cauldron boils—

EPIGRAM ON PARTING WITH A KIND HOST IN THE HIGHLANDS

When death's dark stream I ferry o'er—
A time that surely *shall* come—
In Heaven itself I'll ask no more
Than just a Highland welcome!

STRATHALLAN'S LAMENT[1]

'This air is the composition of one of the worthiest and best men living—Allan Masterton, schoolmaster in Edinburgh. As he and I were both sprouts of Jacobitism, we agreed to dedicate the words and air to that cause. But . . . except when my passions were heated by some accidental cause, my Jacobtism was merely by way of *vive la bagatelle*.'—R.B.

Thickest night, surround my dwelling!
    Howling tempests, o'er me rave!
Turbid torrents, wintry swelling,
    Roaring by my lonely cave.
Crystal streamlets gently flowing,
    Busy haunts of base mankind,
Western breezes softly blowing,
    Suit not my distracted mind.

In the cause of Right engagéd,
    Wrongs injurious to redress,
Honour's war we strongly wagéd,
    But the heavens denied success.
Ruin's wheel has driven o'er us,
    Not a hope that dare attend,
The wide world is all before us—
    But a world without a friend.

[1] The words are descriptive of the feelings of James Drummond, Viscount of Strathallan, who, after his father's death at Culloden, escaped to France, where he died.

TO THE MEMORY OF THE UNFORTUNATE MISS BURNS[1]

Like to a fading flower in May,
    Which Gardner cannot save,
So Beauty must, sometime, decay
    And drop into the grave.

Think, fellow sisters, on her fate!
    Think, think how short her days!
O! think, and, e'er it be too late,
    Turn from your evil ways.

Fair Burns, for long the talk and toast
    Of many a gaudy Beau,
That Beauty has forever lost
    That made each bosom glow.

Beneath this cold, green sod lies dead
    That once bewitching dame
That fired Edina's lustful sons
    And quench'd their glowing flame.

[1] *See* note, page 203.

CASTLE GORDON

Streams that glide in orient plains,
Never bound by winter's chains;
    Glowing here on golden sands,
There immix'd with foulest stains
    From tyranny's empurpled hands;

These, their richly gleaming waves,
I leave to tyrants and their slaves;
Give me the stream that sweetly laves
    The banks by Castle Gordon.

Spicy forests, ever gay,
Shading from the burning ray
    Hapless wretches sold to toil,
Or the ruthless native's way,
    Bent on slaughter, blood, and spoil:
Woods that ever verdant wave,
I leave the tyrant and the slave;
Give me the groves that lofty brave
    The storms by Castle Gordon.

Wildly here, without control,
Nature reigns and rules the whole;
    In that sober pensive mood,
Dearest to the feeling soul,
    She plants the forest, pours the flood:
Life's poor day I'll musing rave
And find at night a sheltering cave,
Where waters flow and wild woods wave,
    By bonnie Castle Gordon.

LADY ONLIE, HONEST LUCKY
Tune—*Ruffian's rant*

Chorus: Lady Onlie, honest Lucky,
    Brews gude ale at shore o' Bucky;
I wish her sale for her gude ale,
    The best on a' the shore o' Bucky.

A' the lads o' Thorniebank,
    When they gae to the shore o' Bucky,
They'll step in and tak a pint
    Wi' Lady Onlie, honest Lucky.

Her house sae bien, her curch sae clean
    I wat she is a daintie chuckie!
And cheery blinks the ingle-gleed
    O' Lady Onlie, honest Lucky!

THENIEL MENZIES' BONNIE MARY
Air—*Ruffian's rant*

Chorus: Theniel Menzies' bonnie Mary,
    Theniel Menzies' bonnie Mary,
Charlie Gregor tint his plaidie,
    Kissin' Theniel's bonnie Mary.

Her een sae bright, her brow sae white,
    Her haffet locks as brown's a berry;
And aye they dimpl't wi' a smile,
    The rosy cheeks o' bonnie Mary.

In coming by the brig o' Dye,
    At Darlet we a blink did tarry;
As day was dawnin in the sky,
    We drank a health to bonnie Mary.

We lap and danc'd the lee-lang day,
    Till piper lads were wae and weary:
But Charlie gat the spring to pay
    For kissin' Theniel's bonnie Mary.

THE BONNIE LASS OF ALBANY[1]
Tune—*Mary's dream*

My heart is wae, and unco wae,
    To think upon the raging sea,
That roars between her gardens green
    And the bonnie Lass of Albany.

This lovely maid's of royal blood
    That ruléd Albion's kingdoms three;
But oh, alas! for her bonnie face,
    They hae wrang'd the Lass of Albany.

In the rolling tide of spreading Clyde
    There sits an isle of high degree,
And a town of fame whose princely name
    Should grace the Lass of Albany.[2]

But there's a youth, a witless youth,[3]
    That fills the place where she should be;
We'll send him o'er to his native shore,
    And bring our ain sweet Albany.

Alas the day, and woe the day,
    A false usurper wan the gree,
Who now commands the towers and lands—
    The royal right of Albany.

We'll daily pray, we'll nightly pray,
    On bended knees most fervently,
That the time may come, with pipe and drum,
    We'll welcome hame fair Albany.

[1] Illegitimate daughter of Prince Charles Edward, the 'Young Pretender'.
[2] Rothesay, on the Isle of Bute, gave the title Duke of Rothesay to the eldest sons of the kings of Scotland.
[3] George, Prince of Wales.

ON SCARING SOME WATER-FOWL IN LOCH TURIT
A Wild Scene among the Hills of Oughtertyre.

'This was the production of a solitary forenoon's walk from Oughtertyre House. I lived there, the guest of Sir William Murray, for two or three weeks, and was much flattered by my hospitable reception. What a pity that the mere emotions of gratitude are so impotent in this world. 'Tis lucky that, as we are told, they will be of some avail in the world to come.'—R.B.

Why, ye tenants of the lake,
For me your wat'ry haunt forsake?
Tell me, fellow-creatures, why
At my presence thus you fly?
Why disturb your social joys,
Parent, filial, kindred ties?—
Common friend to you and me,

Nature's gifts to all are free;
Peaceful keep your dimpling wave,
Busy feed, or wanton lave;
Or, beneath the sheltering rock,
Bide the surging billow's shock.

Conscious, blushing for our race,
Soon, too soon, your fears I trace:
Man, your proud, usurping foe,
Would be lord of all below:
Plumes himself in Freedom's pride,
Tyrant stern to all beside.

The eagle, from the cliffy brow,
Marking you his prey below,
In his breast no pity dwells,
Strong Necessity compels:
But Man, to whom alone is given
A ray direct from pitying Heaven,
Glories in his heart humane—
And creatures for his pleasure slain!

In these savage, liquid plains,
Only known to wandering swains,
Where the mossy riv'let strays,
Far from human haunts and ways;
All on Nature you depend,
And life's poor season peaceful spend.

Or, if man's superior might
Dare invade your native right,
On the lofty ether borne,
Man with all his powers you scorn;
Swiftly seek, on clanging wings,
Other lakes and other springs;
And the foe you cannot brave,
Scorn at least to be his slave.

BLYTHE WAS SHE[1]
Tune—*Andro and his cutty gun*

Chorus: Blythe, blythe and merry was she,
    Blythe was she butt and ben;
Blythe by the banks of Earn,
    And blythe in Glenturit glen.

By Oughtertyre grows the aik,
   On Yarrow banks the birken shaw;
But Phemie was a bonnier lass
   Than braes o' Yarrow ever saw.

Her looks were like a flow'r in May,
   Her smile was like a simmer morn:
She trippéd by the banks o' Earn,
   As light's a bird upon a thorn.

[1] Miss Euphemia Murray, a cousin of Sir William Murray of Oughtertyre and then about eighteen years old.

Her bonnie face it was as meek
　　As ony lamb upon a lea;
The evening sun was ne'er sae sweet,
　　As was the blink o' Phemie's e'e.

The Highland hills I've wander'd wide,
　　And o'er the Lawlands I hae been;
But Phemie was the blythest lass
　　That ever trod the dewy green.

A Rosebud By My Early Walk

'This song I composed on Miss Jenny Cruickshank, only child to my worthy friend, Mr Wm Cruickshank of the High School, Edinburgh.'—R.B.

A rosebud by my early walk,
Adown a corn-encloséd bawk,
Sae gently bent its thorny stalk,
　　All on a dewy morning.
Ere twice the shades o' dawn are fled,
In a' its crimson glory spread,
And drooping rich the dewy head,
　　It scents the early morning.

Within the bush her covert nest
A little linnet fondly prest;
The dew sat chilly on her breast,
　　Sae early in the morning.
She soon shall see her tender brood,
The pride, the pleasure o' the wood,
Amang the fresh green leaves bedew'd,
　　Awake the early morning.

So thou, dear bird, young Jenny fair,
On trembling string or vocal air,
Shall sweetly pay the tender care
　　That tents thy early morning.
So thou, sweet Rosebud, young and gay,
Shalt beauteous blaze upon the day,
And bless the parent's evening ray
　　That watch'd thy early morning.

The Banks Of The Devon

Tune—*Bhannerach dhon na chri*

'These verses were composed on a charming girl, Miss Charlotte Hamilton. . . . . She is sister to my worthy friend, Gavin Hamilton of Mauchline, and was born on the banks of Ayr; but was, at the time I wrote these lines, residing at Harvieston in Clackmannanshire, on the romantic banks of the little river Devon.'—R.B.

How pleasant the banks of the clear winding Devon,
　　With green spreading bushes and flow'rs blooming fair!
But the bonniest flow'r on the banks of the Devon
　　Was once a sweet bud on the braes of the Ayr.
Mild be the sun on this sweet blushing flower,
　　In the gay rosy morn, as it bathes in the dew;
And gentle the fall of the soft vernal shower,
　　That steals on the evening each leaf to renew!

O spare the dear blossom, ye orient breezes,
　　With chill hoary wing as ye usher the dawn!
And far be thou distant, thou reptile that seizes
　　The verdure and pride of the garden or lawn!
Let Bourbon exult in his gay gilded lilies,
　　And England triumphant display her proud rose:
A fairer than either adorns the green valleys,
　　Where Devon, sweet Devon, meandering flows.

WHERE BRAVING ANGRY WINTER'S STORMS
Tune—*Neil Gow's lament for Abercairny*

Where, braving angry winter's storms,
　　The lofty Ochils rise,
Far in their shade my Peggy's[1] charms
　　First blest my wondering eyes—
As one who by some savage stream,
　　A lonely gem surveys,
Astonish'd, doubly marks it beam,
　　With art's most polish'd blaze.

Blest be the wild, sequester'd shade,
　　And blest the day and hour,
Where Peggy's charms I first survey'd,
　　When first I felt their pow'r!
The tyrant Death, with grim control,
　　May seize my fleeting breath;
But tearing Peggy from my soul
　　Must be a stronger death.

[1] Margaret Chalmers, who about a year after the poem was composed became the wife of Lewis Hay, an Edinburgh banker. The next poem is also in her honour.

MY PEGGY'S CHARMS
Tune—*Tha a' chailleach air mo dheigh*

My Peggy's face, my Peggy's form,
The frost of hermit age might warm;
My Peggy's worth, my Peggy's mind,
Might charm the first of human kind.
I love my Peggy's angel air,
Her face so truly, heavenly fair,
Her native grace so void of art,
But I adore my Peggy's heart.

The lily's hue, the rose's dye,
The kindling lustre of an eye;
Who but owns their magic sway?
Who but knows they all decay?
The tender thrill, the pitying tear,
The generous purpose, nobly dear,
The gentle look that rage disarms—
These are all immortal charms.

THE YOUNG HIGHLAND ROVER
Tune—*Morag*

Loud blaw the frosty breezes,
    The snaws the mountains cover;
Like winter on me seizes,
    Since my young Highland rover
    Far wanders nations over.
Where'er he go, where'er he stray,
    May heaven be his warden;
Return him safe to fair Strathspey,
    And bonnie Castle Gordon!

The trees now naked groaning,
    Shall soon wi' leaves be hinging,
The birdies dowie moaning,
    Shall a' be blythely singing,
    And every flower be springing;
Sae I'll rejoice the lee-lang day,
    When by his mighty Warden
My youth's return'd to fair Strathspey,
    And bonnie Castle Gordon.

BIRTHDAY ODE FOR 31ST DECEMBER 1787[1]

Afar the illustrious Exile roams,
    Whom kingdoms on this day should hail;
An inmate in the casual shed,
On transient pity's bounty fed,
    Haunted by busy memory's bitter tale!
Beasts of the forest have their savage homes,
    But he, who should imperial purple wear,
Owns not the lap of earth where rests his royal head!
    His wretched refuge, dark despair,
    While ravening wrongs and woes pursue,
    And distant far the faithful few
    Who would his sorrows share.

False flatterer, Hope, away!
    Nor think to lure us as in days of yore:
We solemnise this sorrowing natal day,
    To prove our loyal truth—we can no more,
And owning Heaven's mysterious sway,
    Submissive, low adore.
Ye honoured, mighty Dead,
    Who nobly perished in the glorious cause,
    Your KING, your Country, and her laws,
From great DUNDEE, who smiling Victory led,
And fell a Martyr in her arms,
(What breast of northern ice but warms!)
To bold BALMERINO's undying name,
    Whose soul of fire, lighted at Heaven's high flame,
Deserves the proudest wreath departed heroes claim:
    Not unrevenged your fate shall lie,
    It only lags, the fatal hour,
    Your blood shall, with incessant cry,
    Awake at last, th' unsparing Power;
As from the cliff, with thundering course,
    The snowy ruin smokes along

[1] The last birthday of Prince Charles Edward. He died precisely one month later.

With doubling speed and gathering force,
Till deep it, crushing, whelms the cottage in the vale;
    So Vengeance' arm, ensanguin'd, strong,
Shall with resistless might assail,
Usurping Brunswick's pride shall lay,
And STUART's wrongs and yours, with tenfold weight, repay.

Perdition, baleful child of night!
Rise and revenge the injured right
    Of STUART's royal race:
Lead on the unmuzzled hounds of hell,
Till all the frighted echoes tell
    The blood-notes of the chase!
Full on the quarry point their view,
Full on the base usurping crew,
The tools of faction, and the nation's curse!
    Hark how the cry grows on the wind;
    They leave the lagging gale behind,
    Their savage fury, pitiless, they pour;
With murdering eyes already they devour;
See Brunswick spent, a wretched prey,
His life one poor despairing day,
Where each avenging hour still ushers in a worse!
    Such havock, howling all abroad,
        Their utter ruin bring,
The base apostates to their GOD,
        Or rebels to their KING.

ON THE DEATH OF ROBERT DUNDAS, ESQ., OF ARNISTON

Late Lord President of the Court of Session.

'I have two or three times in my life composed from the wish rather than from the impulse, but I never succeeded to any purpose. One of these times I shall ever remember with gnashing of teeth. 'Twas on the death of the late Lord President Dundas. My very worthy and respected friend, Mr Alex. Wood, surgeon, urged me to pay a compliment in the way of my trade to his lordship's memory. Well, to work I went, and produced a copy of elegiac verses. . . . On the whole, though they were far from being in my best manner, they were tolerable, and would, by some, have been thought very clever. I wrote a letter which, however, was in my very best manner, and enclosing my poem. . . . [Burns received no acknowledgment.] From that time, highly as I respect the talents of their family, I never see the name Dundas in the column of a newspaper, but my heart seems straitened for room in my bosom; and if I am obliged to read aloud a paragraph relating to one of them, I feel my forehead flush, and my nether lip quiver.'—R.B.

Lone on the bleaky hills the straying flocks
Shun the fierce storms among the sheltering rocks;
Down from the rivulets, red with dashing rains,
The gathering floods burst o'er the distant plains;
Beneath the blast the leafless forests groan,
The hollow caves return a hollow moan.

Ye hills, ye plains, ye forests, and ye caves,
Ye howling winds, and wintry swelling waves!
Unheard, unseen, by human ear or eye,

Sad to your sympathetic glooms I fly;
Where to the whistling blast and waters' roar
Pale Scotia's recent wound I may deplore.

O heavy loss, thy country ill could bear!
A loss these evil days can ne'er repair!
Justice, the high vicegerent of her God,
Her doubtful balance eyed, and sway'd her rod:
Hearing the tidings of the fatal blow,
She sank, abandon'd to the wildest woe.

Wrongs, injuries, from many a darksome den,
Now gay in hope explore the paths of men:
See from his cavern grim Oppression rise,
And throw on poverty his cruel eyes;
Keen on the helpless victim see him fly,
And stifle, dark, the feebly bursting cry:

Mark ruffian Violence, ingrain'd with crimes,
Rousing elate in these degenerate times,
View unsuspecting Innocence a prey,
As guileful Fraud points out the erring way:
While subtle Litigation's pliant tongue
The life-blood equal sucks of Right and Wrong:
Hark, injur'd Want recounts th' unlisten'd tale,
And much wrong'd Mis'ry pours the unpitied wail!

Ye dark waste hills, ye brown unsightly plains,
To you I sing my grief-inspiréd strains:
Ye tempests, rage! ye turbid torrents, roll!
Ye suit the joyless tenor of my soul.
Life's social haunts and pleasures I resign,
Be nameless wilds and lonely wanderings mine,
To mourn the woes my country must endure—
That would degenerate ages cannot cure.

Sylvander To Clarinda
Extempore Reply to Verses addressed to the Author by a Lady, under the
Signature of 'Clarinda'[1]

When dear Clarinda, matchless fair,
　　First struck Sylvander's raptur'd view,
He gaz'd, he listened to despair,
　　Alas! 'twas all he dared to do.

Love, from Clarinda's heavenly eyes,
　　Transfixed his bosom thro' and thro';
But still in Friendship's guarded guise,
　　For more the demon fear'd to do.

[1] Mrs Nancy M'Lehose, a young grass widow whom Burns had met in Edinburgh. This and the following three poems were inspired by correspondence with her.

That heart, already more than lost,
    The imp beleaguer'd all *perdu*;
For frowning Honour kept his post—
    To meet that frown he shrunk to do.

His pangs the Bard refused to own,
    Tho' half he wish'd Clarinda knew;
But Anguish wrung the unweeting groan—
    Who blames what frantic Pain must do?

That heart, where motley follies blend,
    Was sternly still to Honour true:
To prove Clarinda's fondest friend,
    Was what a lover sure might do.

The Muse his ready quill employed,
    No nearer bliss he could pursue;
That bliss Clarinda cold deny'd—
    'Send word by Charles how you do!'

The chill behest disarm'd his muse,
    Till passion all impatient grew:
He wrote, and hinted for excuse,
    'Twas, 'cause 'he'd nothing else to do.'

But by those hopes I have above!
    And by those faults I dearly rue!
The deed, the boldest mark of love,
    For thee that deed I dare uo do!

O could the Fates but name the price
    Would bless me with your charms and you!
With frantic joy I'd pay it thrice,
    If human art and power could do!

Then take, Clarinda, friendship's hand,
    (Friendship, at least, I may avow;)
And lay no more your chill command—
    I'll write whatever I've to do.
                            SYLVANDER.

INTERPOLATION

Your friendship much can make me blest,
    O why that bliss destroy!
Why urge the only, one request
    You know I will deny!

Your thought, if Love must harbour there,
    Conceal it in that thought;
Nor cause me from my bosom tear
    The very friend I sought.

To A Blackbird

Go on, sweet bird, and soothe my care,
Thy tuneful notes will hush despair;
Thy plaintive warblings, void of art,
Thrill sweetly thro' my aching heart.
Now choose thy mate, and fondly love,
And all the charming transport prove;
While I a lovelorn exile live,
Nor transport or recieve or give.

For thee is laughing Nature gay,
For thee she pours the vernal day;
For me in vain is Nature drest,
While Joy's a stranger to my breast!
These sweet emotions all enjoy;
Let Love and Song thy hours employ!
Go on, sweet bird, and soothe my care,
Thy tuneful notes will hush despair.

Clarinda, Mistress Of My Soul

Clarinda, mistres of my soul,
    The measur'd time is run!
The wretch beneath the dreary pole
    So marks his latest sun.

To what dark cave of frozen night
    Shall poor Sylvander hie;
Depriv'd of thee, his life and light,
    The sun of all his joy?

We part—but by these precious drops,
    That fill thy lovely eyes!
No other light shall guide my steps,
    Till thy bright beams arise.

She, the fair sun of all her sex,
    Has blest my glorious day;
And shall a glimmering planet fix
    My worship to its ray?

I'm O'er Young To Marry Yet

Chorus: I'm o'er young, I'm o'er young,
    I'm o'er young to marry yet;
I'm o'er young, 'twad be a sin
    To tak me frae my mammy yet.

I am my mammy's ae bairn,
    Wi' unco folk I weary, sir;
And lying in a man's bed,
    I'm fley'd it make me eerie, sir.

Hallowmass is come and gane,
    The nights are lang in winter, sir;
And you an' I in ae bed,
    In trowth, I dare na venture, sir.

Fu' loud and shill the frosty wind
    Blaws thro' the leafless timmer, sir;
But if ye come this gate again,
    I'll aulder be gin simmer, sir.

To The Weaver's Gin Ye Go

Chorus: To the weaver's gin ye go, fair maids,
    To the weaver's gin ye go;
I rede you right, gang ne'er at night,
    To the weaver's gin ye go.

My heart was ance as blithe and free
    As simmer days were lang,
But a bonnie, westlin weaver lad
    Has gart me change my sang.

My mither sent me to the town
    To warp a plaiden wab;
But the weary, weary warpin' o't
    Has gart me sigh and sab.

A bonnie, westlin weaver lad
    Sat working at his loom;
He took my heart as wi' a net,
    In every knot and thrum.

I sat beside my warpin'-wheel,
    And aye I ca'd it roun';
But every shot and every knock,
    My heart it gae a stoun.

The moon was sinking in the west,
    Wi' visage pale and wan,
As my bonnie, westlin weaver lad
    Convoy'd me thro' the glen.

But what was said, or what was done,
    Shame fa' me gin I tell;
But Oh! I fear the kintra soon
    Will ken as weel's mysel!

McPherson's[1] Farewell

Chorus: Sae rantingly, sae wantonly,
    Sae dauntingly gaed he:
He play'd a spring, and danc'd it round,
    Below the gallows-tree.

Farewell, ye dungeons dark and strong,
    The wretch's destinie!
McPherson's time will not be long
    On yonder gallows-tree.

O what is death but parting breath?
    On many a bloody plain
I've dared his face, and in this place
    I scorn him yet again!

Untie these bands from off my hands,
    And bring to me my sword;
And there's no a man in all Scotland,
    But I'll brave him at a word.

I've liv'd a life of sturt and strife;
    I die by treacherie:
It burns my heart I must depart,
    And not avengéd be.

Now farewell light, thou sunshine bright,
    And all beneath the sky!
May coward shame distain his name,
    The wretch that dares not die!

[1] James McPherson, a Highland freebooter, who is said to have been an excellent violinist.

Stay, My Charmer
Tune—*An gille dubh ciar dhubh*

Stay, my charmer, can you leave me?
Cruel, cruel to deceive me!
Well you know how much you grieve me:
    Cruel charmer, can you go!
    Cruel charmer, can you go!

By my love so ill requited,
By the faith you fondly plighted;
By the pangs of lovers slighted,
    Do not, do not leave me so!
    Do not, do not leave me so!

My Hoggie

What will I do gin my Hoggie die?
   My joy, my pride, my Hoggie!
My only beast, I had nae mae,
   And vow but I was vogie!
The lee-lang night we watch'd the fauld,
   Me and my faithfu' doggie;
We heard nocht but the roaring linn,
   Amang the braes sae scroggie.

But the houlet cry'd frae the castle wa',
   The blitter frae the boggie;
The tod reply'd upon the hill,
   I trembled for my Hoggie.
When day did daw, and cocks did craw,
   The morning it was foggie;
An unco tyke, lap o'er the dyke,
   And maist has kill'd my Hoggie!

Raving Winds Around Her Blowing
Tune—McGrigor of Roro's lament

Raving winds around her blowing,
Yellow leaves the woodlands strowing,
By a river hoarsely roaring,
Isabella stray'd deploring—

'Farewell, hours that late did measure
Sunshine days of joy and pleasure;
Hail, thou gloomy night of sorrow—
Cheerless night that knows no morrow.

'O'er the past too fondly wandering,
On the hopeless future pondering,
Chilly grief my life-blood freezes,
Fell despair my fancy seizes.

'Life, thou soul of every blessing,
Load to misery most distressing,
Gladly how would I resign thee,
And to dark oblivion join thee!'

Up In The Morning Early

Chorus: Up in the morning's no for me,
   Up in the morning early;
When a' the hills are covered wi' snaw,
   I'm sure it's winter fairly.

Cauld blaws the wind frae east to west,
   The drift is driving sairly;

Sae loud and shill's I hear the blast,
    I'm sure it's winter fairly.

The birds sit chittering in the thorn,
    A' day they fare but sparely;
And lang's the night frae e'en to morn,
    I'm sure it's winter fairly.

How Long And Dreary Is The Night[1]
Tune—*Cauld kail*

How long and dreary is the night,
    When I am frae my dearie!
I sleepless lie frae e'en to morn,
    Tho' I were ne'er so weary:
I sleepless lie frae e'en to morn,
    Tho' I were ne'er so weary:

When I think on the happy days
    I spent wi' you my dearie:
And now what lands between us lie,
    How can I be but eerie!
And now what lands between us lie,
    How can I be but eerie!

How slow ye move, ye heavy hours,
    As ye were wae and weary!
It wasna sae, ye glinted by,
    When I was wi' my dearie!
It wasna sae, ye glinted by,
    When I was wi' my dearie!

[1] Burns later wrote another version, *see* page 408.

Dusty Miller

Hey, the dusty Miller,
    And his dusty coat,
He will win a shilling,
    Or he spend a groat:
Dusty was the coat,
    Dusty was the colour,
Dusty was the kiss
    That I gat frae the Miller.

Hey, the dusty Miller,
    And his dusty sack;
Leeze me on the calling
    Fills the dusty peck:
Fills the dusty peck,
    Brings the dusty siller;
I wad gie my coatie
    For the dusty Miller.

Duncan Davison

There was a lass, they ca'd her Meg,
    And she held o'er the moors to spin;
There was a lad that follow'd her,
    They ca'd him Duncan Davison.
The moor was dreigh, and Meg was skeigh,
    Her favour Duncan could na win;

For wi' the rock she wad him knock,
    And aye she shook the temper-pin.

As o'er the moor they lightly foor,
    A burn was clear, a glen was green,
Upon the banks they eas'd their shanks,
    And aye she set the wheel between:
But Duncan swoor a haly aith,
    That Meg should be a bride the morn,
Then Meg took up her spinning-graith,
    And flang them a' out o'er the burn.

We will big a wee, wee house,
    And we will live like king and queen;
Sae blythe and merry's we will be,
    When ye set by the wheel at e'en.
A man may drink, and no be drunk,
    A man may fight, and no be slain;
A man may kiss a bonnie lass,
    And aye be welcome back again!

The Lad They Ca' Jumpin John

Chorus: The lang lad they ca' Jumpin John
    Beguil'd the bonnie lassie,
The lang lad they ca' Jumpin John
    Beguil'd the bonnie lassie.

Her daddie forbad, her minnie forbad,
    Forbidden she wadna be:
She wadna trow't, the browst she brew'd
    Wad taste sae bitterlie.

A cow and a cauf, a yowe and a hauf,
    And thretty gude shillin's and three;
A vera gude tocher, a cotter-man's dochter,
    The lass wi' the bonnie black e'e.

Talk Of Him That's Far Awa
Tune—*Druimion dubh*

Musing on the roaring ocean,
    Which divides my love and me!
Wearying Heav'n in warm devotion,
    For his weal where'er he be.

Hope and Fear's alternate billow
    Yielding late to Nature's law,
Whisp'ring spirits round my pillow
    Talk of him that's far awa.

Ye whom Sorrow never wounded,
    Ye who never shed a tear,
Care-untroubled, joy-surrounded,
    Gaudy Day to you is dear.

Gentle night, do thou befriend me;
    Downy Sleep, the curtain draw;
Spirits kind, again attend me,
    Talk of him that's far awa!

To Daunton Me

Chorus: To daunton me, to daunton me,
An auld man shall never daunton me.

The bluid-red rose at Yule may blaw,
The simmer lilies bloom in snaw,
The frost may freeze the deepest sea;
But an auld man shall never daunton me.

To daunton me, and me sae young,
Wi' his fause heart and flatt'ring tongue!
That is the thing you ne'er shall see,
For an auld man shall never daunton me.

For a' his meal and a' his maut,
For a' his fresh beef and his saut,
For a' his gold and white monie,
An auld man shall never daunton me.

His gear may buy him kye and yowes,
His gear may buy him glens and knowes;
But me he shall not buy nor fee,
For an auld man shall never daunton me.

He hirples twa-fauld as he dow,
Wi' his teethless gab and his auld beld pow,
And the rain rains down frae his red-blear'd e'e—
That auld man shall never daunton me.

The Winter It Is Past

The winter it is past, and the summer comes at last
    And the little birds, they sing on ev'ry tree;
Now ev'ry thing is glad, while I am very sad,
    Since my true love is parted from me.

The rose upon the breer, by the waters running clear,
    May have charms for the linnet or the bee;
Their little loves are blest, and their little hearts at rest,
    But my true love is parted from me.

My love, like yonder sun, in the firmament doth run,
    Ever bright, ever constant and true;
But his is like the moon that wanders up and down,
    And every month it is new.

O do not think it strange that the world I would range
    To secure for my soul its delight;
For, bound as with a chain, Love's captive I remain,
    And my tears are the dew-drops of Night.

Ye maidens cross'd in love—and the cross will not remove—
    Take my pity for the pains ye endure!
When true love's unreturn'd, let the poor heart break unmourn'd—
    In the kind grave Love hath its cure!

THE BONNIE LAD THAT'S FAR AWA

O how can I be blythe and glad,
    Or how can I gang brisk and braw,
When the bonnie lad that I lo'e best
    Is o'er the hills and far awa!

It's no the frosty winter wind,
    It's no the driving drift and snaw;
But aye the tear comes in my e'e,
    To think on him that's far awa.

My father pat me frae his door,
    My friends they hae disown'd me a';
But there is ane will tak my part—
    The bonnie lad that's far awa.

A pair o' gloves he bought to me,
    And silken snoods he gae me twa,
And I will wear them for his sake—
    The bonnie lad that's far awa.

O weary winter soon will pass,
    And spring will cleed the birken shaw;
And my young babie will be born,
    And he'll be hame that's far awa.

VERSES TO CLARINDA
With a Present of a Pair of Drinking Glasses

Fair Empress of the Poet's soul,
    And Queen of Poetesses;
Clarinda, take this little boon,
    This humble pair of glasses:

And fill them up with generous juice,
    As generous as your mind;
And pledge me in the generous toast—
    'The whole of human kind!'

'To those who love us!'—second fill;
    But not to those whom we love;
Lest we love those who love not us!—
    A third—'To thee and me, Love!'

Long may we live! long may we love!
    And long may we be happy!
And may we never want a glass
    Well charg'd with generous nappy!

THE CHEVALIER'S LAMENT
Tune—*Captain O'Kean*

The small birds rejoice in the green leaves returning,
The murmuring streamlet winds clear thro' the vale;
The primroses blow in the dews of the morning,
And wild scatter'd cowslips bedeck the green dale:
But what can give pleasure, or what can seem fair,
While the lingering moments are numbered by care?
No flow'rs faily springing, nor birds sweetly singing,
Can soothe the sad bosom of joyless despair.

The deed that I dared, could it merit their malice—
A king and a father to place on his throne?
His right are these hills, and his right are these valleys,
Where the wild beasts find shelter, but I can find none:
But 'tis not my suff'rings thus wretched, forlorn;
My brave gallant friends! 'tis your ruin I mourn;
Your faith proved so loyal in hot bloody trial—
Alas! I can make it no better return!

EPISTLE TO HUGH PARKER

In this strange land, this uncouth clime,
A land unknown to prose or rhyme;
Where words ne'er cross't the Muse's heckles,
Nor limpit in poetic shackles:
A land that Prose did never view it,
Except when drunk he stacher't thro' it;
Here, ambush'd by the chimla cheek,
Hid in an atmosphere of reek,
I hear a wheel thrum i' the neuk,
I hear it—for in vain I leuk.
The red peat gleams, a fiery kernel,
Enhusked by a fog infernal:
Here, for my wonted rhyming raptures,
I sit and count my sins by chapters;
For life and spunk like ither Christians,
I'm dwindled down to mere existence—
Wi' nae converse but Gallowa' bodies,
Wi' nae kenn'd face but Jenny Geddes,
Jenny—my Pegasean pride!—
Dowie she saunters down Nithside,
And aye a westlin leuk she throws,
While tears hap o'er her auld brown nose!
Was it for this, wi' cannie care,
Thou bure the Bard through many a shire?
At howes or hillocks never stumbled,
And late or early never grumbled?—
O, had I power like inclination,
I'd heeze thee up a constellation,
To canter with the Sagitarre,
Or loup the ecliptic like a bar;
Or turn the pole like any arrow;
Or, when auld Phoebus bids good morrow,
Down the zodiac urge the race,
And cast dirt on his godship's face;
For I could lay my bread and kail
He'd ne'er cast saut upo' thy tail!—
Wi' a' this care and a' this grief,
And sma', sma' prospect of relief,
And nought but peat reek i' my head,
How can I write what ye can read?—

Tarbolton, twenty-fourth o' June,
Ye'll find me in a better tune;
But till we meet and weet our whistle,
Tak this excuse for nae epistle.
ROBERT BURNS.

I LOVE MY JEAN
Tune—*Miss Admiral Gordon's strathspey*
'The air is by Marshall, the song I composed out of compliment to Mrs Burns. N.B.—It was during the honeymoon'—R.B.

Of a' the airts the wind can blaw,
    I dearly like the west,
For there the bonnie lassie lives,
    The lassie I lo'e best:
There's wild-woods grow, and rivers row,
    And mony a hill between:
But day and night my fancys' flight
    Is ever wi' my Jean.

I see her in the dewy flowers,
    I see her sweet and fair:
I hear her in the tunefu' birds,
    I hear her charm the air:
There's not a bonnie flower that springs,
    By fountain, shaw, or green;
There's not a bonnie bird that sings,
    But minds me o' my Jean.

I HAE A WIFE O' MY AIN

I hae a wife o' my ain,
    I'll partake wi' naebody;
I'll take cuckold frae nane,
    I'll gie cuckold to naebody.

I am naebody's lord,
    I'll be slave to naebody;
I hae a gude braid sword,
    I'll tak dunts frae naebody.

I hae a penny to spend—
    There—thanks to naebody;
I hae naething to lend,
    I'll borrow frae naebody.

I'll be merry and free,
    I'll be sad for naebody;
Naebody cares for me,
    I care for naebody.

WRITTEN IN FRIARS CARSE HERMITAGE, NITHSDALE
First Version

Thou whom chance may hither lead,
Be thou clad in russet weed,
Be thou deckt in silken stole,
Grave these maxims on thy soul:—

Life is but a day at most,
Sprung from night, in darkness lost:

Hope not sunshine every hour,
Fear not clouds will always lour.
Happiness is but a name,
Make content and ease thy aim;
Ambition is a meteor-gleam;
Fame—a restless, airy dream;
Pleasures—insects on the wing;
Peace—the tenderest flower in spring;
Those that sip the dew alone,
Make the butterflies thy own:
Those that would the bloom devour—
Crush the locusts! save the flower.
For the future be prepar'd,
Guard, wherever thou canst guard;
But thy utmost duly done,
Welcome what thou canst not shun:
Follies past, give thou to air,
Make their consequence thy care.
Keep the name of Man in mind,
And dishonour not thy kind:
Reverence with lowly heart
Him whose wondrous work thou art;
Keep His Goodness still in view,
Thy trust—and thy example, too.

Stranger, go! Heaven be thy guide!
Quod the Beadsman on Nithside.

WRITTEN IN FRIARS CARSE HERMITAGE, NITHSDALE
Second Version

Thou whom chance may hither lead,
Be thou clad in russet weed,
Be thou deckt in silken stole,
Grave these counsels on thy soul:—

Life is but a day at most,
Sprung from night, in darkness lost;
Hope not sunshine every hour,
Fear not clouds will always lour.

As Youth and Love with sprightly dance,
Beneath thy morning star advance,
Pleasure with her siren air
May delude the thoughtless pair;
Let Prudence bless Enjoyment's cup,
Then raptur'd sip and sip it up.

As thy day grows warm and high,
Life's meridian flaming nigh,
Dost thou spurn the humble vale?
Life's proud summits wouldst thou scale?

Check thy climbing step, elate,
Evils lurk in felon wait:
Dangers, eagle-pinion'd, bold,
Soar around each cliffy hold,
While cheerful peace, with linnet song,
Chants the lowly dells among.

    As the shades of evening close,
Beckoning thee to long repose;
As life itself becomes disease,
Seek the chimney nook of ease.
There, ruminate with sober thought
On all thou'st seen, and heard, and wrought;
And teach the sportive younkers round,
Saws of experience, sage and sound.—
Say, Man's true, genuine estimate,
The grand criterion of his fate,
Is not, art thou high or low?
Did thy fortune ebb or flow?
Did many talents gild thy span?
Or frugal Nature grudge thee one?
Tell them, and press it on their mind,
As thou thyself must shortly find,
The smile, or frown, of aweful Heaven,
To Virtue or to Vice is given.
Say, to be just, and kind, and wise,
There solid self-enjoyment lies;
That foolish, selfish, faithless ways,
Lead to be wretched, vile, and base.

Thus, resign'd and quiet, creep
To the bed of lasting sleep;
Sleep, whence thou shalt ne'er awake,
Night, where dawn shall never wake,
Till Future Life, future no more,
To light and joy the good restore,
To light and joy unknown before.

Stranger, go! Heaven be thy guide!
Quod the Beadsman of Nithside.

TO ALEX. CUNNINGHAM, ESQ., WRITER

My godlike friend—nay, do not stare,
    You think the phrase is odd-like;
But 'God is love,' the saints declare,
    Then surely thou art god-like.

And is thy ardour still the same?
    And kindled still in ANNA?
Others may boast a partial flame,
    But thou art a volcano!

Ev'n Wedlock asks not love beyond
Death's tie-dissolving portal;
But thou, omnipotently fond,
May'st promise love immortal!

Thy wounds such healing powers defy,
Such symptoms dire attend them,
That last great antihectic try—
Marriage perhaps may mend them.

Sweet Anna has an air—a grace,
Divine, magnetic, touching:
She talks, she charms—but who can trace
The process of bewitching?

ANNA, THY CHARMS

Anna, thy charms my bosom fire,
And waste my soul with care;
But ah! how bootless to admire,
When fated to despair!

Yet in thy presence, lovely Fair,
To hope may be forgiven;
For sure 'twere impious to despair
So much in sight of heaven.

THE FÊTE CHAMPÊTRE
Tune—*Killiecrankie*

O wha will to Saint Stephen's House,
To do our errands there, man?
O wha will to Saint Stephen's House
O' th' merry lads of Ayr, man?
Or will we send a man o' law?
Or will we send a sodger?
Or him wha led o'er Scotland a'
The meikle Ursa-Major?[1]

Come, will ye court a noble lord,
Or buy a score o'lairds, man?
For worth and honour pawn their word,
Their vote shall be Glencaird's,[2] man.
Ane gies them coin, ane gies them wine,
Anither gies them clatter:
Annbank,[3] wha guessed the ladies' taste,
He gies a Fête Champêtre.

When Love and Beauty heard the news,
The gay green woods amang, man;
Where, gathering flowers, and busking bowers,
They heard the blackbird's sang, man:
A vow, they seal'd it with a kiss,
Sir Politics to fetter,

[1] James Boswell, who accompanied Dr Johnson on his Scottish tour.
[2] Sir John Whitefoord, then residing at Cloncaird or 'Glencaird'.
[3] William Cunninghame, Esq., of Annbank and Enterkin, the host of the fête, who was thought to be considering standing in a forthcoming country election.

As theirs alone, the patent-bliss,
    To hold a Fête Champêtre.

Then mounted Mirth on gleesome wing,
    O'er hill and dale she flew, man;
Ilk wimpling burn, ilk crystal spring,
    Ilk glen and shaw she knew, man:
She summon'd every social sprite,
    That sports by wood or water,
On the bonnie banks of Ayr to meet,
    And keep this Fête Champêtre.

Cauld Boreas, wi' his boisterous crew,
    Were bound to stakes like kye, man;
And Cynthia's car, o' silver fu',
    Clamb up the starry sky, man:
Reflected beams dwell in the streams,
    Or down the current shatter;
The western breeze steals thro' the trees,
    To view this Fête Champêtre.

How many a robe sae gaily floats!
    What sparkling jewels glance, man!
To Harmony's enchanting notes,
    As moves the mazy dance, man.
The echoing wood, the winding flood,
    Like Paradise did glitter,
When angels met, at Adam's yett,
    To hold their Fête Champêtre.

When Politics came there, to mix
    And make his ether-stane, man!
He circled round the magic ground,
    But entrance found he nane, man;
He blush'd for shame, he quat his name,
    Forswore it, every letter,
Wi' humble prayer to join and share
    This festive Fête Champêtre.

EPISTLE TO ROBERT GRAHAM, ESQ., OF FINTRY
Requesting a Favour

When Nature her great Masterpiece design'd,
And fram'd her last, best work, the Human Mind—
Her eye intent on all the mazy Plan—
She form'd of various parts the various Man.
The Useful Many first, she calls them forth—
Plain plodding Industry and sober Worth;
Thence peasants, farmers, native sons of earth,
And Merchandise' whole genus take their birth:
Each prudent Cit a warm existence finds,
And all Mechanics' many-apron'd kinds.

Some other rarer Sorts are wanted yet,
The lead and buoy are needful to the net:
The *caput mortuum* of gross desires
Makes a material for mere knights and squires;
The Martial Phosphorus is taught to flow;
She kneads the lumpish philosophic dough,
Then marks th' unyielding mass with grave Designs—
Law, Physics, Politics, and deep Divines;
Last, she sublimes th' Aurora of the Poles—
The flashing elements of Female Souls.

 The order'd system fair before her stood,
Nature, well pleas'd, pronounc'd it very good;
Yet ere she gave creating labour o'er,
Half-jest, she tried one curious labour more:
Some spumy, fiery, *ignis fatuus* matter,
Such as the slightest breath of air might scatter,
With arch-alacrity and conscious glee
(Nature may have her whim as well as we,
Her Hogarth-art perhaps she meant to show it)
She forms the Thing and christens it—a Poet!—
Creature, tho' oft the prey of Care and Sorrow,
When blest today, unmindful of tomorrow—
A being form'd t' amuse his graver friends,
Admir'd and prais'd—and there the homage ends—
A mortal quite unfit for Fortune's strife,
Yet oft the sport of all the ills of life—
Prone to enjoy each pleasure riches give,
Yet haply wanting wherewithal to live—
Longing to wipe each tear, to heal each groan,
Yet frequent all unheeded in his own.

 But honest Nature is not quite a Turk,
She laugh'd at first, then felt for her poor Work:
Viewing the propless Climber of mankind,
She cast about a standard tree to find;
And to support his helpless woodbine state,
She clasp'd his tendrils round the Truly Great—
A title, and the only one I claim,
To lay strong hold for help on bounteous Graham.

 Pity the tuneful Muses' hapless train,
Weak, timid Landsmen on life's stormy main!
Their hearts no selfish stern absorbent stuff,
That never gives, tho' humbly takes enough;
The little Fate allows, they share as soon:
Unlike sage proverb'd wisdom's hard-wrung boon:
The world were blest did bliss on them depend—
Ah, that 'the Friendly e'er should want a Friend!'

Let Prudence number o'er each sturdy son
Who life and wisdom at one race begun,
Who feel by reason and who give by rule,

(Instinct's a brute, and Sentiment a fool!)
Who make poor 'Will do' wait upon 'I should'—
We own they're prudent, but who owns they're good?
Ye Wise Ones, hence! ye hurt the social eye;
God's image rudely etch'd on base alloy!
But come, ye who the godlike pleasure know—
Heaven's attribute distinguished—to bestow,
Whose arms of love would grasp all human race;
Come, thou who giv'st with all a courtier's grace,
Friend of my life, true Patron of my rhymes,
Prop of my dearest hopes for future times:

Why shrinks my soul, half blushing, half afraid,
Backward, abash'd to ask thy friendly aid?
I know my need, I know thy giving hand,
I tax thy friendship at thy kind command.
But there are such who court the tuneful Nine—
(Heavens! should the branded character be mine!)
Whose verse in manhood's pride sublimely flows,
Yet vilest reptiles in their begging prose.
Mark how their lofty independent spirit
Soars on the spurning wing of injur'd Merit!
Seek you the proofs in private life to find?
Pity the best of words should be but wind!
So, to heaven's gates the lark's shrill song ascends,
But grovelling on the earth the carol ends.
In all the clamorous cry of starving Want,
They dun Benevolence with shameless front:
Oblige them, patronise their tinsel lays,
They persecute you all your future days!—

Ere my poor soul such deep damnation stain
My horny fist assume the plough again;
The piebald jacket let me patch once more,
On eighteenpence a week I've liv'd before—
Tho', thanks to Heaven! I dare even that last shift,
I trust, meantime, my boon is in thy gift:
That, plac'd by thee upon the wish'd-for height,
Where—Man and Nature fairer in her sight—
My Muse may imp her wing for some sublimer flight.

THE DAY RETURNS
Tune—*Seventh of November*

The day returns, my bosom burns,
    The blissful day we twa did meet:
Tho' winter wild in tempest toil'd,
    Ne'er summer-sun was half sae sweet.
Than a' the pride that loads the tide,
    And crosses o'er the sultry line;
Than kingly robes, than crowns and globes,
    Heav'n gave me more—it made thee mine!

While day and night can bring delight,
 Or nature aught of pleasure give;
While joys above, my mind can move,
 For thee and thee alone I live!
When that grim foe of life below
 Comes in between to make us part,
The iron hand that breaks our band,
 It breaks my bliss—it breaks my heart!

A MOTHER'S LAMENT FOR THE DEATH OF HER SON
Tune—*Finlayston House*

Fate gave the word—the arrow sped,
 And pierc'd my darling's heart;
And with him all the joys are fled
 Life can to me impart.
By cruel hands the sapling drops,
 In dust dishonour'd laid;
So fell the pride of all my hopes—
 My age's future shade.

The mother-linnet in the brake
 Bewails her ravish'd young;
So I, for my lost darling's sake,
 Lament the live-day long.
Death, oft I've feared thy fatal blow.
 Now, fond, I bare my breast;
O, do thou kindly lay me low
 With him I love, at rest!

O WERE I ON PARNASSUS HILL
Tune—*My love is lost to me*

O were I on Parnassus hill,
Or had o' Helicon my fill,
That I might catch poetic skill,
 To sing how dear I love thee!
But Nith maun be my Muse's well,
My Muse maun be thy bonnie sel':
On Corsincon I'll glowr and spell,
 And write how dear I love thee.

Then come, sweet Muse, inspire my lay!
For a' the lee-lang simmer's day,
I couldna sing, I couldna say,
 How much, how dear, I love thee.
I see thee dancing o'er the green—
Thy waist sae jimp, thy limbs sae clean,
Thy tempting lips, thy roguish een—
 By Heaven and Earth I love thee!

By night, by day, a-field, at hame,
The thoughts o' thee my breast inflame;
And aye I muse and sing thy name—
    I only live to love thee!
Tho' I were doom'd to wander on,
Beyond the sea, beyond the sun;
Till my last weary sand was run—
    Till then—and then I love thee!

THE FALL OF THE LEAF

The lazy mist hangs from the brow of the hill,
Concealing the course of the dark-winding rill;
How languid the scenes, late so sprightly, appear,
As Autumn to Winter resigns the pale year.

The forests are leafless, the meadows are brown,
And all the gay foppery of summer is flown:
Apart let me wander, apart let me muse,
How quick Time is flying, how keen Fate pursues.

How long I have liv'd—but how much liv'd in vain;
How little of life's scanty span may remain;
What aspects, old Time, in his progress has worn;
What ties, cruel Fate, in my bosom has torn;
How foolish, or worse, till our summit is gain'd!
And downward, how weaken'd, how darken'd, how pain'd!
Life is not worth having with all it can give—
For something beyond it poor man sure must live.

I REIGN IN JEANIE'S BOSOM

Louis, what reck I by thee,
    Or Geordie on his ocean?
Dyvor, beggar louns to me—,
    I reign in Jeanie's bosom!

Let her crown my love her law,
    And in her breast enthrone me:
Kings and nations—swith, awa!
    Reif randies, I disown ye!

IT IS NA, JEAN, THY BONNIE FACE[1]

It is na, Jean, thy bonnie face,
    Nor shape that I admire;
Altho' thy beauty and thy grace
    Might weel awauk desire.

Something, in ilka part o' thee,
    To praise, to love, I find;
But dear as is thy form to me,
    Still dearer is thy mind.

Nae mair ungenerous wish I hae,
    Nor stronger in my breast,
Than, if I canna make thee sae,
    At least to see thee blest.

Content am I, if heaven shall give
    But happiness, to thee;
And as wi' thee I'd wish to live,
    For thee I'd bear to die.

[1] 'These were originally English verses: I gave them their Scots dress.'—R.B.

AULD LANG SYNE

Chorus: For auld lang syne, my dear,
    For auld lang syne.
We'll tak a cup o' kindness yet,
    For auld lang syne.

Should auld acquaintance be forgot
    And never brought to mind?
Should auld acquaintance be forgot,
    And auld lang syne?

And surely ye'll be your pint stoup,
    And surely I'll be mine;
And we'll tak a cup o' kindness yet,
    For auld lang syne.

We twa hae run about the braes,
    And pou'd the gowans fine;
But we've wander'd mony a weary fit,
    Sin' auld lang syne.

We twa hae paidl'd in the burn,
    Frae morning sun till dine;
But seas between us braid hae roar'd
    Sin' auld lang syne.

And there's a hand, my trusty fiere!
    And gie's a hand o' thine!
And we'll tak a right gude-willie waught,
    For auld lang syne.

MY BONNIE MARY
Tune—*The secret kiss*

Go, fetch to me a pint o' wine,
    And fill it in a silver tassie,
That I may drink before I go,
    A service to my bonnie lassie.
The boat rocks at the pier o' Leith,
    Fu' loud the wind blaws frae the Ferry;
The ship rides by the Berwick-law,
    And I maun leave my bonnie Mary.

The trumpets sound, the banners fly,
    The glittering spears are rankéd ready:
The shouts o' war are heard afar,
    The battle closes deep and bloody;
It's not the roar o' sea or shore,
    Wad mak me langer wish to tarry;
Nor shouts o' war that's heard afar—
    It's leaving thee, my bonnie Mary!

ELEGY ON THE YEAR 1788

For lords or kings I dinna mourn,
E'en let them die—for that they're born:
But oh! prodigious to reflect,
A towmont, sirs, is gane to wreck!
O Eighty-eight, in thy sma' space,
What dire events hae taken place!
Of what enjoyments thou hast reft us!
In what a pickle thou has left us!

The Spanish empire's tint a head,[1]
An' my auld teethless Bawtie's dead:
The tulzie's teugh 'tween Pitt an' Fox,
An' our gudewife's wee birdie cocks;
The tane is game, a bluidy devil,
But to the hen-birds unco civil;
The tither's dour, has nae sic breedin',
But better stuff ne'er claw'd a middin.

Ye ministers, come mount the pu'pit,
And cry till ye be hearse and roupit,
For Eighty-eight he wished you weel,
An' gied ye a' baith gear an' meal;
E'en mony a plack, and mony a peck,
Ye ken yoursels, for little feck!

Ye bonnie lasses, dight your een,
For some o' you hae tint a frien';
In Eighty-eight, ye ken, was ta'en,
What ye'll ne'er hae to gie again.

Observe the very nowt and sheep,
How dowff an' dowie now they creep;
Nay, even the yirth itsel' does cry,
For Embro' wells are grutten dry.[2]

O Eighty-nine, thou's but a bairn,
An' no owre auld, I hope, to learn!
Thou beardless boy, I pray tak care,
Thou now hast got thy daddy's chair;
Nae handcuff'd, mizzl'd, hap-shackl'd Regent,[3]
But, like himsel', a full free agent.
Be sure ye follow out the plan
Nae waur than he did, honest man!
As muckle better as you can.

January, 1, 1789.

---

[1] Charles III of Spain died 13 December 1788.
[2] The Edinburgh newspapers in December 1788 refer to the hard frost having frozen up the wells.
[3] In November 1788, King George III showed symptoms of mental disease, and proposals for a regent were discussed.

THE HENPECK'D HUSBAND

Curs'd be the man, the poorest wretch in life,
The crouching vassal to the tyrant wife,
Who has no will but by her high permission;
Who has not sixpence but in her possession;
Who must to her his dear friend's secret tell;
Who dreads a curtain lecture worse than hell.
Were such the wife had fallen to my part,
I'd break her spirit or I'd break her heart;
I'd charm her with the magic of a switch,
I'd kiss her maids, and kick the perverse bitch.

VERSICLES ON SIGNPOSTS

He looked just as your signpost Lions do,
With aspect fierce, and quite as harmless too.

So heavy, passive to the tempest's shocks,
Dull on the sign-post stands the stupid ox.

His face with smile eternal drest,
Just like the landlord's to his guest,
High as they hang with creaking din,
To index out the country Inn.

A head, pure, sinless quite of brain and soul,
The very image of a barber's poll;
Just shews a human face, and wears a wig,
And looks, when well friseur'd, amazing big.

ROBIN SHURE IN HAIRST

Chorus: Robin shure in hairst,
   I shure wi' him;
Fient a heuk had I,
   Yet I stack by him.

I gaed up to Dunse,
   To warp a wab o' plaiden,
At his daddie's yett,
   Wha met me but Robin:

Was na Robin bauld,
   Though I was a cotter,
Play'd me sic a trick,
   An' me the El'er's dochter?

Robin promis'd me
   A' my winter vittle;
Fient haet he had but three
   Goose-feathers and a whittle!

ODE
Sacred to the Memory of Mrs Oswald of Auchencruive

Dweller in yon dungeon dark,
Hangman of creation! mark,
Who in widow-weeds appears,
Laden with unhonour'd years,
Noosing with care a bursting purse,
Baited with many a deadly curse?

Strophe

View the wither'd beldam's face—
Can thy keen inspection trace
Aught of Humanity's sweet, melting grace?
Note that eye, 'tis rheum o'erflows;
    Pity's flood there never rose.
    See those hands, ne'er stretch'd to save,
    Hands that took—but never gave.
    Keeper of Mammon's iron chest,
    Lo, there she goes, unpitied and unblest,
She goes, but not to realms of everlasting rest!

Antistrophe

Plunderer of Armies, lift thine eyes,
    (A while forbear, ye torturing fiends),
Seest thou whose step, unwilling, hither bends?
No fallen angel, hurl'd from upper skies;
    'Tis thy trusty quondam Mate,
    Doom'd to share thy fiery fate;
    She, tardy, hell-ward plies.

Epode

And are they of no more avail,
Ten thousand glittering pounds a year?
    In other worlds can Mammon fail,
        Omnipotent as he is here!
O, bitter mockery of the pompous bier,
    While down the wretched vital part is driven!
The cave-lodg'd beggar, with a conscience clear,
    Expires in rags, unknown, and goes to Heaven.

Pegasus at Wanlockhead

With Pegasus upon a day,
    Apollo, weary flying,
(Thro' frosty hills the journey lay),
    On foot the way was plying.

Poor slipshod giddy Pegasus
    Was but a sorry walker;
To Vulcan then Apollo gaes,
    To get a frosty caulker.

Obliging Vulcan fell to wark,
    Threw by his coat and bonnet,
And did Sol's business in a crack;
    Sol paid him with a sonnet.

Ye Vulcan's sons of Wanlockhead,
    Pity my sad disaster;
My Pegasus is poorly shod—
    I'll pay you like my master.

PASSION'S CRY

'I cannot but remember such things were,
And were most dear to me'

In vain would Prudence with decorous sneer
Point out a cens'ring world, and bid me fear:
Above that world on wings of love I rise:
I know its worst and can that worst despise—
Wrong'd, injur'd, shunn'd, unpitied, unredrest.
'The mock'd quotation of the scorner's jest,'
Let Prudence' direst bodements on me fall,
Clarinda, rich reward! o'erpays them all.
As low-borne mists before the sun remove,
So shines, so reigns unrivalled mighty LOVE.
In vain the laws their feeble force oppose;
Chain'd at his feet, they groan Love's vanquish'd foes;
In vain Religion meets my shrinking eye;
I dare not combat, but I turn and fly:
Conscience in vain upbraids th' unhallowed fire;
Love grasps his scorpions, stifl'd they expire:
Reason drops headlong from his sacred throne,
Thy dear idea reigns, and reigns alone;
Each thought intoxicated homage yields,
And riots wanton in forbidden fields.

By all on High, adoring mortals know!
By all the conscious villain fears below!
By what, Alas! much more my soul alarms,
My doubtful hopes once more to fill thy arms!
E'en shouldst thou, false, forswear each guilty tie,
Thine, and thine only, I must live and die!

SHE'S FAIR AND FAUSE

She's fair and fause that causes my smart,
    I lo'ed her meikle and lang;
She's broken her vow, she's broken my heart,
    And I may e'en gae hang.
A coof cam in wi' routh o' gear,
And I hae tint my dearest dear;
But woman is but warld's gear,
    Sae let the bonnie lass gang.

Whae'er ye be that woman love,
    To this be never blind;
Nae ferlie 'tis tho' fickle she prove,
    A woman has 't by kind.
O woman lovely, woman fair,
An angel form's faun to thy share,
'Twad been o'er meikle to gi'en thee mair—
    I mean an angel mind.

IMPROMPTU LINES TO CAPTAIN RIDDELL
On returning a Newspaper.

Ellisland, Monday morning.
 Your News and Review, Sir.
 I've read through and through, Sir,
With little admiring or blaming;
 The Papers are barren
 Of home-news or foreign,
No murders or rapes worth the naming.

 Our friends the Reviewers,
 Those chippers and hewers,
Are judges of mortar and stone, Sir;
 But of *meet* or *unmeet*,
 In a fabric complete,
I'll boldly pronounce they are none, Sir;

 My goose-quill too rude is
 To tell all your goodness
Bestow'd on your servant, the Poet;
 Would to God I had one
 Like a beam of the Sun,
And then all the World, Sir, should know it!
Robt. Burns

LINES TO JOHN McMURDO, ESQ. OF DRUMLANRIG[1]
Sent with some of the Author's Poems.

 O could I give thee India's wealth,
  As I this trifle send!
 Because thy joy in both would be—
  To share them with a friend.

 But golden sands did never grace
  The Heliconian stream;
 Then take what Gold could never buy—
  An honest Bard's esteem.

[1] Chamberlain at Drumlanrig Castle, seat of the Duke of Queensberry.

RHYMING REPLY TO A NOTE FROM CAPTAIN RIDDELL

Ellisland
 Dear Sir, at onie time or tide,
 I'd rather sit wi' you than ride,
  Though 'twere wi' royal Geordie:
 And trowth, your kindness, soon and late,
 Aft gars me to mysel' look blate—
  The Lord in Heav'n reward ye!
R. Burns.

CALEDONIA—A BALLAD
Tune—*Caledonian Hunt's delight*

There was once a time, but old Time was then young,
    That brave Caledonia, the chief of her line,
From some of your northern deities sprung,
    (Who knows not that brave Caledonia's divine?)
From Tweed to the Orcadés was her domain,
    To hunt, or to pasture, or do what she would:
Her heav'nly relations there fixed her reign,
    And pledg'd her their godheads to warrant it good.

A lambkin in peace, but a lion in war,
    The pride of her kindred, the heroine grew:
Her grandsire, old Odin, triumphantly swore,
    'Whoe'er shall provoke thee, th' encounter shall rue!'
With tillage or pasture at times she would sport,
    To feed her fair flocks by her green rustling corn;
But chiefly the woods were her fav'rite resort,
    Her darling amusement, the hounds and the horn.

Long quiet she reign'd; till thitherward steers
    A flight of bold eagles from Adria's strand:[1]
Repeated, successive, for many long years,
    They darken'd the air, and they plunder'd the land:
Their pounces were murder, and terror their cry,
    They'd conquer'd and ruin'd a world beside;
She took to her hills, and her arrows let fly,
    The daring invaders they fled or they died.

The Cameleon-Savage disturb'd her repose,[2]
    With tumult, disquiet, rebellion and strife;
Provok'd beyond bearing, at last she arose,
    And robb'd him at once of his hopes and his life:
The Anglian lion, the terror of France,
    Oft prowling, ensanguin'd the Tweed's silver flood;
But, taught by the bright Caledonian lance,
    He learned to fear in his own native wood.

The fell Harpy-raven took wing from the north,
    The scourge of the seas and the dread of the shore;[3]
The wild Scandinavian boar[4] issu'd forth
    To wanton in carnage and wallow in gore:
O'er countries and kingdoms their fury prevail'd,
    No arts could appease them, no arms could repel;
But brave Caledonia in vain they assail'd,
    As Largs well can witness, and Loncartie tell.[5]

[1] The Romans.
[2] The Picts.
[3] The Saxons.
[4] The Danes.
[5] Two famous battles in which the Vikings were defeated.

Thus bold, independent, unconquer'd and free,
    Her bright course of glory for ever shall run:
For brave Caledonia immortal must be;
    I'll prove it from Euclid as clear as the sun:
Rectangle-triangle, the figure we'll chuse:
    The upright is Chance, and old Time is the Base;
But brave Caledonia's the Hypothenuse;
    Then, ergo, she'll match them and match them always!

TO MISS CRUICKSHANK, A VERY YOUNG LADY
Written on the Blank Leaf of a Book, presented to her by the Author.

Beauteous Rosebud, young and gay,
Blooming in thy early May,
Never may'st thou, lovely flower,
Chilly shrink in sleety shower!
Never Boreas' hoary path,
Never Eurus' pois'nous breath,
Never baleful stellar lights,
Taint thee with untimely blights!
Never, never reptile thief
Riot on thy virgin leaf!
Nor even Sol too fiercely view
Thy bosom blushing still with dew!

May'st thou long, sweet crimson gem,
Richly deck thy native stem;
Till some evening, sober, calm,
Dropping dews, and breathing balm,
While all around the woodland rings,
And every bird thy requiem sings;
Thou, amid the dirgeful sound,
Shed thy dying honours round,
And resign to parent Earth
The loveliest form she e'er gave birth.

BEWARE O' BONNIE ANN

Ye gallants bright, I rede you right,
    Beware o' bonnie Ann;
Her comely face sae fu' o' grace,
    Your heart she will trepan:
Her een sae bright, like stars by night,
    Her skin is like the swan;
Sae jimply lac'd her genty waist,
    That sweetly ye might span.

Youth, grace and love attendant move,
    And pleasure leads the van:
In a' their charms, and conquering arms,
    They wait on bonnie Ann.

The captive bands may chain the hands,
    But love enslaves the man:
Ye gallants braw, I rede you a',
    Beware o' bonnie Ann!

ODE TO THE DEPARTED REGENCY BILL[1]
March 1789

Daughter of Chaos' doting years,
Nurse of ten thousand hopes and fears,
Whether thy airy, insubstantial shade
(The rights of sepulture now duly paid)
    Spread abroad its hideous form
    On the roaring civil storm,
    Deafening din and warring rage
    Factions wild with factions wage;
Or underground, deep-sunk, profound,
    Among the demons of the earth,
With groans that make the mountains shake,
    Thou mourn thy ill-starr'd, blighted birth;
Or in the uncreated Void,
    Where seeds of future being fight,
With lighten'd step thou wander wide,
    To greet thy Mother—Ancient Night,
    And as each jarring, monster mass is past,
    Fond recollect what once thou wast:
In manner due, beneath this sacred oak,
Hear, Spirit, hear! thy presence I invoke!

    By a Monarch's heaven-struck fate,
    By a disunited State;
    By a generous Prince's wrongs;
    By a Senate's strife of tongues;
    By a Premier's sullen pride,
    Louring on the changing tide;
    By dread Thurlow's powers to awe
    Rhetoric, blasphemy and law;
        By the turbulent ocean—
        A Nation's commotion,
        By the harlot-caresses
        Of borough addresses,
        By days few and evil,
        (Thy portion, poor devil!)
By Power, Wealth, and Show,
    (The Gods by men adored,)
By nameless Poverty,
    (Their hell abhorred,)
    By all they hope, by all they fear,
    Hear! and appear!

[1] This poem alludes to Charles Fox and the Portland Party and their debates with Pitt and schemings during the illness and on to the 'convalescence' of King George III.

Stare not on me, thou ghastly Power!
   Nor grim with chain'd defiance lour:
No Babel-structure would I build
   Where, order exil'd from his native sway,
Confusion may the REGENT-sceptre wield,
   While all would rule and none obey:
Go, to the world of Man relate
The story of thy sad, eventful fate;
And call presumptuous Hope to hear
And bid him check his blind career;
And tell the sore-prest sons of Care,
Never, never to despair!

Paint Charles' speed on wings of fire,
The object of his fond desire,
Beyond his boldest hopes, at hand:
Paint all the triumph of the Portland Band;
Mark how they lift the joy-elated voice
And how their num'rous creditors rejoice:
But just as hopes to warm enjoyment rise,
Cry CONVALESCENCE! and the vision flies.

Then next pourtray a dark'ning twilight gloom,
   Eclipsing sad a gay, rejoicing morn,
While proud Ambition to th' untimely tomb
   By gnashing, grim, despairing fiends is borne:
Paint ruin, in the shape of high D[undas]
   Gaping with giddy terror o'er the brow;
In vain he struggles, the Fates behind him press,
   And clamorous Hell yawns for her prey below:
How fallen That, whose pride late scal'd the skies!
And This, like Lucifer, no more to rise!
   Again pronounce the powerful word;
See Day, triumphant from the night, restored.

Then know this truth, ye Sons of Men!
   (Thus ends thy moral tale),
Your darkest terrors may be vain,
   Your brightest hopes may fail.

EPISTLE TO JAMES TENNANT OF GLENCONNER[1]

Auld comrade dear and brither sinner,
How's a' the folk about Glenconner?
How do ye this blae eastlin win',
That's like to blaw a body blin'?
For me, my faculties are frozen,
My dearest member nearly dozen'd.
I've sent you here, by Johnie Simson,
Twa sage philosophers to glimpse on:

[1] An old friend of Burns, who assisted him in the choice of Ellisland.

Smith,[1] wi' his sympathetic feeling,
An' Reid,[2] to common sense appealing.
Philosophers have fought an' wrangled,
An' meikle Greek an' Latin mangled,
Till wi' their logic-jargon tir'd,
An' in the depth of science mir'd,
To common sense they now appeal,
What wives and wabsters see an' feel.
But, hark ye, friend! I charge you strictly,
Peruse them, an' return them quickly:
For now I'm grown sae cursèd douce
I pray an' ponder butt the house;
My shins, my lane, I there sit roastin',
Perusing Bunyan, Brown[3] an' Boston,[4]
Till by an' by, if I haud on,
I'll grunt a real gospel groan:
Already I begin to try it,
To cast my e'en up like a pyet,
When by the gun she tumbles o'er,
Flutt'ring an' gasping in her gore:
Sae shortly you shall see me bright,
A burning an' a shining light.

My heart-warm love to guid auld Glen,[5]
The ace an' wale of honest men:
When bending down wi' auld grey hairs,
Beneath the load of years and cares,
May He who made him still support him,
An' views beyond the grave comfort him;
His worthy fam'ly far and near,
God bless them a' wi' grace and gear!

My auld schoolfellow, Preacher Willie,[6]
The manly tar, my mason billie,[7]
And Auchenbay,[8] I wish him joy;
If he's a parent, lass or boy,
May he be dad, and Meg the mither,[9]
Just five and forty years thegither!
And no forgetting wabster Charlie,
I'm tauld he offers very fairly.
An' Lord, remember singing Sannock,[10]
Wi' hale breeks, saxpence an' a bannock!
And next, my auld acquaintance, Nancy,[11]
Since she is fitted to her fancy,
An' her kind stars hae airted till her
A guid chiel wi' a pickle siller.
My kindest, best respects, I sen' it,

---

[1] Adam Smith.
[2] Dr Thomas Reid.
[3] John Brown.
[4] Thomas Boston.
[5] John Tennant.
[6] Reverend William Tennant.
[7] David Tennant.
[8] John Tennant Jr.
[9] Margaret Colville.
[10] Robert Tennant.
[11] Agnes Tennant.

To cousin Kate, an' sister Janet:
Tell them, frae me, wi' chiels be cautious,
For, faith, they'll aiblins fin' them fashious;
To grant a heart is fairly civil,
But to grant a maidenhead's the devil!
An' lastly, Jamie, for yoursel,
May guardian angels tak a spell,
An' steer you seven miles south o' hell;
But first, before you see heaven's glory,
May ye get monie a merry story,
Monie a laugh, and monie a drink,
An' aye eneugh o' needfu' clink.

    Now fare ye weel, an' joy be wi' you:
For my sake this I beg it o' you,
Assist poor Simson a' ye can;
Ye'll fin' him just an honest man.
Sae I conclude, and quat my chanter,
Your's, saint or sinner,
                    Rob the Ranter.

A New Psalm For The Chapel Of Kilmarnock
On the Thanksgiving-Day for His Majesty's Recovery[1]

O sing a new song to the Lord!
    Make, all and every one,
A joyful noise, even for the king
    His restoration.

The sons of Belial in the land
    Did set their heads together;
Come, let us sweep them off, said they,
    Like an o'erflowing river.

They set their heads together, I say,
    They set their heads together;
On right, on left, on every hand,
    We saw none to deliver.

Thou madest strong two chosen Ones
    To quell the Wicked's pride;
That Young Man, great in Issachar,
    The burden-bearing tribe.

And him, among the Princes chief
    In our Jerusalem,
The judge that's mighty in thy law,
    The man that fears thy name.

[1] King George III went on 23 April 1789 to St Paul's Cathedral in London to return thanks for his recovery. These pompous ceremonies were by no means pleasing to Burns.

Yet they, even they, with all their strength,
    Began to faint and fail:
Even as two howling, ravening wolves
    To dogs do turn their tail.

Th' ungodly o'er the just prevail'd,
    For so thou hadst appointed;
That thou might'st greater glory give
    Unto thine own anointed.

And now thou hast restor'd our State,
    Pity our Kirk also;
For she by tribulations
    Is now brought very low.

Consume that high-place, Patronage,
    From off thy holy hill;
And in thy fury burn the book—
    Even of that man McGill.[1]

Now hear our prayer, accept our song,
    And fight thy chosen's battle:
We seek but little, Lord, from thee,
    Thou kens we get as little.

[1] Dr William McGill of Ayr, who published in 1784 an essay on the death of Jesus Christ, which led to a charge of heresy against him. Burns took up his cause in 'The Kirk Of Scotland's Alarm' (*see* page 262).

SKETCH IN VERSE
Inscribed to the Right Hon. C. J. Fox

How Wisdom and Folly meet, mix and unite,
How Virtue and Vice blend their black and their white,
How Genius, th' illustrious father of fiction,
Confounds rule and law, reconciles contradiction,
I sing: If these mortals, the critics, should bustle,
I care not, not I—let the critics go whistle!

    But now for a Patron whose name and whose glory
At once may illustrate and honour my story.

    Thou first of our orators, first of our wits;
Yet whose parts and acquirements seem just lucky hits;
With knowledge so vast and with judgment so strong,
No man with the half of 'em e'er could go wrong;
With passions so potent and fancies so bright,
No man with the half of 'em e'er could go right;
A sorry, poor, misbegot son of the Muses,
For using thy name, offers fifty excuses.

    Good Lord, what is Man! for as simple he looks,
Do but try to develop his hooks and his crooks,
With his depths and his shallows, his good and his evil,
All in all he's a problem must puzzle the devil.

On his one ruling passion Sir Pope hugely labours,
That, like th' old Hebrew walking switch, eats up its neighbours:
Human nature's his show-box—your friend, would you know him?
Pull the string, Ruling Passion the picture will show him.
What pity in rearing so beauteous a system,
One trifling particular, Truth, should have miss'd him;
For spite of his fine theoretic positions,
Mankind is a science defies definitions.

Some sort all our qualities each to its tribe,
And think human nature they truly describe;
Have you found this or t'other? There's more in the wind,
As by one drunken fellow his comrades you'll find.
But such is the flaw, or the depth of the plan,
In the make of that wonderful creature called Man,
No two virtues, whatever relation they claim,
Nor even two different shades of the same,
Though like as was ever twin brother to brother,
Possessing the one shall imply you've the other.

But truce with abstraction, and truce with a Muse,
Whose rhymes you'll perhaps, Sir, ne'er deign to peruse:
Will you leave your justings, your jars and your quarrels,
Contending with Billy for proud-nodding laurels?
(My much honour'd Patron, believe your poor Poet,
Your courage much more than your prudence you show it;
In vain with Squire Billy for laurels you struggle,
He'll have them by fair trade, if not, he will smuggle;
Not cabinets even of kings would conceal 'em,
He'd up the back stairs and by God he would steal 'em!
Then feats like Squire Billy's you ne'er can achieve 'em;
It is not, outdo him—the task is, out-thieve him!)

THE WOUNDED HARE

'I have just put the last hand to a little poem, which I think will be something to your taste. One morning lately, as I was out pretty early in the fields, sowing aome grass-seeds, I heard the burst of a shot from a neighbouring plantation, and presently a poor little wounded hare came crippling by me. You will guess my indignation at the inhuman fellow who could shoot a hare at this season, when all of them have young ones. Indeed, there is something in this business of destroying, for our sport, individuals in the animal creation that do not injure us materially, which I could never reconcile to my ideas of virtue.'

Inhuman man! curse on thy barb'rous art,
   And blasted be thy murder-aiming eye;
   May never pity soothe thee with a sigh,
Nor ever pleasure glad thy cruel heart!

Go live, poor wanderer of the wood and field,
   The bitter little that of life remains:
   No more the thickening brakes and verdant plains
To thee shall home, or food, or pastime yield.

Seek, mangled wretch, some place of wonted rest,
    No more of rest, but now thy dying bed!
    The sheltering rushes whistling o'er thy head,
The cold earth with thy bloody bosom prest.

Oft as by winding Nith I, musing, wait
    The sober eve, or hail the cheerful dawn,
    I'll miss thee sporting o'er the dewy lawn,
And curse the ruffian's aim and mourn thy hapless fate.

DELIA, AN ODE

'To the Editor of *The Star.*—Mr Printer—If the productions of a simple ploughman can merit a place in the same paper with Sylvester Otway, and the other favourites of the Muses who illuminate the *Star* with the lustre of genius, your insertion of the enclosed trifle will be succeeded by future communications from—Yours, etc, R. Burns.'

Fair the face of orient day,
    Fair the tints of op'ning rose;
But fairer still my Delia dawns,
    More lovely far her beauty blows.

Sweet the lark's wild-warbled lay,
    Sweet the tinkling rill to hear;
But, Delia, more delightful still,
    Steal thine accents on mine ear.

The flower-enamour'd busy bee
    The rosy banquet loves to sip;
Sweet the streamlet's limpid lapse
    To the sun-brown'd Arab's lip.

But, Delia, on thy balmy lips
    Let me, no vagrant insect, rove!
O let me steal one liquid kiss,
    For Oh! my soul is parch'd with love!

THE GARD'NER WI' HIS PAIDLE
Tune—*The gardener's march*

When rosy May comes in wi' flowers,
To deck her gay, green-spreading bowers,
Then busy, busy are his hours,
    The Gard'ner wi' his paidle.

The crystal waters gently fa',
The merry bards are lovers a',
The scented breezes round him blaw—
    The Gard'ner wi' his paidle.

When purple morning starts the hare
To steal upon her early fare,
Then thro' the dews he maun repair—
    The Gard'ner wi' his paidle.

When Day, expiring in the west,
The curtain draws o' Nature's rest,
He flies to her arms he lo'es the best,
    The Gard'ner wi' his paidle.

ON A BANK OF FLOWERS

On a bank of flowers, in a summer day,
    For summer lightly drest,
The youthful, blooming Nelly lay,
    With love and sleep opprest;

When Willie, wand'ring thro' the wood,
Who for her favour oft had sued;
    He gaz'd, he wish'd
    He fear'd, he blush'd,
And trembled where he stood.

Her closéd eyes, like weapons sheath'd,
    Were seal'd in soft repose;
Her lip, still as she fragrant breath'd,
    It richer dyed the rose;
The springing lilies, sweetly prest,
Wild-wanton kiss'd her rival breast;
    He gaz'd, he wish'd,
    He mear'd, he blush'd,
His bosom ill at rest.

Her robes light-waving in the breeze,
    Her tender limbs embrace;
Her lovely form, her native ease,
    All harmony and grace;
Tumultuous tides his pulses roll,
A faltering, ardent kiss he stole;
    He gaz'd, he wish'd,
    He fear'd, he blush'd,
And sigh'd his very soul.

As flies the partridge from the brake,
    On fear-inspiréd wings,
So Nelly, starting, half-awake,
    Away affrighted springs;
But Willie follow'd, as he should;
He overtook her in the wood;
    He vow'd, he pray'd,
    He found the maid
Forgiving all and good.

YOUNG JOCKIE WAS THE BLYTHEST LAD

Young Jockie was the blythest lad,
    In a' our town or here awa;
Fu' blythe he whistled at the gaud,
    Fu' lightly danc'd he in the ha'.
He roos'd my een sae bonnie blue,
    He roos'd my waist sae genty sma';
An' aye my heart cam to my mou',
    When ne'er a body heard or saw.

My Jockie toils upon the plain,
    Thro' wind and weet, thro' frost and snaw;
And o'er the lea I leuk fu' fain
    When Jockie's owsen hameward ca'.

An' aye the night comes round again,
 When in his arms he taks me a';
An' aye he vows he'll be my ain
 As lang's he has a breath to draw.

THE BANKS OF NITH
Tune—*Robie donna gorach*

The Thames flows proudly to the sea,
 Where royal cities stately stand;
But sweeter flows the Nith to me,
 Where Comyns ance had high command.
When shall I see that honour'd land,
 That winding stream I love so dear!
Must wayward Fortune's adverse hand
 For ever, ever keep me here?

How lovely, Nith, thy fruitful vales,
 Where bounding hawthorns gaily bloom;
And sweetly spread thy sloping dales,
 Where lambkins wanton through the broom!
Tho' wandering now must be my doom,
 Far from thy bonnie banks and braes,
May there my latest hours consume,
 Amang the friends of early days!

JAMIE, COME TRY ME

Chorus: Jamie, come try me,
 Jamie, come try me,
 If thou would win my love,
 Jamie, come try me.

If thou should ask my love,
 Could I deny thee?
If thou would win my love,
 Jamie, come try me!

If thou should kiss me, love,
 Wha could espy thee?
If thou wad be my love,
 Jamie, come try me!

I LOVE MY LOVE IN SECRET

Chorus: My Sandy O, my Sandy O,
My bonnie, bonnie Sandy O;
Tho' the love that I owe to thee I dare na show,
Yet I love my love in secret, my Sandy O.

My Sandy gied to me a ring,
Was a' beset wi' diamonds fine;
But I gied him a far better thing,
I gied my heart in pledge o' his ring.

My Sandy brak a piece o' gowd,
While down his cheeks the saut tears row'd;
He took a hauf, and gied it to me,
And I'll keep it till the hour I die.

SWEET TIBBIE DUNBAR
Tune—*Johny McGill*

O wilt thou go wi' me, sweet Tibbie Dunbar?
O wilt thou go wi' me, sweet Tibbie Dunbar?
Wilt thou ride on a horse, or be drawn in a car,
Or walk by my side, O sweet Tibbie Dunbar?

I care na thy daddie, his lands and his money;
I care na thy kin, sae high and sae lordly;
But sae that thou'lt hae me for better for waur,
And come in thy coatie, sweet Tibbie Dunbar.

THE CAPTAIN'S LADY
Tune—*Mount your baggage*

Chorus: O mount and go,
Mount and make you ready,
O mount and go,
And be the Captain's lady.

When the drums do beat,
And the cannons rattle,
Thou shalt sit in state,
And see thy love in battle.

When the vanquish'd foe
Sues for peace and quiet,
To the shades we'll go,
And in love enjoy it.

JOHN ANDERSON, MY JO

John Anderson, my jo, John,
When we were first acquent,
Your locks were like the raven,
Your bonnie brow was brent;
But now your brow is beld, John,
Your locks are like the snaw;
But blessings on your frosty pow,
John Anderson, my jo.

John Anderson, my jo, John,
We clamb the hill thegither;
And monie a cantie day, John,
We've had wi' ane anither:
Now we maun totter down, John,
And hand in hand we'll go,
And sleep thegither at the foot,
John Anderson, my jo.

MY LOVE, SHE'S BUT A LASSIE YET
Tune—*Lady Badinscoth's reel*

My love, she's but a lassie yet,
My love, she's but a lassie yet;
We'll let her stand a year or twa,
She'll no be half sae saucy yet.

I rue the day I sought her, O!
I rue the day I sought her, O!
Wha gets her needs na say she's woo'd,
    But he may say he's bought her, O.

Come draw a drap o' the best o't yet,
Come draw a drap o' the best o't yet,
Gae seek for pleasure whare you will,
    But here I never miss'd it yet,

We're a' dry wi' drinkin o't,
We're a' dry wi' drinkin o't;
The minister kiss'd the fiddler's wife;
    He could na preach for thinkin o't.

TAM GLEN
Tune—*The mucking o' Geordie's byre*

My heart is a-breaking, dear tittie,
    Some counsel unto me come len',
To anger them a' is a pity,
    But what will I do wi' Tam Glen?

I'm thinking, wi' sic a braw fellow,
    In poortith I might mak a fen';
What care I in riches to wallow,
    If I mauna marry Tam Glen.

There's Lowrie the Laird o' Dumeller—
    'Gude day to you, brute!' he comes ben:
He brags and he blaws o' his siller,
    But when will he dance like Tam Glen?

My minnie does constantly deave me
    And bids me beware o' young men;
They flatter, she says, to deceive me,
    But wha can think sae o' Tam Glen?

My daddie says, gin I'll forsake him,
    He'd gie me gude hunder marks ten;
But, if it's ordain'd I maun take him,
    O wha will I get but Tam Glen?

Yestreen at the Valentine's dealing,
    My heart to my mou' gied a sten';
For thrice I drew ane without failing,
    And thrice it was written 'Tam Glen'!

The last Halloween I was waukin
    My droukit sark-sleeve, as ye ken,
His likeness came up the house staukin,
    And the very grey breeks o' Tam Glen!

Come, counsel, dear tittie, don't tarry;
　　I'll gie ye my bonnie black hen,
Gif ye will advise me to marry
　　The lad I lo'e dearly, Tam Glen.

CARL, AN THE KING COME

Chorus: Carl, an the King come,
　　Carl, an the King come,
Thou shalt dance, and I will sing,
　　Carl, an the King come.

An somebodie were come again,
Then somebodie maun cross the main,
And every man shall hae his ain,
　　Carl, an the King come.

I trow we swappéd for the worse,
We gae the boot and better horse;
And that we'll tell them at the cross,
　　Carl, an the King come.

Coggie, an the King come,
Coggie, an the King come,
I'se be fou, and thou'se be toom
　　Coggie, an the King come.
　　　　Coggie, an the King come, etc.

THE LADDIE'S DEAR SEL'[1]
Tune—*A Gaelic air*

There's a youth in this city, it were a great pity
　　That he from our lassies should wander awa';
For he's bonnie and braw, weel-favour'd with a',
　　An' his hair has a natural buckle an' a'.
His coat is the hue o' his bonnet sae blue;
　　His fecket is white as the new-driven snaw;
His hose they are blae, and his shoon like the slae,
　　And his clear siller buckles, they dazzle us a'.

For beauty and fortune the laddie's been courtin;
　　Weel-featur'd, weel-tocher'd, weel-mounted an' braw;
But chiefly the siller that gars him gang till her—
　　The penny's the jewel that beautifies a'.
There's Meg wi' the mailen that fain wad a haen him,
　　And Susie, wha's daddie was laird o' the Ha';
There's lang-tocher'd Nancy maist fetters his fancy—
　　But the laddie's dear sel', he loes dearest of a'.

---

[1] The first half stanza of the song is old, and the rest is mine. The air is claimed by Neil Gow, who calls it the lament for his brother.—R.B.

WHISTLE O'ER THE LAVE O'T

First when Maggie was my care,
Heaven, I thought, was in her air;
Now we're married—speir nae mair—
    But whistle o'er the lave o't!

Meg was meek, and Meg was mild,
Sweet and harmless as a child—
Wiser men than me's beguil'd;
    Whistle o'er the lave o't!

How we live, my Meg and me,
How we love, and how we gree,
I carena by how few may see—
    Whistle o'er the lave o't!

Wha I wish were maggot's meat,
Dish'd up in her winding sheet,
I could write—but Meg maun see't—
    Whistle o'er the lave o't!

EPPIE ADAIR

Chorus: An' O, my Eppie,
My jewel, my Eppie!
Wha wad na be happy
    Wi' Eppie Adair?

By love and by beauty,
By law and by duty,
I swear to be true to
    My Eppie Adair!

A' pleasure exile me,
Dishonour defile me,
If e'er I beguile ye,
    My Eppie Adair!

EPIGRAM ON FRANCIS GROSE THE ANTIQUARY[1]

The devil got notice that Grose was a-dying,
So whip! at the summons, old-Satan came flying;
But when he approach'd where poor Francis lay moaning,
And saw each bed-post with its burden a-groaning,
Astonish'd, confounded, cries Satan—'By God,
I'll want 'im ere I take such a damnable load!'

[1] Francis Grose, an Englishman who had seen better days and taken up authorship. He wrote works on antiquities, was fat in person, small in stature and 'very facetious'.

ON THE LATE CAPTAIN GROSE'S PEREGRINATIONS THRO' SCOTLAND
Collecting the Antiquities of that Kingdom

Hear, Land o' Cakes, and brither Scots,
Frae Maidenkirk[1] to Johnie Groat's,
If there's a hole in a' your coats,
        I rede you tent it:
A child's amang you, taking notes,
        And, faith, he'll prent it:

If in your bounds ye chance to light
Upon a fine, fat fodgel wight,
O' stature short but genius bright,
        That's he, mark weel—
And wow! he has an unco sleight
        O' cauk and keel.

[1] Kirkmaiden, in Wigtownshire, the most southerly parish in Scotland.

By some auld, houlet-haunted biggin,[1]
Or kirk deserted by its riggin,
It's ten to ane ye'll find him snug in
        Some eldritch part,
Wi' deils, they say, Lord safe's! colleaguin
        At some black art.

Ilk ghaist that haunts auld ha' or chaumer,
Ye gipsy-gang that deal in glamour,
And you, deep-read in hell's black grammar,
        Warlocks and witches,
Ye'll quake at his conjuring hammer,
        Ye midnight bitches.

It's tauld he was a sodger bred,
And ane wad rather fa'n than fled;
But now he's quat the spurtle blade,
        And dog-skin wallet,
And taen the—Antiquarian trade,
        I think they call it.

He has a fouth o' auld nick-nackets:
Rusty airn caps and jinglin jackets,[2]
Wad haud the Lothians three in tackets,
        A towmont gude;
And parritch-pats and auld saut-backets,
        Before the Flood.

Of Eve's first fire he has a cinder;
Auld Tubalcain's fire-shool and fender;
That which distinguished the gender
        O' Balaam's ass;
A broomstick o' the witch of Endor,
        Weel shod wi' brass.

Forbye, he'll shape you aff fu' gleg
The cut of Adam's philibeg;
The knife that nickit Abel's craig
        He'll prove you fully,
It was a faulding jocteleg,[3]
        Or lang-kail gullie.

But wad ye see him in his glee,
For meikle glee and fun has he,
Then set him down, and twa or three
        Gude fellows wi' him:
And *port, O port*! shine thou a wee,
        And THEN ye'll see him!

[1] *Vide* his Antiquities of Scotland.—R.B., 1793.
[2] *Vide* his treatise on ancient armour and weapons.—R. B., 1793.
[3] The etymology of this word was unknown till recently, when an old knife was found with the cutler's name marked 'Jacques de Liege'. Thus it is in exact analogy with 'Andrea di Ferrara'.—Lord Hailes.

Now, by the Pow'rs o' verse and prose!
Thou art a dainty chield, O Grose!—
Whae'er o' thee shall ill suppose,
        They sair misca' thee;
I'd take the rascal by the nose,
        Wad say, 'Shame fa' thee!'

THE KIRK OF SCOTLAND'S ALARM[1]
A Ballad
Tune—*Come rouse, Brother Sportsman!*

Orthodox! Orthodox! Wha believe in John Knox,
    Let me sound an alarm to your conscience:
A heretic blast has been blown in the Wast,
    'That what is not sense must be nonsense,'
Orthodox! That what is not sense must be nonsense.

Doctor Mac! Doctor Mac, ye should streek on a rack,
    To strike evildoers wi' terror:
To join Faith and Sense upon any pretence
    Was heretic, damnable error,
Doctor Mac![2] 'Twas heretic, damnable error.

Town of Ayr! Town of Ayr, it was mad, I declare,
    To meddle wi' mischief a-brewing,[3]
Provost John[4] is still deaf to the Church's relief,
    And Orator Bob[5] is its ruin,
Town of Ayr! Yes, Orator Bob is its ruin.

D'rymple mild! D'rymple mild, tho' your heart's like a child,
    And your life like the new-driven snaw,
Yet that winna save you, auld Satan maun have ye,
    For preaching that three's ane an' twa,
D'rymple mild![6] For preaching that three's ane an' twa.

Rumble John! Rumble John, mount the steps with a groan,
    Cry the book is with heresy cramm'd;
Then out wi' your ladle, deal brimstone like aidle,
    And roar ev'ry note of the damn'd.
Rumble John![7] And roar ev'ry note of the damn'd.

Simper James! Simper James, leave your fair Killie dames,
    There's a holier chase in your view:
I'll lay on your head, that the pack you'll soon lead,
    For puppies like you there's but few,
Simper James![8] For puppies like you there's but few.

---

[1] Written a short time after the publication of Dr McGill's essay on the death of Jesus Christ and referring to the polemical warfare that it excited.
[2] Dr McGill, Ayr.—R.B.
[3] See the advertisement.—R.B.
[4] John Ballantine.—R.B.
[5] Robert Aiken.—R.B.
[6] Dr Dalrymple, Ayr.—R.B.
[7] John Russell, Kilmarnock.—R.B.
[8] James Mackinlay, Kilmarnock.—R.B.

Singet Sawnie! Singet Sawnie, are ye herdin the penny,
    Unconscious whatdanger awaits?
With a jump, yell and howl, alarm ev'ry soul,
    For the foul fiend is just at your gates.
Singet Sawnie![1] For the foul fiend is just at your gates.

Poet Willie! Poet Willie, gie the Doctor a volley,
    Wi' your 'Liberty's Chain' and your wit;
O'er Pegasus' side ye ne'er laid a stride,
    Ye but smelt, man, the place where he shit.
Poet Willie![2] Ye but smelt, man, the place where he shit.

Barr Steenie! Barr Steenie, what mean ye, what mean ye?
    If ye'll meddle nae mair wi' the matter,
Ye may hae some pretence to havins and sense,
    Wi' people wha ken ye nae better,
Barr Steenie![3] Wi'people wha ken ye nae better.

Jamie Goose! Jamie Goose, ye hae made but toom roose,
    In hunting the wicked Lieutenant;
But the Doctor's your mark, for the Lord's holy ark,
    He has cooper'd an' ca'd a wrang pin in't,
Jamie Goose![4] He has cooper'd an' ca'd a wrang pin in't.

Davie Rant! Davie Rant, wi' a face like a saunt,
    And a heart that wad poison a hog;
Raise an impudent roar, like a breaker lee-shore,
    Or the Kirk will be tint in a bog,
Davie Rant![5] Or the Kirk will be tint in a bog.

Irvine-side! Irvine-side, wi' your turkey-cock pride
    Of manhood but sma' is your share:
Ye've the figure, 'tis true, ev'n your faes maun allow,
    An' your friends daurna say ye hae mair,
Irvine Side![6] Your friends daurna say ye hae mair.

Muirland Jock! Muirland Jock, whom the Lord made a rock
    To crush common sense for her sins;
If ill-manners were wit, there's no mortal so fit
    To confound the poor Doctor at ance,
Muirland Jock![7] To confound the poor Doctor at ance.

Andro Gowk! Andro Gowk, ye may slander the Book,
    And the Book nought the waur, let me tell ye;
Ye're rich and look big, but lay by hat an' wig,
    And ye'll hae a calf's-head o' sma' value,
Andro Gowk![8] Ye'll hae a calf's-head o' sma value.

[1] Alexander Moodie of Riccarton.—R.B.
[2] William Peebles, in Newton-upon-Ayr, a poetaster, who, among many other things, published an ode on the 'Centenary of the Revolution,' in which was the line: 'And bound in Liberty's endering chain.'—R.B.
[3] Stephen Young of Barr.—R.B.
[4] James Young, in New Cumnock, who had lately been foiled in an ecclesiastical prosecution against a Lieutenant Mitchel—R.B.
[5] David Grant, Ochiltree.—R.B.
[6] George Smith, Galston.—R.B.
[7] John Shepherd, Muirkirk.—R.B.
[8] Dr Andrew Mitchel, Monkton.—R.B.

Daddie Auld! Daddie Auld, there's a tod in the fauld,
    A tod meikle waur than the clerk;
Tho' ye do little skaith ye'll be in at the death,
    And gif ye canna bite, ye may bark,
Daddie Auld![1] For gif ye canna bite, ye may bark.

Holy Will! Holy Will, there was wit in your skull,
    When ye pilfer'd the alms o' the poor;
The timmer is scant when ye're taen for a saunt,
    Wha should swing in a rape for an hour,
Holy Will![2] Ye should swing in a rape for an hour.

Calvin's Sons! Calvin's Sons, seize your spiritual guns,
    Ammunition you never can need;
Your hearts are the stuff will be powder enough,
    And your skulls are a storehouse o' lead,
Calvin's Sons! Your skulls are a storehouse o' lead.

Poet Burns! Poet Burns, wi' your priest-skelpin turns,
    Why desert ye your auld native shire?
Tho' your Muse is a gipsy, yet were she e'en tipsy,
    She could ca' us nae waur than we are,
Poet Burns! She could ca' us nae waur than we are.

Presentation Stanzas to Correspondents

Factor John! Factor John, whom the Lord made alone,
    And ne'er made anither thy peer,
Thy poor servant, the Bard, in respectful regard,
    He presents thee this token sincere,
Factor John![3] He presents thee this token sincere.

Afton's Laird! Afton's Laird, when your pen can be spar'd,
    A copy o' this I bequeath,
On the same sicker score as I mention'd before,
    To that trusty auld worthy, Clackleith,
Afton's Laird![4] To that trusty auld worthy, Clackleith.

[1] William Auld, Mauchline; for the Clerk, see 'Holy Willie's Prayer.'—R.B.
[2] *Vide* the 'Prayer' of this saint.—R.B.
[3] John Kennedy, factor to the last Earl of Dumfries, or John McMurdo, Chamberlain of the Duke of Queensberry at Drumlanrig.
[4] Mr Johnston of Clackleith.

EXTEMPORANEOUS EFFUSION ON BEING APPOINTED TO AN EXCISE DIVISION

Searching auld wives' barrels,
    Ochon, the day!
That clarty barm should stain my laurels;
    But—what'll ye say?
These movin' things ca'd wives an' weans
Wad move the very hearts o' stanes!

SONNET ON RECEIVING A FAVOUR
10 August 1989
Addressed to Robert Graham, Esq. of Fintry

I call no goddess to inspire my strains,
A fabled Muse may suit a bard that feigns:
'Friend of my life!' my ardent spirit burns,
And all the tribute of my heart returns,
For boons accorded, goodness ever new,
The gifts still dearer, as the giver you.
Thou orb of day! thou other paler light!
And all ye many sparkling stars of night!
If aught that giver from my mind efface,
If I that giver's bounty e'er disgrace,
Then roll to me along your wand'ring spheres,
Only to number out a villain's years!
I lay my hand upon my swelling breast,
And grateful would—but cannot speak the rest.

WILLIE BREW'D A PECK O' MAUT

'The air is Masterton's, the song mine. The occasion of it was this: Mr William Nicol, of the High School, Edinburgh, during the Autumn vacation being at Moffat, honest Allan (who was at that time on a visit to Dalswinton), and I went to pay Nicol a visit. We had such a joyous meeting that Mr Masterton and I agreed, each in our own way, that we should celebrate the business.'— R. B.

> *Chorus*: We are na fou, we're nae that fou,
>   But just a drappie in our e'e;
> The cock may craw, the day may daw
>   And aye we'll taste the barley bree.

O Willie brew'd a peck o' maut,
    And Rob and Allan cam to see;
Three blyther hearts, that lee-lang night,
    Ye wadna found in Christendie.

Here are we met, three merry boys,
    Three merry boys I trow are we;
And monie a night we've merry been,
    And monie mae we hope to be!

It is the moon, I ken her horn,
    That's blinkin' in the lift sae hie;
She shines sae bright to wyle us hame,
    But, by my sooth, she'll wait a wee!

Wha first shall rise to gang awa,
    A cuckold, coward loun is he!
Wha first beside his chair shall fa',
    He is the King amang us three.

CA' THE YOWES TO THE KNOWES
First Version

Chorus: Ca' the yowes to the knowes,
Ca' them where the heather grows,
Ca' them where the burnie rowes,
    My bonnie dearie.

As I gaed down the waterside,
There I met my shepherd lad:
He row'd me sweetly in his plaid,
    And he ca'd me his dearie.

'Will ye gang down the waterside,
And see the waves sae sweetly glide
Beneath the hazels spreading wide?
    The moon it shines fu' clearly.'

'I was bred up in nae sic school,
My shepherd lad, to play the fool,
An' a' the day to sit in dool,
    An' naebody to see me.'

'Ye sall get gowns and ribbons meet,
Cauf-leather shoon upon your feet,
And in my arms thou'lt lie and sleep,
    An' ye sall be my dearie.'

'If ye'll but stand to what ye've said,
I'se gang wi' thee, my shepherd lad,
And ye may row me in your plaid,
    And I sall be your dearie.'

'While waters wimple to the sea,
While day blinks in the lift sae hie,
Till clay-cauld death sall blin' my e'e,
    Ye sall be my dearie.'

CA' THE YOWES TO THE KNOWES
Second Version

Chorus: Ca' the yowes to the knowes,
Ca' them where the heather grows,
Ca' them where the burnie rowes,
My bonnie dearie.

Hark, the mavis' e'ening sang,
Sounding Clouden's[1] woods amang!
Then a-faulding let us gang,
My bonnie dearie.

We'll gae down by Clouden side,
Through the hazels spreading wide,
O'er the waves that sweetly glide
To the moon sae clearly.

Yonder Clouden's silent towers,[2]
Where at moonshine's midnight hours
O'er the dewy-bending flowers
    Fairies dance sae cheery.

Ghaist nor bogle shalt thou fear,
Thou'rt to love and heaven sae dear,
Nocht of ill may come thee near;
    My bonnie dearie.

Fair and lovely as thou art,
Thou hast stown my very heart;
I can die—but canna part,
    My bonnie dearie.

[1] The Clouden is a tributary to the Nith.
[2] An old ruin in a sweet situation at the confluence of the Clouden and the Nith.—R.B.

THE BLUE-EYED LASSIE

I gaed a waefu' gate yestreen,
    A gate, I fear, I'll dearly rue;
I gat my death frae twa sweet een,
    Twa lovely een o'bonnie blue.

'Twas not her golden ringlets bright,
   Her lips like roses wat wi' dew,
Her heaving bosom, lily-white—
   It was her een sae bonnie blue.[1]

She talk'd, she smil'd, my heart she wyl'd;
   She charm'd my soul I wist na how;
And aye the stound, the deadly wound,
   Cam frae her een so bonnie blue.
But 'spare to speak, and spare to speed;'
   She'll aiblins listen to my vow:
Should she refuse, I'll lay my dead
   To her twa een sae bonnie blue.

[1] Miss Jeanie Jaffrey, a daughter of Rev. Jaffrey of Lochmaben. She married a Mr Renwick of New York, and in 1822, when met by a son of George Thomson, Burns' friend, her eyes were as blue and bright as ever. She talked of Burns with great respect and affection.

HIGHLAND HARRY BACK AGAIN

'The oldest title I ever heard to this air was *The Highland Watch's Farewell to Ireland*. The chorus I picked up from an old woman in Dunblane;[1] the rest of the song is mine.'—R.B.

Chorus: O for him back again!
   O for him back again!
I wad gie a' Knockhaspie's[2] land
   For Highland Harry back again.

My Harry was a gallant gay,
   Fu' stately strade he on the plain;
But now he's banish'd far away,
   I'll never see him back again.

When a' the lave gae to their bed,
   I wander dowie up the glen;
I set me down and greet my fill,
   And aye I wish him back again.

O were some villains hangit high,
   And ilka body had their ain!
Then I might see the joyfu' sight,
   My Highland Harry back again.

[1] Burns picked up the chorus from an old woman in Dunblane. He understood it in a Jacobite sense. It is said, however, to be founded on an old love story in Aberdeenshire.
[2] Part of Mossgiel farm was so called.

THE BATTLE OF SHERRAMUIR[1]
Tune—*The Cameronian rant*

'O cam ye here the fight to shun,
   Or herd the sheep wi' me, man?
Or were ye at the Sherra-moor,
   Or did the battle see, man?'
'I saw the battle, sair and teugh,
And reekin-red ran monie a sheugh;
My heart, for fear, gaed sough for sough,
To hear the thuds and see the cluds
O' clans frae woods in tartan duds,
   Wha glaum'd at kingdoms three, man.

[1] The battle of Dunblane, or Sheriffmuir, was fought on 13 November 1715, between the Earl of Mar, for the Chevalier, and the Duke of Argyle, for the Government; both sides claimed the victory, the left wing of either army being routed.

'The red-coat lads, wi' black cockauds,
    To meet them were na slaw, man;
They rush'd and push'd, and bluid outgush'd,
    And monie a bouk did fa', man;
The great Argyle led on his files,
I wat they glanc'd for twenty miles;
They hough'd the clans like ninepin kyles,
They hack'd an' hash'd while braid-swords, clash'd,
And thro' they dash'd, and hew'd and smash'd,
    Till fey men died awa, man.

But had ye seen the philibegs,
    And skyrin tartan trews, man;
When in the teeth they dar'd our Whigs,
    And Covenant trueblues, man!
In lines extended lang and large,
When baig'nets o'erpower'd the targe,
And thousands hasten'd to the charge.
Wi' Highland wrath they frae the sheath
Drew blades o' death, till, out o' breath,
    They fled like frighted dows, man!'

'O, how deil, Tam, can that be true?
    The chase gaed frae the north, man!
I saw mysel, they did pursue,
    The horsemen back to Forth, man;
And at Dunblane, in my ain sight,
They took the brig wi' a' their might,
And straught to Stirling wing'd their flight;
But, curséd lot! the gates were shut,
And monie a huntit poor red-coat,
    For fear amaist did swarf, man!'

'My sister Kate cam up the gate
    Wi' crowdie unto me, man;
She swoor she saw some rebels run
    To Perth and to Dundee, man!
Their left-hand general had nae skill;
The Angus lads had nae good will
That day their neibors' blude to spill;
For fear, by foes, that they should lose
Their cogs o' brose; they scar'd at blows,
    And hameward fast did flee, man.

'They've lost some gallant gentlemen,
    Amang the Highland clans, man!
I fear my Lord Panmure is slain,
    Or in his en'mies hands, man,
Now wad ye sing this double flight,
Some fell for wrang, and some for right;

But monie bade the world guid-night;
Say pell and mell, wi' muskets knell,
How Tories fell, and Whigs to hell
Flew off in frighted bands, man!'

KILLIECRANKIE
Tune—*An ye had been whare I hae been*

Chorus: An ye had been whare I hae been,
  Ye wad na been sae cantie, O!
An ye had seen what I hae seen,
  I' the braes o' Killiecrankie, O!

'Whare hae ye been sae braw, lad?
  Whare hae ye been sae brankie, O?
Whare hae ye been sae braw, lad?
  Cam ye by Killiecrankie, O?'

'I faught at land, I faught at sea,
  At hame I faught my auntie, O;
But I met the devil and Dundee
  On the braes o' Killiecrankie, O.

'The bauld Pitcur fell in a furr,
  An' Clavers gat a clankie, O,
Or I had fed an Athole gled
  On the braes o' Killiecrankie, O!

AWA' WHIGS, AWA'

Chorus: Awa' Whigs, awa'!
  Awa' Whigs, awa'!
Ye're but a pack o' traitor louns,
  Ye'll do nae gude at a'.

Our thrissles flourish'd fresh and fair,
  And bonnie bloom'd our roses;
But Whigs cam' like a frost in June,
  An' wither'd a' our posies.

Our ancient crown's fa'en in the dust—
  Deil blin' them wi' the stoure o't!
An' write their names in his black beuk,
  Wha gae the Whigs the power o't.

Our sad decay in church and state
  Surpasses my descriving:
The Whigs cam' o'er us for a curse,
  An' we hae done wi' thriving.

Grim vengeance lang has taen a nap,
  But we may see him wauken:
Gude help the day when royal heads
  Are hunted like a maukin!

A WAUKRIFE MINNIE
'I picked up this old song and tune from a country girl in Nithsdale. I never met with it elsewhere in Scotland.'—R. B.

'Whare are you gaun, my bonnie lass,
  Whare are you gaun, my hinnie?'
She answered me right saucilie,
  'An errand for my minnie.'

'O whare live ye, my bonnie lass,
  O whare live ye, my hinnie?'
'By yon burnside, gin ye maun ken,
  In a wee house wi' my minnie.'

But I foor up the glen at e'en.
  To see my bonnie lassie;
And lang before the grey morn cam,
  She was na hauf sae saucie.

O weary fa' the waukrife cock,
  And the foumart lay his crawin!
He wauken'd the auld wife frae her sleep,
  A wee blink or the dawin.

An angry wife I wat she raise,
  And o'er the bed she brocht her,
And wi' a meikle hazel rung
  She made her a weel-pay'd dochter.

'O. fare thee weel, my bonnie lass,
  O. fare thee well, my hinnie!
Thou art a gay an' a bonnie lass,
  But thou has a waukrife minnie!'

My Heart's In The Highlands
Tune—*Failte na miosg*

Chorus: My heart's in the Highlands, my heart is not here,
My heart's in the Highlands, a-chasing the deer;
Chasing the wild deer and following the roe;
My heart's in the Highlands, wherever I go.

Farewell to the Highlands, farewell to the North,
The birthplace of Valour, the country of Worth;
Wherever I wander, wherever I rove,
The hills of the Highlands for ever I love.

Farewell to the mountains, high-cover'd with snow;
Farewell to the straths and green vallies below;
Farewell to the forests and wild-hanging woods;
Farewell to the torrents and loud-pouring floods.

The Whistle—A Ballad

'As the authentic *prose* history of the Whistle is curious, I shall here give it.—In the train of Anne of Denmark, when she came to Scotland with our James the Sixth, there came over also a Danish gentleman of gigantic stature and great prowess, and a matchless champion of Bacchus. He had a curious ebony ca' or Whistle, which, at the commencement of the orgies, he laid on the table; and whoever was last able to blow it, every body else being disabled by the potency of the bottle, was to carry off the Whistle as a trophy of victory. The Dane produced credentials of his victories, without a single defeat, at the courts of Copenhagen, Stockholm, Moscow, Warsaw, and several of the petty courts in Germany; and challenged the Scots Bacchanalians to the alternative of trying his prowess, or else acknowledging their inferiority.—After many overthrows on the part of the Scots, the Dane was encountered by Sir Robert Laurie of Maxwelton, ancestor of the present worthy baronet of that name: who, after three days and nights' hard contest, left the Scandinavian under the table, "And blew on the Whistle his Requiem shrill".

'Sir Walter, son to Sir Robert before-mentioned, afterwards lost the Whistle to Walter Riddel of Glenriddell, who had married a sister of Sir Walter's.—On Friday, the 16th of October, 1790, at Friars Carse, the Whistle was once more contended for, as related in the ballad, by the present Sir Robert Laurie; Robert Riddel, Esq., of Glenriddel, lineal descendant and representative of Walter Riddel, who won the Whistle, and in whose family it had continued; and Alexander Ferguson, Esq. of Craigdarroch, likewise descended of the great Sir Robert; which last gentleman carried off the hard-won honours of the field.'—R.B.

I sing of a Whistle, a Whistle of worth,
I sing of a Whistle, the pride of the North.
Was brought to the court of our good Scottish King,
And long with this Whistle all Scotland shall ring.

Old Loda,[1] still rueing the arm of Fingal,
The god of the bottle sends down from his hall—
'This Whistle's your challenge, to Scotland get o'er,
And drink them to hell, Sir! or ne'er see me more!'

[1] See Ossian's 'Caric-thura'.—R.B.

Old poets have sung, and old chronicles tell,
What champions ventur'd, what champions fell:
The son of great Loda was conqueror still,
And blew on the Whistle their requiem shrill.

Till Robert, the lord of the Cairn and the Scaur,[1]
Unmatch'd at the bottle, unconquer'd in war,
He drank his poor god-ship as deep as the sea;
No tide of the Baltic e'er drunker than he.

Thus Robert, victorious, the trophy has gain'd,
Which now in his house has for ages remain'd;
Till three noble chieftains, and all of his blood,
The jovial contest again have renew'd.

Three joyous good fellows, with hearts clear of flaw
Craigdarroch, so famous for wit, worth and law;
And trusty Glenriddel, so skill'd in old coins;
And gallant Sir Robert, deep-read in old wines.

Craigdarroch began, with a tongue smooth as oil,
Desiring Glenriddel to yield up the spoil;
Or else he would muster the heads of the clan,
And once more, in claret, try which was the man.

'By the gods of the ancients!' Glenriddel replies,
'Before I surrender so glorious a prize,
I'll conjure the ghost of the great Rorie More,[2]
And bumper his horn with him twenty times o'er.'

Sir Robert, a soldier, no speech would pretend,
But he ne'er turn'd his back on his foe—or his friend,
Said, 'Toss down the Whistle, the prize of the field,'
And, knee-deep in claret, he'd die ere he'd yield.

To the board of Glenriddel our heroes repair,
So noted for drowning of sorrow and care;
But for wine and for welcome not more known to fame
Than the sense, wit and taste, of a sweet lovely dame.

A bard was selected to witness the fray
And tell future ages the feats of the day;
A Bard who detested all sadness and spleen
And wish'd that Parnassus a vineyard had been.

The dinner being over, the claret they ply,
And ev'ry new cork is a new spring of joy;
In the bands of old friendship and kindred so set,
And the bands grew the tighter the more they were wet.

---

[1] Tributaries to the Nith.—R.B.   [2] See Johnson's 'Tour in the Hebrides'.—R.B.

Gay Pleasure ran riot as bumpers ran o'er:
Bright Phoebus ne'er witness'd so joyous a corps,
And vow'd that to leave them he was quite forlorn,
Till Cynthia hinted he'd see them next morn.

Six bottles a-piece had well wore out the night,
When gallant Sir Robert, to finish the fight,
Turn'd o'er in one bumper a bottle of red,
And swore 'twas the way that their ancestor did.

Then worthy Glenriddel, so cautious and sage,
No longer the warfare ungodly would wage;
A high ruling elder to wallow in wine!
He left the foul business to folks less divine.

The gallant Sir Robert fought hard to the end;
But who can with Fate and quart bumpers contend?
Though Fate said, a hero should perish in light;
So uprose bright Phoebus—and down fell the knight.

Next uprose our Bard, like a prophet in drink—
'Craigdarroch, thou'lt soar when creation shall sink!
But if thou would flourish immortal in rhyme,
Come—one bottle more—and have at the sublime!

'Thy line, that have struggled for freedom with Bruce,
Shall heroes and patriots ever produce:
So thine be the laurel, and mine be the bay;
The field thou hast won, by yon bright god of day!'

To Mary In Heaven
Tune—*The death of Captain Cook*

Thou ling'ring star with lessening ray
 That lov'st to greet the early morn,
Again thou usher'st in the day
 My Mary from my soul was torn.
O Mary! dear departed shade!
 Where is thy place of blissful rest?
See'st thou thy lover lowly laid?
 Hear'st thou the groans that rend his breast?

That sacred hour can I forget,
 Can I forget the hallow'd grove,
Where, by the winding Ayr we met,
 To live one day of parting love?
Eternity cannot efface
 Those records dear of transports past;
Thy image at our last embrace,
 Ah! little thought we 'twas our last!

Ayr, gurgling, kiss'd his pebbled shore,
 O'erhung with wild-woods, thick'ning green;

The fragrant birch and hawthorn hoar,
 'Twin'd amorous round the raptur'd scene:
The flowers sprang wanton to be prest,
 The birds sang love on every spray;
Till too, too soon, the glowing west
 Proclaim'd the speed of wingéd day.

Still o'er these scenes my mem'ry wakes
 And fondly broods with miser-care;
Time but th' impression stronger makes,
 As streams their channels deeper wear,
My Mary! dear departed shade!
 Where is thy blissful place of rest?
See'st thou thy lover lowly laid?
 Hear'st thou the groans that rend his breast?

Epistle To Dr Blacklock

Ellisland, 21st Oct., 1789
My Revd. and dear Friend
Wow, but your letter made me vauntie!
And are ye hale, and weel and cantie?
I kend it still, your wee bit jauntie
   Wad bring ye to:
Lord send you aye as weel's I want ye,
   And then ye'll do!

The ill-thief blaw the Heron[1] south!
And never drink be near his drouth!
He tauld mysel' by word o' mouth,
   He'd tak my letter;
I lippen'd to the chiel in trouth,
   And bade nae better.

But aiblins, honest Master Heron
Had, at the time, some dainty fair one
To ware this theologic care on,
   And holy study;
And tired o' sauls to waste his lear on,
   E'en tried the body.[2]

But what d'ye think, my trusty fier,
I'm turned a gauger—Peace be here!
Parnassian quines, I fear, I fear,
   Ye'll now disdain me,
And then my fifty pounds a year
   Will little gain me!

Ye glaikit, gleesome, dainty damies,
Wha by Castalia's wimplin streamies

---

[1] Robert Heron, author of a history of Scotland and of a life of Burns.
[2] 'He ventur'd the soul, and I risk'ed the body'.—*Jolly Beggars.*

Lowp, sing and lave your pretty limbies,
    Ye ken, ye ken,
That strang necessity supreme is
    'Mang sons o' men.

I hae a wife and twa wee laddies;
They maun hae brose and brats o' duddies;
Ye ken yoursels my heart right proud is—
    I need na vaunt
But I'll sned besoms, thraw saugh woodies,
    Before they want.

Lord help me thro' this warld o' care!
I'm weary sick o't late and air!
Not but I hae a richer share
    Than monie ithers;
But why should ae man better fare,
    And a' men brithers?

Come, Firm Resolve, take thou the van,
Thou stalk o' carl-hemp in man!
And let us mind, faint heart ne'er wan
    A lady fair:
Wha does the utmost that he can,
    Will whyles do mair.

But to conclude my silly rhyme
(I'm scant o' verse and scant o' time),
To make a happy fireside clime
    To weans and wife,
That's the true pathos and sublime
    Of human life.

My compliments to sister Beckie,
And eke the same to honest Lucky;
I wat she is a daintie chuckie
    As e'er tread clay;
And gratefully, my guid auld cockie,
    I'm yours for aye.
                      Robert Burns

THE FIVE CARLINS—AN ELECTION BALLAD
Tune—*Chevy chase*

There was five Carlins[1] in the South,
    They fell upon a scheme,
To send a lad[2] to London town
    To bring them tidings hame.

Nor only bring them tidings hame,
    But do their errands there;

---

[1] The five Dumfries boroughs.   [2] A member of parliament.

And aiblins gowd and honour baith
  Might be that laddie's share.

There was Maggy by the banks o' Nith,[1]
  A dame wi' pride eneugh;
And Marjory o' the monie Lochs,[2]
  A Carlin auld and teugh.

And blinkin Bess o' Annandale,
  That dwelt near Solway-side;[3]
And Whisky Jean, that took her gill,
  In Galloway sae wide.[4]

And Black Jöan frae Crichton Peel,[5]
  O' gipsy kith an' kin;
Five wighter Carlins were na found
  The South countrie within.

To send a lad to London town,
  They met upon a day;
And monie a knight and monie a laird
  This errand fain wad gae.

O monie a knight and monie a laird
  This errand fain wad gae;
But nae ane could their fancy please,
  O ne'er a ane but twae.

The first ane was a belted Knight,
  Bred of a Border band;[6]
And he wad gae to London town,
  Might nae man him withstand.

And he wad do their errands weel,
  And meikle he wad say;
And ilka ane at London court
  Wad bid to him guid day.

The neist cam in a Soger youth[7]
  Who spak wi' modest grace,
And he wad gae to London town,
  If sae their pleasure was.

He wad na hecht them courtly gifts,
  Nor meikle speech pretend;
But he wad hecht an honest heart
  Wad ne'er desert his friend.

[1] Dumfries.
[2] Lochmaben.
[3] Annan.
[4] Kirkcudbright.
[5] Sanquhar.
[6] Sir James Johnston of Westerhall.
[7] Captain Patrick Miller of Dalswinton.

Now wham to chuse and wham refuse,
    At strife thir Carlins fell;
For some had Gentlefolks to please,
    And some wad please themsel'.

Then out spak mim-mou'd Meg o' Nith,
    And she spak up wi' pride,
And she wad send the Soger lad,
    Whatever might betide.

For the auld Guidman o' London court[1]
    She didna care a pin;
But she wad send the Soger lad,
    To greet his eldest son.[2]

Then started Bess o' Annandale,
    A deadly aith she's ta'en
That she wad vote the Border Knight,
    Though she should vote her lane.

'For far-off fowls hae feathers fair,
    And fools o' change are fain;
But I hae tried this Border Knight,
    I'll try him yet again.'

Says Black Jöan frae Crichton Peel,
    A Carlin stoor and grim;
'The auld Guidman or the young Guidman,
    For me may sink or swim;

'For fools will prate o' right or wrang,
    While knaves laugh them to scorn;
But the Soger's friends hae blawn the best,
    So he shall bear the horn.'

Then Whisky Jean spak o'er her drink,
    'Ye weel ken, kimmers a',
The Auld Guidman o' London court,
    His back's been at the wa';

'And monie a friend that kiss'd his caup
    Is now a fremit wight;
But it's ne'er be sae wi' Whisky Jean—
    We'll send the Border Knight.'

Then slaw raise Marjory o' the Lochs,
    And wrinkled was her brow;
Her ancient weed was russet grey,
    Her auld Scots heart was true;

[1] King George III.   [2] The Prince of Wales.

'There's some great folk set light by me,
    I set as light by them;
But I will send to London town
    Wham I like best at hame.'

Sae how this mighty plea may end,
    Nae mortal wight can tell:
God grant the king and ilka man
    May look weel to themsel'.

ELECTION BALLAD FOR WESTERHA'
Tune—*Up and waur them a'*

Chorus: Up and waur them a', Jamie,
    Up and waur them a';
The Johnstones hae the guidin o't,
    Ye turncoat Whigs, awa'!

The Laddies by the banks o' Nith
    Wad trust his Grace[1] wi a', Jamie;
But he'll sair them, as he sair'd the King—
    Turn tail and rin awa', Jamie.

The day he stude his country's friend
    Or gied her faes a claw, Jamie,
Or frae puir man a blessin wan,
    That day the Duke ne'er saw, Jamie.

But wha is he, his country's boast?
    Like him there is na twa, Jamie;
There's no a callent tents the kye
    But kens o' Westerha', Jamie.

To end the wark, here's Whistlebirk,
    Lang may his whistle blaw, Jamie;
And Maxwell true, o' sterling blue;
    And we'll be Johnstones a', Jamie.

[1] The fourth Duke of Queensberry, who had voted with the Whig Party against King George III and for the Prince of Wales in the struggle for the regency during the king's illness.

PROLOGUE SPOKEN AT THE THEATRE OF DUMFRIES
On New Year's Day evening 1790.

No song nor dance I bring from yon great city
That queens it o'er our taste—the more's the pity:
Tho' by the bye, abroad why will you roam?
Good sense and taste are natives here at home;
But not for panegyric I appear,
I come to wish you all a good New Year!
Old Father Time deputes me here before ye,
Not for to preach but tell his simple story:
The sage, grave Ancient cough'd and bade me say,

'You're one year older this important day,'
If *wiser too*—he hinted some suggestion,
But 'twould be rude, you know, to ask the question;
And with a would-be roguish leer and wink,
He bade me on you press this one word—'Think!'

　　Ye sprightly youths, quite flush with hope and spirit,
Who think to storm the world by dint of merit,
To you the dotard has a deal to say
In his sly, dry, sententious, proverb way!
He bids you mind, amid your thoughtless rattle,
That the first blow is ever half the battle;
That tho' some by the skirt may try to snatch him,
Yet by the forelock is the hold to catch him;
That whether doing, suffering or forbearing,
You may do miracles by persevering.

　　Last, tho' not least in love, ye youthful fair,
Angelic forms, high Heaven's peculiar care!
To you old Bald-pate smoothes his wrinkled brow
And humbly begs you'll mind the important—Now!
To crown your happiness he asks your leave,
And offers, bliss to give and to receive.

　　For our sincere, tho' haply weak endeavours,
With grateful pride we own your many favours;
And howsoe'er our tongues may ill reveal it,
Believe our glowing bosoms truly feel it.

NEW YEAR'S DAY—A SKETCH
To Mrs Dunlop

　　This day, Time winds th' exhausted chain
　　To run the twelvemonth's length again:
　　I see, the old bald-pated fellow,
　　With ardent eyes, complexion sallow,
　　Adjust the unimpair'd machine
　　To wheel the equal, dull routine.

　　　　The absent lover, minor heir,
　　In vain assail him with their prayer;
　　Deaf as my friend, he sees them press,
　　Nor makes the hour one moment less.
　　Will you (the Major's[1] with the hounds,
　　The happy tenants share his rounds;
　　Coila's fair Rachel's[2] care today,
　　And blooming Keith's engaged with Gray);
　　From housewife cares a minute borrow
　　(That grandchild's cap will do tomorrow)
　　And join with me a-moralising;
　　This day's propitious to be wise in.

[1] Afterwards General Dunlop of Dunlop.
[2] Rachel, daughter of Mrs Dunlop, was drawing a picture of Coila from 'The Vision'.

First, what did yesternight deliver?
'Another year has gone for ever.'
And what is this day's strong suggestion?
'The passing moment's all we rest on!'
Rest on—for what? what do we here?
Or why regard the passing year?
Will Time, amus'd with proverb'd lore,
Add to our date one minute more?
A few days may—a few years must—
Repose us in the silent dust.
Then is it wise to damp our bliss?
Yes—all such reasonings are amiss!
The voice of Nature loudly cries,
And many a message from the skies,
That something in us never dies:
That on his frail, uncertain state,
Hang matters of eternal weight:
That future life in worlds unknown
Must take its hue from this alone;
Whether as heavenly glory bright
Or dark as Misery's woeful night.

Since then, my honour'd first of friends,
On this poor being all depends;
Let us th' important *now* employ
And live as those who never die.
Tho' you, with days and honours crown'd,
Witness that filial circle round
(A sight life's sorrows to repulse,
A sight pale Envy to convulse),
Others now claim your chief regard;
Yourself, you wait your bright reward.

Scots Prologue For Mrs Sutherland
On her Benefit Night at the Theatre, Dumfries

What needs this din about the town o' Lon'on,
How this new play an' that new sang is comin?
Why is outlandish stuff sae meikle courted?
Does nonsense mend, like brandy, when imported?
Is there nae poet, burning keen for fame,
Will bauldly try to gie us plays at hame?
For comedy abroad he need na toil,
A fool and knave are plants of every soil;
Nor need he hunt as far as Rome or Greece
To gather matter for a serious piece;
There's themes enow in Caledonian story
Wad shew the tragic muse in a' her glory.

Is there no daring bard will rise and tell
How glorious Wallace stood, how hapless fell?
Where are the Muses fled that should produce

A drama worthy o' the name o' Bruce?
How here, even here, he first unsheath'd the sword
'Gainst mighty England and her guilty Lord;
And after monie a bloody, deathless doing,
Wrench'd his dear country from the jaws of ruin!
O! for a Shakespeare or an Otway scene
To draw the lovely, hapless Scottish Queen!
Vain all th' omnipotence of female charms
'Gainst headlong, ruthless, mad rebellion's arms:
She fell, but fell with spirit truly Roman,
To glut that direst foe—a vengeful woman;
A woman (tho' the phrase may seem uncivil)
As able and as wicked as the devil!
One Douglas lives in Home's immortal page,
But Douglasses were heroes every age:
And tho' your fathers, prodigal of life,
A Douglas followed to the martial strife,
Perhaps, if bowls row right, and Right succeeds,
Ye yet may follow where a Douglas leads!

As ye hae generous done, if a' the land
Would take the Muses' servants by the hand,
Not only hear, but patronise, befriend them,
And where ye justly can commend, commend them;
And aiblins when they winna stand the test,
Wink hard and say, 'The folks hae done their best!'
Would a' the land do this, then I'll be caition,
Ye'll soon hae poets o' the Scottish nation
Will gar Fame blaw until her trumpet crack,
And warsle Time an' lay him on his back!

For us and for our stage, should onie spier,
'Whase aught thae chiels maks a' this bustle here?'
My best leg foremost, I'll set up my brow—
We have the honour to belong to you!
We're your ain bairns, e'en guide us as ye like,
But, like good mithers, shore before ye strike;
And gratefu' still, I trust ye'll ever find us,
For gen'rous patronage, and meikle kindness
We've got frae a' professions, sorts and ranks:
God help us! we're but poor—ye'se get but thanks.

To A Gentleman[1]
Who had sent the Poet a Newspaper and offered to continue it free of Expense.

Kind Sir, I've read your paper through,
And faith, to me, 'twas really new!
How guessed ye, Sir, what maist I wanted?
This monie a day I've grain'd and gaunted,
To ken what French mischief was brewin;

[1] Peter Stuart of the London *Star*.

Or what the drumlie Dutch were doin;
That vile doup-skelper, Emperor Joseph,
If Venus yet had got his nose off;
Or how the collieshangie works
Atween the Russians and the Turks,
Or if the Swede, before he halt,
Would play anither Charles the twalt;[1]
If Denmark, any body spak o't;
Or Poland, wha had now the tack o't:
How cut-throat Prussian blades were hingin;
How libbet Italy was singin;
If Spaniard, Portuguese or Swiss
Were sayin' or takin' aught amiss;
Or how our merry lads at hame
In Britain's court kept up the game;
How royal George, the Lord leuk o'er him!
Was managing St Stephen's quorum;
If sleekit Chatham Will was livin,
Or glaikit Charlie got his nieve in;
How daddie Burke the plea was cookin,
If Warren Hasting's neck was yeukin;
How cesses, stents and fees were rax'd.
Or if bare arses yet were tax'd;
The news o' princes, dukes and earls,
Pimps, sharpers, bawds and opera-girls;
If that daft buckie, Geordie Wales,
Was threshing still at hizzies' tails,
Or if he was grown oughtlins douser,
And no a perfect kintra cooser:
A' this and mair I never heard of;
And but for you I might despair'd of.
So, gratefu', back your news I send you,
And pray a' guid things may attend you.
Ellisland, Monday Morning, 1790.

REMONSTRANCE ON IRREGULAR DELIVERY

Dear Peter, Dear Peter,
    We poor sons of metre
Are often negleckit, ye ken;
    For instance, your sheet, man,
    (Tho' glad I'm to see 't, man),
I get it no ae day in ten.—R.B.

ELEGY ON WILLIE NICOL'S MARE

Peg Nicholson[1] was a good bay mare
    As ever trod on airn;
But now she's floating down the Nith,
    And past the mouth o' Cairn.

[1] The name of the horse was derived from Margaret Nicholson, the insane woman who attempted to stab King George III in 1786.

Peg Nicholson was a good bay mare
 And rode thro' thick and thin;
But now she's floating down the Nith,
 And wanting even the skin.

Peg Nicholson was a good bay mare
 And ance she bore a priest;[1]
But now she's floating down the Nith,
 For Solway fish a feast.

Peg Nicholson was a good bay mare,
 An' the priest he rode her sair;
And much oppress'd and bruis'd she was,
 As priest-rid cattle are.

---

[1] William Nicol, schoolteacher, was originally intended for the church and had been licensed to preach.

THE GOWDEN LOCKS OF ANNA
Tune—*Banks of Banna*

Yestreen I had a pint o' wine,
 A place where body saw na;
Yestreen lay on this breast o' mine
 The gowden locks of Anna.

The hungry Jew in wilderness,
 Rejoicing o'er his manna,
Was naething to my hinny bliss
 Upon the lips of Anna.

Ye monarchs, take the East and West
 Frae Indus to Savannah;
Gie me, within my straining grasp,
 The melting form of Anna:

There I'll despise Imperial charms,
 An Empress or Sultana,
While dying raptures in her arms
 I give and take wi' Anna!

Awa, thou flaunting god o' day!
 Awa, thou pale Diana!
Ilk star, gae hide thy twinkling ray,
 When I'm to meet my Anna!

Come, in thy raven plumage, Night,
 Sun, moon and stars withdrawn a';
And bring an angel pen to write
 My transports with my Anna!

GUIDWIFE, COUNT THE LAWIN

Chorus: Then, guidwife, count the lawin,
The lawin, the lawin,
Then, guidwife, count the lawin,
 And bring a coggie mair.

Gane is the day and mirk's the night,
But we'll ne'er stray for faut o' light;
Guid ale and brandy's stars and moon,
And bluid-red wine's the risin' sun.

There's wealth and ease for gentlemen,
And simple folk maun fecht and fen';
But here we're a' in ae accord,
For ilka man that's drunk's a lord.

My coggie is a haly pool
That heals the wounds o' care and dool;
And pleasure is a wanton trout,
An ye drink it a', ye'll find him out.

ELECTION BALLAD
At the Close of the Contest for representing the Dumfries Burghs, 1790.[1]
Addressed to R. Graham, Esq. of Fintry.

Fintry, my stay in wordly strife,
Friend o' my Muse, friend o' my life,
   Are ye as idle 's I am?
Come then, wi' uncouth kintra fleg,
O'er Pegasus I'll fling my leg,
   And ye shall see me try him.

But where shall I go rin or ride,
That I may splatter nane beside?
   I wad na be uncivil:
In mankind's various paths and ways
There's aye some doytin' body strays,
   And *I* ride like a devil.

Thus I break aff wi' a' my birr,
An' down yon dark, deep alley spur,
   Where Theologics dander:
Alas! curst wi' eternal fogs,
And damn'd in everlasting bogs,
   As sure's the Creed I'll blunder!

I'll stain a band, or jaup a gown,
Or rin my reckless, guilty crown
   Against the haly door!
Sair do I rue my luckless fate,
When, as the Muse an' Deil wad hae 't,
   I rade that road before!

Suppose I take a spurt and mix
Amang the wilds o' Politics—
   Electors and elected—
Where dogs at Court (sad sons o' bitches!)
Septennially a madness touches,
   Till all the land's infected?

All hail! Drumlanrig's haughty Grace,[2]
Discarded remnant of a race
   Once godlike—great in story!
Thy fathers' virtues all contrasted,
The very name of Douglas blasted,
   Thine that inverted glory!

Hate, envy, oft the Douglas bore,
But thou hast superadded more,
   And sunk them in contempt!
Follies and crimes have stain'd the name,
But, Queensberry, thine the virgin claim,
   From aught that's good exempt!

[1] A contested election between Sir J. Johnston and Captain Miller for the Dumfries burghs. *See also* page 274.
[2] Second title of the Duke of Queensberry.

I'll sing the zeal Drumlanrig bears,
Who left the all-important cares
        Of fiddlers, whores and hunters,
And, bent on winning borough towns,
Came shaking hands wi' wabster-loons,
        And kissing barefit bunters.

Combustion thro' our boroughs rode,
Whistling his roaring pack abroad
        Of mad unmuzzl'd lions,
As Queensberry blue and buff[1] unfurl'd,
And Westerha'[2] and Hopetoun[3] hurl'd
        To every Whig defiance.

But cautious Queensberry left the war
(Th' unmanner'd dust might soil his star,
        Besides, he hated *bleeding*),
But left behind him heroes bright,
Heroes in Caesarean fight
        Or Ciceronian pleading.

O, for a throat like huge Mons-Meg,[4]
To muster o'er each ardent Whig
        Beneath Drumlanrig's banner!
Heroes and heroines commix,
All in the field of politics,
        To win immortal honour!

McMurdo[5] and his lovely spouse
(Th' enamour'd laurels kiss her brows!)
        Led on the Loves and Graces:
She won each gaping burgess' heart,
While he, *sub rosa*, played his part
        Among their wives and lasses.

Craigdarroch[6] led a light-arm'd core,
Tropes, metaphors and figures pour,
        Like Hecla streaming thunder.
Glenriddel,[7] skill'd in rusty coins,
Blew up each Tory's dark designs,
        And bared the treason under.

In either wing two champions fought:
Redoubted Staig,[8] who set at nought
        The wildest savage Tory;
And Welsh,[9] who ne'er yet flinch'd his ground,
High-wav'd his magnum-bonum round
        With Cyclopeian fury.

---

[1] The Fox or Whig livery.
[2] The Tory candidate.
[3] The Earl of Hopetoun.
[4] A gigantic piece of ordnance at Edinburgh Castle, made in the reign of James IV.
[5] John McMurdo, Esq. (*see* note page 245).
[6] Fergusson of Craigdarroch, champion of 'The Whistle' (*see* page 270).
[7] Robert Riddell, Esq., of Carse.
[8] Provost of Dumfries.
[9] Sheriff of the county.

Miller[1] brought up th' artillery ranks,
The many-pounders of the Banks,
      Resistless desolation!
While Maxwelton,[2] that baron bold,
'Mid Lawson's[3] port entrench'd his hold,
      And threaten'd worse damnation.

To these what Tory hosts oppos'd,
With these what Tory warriors clos'd,
      Surpasses my descriving;
Squadrons, extended long and large,
With furious speed rush to the charge,
      Like furious devils driving.

What verse can sing, what prose narrate,
The butcher deeds of bloody Fate
      Amid this mighty tulyie?
Grim Horror girn'd, pale Terror roar'd,
As Murther at his thrapple shor'd,
      And Hell mix'd in the brulyie.

As Highland craigs by thunder cleft,
When lightnings fire the stormy lift,
      Hurl down with crashing rattle,
As flames among a hundred woods,
As headlong foam from a hundred floods—
      Such is the rage of Battle!

The stubborn Tories dare to die:
As soon the rooted oaks would fly
      Before th' approaching fellers!
The Whigs come on like Ocean's roar,
When all his wintry billows pour
      Against the Buchan Bullers.[4]

Lo, from the shades of Death's deep night
Departed Whigs enjoy the fight,
      And think on former daring!
The muffled murtherer of Charles[5]
The Magna Charter flag unfurls,
      All deadly gules its bearing.

Nor wanting ghosts of Tory fame:
Bold Scrimgeour[6] follows gallant Graham;[7]
      Auld Covenanters shiver—
Forgive! forgive! much wrong'd Montrose!
Now Death and Hell engulf thy foes,
      Thou liv'st on high for ever!

[1] Patrick Miller of Dalswinton, father of the Whig candidate, who had been a banker.
[2] Sir Robert Lawrie of Maxwellton, MP for the county.
[3] Lawson, an eminent wine merchant.
[4] Remarkable rock caverns, on the coast near Peterhead.
[5] The executioner of Charles I was masked.
[6] Scrimgeour, Lord Dundee.
[7] Graham, Marquis of Montrose.

Still o'er the field the combat burns;
The Tories, Whigs, give way by turns;
      But Fate the word has spoken;
For woman's wit and strength o' man,
Alas! can do but what they can:
      The Tory ranks are broken.

O, that my een were flowing burns!
My voice a lioness that mourns
      Her darling cubs' undoing!
That I might greet, that I might cry,
While Tories fall, while Tories fly
      From furious Whigs pursuing!

What Whig but melts for good Sir James,
Dear to his country, by the names,
      Friend, Patron, Benefactor?
Not Pulteney's wealth can Pulteney save;
And Hopetoun falls—the generous, brave!—
      And Stewart[1] bold as Hector.

Thou, Pitt, shalt rue this overthrow,
And Thurlow growl a curse of woe,
      And Melville melt in wailing!
Now Fox and Sheridan rejoice,
And Burke shall sing, 'O Prince, arise!
      Thy power is all-prevailing!'

For your poor friend, the Bard, afar
He sees and hears the distant war,
      A cool spectator purely:
So, when the storm the forest rends,
The robin in the hedge descends,
      And, patient, chirps securely.

Now, for my friends' and brethren's sakes,
And for my dear-lov'd Land o' Cakes,
      I pray with holy fire—
Lord, send a rough-shod troop o' Hell
O'er a' wad Scotland buy or sell,
      To grind them in the mire!

[1] Stewart of Hillside.

Elegy On Captain Matthew Henderson[1]
A Gentleman who held the Patent for his Honours immediately from Almighty God

Should the poor be flattered?—Shakespeare.

O Death! thou tyrant fell and bloody!
The meikle devil wi' a woodie
Haurl thee hame to his black smiddie,
      O'er hurcheon hides,

[1] An Edinburgh *bon vivant* and boon companion of Burns, called 'Captain' as a pet name.

And like stock-fish come o'er his studdie
        Wi' thy auld sides!

He's gane, he's gane! he's frae us torn,
The ae best fellow e'er was born!
Thee, Matthew, Nature's sel' shall mourn,
        By wood and wild,
Where, haply, Pity strays forlorn,
        Frae man exil'd.

Ye hills, near neighbours o' the starns,
That proudly cock your cresting cairns!
Ye cliffs, the haunts of sailing yearns,
        Where Echo slumbers!
Come join, ye Nature's sturdiest bairns,
        My wailing numbers!

Mourn, ilka grove the cushat kens!
Ye hazly shaws and briery dens!
Ye burnies, wimplin' down your glens,
        Wi' toddlin din,
Or foaming, strang, wi' hasty stens,
        Frae lin to lin.

Mourn, little harebells o'er the lea;
Ye stately foxgloves, fair to see;
Ye woodbines hanging bonilie
        In scented bowers;
Ye roses on your thorny tree,
        The first o' flowers.

At dawn, when every grassy blade
Droops with a diamond at his head,
At even, when beans their fragrance shed,
        I' th' rustling gale,
Ye maukins, whiddin thro' the glade,
        Come join my wail.

Mourn, ye wee songsters o' the wood;
Ye grouse that crap the heather bud;
Ye curlews, calling thro' a clud;
        Ye whistling plover;
And mourn, ye whirring paitrick brood;
        He's gane for ever!

Mourn, sooty coots and speckled teals;
Ye fisher herons, watching eels;
Ye duck and drake, wi' airy wheels
        Circling the lake;
Ye bitterns, till the quagmire reels,
        Rair for his sake.

Mourn, clam'ring craiks at close o' day,
'Mang fields o' flowering clover gay;

And when ye wing your annual way
      Frae our claud shore,
Tell thae far warlds wha lies in clay,
      Wham we deplore.

Ye houlets, frae your ivy bower
In some auld tree or eldritch tower,
What time the moon, wi' silent glow'r,
      Sets up her horn,
Wail thro' the dreary midnight hour
      Till waukrife morn.

O, rivers, forests, hills and plains!
Oft have ye heard my canty strains:
But now, what else for me remains
      But tales of woe;
And frae my een the drapping rains
      Maun ever flow.

Mourn, Spring, thou darling of the year!
Ilk cowslip cup shall kep a tear:
Thou, Simmer, while each corny spear
      Shoots up its head,
Thy gay, green, flowery tresses shear,
      For him that's dead!

Thou, Autumn, wi' thy yellow hair,
In grief thy sallow mantle tear!
Thou, Winter, hurling thro' the air
      The roaring blast,
Wide o'er the naked world declare
      The worth we've lost!

Mourn him, thou Sun, great source of light!
Mourn, Empress of the silent night!
And you, ye twinkling starnies bright,
      My Matthew mourn!
For through your orbs he's ta'en his flight,
      Ne'er to return.

O Henderson! the man! the brother!
And art thou gone, and gone for ever!
And hast thou crost that unknown river,
      Life's dreary bound!
Like thee, where shall I find another,
      The world around!

Go to your sculptur'd tombs, ye Great,
In a' the tinsel trash o' state!
But by thy honest turf I'll wait,
      Thou man of worth!
And weep the ae best fellow's fate
      E'er lay in earth.

The Epitaph

Stop, passenger! my story's brief,
    And truth I shall relate, man;
I tell nae common tale o' grief,
    For Matthew was a great man.

If thou uncommon merit hast,
    Yet spurn'd at Fortune's door, man;
A look of pity hither cast,
    For Matthew was a poor man.

If thou a noble sodger art,
    That passest by this grave, man;
There moulders here a gallant heart,
    For Matthew was a brave man.

If thou on men, their works and ways,
    Canst throw uncommon light, man;
Here lies wha weel had won thy praise,
    For Matthew was a bright man.

If thou at Friendship's sacred ca'
    Wad life itself resign, man;
Thy sympathetic tear maun fa',
    For Matthew was a kind man.

If thou art staunch, without a stain,
    Like the unchanging blue, man;
This was a kinsman o' thy ain,
    For Matthew was a true man.

If thou hast wit, and fun, and fire,
    And ne'er guid wine did fear, man;
This was thy billie, dam and sire,
    For Matthew was a queer man.

If onie whiggish, whingin' sot,
    To blame poor Matthew dare, man;
May dool and sorrow be his lot,
    For Matthew was a rare man.

VERSES ON CAPTAIN GROSE[1]
Written on an Envelope enclosing a Letter to him

Ken ye aught o' Captain Grose?
    Igo and ago
If he's amang his friends or foes?
    Iram, coram, dago
Is he south or is he north?
    Igo and ago
Or drownéd in the river Forth?
    Iram, coram dago

[1] *See* note page 260.

Is he slain by Hielan' bodies?
 Igo and ago
And eaten like a wether haggis?
 Iram, coram, dago
Is he to Abra'm's bosom gane?
 Igo and ago
Or haudin Sarah by the wame?
 Iram, coram dago

Where'er he be, the Lord be near him!
 Igo and ago
As for the deil, he daur na steer him.
 Iram, coram, dago
But please transmit th' encloséd letter,
 Igo and ago
Which will oblige your humble debtor.
 Iram, coram, dago

So may ye hae auld stanes in store,
 Igo and ago
The very stanes that Adam bore!
 Iram, coram, dago
So may ye get in glad possession,
 Igo and ago
The coins o' Satan's coronation!
 Iram coram dago

TAM O' SHANTER
A Tale

Of Brownyis and of Bogillis full is this Buke—Gawin Douglas

When chapman billies leave the street,
And drouthy neibors, neibors meet;
As market days are wearing late,
And folk begin to tak the gate,
While we sit bousing at the nappy,
An' getting fou and unco happy,
We think na on the lang Scots miles,
The mosses, waters, slaps and stiles
That lie between us and our hame,
Where sits our sulky, sullen dame,
Gathering her brows like gathering storm,
Nursing her wrath to keep it warm.

 This truth fand honest Tam o' Shanter,
As he frae Ayr ae night did canter:
(Auld Ayr, wham ne'er a town surpasses,
For honest men and bonnie lasses).

 O Tam! had'st thou but been sae wise
As ta'en thy ain wife Kate's advice!
She tauld thee weel thou was a skellum,

A blethering, blustering, drunken blellum;
That frae November till October,
Ae market-day thou was nae sober;
That ilka melder wi' the miller,
Thou sat as lang as thou had siller;
That every naig was ca'd a shoe on
The smith and thee gat roaring fou on;
That at the Lord's[1] house, even on Sunday,
Thou drank wi' Kirkton[2] Jean till Monday.
She prophesied that late or soon,
Thou wad be found, deep drown'd in Doon,
Or catch'd wi' warlocks in the mirk,
By Alloway's auld, haunted kirk.

    Ah, gentle dames! it gars me greet
To think how monie counsels sweet,
How monie lengthen'd, sage advices,
The husband frae the wife despises!

    But to our tale: Ae market night,
Tam had got planted unco right,
Fast by an ingle, bleezing finely,
Wi reaming swats, that drank divinely;
And at his elbow, Souter Johnie,
His ancient, trusty, drouthy crony;
Tam lo'ed him like a very brither;
They had been fou for weeks thegither.
The night drave on wi' sangs and clatter;
And aye the ale was growing better:
The landlady and Tam grew gracious,
Wi' favours secret, sweet and precious:
The Souter tauld his queerest stories;
The landlord's laugh was ready chorus:
The storm without might rair and rustle,
Tam did na mind the storm a whistle.

    Care, mad to see a man sae happy,
E'en drown'd himsel amang the nappy.
As bees flee hame wi' lades o' treasure,
The minutes wing'd their way wi' pleasure:
Kings may be blest, but Tam was glorious,
O'er a' the ills o' life victorious!

    But pleasures are like poppies spread:
You seize the flower, its bloom is shed;
Or like the snow falls in the river,
A moment white—then melts for ever;
Or like the borealis race,
That flit ere you can point their place;
Or like the rainbow's lovely form

---

[1] Possibly Leddie's House, a tavern kept by the two sisters Kennedy, one of them called Kirkton Jean.
[2] Any little village where a parish church is erected is called 'the Kirkton'.

Evanishing amid the storm.—
Nae man can tether time nor tide,
The hour approaches Tam maun ride;
That hour, o' night's black arch the keystane,
That dreary hour he mounts his beast in;
And sic a night he taks the road in,
As ne'er poor sinner was abroad in.

The wind blew as 'twad blawn its last;
The rattling showers rose on the blast;
The speedy gleams the darkness swallow'd;
Loud, deep and lang the thunder bellow'd:
That night, a child might understand,
The Deil had business on his hand.

Weel-mounted on his grey mare, Meg,
A better never lifted leg,
Tam skelpit on thro' dub and mire,
Despising wind, and rain, and fire;
Whiles holding fast his guid blue bonnet,
Whiles crooning o'er some auld Scots sonnet,
Whiles glow'ring round wi' prudent cares,
Lest bogles catch him unawares;
Kirk-Alloway was drawing nigh,
Where ghaists and houlets nightly cry.

By this time he was cross the ford,
Whare in the snaw the chapman smoor'd;
And past the birks and meikle stane,
Whare drunken Charlie brak 's neck-bane;
And thro' the whins, and by the cairn,
Whare hunters fand the murder'd bairn;
And near the thorn, aboon the well,
Whare Mungo's mither hang'd hersel'.
Before him Doon pours all his floods;
The doubling storm roars thro' the woods;
The lightnings flash from pole to pole;
Near and more near the thunders roll:
When, glimmering thro' the groaning trees,
Kirk-Alloway seem'd in a bleeze;
Thro' ilka bore the beams were glancing,
And loud resounded mirth and dancing.

Inspiring bold John Barleycorn!
What dangers thou canst make us scorn!
Wi' tippenny, we fear nae evil;
Wi' usquabae, we'll face the devil!
The swats sae ream'd in Tammie's noddle,
Fair play, he car'd na deils a boddle.
But Maggie stood right sair astonish'd,
Till, by the heel and hand admonish'd,

She ventur'd forward on the light;
And, vow! Tam saw an unco sight!

    Warlocks and witches in a dance:
Nae cotillon brent new frae France,
But hornpipes, jigs, strathspeys and reels
Put life and mettle in their heels.
A winnock-bunker in the east,
There sat Auld Nick, in shape o' beast;
A towzie tyke, black, grim and large,
To gie them music was his charge:
He screw'd the pipes and gart them skirl,
Till roof and rafters a' did dirl.—
Coffins stood round, like open presses,
That shaw'd the Dead in their last dresses;
And by some devilish cantraip sleight
Each in its cauld hand held a light—
By which heroic Tam was able
To note upon the haly table
A murderer's banes in gibbet airns;
Twa span-lang, wee, unchristen'd bairns;
A thief, new-cutted frae a rape,
Wi' his last gasp his gab did gape;
Five tomahawks, wi' bluid red-rusted;
Five scimitars, wi' murder crusted;
A garter, which a babe had strangled;
A knife, a father's throat had mangled,
Whom his ain son o' life bereft,
The grey hairs yet stack to the heft;
Wi' mair of horrible and awfu',
Which even to name wad be unlawfu'.[1]

    As Tammie glowr'd, amaz'd and curious,
The mirth and fun grew fast and furious:
The piper loud and louder blew,
The dancers quick and quicker flew;
They reel'd, they set, they cross'd, they cleekit,
Till ilka carlin swat and reekit,
And coost her duddies to the wark,
And linkit at it in her sark!

    Now Tam, O Tam! had thae been queans,
A' plump and strapping in their teens,
Their sarks, instead o' creeshie flannen,
Been snaw-white seventeen hunder linen![2]
Thir breeks o' mine, my only pair,
That ance were plush o' guid blue hair,
I wad hae gi'en them off my hurdies,

---

[1] 'Sae, tho' the aith we took was awfu',
  To keep it now appears unlawfu'.'—Ramsay's 'Three Bonnets'.
[2] The manufacturer's term for very fine linen, woven in a reed of 1700 divisions.

For ae blink o' the bonnie burdies!
But wither'd beldams, auld and droll,
Rigwoodie hags wad spean a foal,
Louping and flinging on a crummock.
I wonder did na turn thy stomach.

But Tam kend what was what fu' brawlie:
There was ae winsome wench and wawlie,[1]
That night enlisted in the core,
Lang after kend on Carrick shore;
(For monie a beast to dead she shot,
And perish'd monie a bonnie boat,
And shook baith meikle corn and bear,
And kept the countryside in fear);
Her cutty sark, o' Paisley harn,
That while a lassie she had worn,
In longitude tho' sorely scanty,
It was her best, and she was vauntie.
Ah! little kend thy reverend grannie,
That sark she coft for her wee Nannie,
Wi twa pund Scots ('twas a' her riches),
Wad ever grac'd a dance of witches!

But here my Muse her wing maun cour.
Sic flights are far beyond her power;
To sing how Nannie lap and flang,
(A souple jade she was and strang),
And how Tam stood, like ane bewitch'd,
And thought his very een enrich'd;
Even Satan glowr'd, and fidg'd fu' fain,
And hotch'd and blew wi' might and main:
Till first ae caper, syne anither,
Tam tint his reason a thegither,
And roars out, 'Weel done, Cutty-sark!'
And in an instant all was dark:
And scarcely had he Maggie rallied
When out the hellish legion sallied.

As bees bizz out wi' angry fyke
When plundering herds assail their byke;
As open pussie's mortal foes
When, pop! she starts before their nose;
As eager runs the market crowd
When 'Catch the thief!' resounds aloud;
So Maggie runs, the witches follow,
Wi' monie an eldritch skreich and hollow.

Ah, Tam! Ah, Tam! thou'll get thy fairin!
In hell they'll roast thee like a herrin!
In vain thy Kate awaits thy comin!

---

[1] 'She was a winsome wench and waulie
An' could put on her claes fu' brawlie.'—Ramsay's 'Three Bonnets'.

Kate soon will be a woefu' woman!
Now, do thy speedy-utmost, Meg,
And win the keystane o' the brig;[1]
There at them thou thy tail may toss,
A running stream they dare na cross.
But ere the keystane she could make,
The fient a tail she had to shake!
For Nannie, far before the rest,
Hard upon noble Maggie prest
And flew at Tam wi' furious ettle;
But little wist she Maggie's mettle—
Ae spring brought off her master hale,
But left behind her ain grey tail:
The carlin claught her by the rump
And left poor Maggie scarce a stump.

Now, wha this tale o' truth shall read,
Ilk man and mother's son, take heed:
Whene'er to drink you are inclin'd,
Or cutty-sarks rin in your mind,
Think! ye may buy the joys o'er dear:
Remember Tam o' Shanter's mare.

[1] It is a well-known fact that witches, or any evil spirits, have no power to follow a poor wight any farther than the middle of the next running stream. It may be proper likewise to mention to the benighted traveller, that when he falls in with *bogles*, whatever danger may be in his going forward, there is much more hazard in turning back.—R.B.

ON THE BIRTH OF A POSTHUMOUS CHILD[1]
Born in Peculiar Circumstances of Family Distress

Sweet flow'ret, pledge o' meikle love,
    And ward o' monie a prayer,
What heart o' stane wad thou na move,
    Sae helpless, sweet and fair?

November hirples o'er the lea,
    Chill, on thy lovely form:
And gane, alas! the shelt'ring tree
    Should shield thee frae the storm.

May He who gives the rain to pour
    And wings the blast to blaw,
Protect thee frae the driving shower,
    The bitter frost and snaw.

May He, the friend o' woe and want,
    Who heals life's various stounds,
Protect and guard the mother plant
    And heal her cruel wounds.

But late she flourish'd, rooted fast,
    Fair in the summer morn,
Now feebly bends she in the blast,
    Unshelter'd and forlorn.

Blest be thy bloom, thou lovely gem,
    Unscath'd by ruffian hand!
And from thee many a parent stem
    Arise to deck our land!

[1] A grandson of Mrs Dunlop, whose daughter had married M. Henri, a Frenchman, who died before the birth.

ELEGY ON THE LATE MISS BURNET OF MONBODDO[1]

Life ne'er exulted in so rich a prize
    As Burnet, lovely from her native skies;
Nor envious death so triumph'd in a blow,
    As that which laid th' accomplish'd Burnet low.

[1] *See* note, page 193.

Thy form and mind, sweet maid, can I forget?
    In richest ore the brightest jewel set!
In thee, high Heaven above was truest shown,
    As by His noblest work the Godhead best is known.

In vain ye flaunt in summer's pride, ye groves;
    Thou crystal streamlet with thy flowery shore,
Ye woodland choir that chaunt your idle loves,
    Ye cease to charm: Eliza is no more.

Ye heathy wastes immix'd with reedy fens,
    Ye mossy streams with sedge and rushes stor'd,
Ye rugged cliffs o'erhanging dreary glens,
    To you I fly—ye with my soul accord.

Princes whose cumb'rous pride was all their worth,
    Shall venal lays their pompous exit hail;
And thou, sweet Excellence! forsake our earth,
    And not a Muse with honest grief bewail?

We saw thee shine in youth and beauty's pride,
    And Virtue's light, that beams beyond the spheres;
But like the sun eclips'd at morning tide,
    Thou left us darkling in a world of tears.

The parent's heart that nestled fond in thee,
    That heart how sunk, a prey to grief and care!
So deckt the woodbine sweet yon agéd tree;
    So, rudely ravish'd, left it bleak and bare.

LAMENT OF MARY QUEEN OF SCOTS
On the Approach of Spring

Now Nature hangs her mantle green
    On every blooming tree
And spreads her sheets o' daisies white
    Out o'er the grassy lea;
Now Phoebus cheers the crystal streams
    And glads the azure skies;
But nought can glad the weary wight
    That fast in durance lies.

Now laverocks wake the merry morn,
    Aloft on dewy wing;
The merle, in his noontide bower,
    Makes woodland echoes ring;
The mavis wild wi' monie a note
    Sings drowsy day to rest:
In love and freedom they rejoice,
    Wi' care nor thrall opprest.

Now blooms the lily by the bank,
    The primrose down the brae;

The hawthorn's budding in the glen,
And milk-white is the slae:
The meanest hind in fair Scotland
May rove their sweets amang;
But I, the Queen of a' Scotland,
Maun lie in prison strang.

I was the Queen o' bonnie France,
Where happy I hae been;
Fu' lightly rase I in the morn,
As blythe lay down at e'en:
And I'm the sov'reign of Scotland,
And monie a traitor there;
Yet here I lie in foreign bands,
And never-ending care.

But as for thee, thou false woman,
My sister and my fae,
Grim Vengeance yet shall whet a sword
That thro' thy soul shall gae!
The weeping blood in woman's breast
Was never known to thee;
Nor th' balm that draps on wounds of woe
Frae woman's pitying e'e.

My son! my son! may kinder stars
Upon thy fortune shine;
And may those pleasures gild thy reign
That ne'er wad blink on mine!
God keep thee frae thy mother's faes
Or turn their hearts to thee:
And where thou meet'st thy mother's friend,
Remember him for me!

O! soon, to me, may summer suns
Nae mair light up the morn!
Nae mair to me the autumn winds
Wave o'er the yellow corn!
And in the narrow house o' death
Let winter round me rave;
And the next flowers that deck the spring,
Bloom on my peaceful grave.

THERE'LL NEVER BE PEACE TILL JAMIE COMES HAME
Tune—*There's few guid fellows when Jamie's awa'*

By yon castle wa' at the close of the day,
I heard a man sing tho' his head it was grey;
And as he was singing, the tears doon came—
'There'll never be peace till Jamie comes hame.

'The Church is in ruins, the State is in jars,
Delusions, oppressions and murderous wars,
We dare na weel say 't, but we ken wha's to blame—
There'll never be peace till Jamie comes hame!

'My seven braw sons for Jamie drew sword,
But now I greet round their green beds in the yerd;
It brak the sweet heart o' my faithful auld dame—
There'll never be peace till Jamie comes hame!

'Now life is a burden that bows me down,
Sin' I tint my bairns, and he tint his crown;
But till my last moments my words are the same—
There'll never be peace till Jamie comes hame!'

OUT OVER THE FORTH
Tune—*Charles Gordon's welcome home*

Out over the Forth, I look to the north;
     But what is the north and its Highlands to me?
The south nor the east gie ease to my breast,
     The far foreign land, or the wide rolling sea!

But I look to the west when I gae to rest,
     That happy my dreams and my slumbers may be;
For far in the west lives he I lo'e best,
     The man that is dear to my babie and me.

THE BANKS O' DOON
First Version

'Ellisland, 11th March 1791.—I have this evening sketched out a song which I have a good mind to send you. . . . It is intended to be sung to a Strathspey reel of which I am very fond, called in Cumming's Collection, "Ballindalloch's Reel", and in others, "Camdelmore". It takes three stanzas of four lines each, to go through the whole tune.'—In a letter to Alexander Cunningham

Sweet are the banks, the banks o' Doon,
     The spreading flowers are fair,
And everything is blythe and glad,
     But I am fu' o' care.
Thou'll break my heart, thou bonnie bird,
     That sings upon the bough!
Thou minds me o' the happy days
     When my fause Luve was true.
Thou'll break my heart, thou bonnie bird,
     That sings beside thy mate,
For sae I sat and sae I sang,
     And wist na o' my fate.

Aft hae I rov'd by bonnie Doon,
     To see the woodbine twine;
And ilka birds sang o' its Luve,
     And sae did I o' mine:
Wi' lightsome heart I pu'd a rose,
     Upon its thorny tree;
But my fause Luver staw my rose
     And left the thorn wi' me:
Wi' lightsome heart I pu'd a rose,
     Upon a morn in June;
And sae I flourished on the morn,
     And sae was pu'd or' noon!

THE BANKS O' DOON
Second Version

[March 1791] 'While here I sit, sad and solitary, by the side of a fire in a little country Inn, and drying my wet clothes, in pops a poor fellow of a soger, and tells me he is going to Ayr. By heavens! say I to myself, with a tide of good spirits which the magic of that sound—"Auld Toon o' Ayr", conjured up, I will send my last song to Mr Ballantine. Here it is.'—Letter to John Ballantine, Esq., Ayr.

Ye flowery banks o' bonnie Doon,
    How can ye blume sae fair?
How can ye chant, ye little birds,
    And I sae fu' o care!

Thou'll break my heart, thou bonnie bird
    That sings upon the bough;
Thou minds me o' the happy days
    When my fause luve was true!

Thou'll break my heart, thou bonnie bird
    That sings beside thy mate;
For sae I sat, and sae I sang,
    And wist na o' my fate.

Aft hae I rov'd by bonnie Doon
    To see the woodbine twine;
And ilka bird sang o' its luve,
    And sae did I o' mine.

Wi' lightsome heart I pu'd a rose
    Frae off its thorny tree,
But my fause luver staw my rose
    And left the thorn wi' me.

Wi' lightsome heart I pu'd a rose
    Upon a morn in June,
And sae I flourished on the morn,
    And sae was pu'd or noon.

THE BANKS O' DOON
Third Version

Ye banks and braes o' bonnie Doon,
    How can ye bloom sae fresh and fair?
How can ye chant, ye little birds,
    And I sae weary fu' o' care!
Thou'll break my heart, thou warbling bird,
    That wantons thro' the flowering thorn:
Thou minds me o' departed joys,
    Departed never to return.

Aft hae I rov'd by Bonnie Doon,
    To see the rose and woodbine twine:
And ilka bird sang o' its Luve,
    And fondly sae did I o' mine;
Wi' lightsome heart I pu'd a rose,
    Fu' sweet upon its thorny tree!
And may fause Luver staw my rose,
    But ah! he left the thorn wi' me.

LAMENT FOR JAMES, EARL OF GLENCAIRN[1]

The wind blew hollow frae the hills,
    By fits the sun's departing beam
Look'd on the fading yellow woods,
    That wav'd o'er Lugar's winding stream:

---

[1] Lord Glencairn, friend of Burns and his patron, died in January 1791 at Falmouth on his way back from a voyage to Lisbon where he had gone in a vain search for health. He was forty-two. Burns put on mourning for him and called one of his sons James Glencairn. *See also* page 199.

Beneath a craigy steep, a Bard,
    Laden with years and meikle pain,
In loud lament bewail'd his lord,
    Whom death had all untimely ta'en.

He lean'd him to an ancient aik,
    Whose trunk was mould'ring down with years;
His locks were bleachéd white with time,
    His hoary cheek was wet wi' tears;
And as he touch'd his trembling harp,
    And as he tuned his doleful sang,
The winds, lamenting thro' their caves,
    To Echo bore the notes alang.

'Ye scatter'd birds that faintly sing,
    The reliques o' the vernal quire;
Ye woods that shed on a' the winds
    The honours of the agéd year:
A few short months, and glad and gay,
    Again ye'll charm the ear and e'e;
But nocht in all-revolving time
    Can gladness bring again to me.

'I am a bending agéd tree
    That long has stood the wind and rain;
But now has come a cruel blast,
    And my last hald of earth is gane;
Nae leaf o' mine shall greet the spring,
    Nae simmer sun exalt my bloom;
But I maun lie before the storm,
    And ithers plant them in my room.

'I've seen sae monie changefu' years,
    On earth I am a stranger grown;
I wander in the ways of men,
    Alike unknowing and unknown:
Unheard, unpitied, unreliev'd,
    I bear alane my lade o' care,
For silent, low, on beds of dust,
    Lie a' that would my sorrows share.

'And last (the sum of a' my griefs!),
    My noble master lies in clay;
The flower amang our barons bold,
    His country's pride, his country's stay:
In weary being now I pine,
    For a' the life of life is dead,
And hope has left may agéd ken,
    On forward wing for ever fled.

'Awake thy last sad voice, my harp!
    The voice of woe and wild despair!
Awake, resound thy latest lay,
    Then sleep in silence evermair!
And thou, my last, best, only, friend,
    That fillest an untimely tomb,
Accept this tribute from the Bard
    Thou brought from Fortune's mirkest gloom.

'In Poverty's low barren vale,
    Thick mists obscure involv'd me round;
Though oft I turn'd the wistful eye,
    Nae ray of fame was to be found:
Thou found'st me, like the morning sun
    That melts the fogs in limpid air,
The friendless Bard and rustic song
    Became alike thy fostering care.

'O! why has Worth so short a date,
    While villains ripen grey with time?
Must thou, the noble, gen'rous, great,
    Fall in bold manhood's hardy prim!
Why did I live to see that day—
    A day to me so full of woe?
O! had I met the mortal shaft
    That laid my benefactor low!

'The bridegroom may forget the bride
    Was made his wedded wife yestreen;
The monarch may forget the crown
    That on his head an hour has been;
The mother may forget the child
    That smiles sae sweetly on her knee;
But I'll remember thee, Glencairn,
    And a' that thou hast done for me!'

LINES TO SIR JOHN WHITEFORD, OF WHITEFOORD, BART[1]
Sent with the Foregoing Poem

Thou, who thy honour as thy God rever'st,
Who, save thy mind's reproach, nought earthly fear'st,
To thee this votive offering I impart,
The tearful tribute of a broken heart.
The Friend thou valued'st, I, the Patron lov'd;
His worth, his honour, all the world approved.
We'll mourn till we too go as he has gone,
And tread the shadowy path to that dark world unknown.

---

[1] Once laird of Ballochmyle, a great friend of the Earl of Glencairn (*see* page 299).

CRAIGIEBURN WOOD
First Version

This song was composed on a passion which a Mr Gillespie, a particular friend of mine, had for a Miss Lorimer, afterwards Mrs Whelpdale. The young lady was born at Craigieburn Wood [near Moffat]. The chorus is part of an old, foolish ballad.—R. B.

Chorus: Beyond thee, dearie, beyond thee, dearie,
    And oh, to be lying beyond thee!
Oh, sweetly, soundly, weel may he sleep
    That's laid in the bed beyond thee!

Sweet closes the evening on Craigieburn Wood,
    And blythely awaukens the morrow;
But the pride o' the spring on the Craigieburn Wood
    Can yield to me nothing but sorrow.

I see the spreading leaves and flowers,
    I hear the wild birds singing;
But pleasure they hae nane for me,
    While care my heart is wringing.

I canna tell, I maunna tell,
    I daurna for your anger;
But secret love will break my heart,
    If I conceal it langer.

I see thee gracefu', straight and tall,
    I see thee sweet and bonnie;
But oh, what will my torments be
    If thou refuse thy Johnie!

To see thee in another's arms,
    In love to lie and languish,
'Twad be my dead, that will be seen,
    My heart wad burst wi' anguish.

But Jeanie, say thou wilt be mine,
    Say thou lo'es nane before me;
And a' my days o' life to come
    I'l gratefully adore thee,

CRAIGIEBURN WOOD
Second Version

Sweet fa's the eve on Craigieburn,
    And blythe awakes the morrow,
But a' the pride o' Spring's return
    Can yield me nocht but sorrow.
I see the flowers and spreading trees,
    I hear the wild birds singing;
But what a weary wight can please,
    And Care his bosom wringing.

Fain, fain would I my griefs impart,
　　Yet dare na for your anger;
But secret love will break my heart,
　　If I conceal it langer.
If thou refuse to pity me;
　　If thou shalt love anither,
When yon green leaves fade frae the tree,
　　Around my grave they'll wither.

BONNIE WEE THING

Chorus: Bonnie wee thing, cannie wee thing,
　　Lovely wee thing, wert thou mine,
I wad wear thee in my bosom,
　　Lest my jewel it should tine.

Wishfully I look and languish
　　In that bonnie face o' thine,
And my heart it stounds wi' anguish,
　　Lest my wee thing be na mine.

Wit, and Grace, and Love, and Beauty,
　　In ae constellation shine;
To adore thee is my duty,
　　Goddess o' this soul o' mine!

EPIGRAM ON MISS DAVIES[1]
On being asked why she had been formed so little, and Mrs A—— so big[2]

Ask why God made the GEM so small
　　And why so huge the granite?
Because God meant mankind should set
　　That higher value on it.

[2] Written on a pane of glass in the inn at Moffat, on observing Miss Davies ride past in company with a woman of portly dimensions.

THE CHARMS OF LOVELY DAVIES[1]
Tune—*Miss Muir*

O how shall I, unskilfu', try
　　The poet's occupation?
The tunefu' powers, in happy hours,
　　That whisper inspiration,
Even they maun dare an effort mair
　　Than aught they ever gave us,
Ere they rehearse, in equal verse,
　　The charms o' lovely Davies.

Each eye it cheers when she appears,
　　Like Phoebus in the morning,
When past the shower, and every flower
　　The garden is adorning:
As the wretch looks o'er Siberia's shore,
　　When winter-bound the wave is;
Sae droops our heart, when we maun part
　　Frae charming, lovely Davies.

[1] Miss Deborah Davis was a young woman from Pembrokeshire, related to the Riddells—very pretty, witty and *wee*. She was forsaken by her lover, a Captain Delany, and drooped and died in consequence.

Her smile's a gift frae 'boon the lift,
    That maks us mair than princes;
A scepter'd hand, a king's command,
    Is in her darting glances;
The man in arms 'gainst female charms
    Even he her willing slave is;
He hugs his chain and owns the reign
    Of conquering, lovely Davies.

My Muse, to dream of such a theme,
    Her feeble powers surrender;
The eagle's gaze alone surveys
    The sun's meridian splendour.
I wad in vain essay the strain,
    The deed too daring brave is;
I'll drap the lyre and mute admire
    The charms o' lovely Davies.

WHAT CAN A YOUNG LASSIE DO WI' AN AULD MAN
Tune—*What shall I do with an auld man*

What can a young lassie, what shall a young lassie,
    What can a young lassie do wi' an auld man?
Bad luck on the penny that tempted my minnie
    To sell her puir Jenny for siller an' lan'!

He's always compleenin' frae mornin' to e'enin',
    He hoasts and he hirples the weary day lang;
He's doylt and he's dozin, his bluid it is frozen—
    O, dreary's the night wi' a crazy auld man!

He hums and he hankers, he frets and he cankers,
    I never can please him do a' that I can;
He's peevish an' jealous o' a' the young fellows,
    O, dool on the day I met wi' an auld man!

My auld auntie Katie upon me taks pity,
    I'll do my endeavour to follow her plan;
I'll cross him an' wrack him until I heartbreak him,
    And then his auld brass will buy me a new pan,

THE POSIE

O luve will venture in where it daur na weel be seen,
O luve will venture in where wisdom ance has been;
But I will doun yon river rove, amang the woods sae green,
    And a' to pu' a posie to my ain dear May.

The primrose I will pu', the firstling o' the year;
And I will pu' the pink, the emblem o' my dear,
For she's the pink o' womankind and blooms without a peer—
    And a' to be a posie to my ain dear May.

I'll pu' the budding rose when Phoebus peeps in view,
For it's like a baumy kiss o' her sweet, bonnie mou;
The hyacinth's for constancy wi' its unchanging blue,
    And a' to be a posie to my ain dear May.

The lily it is pure, and the lily it is fair,
And in her lovely bosom I'll place the lily there;
The daisy's for simplicity and unaffected air,
    And a' to be a posie to my ain dear May.

The hawthorn I will pu', wi' its locks o' siller grey,
Where like an agéd man it stands at break o' day;
But the songster's nest within the bush I winna tak away;
    And a' to be a posie to my ain dear May.

The woodbine I will pu' when the e'ening star is near,
And the diamond draps o' dew shall be her een sae clear;
The violet's for modesty, which weel she fa's to wear,
    And a' to be a posie to my ain dear May.

I'll tie the posie round wi' the silken band o' luve,
And I'll place it in her breast, and I'll swear by a' above
That to my latest draught o' life the band shall ne'er remove,
    And this will be a posie to my ain dear May.

On Glenriddell's Fox Breaking His Chain—A Fragment

Thou, Liberty, thou art my theme;
Not such as idle poets dream,
Who trick thee up a heathen goddess
That a fantastic cap and rod has:
Such stale conceits are poor and silly;
I paint thee out, a Highland filly,
A sturdy, stubborn, handsome dapple,
As sleek 's a mouse, as round 's an apple,
That when thou pleasest canst do wonders;
But when thy luckless rider blunders,
Or if thy fancy should demur there,
Wilt break thy neck ere thou go further.

These things premised, I sing a fox—
Was caught among his native rocks
And to a dirty kennel chain'd,
How he his liberty regain'd.

Glenriddell! a Whig without a stain,
A Whig in principle and grain,
Could'st thou enslave a free-born creature,
A native denizen of Nature?
How could'st thou, with a heart so good
(A better ne'er was sluic'd with blood)
Nail a poor devil to a tree
That ne'er did harm to thine or thee?

The staunchest Whig Glenriddell was,
Quite frantic in his country's cause;
And oft was Reynard's prison passing,
And with his brother Whigs canvassing
The Rights of Men, the Powers of Women,
With all the dignity of Freemen.

Sir Reynard daily heard debates
Of princes', kings' and nations' fates,
With many rueful, bloody stories
Of tyrants, Jacobites, and Tories:
From liberty how angels fell,
That now are galley slaves in hell;
How Nimrod first the trade began
Of binding Slavery's chains on Man;
How fell Semiramis—God damn her!—
Did first with sacrilegious hammer
(All ills till then were trivial matters)
For Man dethron'd forge hen-peck fetters;
How Xerxes, that abandoned Tory,
Thought cutting throats was reaping glory,
Until the stubborn Whigs of Sparta
Taught him great Nature's Magna Charta;
How mighty Rome her fiat hurl'd
Resistless o'er a bowing world,
And, kinder than they did desire,
Polish'd mankind with sword and fire;
With much too tedious to relate
Of ancient and of modern date,
But ending still, how Billy Pitt
(Unlucky boy!) with wicked wit
Has gagg'd old Britain, drain'd her coffer,
As butchers bind and bleed a heifer.

Thus wily Reynard by degrees,
In kennel listening at his ease,
Suck'd in a mighty stock of knowledge,
As much as some folks at a college;
Knew Britain's rights and constitution,
Her aggrandisement, diminution,
How fortune wrought us good from evil;
Let no man then despise the devil,
As who should say, 'I never can need him,'
Since we to scoundrels owe our freedom.

On Pastoral Poetry—A Sketch

Hail, Poesie! thou nymph reserv'd!
In chase o' thee, what crowds hae swerv'd
Frae common sense, or sunk enerv'd
      'Mang heaps o' clavers;

And och! o'er aft thy joes hae starv'd,
      'Mid a' thy favours!

Say, Lassie, why, thy train amang,
While loud the trump's heroic clang,
And sock or buskin skelp alang
      To death or marriage;
Scarce ane has tried the shepherd-sang
      But wi' miscarriage?

In Homer's craft Jock Milton thrives;
Eschylus' pen Will Shakespeare drives;
Wee Pope, the knurlin', 'till him rives
      Horatian fame;
In thy sweet sang, Barbauld, survives
      Even Sappho's flame.

But thee, Theocritus, wha matches?
They're no' herd's ballats, Maro's catches;
Squire Pope but busks his skinklin' patches
      O' heathen tatters:
I pass by hunders, nameless wretches,
      That ape their betters.

In this braw age o' wit and lear,
Will nane the Shepherd's whistle mair
Blaw sweetly in its native air
      And rural grace;
And, wi' the far-fam'd Grecian, share
      A rival place?

Yes! there is ane—a Scottish callan!
There's ane: come forrit, honest Allan!
Thou need na jouk behint the hallan,
      A chiel sae clever;
The teeth o' time may gnaw Tantallan,
      But thou's for ever.

Thou paints auld Nature to the nines
In thy sweet Caledonian lines;
Nae gowden stream thro' myrtle twines
      Where Philomel,
While nightly breezes sweep the vines,
      Her griefs will tell!

Thy rural loves are Nature's sel';
Nae bombast spates o' nonsense swell;
Nae snap conceits, but that sweet spell
      O' witchin love,
That charm that can the strongest quell,
      The sternest move.

In gowany glens thy burnie strays,
Where bonnie lasses bleach their claes;
Or trots by hazelly shaws and braes
 Wi' hawthorns grey,
Where blackbirds join the shepherd's lays
 At close o' day.

THE GALLANT WEAVER
Tune—*The weaver's march*

Where Cart rins rowin' to the sea,
By monie a flower and spreading tree,
There lives a lad, the lad for me,
 He is a gallant Weaver.

O, I had wooers aught or nine,
They gied me rings and ribbons fine;
And I was fear'd my heart wad tine,
 And I gied it to the Weaver.

My daddie sign'd my tocher-band,
To gie the lad that has the land,
But to my heart I'll add my hand,
 And give it to the Weaver.

While birds rejoice in leafy bowers,
While bees delight in opening flowers,
While corn grows green in summer showers,
 I love my gallant Weaver.

EPIGRAM AT BROWNHILL INN

At Brownhill we always get dainty good cheer,
And plenty of bacon each day in the year;
We've a' thing that's nice, and mostly in season—
But why always Bacon[1]—come, tell me a reason?

[1] Bacon was the name of the landlord, who would seem to have been given to intruding on his guests.

YOU'RE WELCOME, WILLIE STEWART[1]

Chorus: You're welcome, Willie Stewart,
 You're welcome, Willie Stewart;
There's ne'er a flower that blooms in May
 That's half sae welcome 's thou art!

Come, bumpers high, express your joy,
 The bowl we maun renew it;
The tappet hen, gae bring her ben,
 To welcome Willie Stewart.

May foes be strang and friends be slack,
 Ilk action may he rue it;
May woman on him turn her back
 That wrangs thee, Willie Stewart.

[1] Written on a tumbler by Burns on the arrival of a friend William Stewart, a factor in Nithsdale and brother-in-law of Bacon, landlord of the Brownhill Inn. The tumbler became Sir Walter Scott's property.

LOVELY POLLY STEWART[1]
Tune—*You're welcome, Charlie Stewart*

Chorus: O lovely Polly Stewart,
 O charming Polly Stewart,
There's ne'er a flower that blooms in May
 That's half so fair as thou art!

[1] Daughter of William Stewart, the Nithsdale factor. She married a large proprietor, fell into bad ways and died in Florence.

The flower it blaws, it fades, it fa's,
    And art can ne'er renew it;
But worth and truth, eternal youth
    Will gie to Polly Stewart,

May he whase arms shall fauld thy charms
    Possess a leal and true heart!
To him be given to ken the heaven
    He grasps in Polly Stewart!

COCK UP YOUR BEAVER

When first my brave Johnie lad came to this town,
He had a blue bonnet that wanted the crown;
But now he has gotten a hat and a feather,
Hey, brave Johnie lad, cock up your beaver!

Cock up your beaver, and cock it fu' sprush;
We'll over the border and gie them a brush;
There's somebody there we'll teach better behaviour,
Hey, brave Johnie lad, cock up your beaver!

EPPIE MACNAB

O, saw ye my dearie, my Eppie Macnab?
O, saw ye my dearie, my Eppie Macnab?
    'She's down in the yard, she's kissin the laird,
She winna come hame to her ain Jock Rab!'

O, come thy ways to me, my Eppie Macnab!
O, come thy ways to me, my Eppie Macnab!
    Whate'er thou hast done, be it late, be it soon,
Thou's welcome again to thy ain Jock Rab.

What says she, my dearie, my Eppie Macnab?
What says she, my dearie, my Eppie Macnab?
    'She let's thee to wit that she has thee forgot,
And for ever disowns thee, her ain Jock Rab.'

O, had I ne'er seen thee, my Eppie Macnab!
O, had I ne'er seen thee, my Eppie Macnab!
    As light as the air and as fause as thou's fair,
Thou's broken the heart o' thy ain Jock Rab.

MY TOCHER'S THE JEWEL

O, meikle thinks my luve o' my beauty,
    And meikle thinks my luve o' my kin;
But little thinks my luve, I ken brawlie,
    My tocher's the jewel has charms for him.
It's a' for the apple he'll nourish the tree,
    It's a' for the hinny he'll cherish the bee;
My laddie's sae meikle in luve wi' the siller,
    He canna hae luve to spare for me.

Your proffer o' luve's an airle-penny,
    My tocher's the bargain ye wad buy;

But an ye be crafty, I am cunnin',
　　Sae ye wi anither your fortune may try.
Ye're like to the timmer o' yon rotten wood,
　　Ye're like to the bark o' yon rotten tree,
Ye'll slip frae me like a knotless thread,
　　And ye'll crack your credit wi' mae nor me.

O For Ane An' Twenty, Tam
Tune—*The moudiewart*

Chorus: An' O, for ane an' twenty, Tam!
　　And hey, sweet ane an' twenty, Tam!
I'll learn my kin a rattlin' sang,
　　An I saw ane an' twenty, Tam.

They snool me sair and haud me down,
　　An' gar me look like bluntie, Tam;
But three short years will soon wheel roun',
　　And then comes ane an' twenty, Tam.

A glieb o' lan', a claut o' gear,
　　Was left me by my auntie, Tam;
At kith or kin I need na spier,
　　An I saw ane an' twenty, Tam.

They'll hae me wed a wealthy coof,
　　Tho' I mysel' hae plenty, Tam;
But hear'st thou, laddie! there's my loof,
　　I'm thine at ane an' twenty, Tam!

Thou Fair Eliza

Turn again, thou fair Eliza!
　　Ae kind blink before we part;
Rue on thy despairing lover,
　　Can'st thou break his faithfu' heart?
Turn again, thou fair Eliza!
　　If to love thy heart denies,
For pity hide the cruel sentence
　　Under friendship's kind disguise!

Thee, sweet maid, hae I offended?
　　My offence is loving thee:
Can'st thou wreck his peace for ever,
　　Wha for thine would gladly die?
While the life beats in my bosom,
　　Thou shalt mix in ilka throe:
Turn again, thou lovely maiden,
　　Ae sweet smile on me bestow.

Not the bee upon the blossom,
　　In the pride o' sinny noon;

Not the little sporting fairy,
 All beneath the simmer moon;
Not the Minstrel in the moment
 Fancy lightens in his e'e,
Kens the pleasure, feels the rapture,
 That thy presence gies to me.

My Bonnie Bell

The smiling spring comes in rejoicing,
 And surly winter grimly flies;
Now crystal clear are the falling waters,
 And bonnie blue are the sunny skies.
Fresh o'er the mountains breaks forth the morning,
 The ev'ning gilds the ocean's swell;
All creatures joy in the sun's returning,
 And I rejoice in my Bonnie Bell.

The flowery spring leads sunny summer,
 The yellow autumn presses near;
Then in his turn comes gloomy winter,
 Till smiling spring again appear:
Thus seasons dancing, life advancing,
 Old Time and Nature their changes tell;
But never ranging, still unchanging,
 I adore my Bonnie Bell.

Sweet Afton

Flow gently, sweet Afton among thy green braes,
Flow gently, I'll sing thee a song in thy praise;
My Mary's asleep by thy murmuring stream—
Flow gently, sweet Afton, disturb not her dream!

Thou stock dove whose echo resounds thro' the glen,
Ye wild whistling blackbirds in yon thorny den,
Thou green-crested lapwing, thy screaming forbear—
I charge you, disturb not my slumbering Fair!

How lofty, sweet Afton, thy neighbouring hills,
Far mark'd with the courses of clear, winding rills;
There daily I wander as noon rises high,
My flocks and my Mary's sweet cot in my eye.

How pleasant thy banks and green valleys below,
Where wild in the woodlands the primroses blow;
There oft, as mild ev'ning weeps over the lea,
The sweet-scented birk shades my Mary and me.

Thy crystal stream, Afton, how lovely it glides,
And winds by the cot where my Mary resides;
How wanton thy waters her snowy feet lave,
As, gathering sweet flowerets she stems thy clear wave!

Flow gently, sweet Afton, among thy green braes,
Flow gently, sweet river, the theme of my lays;
My Mary's asleep by thy murmuring stream—
Flow gently, sweet Afton, disturb not her dream!

Address To The Shade Of Thomson
On crowning his Bust[1] at Ednam, Roxburghshire, with a Wreath of Bays

While virgin Spring by Eden's flood
    Unfolds her tender mantle green,
Or pranks the sod in frolic mood,
    Or tunes Eolian strains between.

While Summer with a matron grace
    Retreats to Dryburgh's cooling shade,
Yet oft, delighted, stops to trace
    The progress of the spiky blade.

While Autumn, benefactor kind,
    By Tweed erects his agéd head,
And sees, with self-approving mind,
    Each creature on his bounty fed.

While maniac Winter rages o'er
    The hills whence classic Yarrow flows,
Rousing the turbid torrent's roar,
    Or sweeping, wild, a waste of snows.

So long, sweet Poet of the year!
    Shall bloom that wreath thou well hast won;
While Scotia, with exulting tear,
    Proclaims that Thomson was her son.

[1] This was in September 1790, under the eye of the Earl of Buchan. Burns was invited but sent this instead of himself—a poor substitute.

Nithsdale's Welcome Hame[1]

The noble Maxwells and their powers
    Are coming o'er the border,
And they'll gae big Terreagles' towers
    And set them a' in order.
And they declare Terreagles fair,
    For their abode they choose it;
There's no a heart in a' the land
    But's lighter at the news o't.

Tho' stars in skies may disappear,
    And angry tempests gather;

[1] Composed when Lady Winifred Maxwell returned to Scotland and rebuilt Terreagles House, near Dumfries. She was descended from the forfeited Earl of Nithsdale.

The happy hour may soon be near
    That brings us pleasant weather:
The weary night o' care and grief
    May hae a joyfu' morrow;
So dawning day has brought relief,
    Fareweel our night o' sorrow.

FRAE THE FRIENDS AND LAND I LOVE
Tune—*Carron-side*

Frae the friends and land I love,
    Driven by Fortune's felly spite,
Frae my best belov'd I rove,
    Never mair to taste delight:
Never mair maun hope to find
    Ease frae toil, relief frae care;
When Remembrance wracks the mind,
    Pleasures but unveil despair.

Brightest climes shall mirk appear,
    Desert ilka blooming shore,
Till the Fates, nae mair severe,
    Friendship, love and peace restore,
Till Revenge, wi' laurell'd head,
    Bring our banished hame again;
And ilk loyal, bonnie lad
    Cross the seas and win his ain.

SUCH A PARCEL OF ROGUES IN A NATION

Fareweel to a' our Scottish fame,
    Fareweel our ancient glory;
Fareweel ev'n to the Scottish name,
    Sae fam'd in martial story.
Now Sark rins over Solway sands,
    An' Tweed rins to the ocean,
To mark where England's province stands—
    Such a parcel of rogues[1] in a nation!

What force or guile could not subdue,
    Thro' many warlike ages,
Is wrought now by a coward few,
    For hireling traitors' wages.
The English steel we could disdain,
    Secure in valour's station;
But English gold has been our bane—
    Such a parcel of rogues in a nation!

O would, or I had seen the day
    That treason thus could sell us,
My auld grey head had lien in clay,
    Wi' Bruce and loyal Wallace!

---

[1] The Scottish commisioners who took part in negotiating the Act of Union of 1707.

But pith and power, till my last hour,
    I'll mak this declaration—
We're bought and sold for English gold—
    Such a parcel of rogues in a nation!

YE JACOBITES BY NAME

Ye Jacobites by name, give an ear, give an ear,
Ye Jacobites by name, give an ear;
    Ye Jacobites by name,
    Your fautes I will proclaim,
Your doctrines I maun blame—you shall hear!

What is Right and what is Wrang, by the law, by the law?
What is Right and what is Wrang, by the law?
    What is Right and what is Wrang?
    A short sword and a lang,
A weak arm and a strang, for to draw!

What makes heroic strife fam'd afar, fam'd afar?
What makes heroic strife fam'd afar?
    What makes heroic strife?
    To whet th' Assassin's knife,
Or hunt a Parent's life wi' bluidy war?

Then let your schemes alone, in the State, in the State,
Then let your schemes alone in the State.
    Then let your schemes alone,
    Adore the rising sun,
And leave a man undone, to his fate.

I HAE BEEN AT CROOKIEDEN
Tune—*The old Highland laddie*

I hae been at Crookieden,
    My bonnie laddie, Highland laddie,
Viewing Willie[1] and his men,
    My bonnie laddie, Highland laddie.
There our foes that burnt and slew,
    My bonnie laddie, Highland laddie,
There, at last, they gat their due,
    My bonnie laddie, Highland laddie.

Satan sits in his black neuk,
    My bonnie laddie, Highland laddie,
Breaking sticks to roast the Duke,
    My bonnie laddie, Highland laddie,
The bloody monster gae a yell,
    My bonnie laddie, Highland laddie.
And loud the laugh gied round a' hell
    My bonnie laddie, Highland laddie.

[1] The Duke of Cumberland.

O, KENMURE'S ON AND AWA', WILLIE

O, Kenmure's on and awa', Willie,
    O, Kenmure's on and awa';
An' Kenmure's lord's the bravest lord
    That ever Galloway saw!

Success to Kenmure's band, Willie,
    Success to Kenmure's band!
There's no a heart that fears a Whig
    That rides by Kenmure's hand.

Here's Kenmure's health in wine, Willie,
    Here's Kenmure's health in wine!
There ne'er was a coward o' Kenmure's bluid,
    Nor yet o' Gordon's line.

O, Kenmure's lads are men, Willie,
    O, Kenmure's lads are men!
Their hearts and swords are metal true,
    And that their foes shall ken.

They'll live or die wi' fame, Willie,
    They'll live or die wi' fame!
But soon wi' sounding victorie
    May Kenmure's lord come hame!

Here's him that's far awa', Willie,
    Here's him that's far awa'!
And here's the flower that I lo'e best,
    The rose that's like the snaw.

EPISTLE TO JOHN MAXWELL, ESQ., OF TERRAUGHTIE
On his Birthday

Health to the Maxwells' veteran Chief!
Health, aye unsour'd by care or grief!
Inspir'd, I turn'd Fate's sibyl leaf,
    This natal morn,
I see thy life is stuff o' prief,
    Scarce quite half-worn.

This day thou metes threescore eleven,
And I can tell that bounteous Heaven
(The second-sight, ye ken, is given
    To ilka Poet)
On thee a tack o' seven times seven
    Will yet bestow it.

If envious buckies view wi' sorrow
Thy lengthen'd days on this blest morrow,

May Desolation's lang-teeth'd harrow,
    Nine miles an hour,
Rake them like Sodom and Gomorrah,
    In brunstane stour.

But for thy friends, and they are monie,
Baith honest men and lassies bonnie,
May couthie Fortune, kind and cannie,
    In social glee,
Wi' mornings blythe and e'enings funny
    Bless them and thee!

Fareweel, auld birkie! Lord be near ye,
And then the deil, he daur na steer ye:
Your friends aye love, your faes aye fear ye!
    For me, shame fa' me,
If neist my heart I dinna wear ye,
    While Burns they ca' me.

THIRD EPISTLE TO ROBERT GRAHAM, ESQ., OF FINTRY
5 October 1791

Late crippl'd of an arm, and now a leg,[1]
About to beg a pass for leave to beg;
Dull, listless, teas'd, dejected and deprest
(Nature is adverse to a cripple's rest);
Will generous Graham list to his Poet's wail?
(It soothes poor Misery, heark'ning to her tale)
And hear him curse the light he first survey'd,
And doubly curse the luckless rhyming trade?

Thou, Nature! partial Nature, I arraign;
Of thy caprice maternal I complain.
The lion and the bull thy care have found,
One shakes the forests, and one spurns the ground;
Thou giv'st the ass his hide, the snail his shell;
Th' envenom'd wasp, victorious, guards his cell.
Thy minions, kings, defend, control, devour,
In all th' omnipotence of rule and power.
Foxes and statesmen subtile wiles ensure;
The cit and polecat stink, and are secure;
Toads with their poison, doctors with their drug,
The priest and hedgehog in their robes, are snug;
Even silly woman has her warlike arts,
Her tongue and eyes—her dreaded spear and darts.

But O! thou bitter stepmother and hard,
To thy poor, fenceless, naked child—the Bard!
A thing unteachable in world's skill,
And half an idiot too, more helpless still.
No heels to bear him from the opening dun;
No claws to dig, his hated sight to shun;

[1] After a fall from his horse.

No horns, but those by luckless Hymen worn,
And those, alas! not Amalthea's horn:
No nerves olfact'ry, Mammon's trusty cur,
Clad in rich Dulness' comfortable fur.
In naked feeling, and in aching pride,
He bears th' unbroken blast from every side:
Vampyre booksellers drain him to the heart,
And scorpion critics cureless venom dart.

Critics—appall'd, I venture on the name,
Those cut-throat bandits in the paths of fame:
Bloody dissectors, worse than ten Monroes;[1]
He hacks to teach, they mangle to expose:

His heart by causeless wanton malice wrung,
By blockheads' daring into madness stung;
His well-won bays, than life itself more dear,
By miscreants torn, who ne'er one sprig must wear:
Foil'd, bleeding, tortur'd in the unequal strife,
The hapless Poet flounders on thro' life.
Till fled each hope that once his bosom fired,
And fled each muse that glorious once inspir'd,
Low sunk in squalid, unprotected age,
Dead even resentment for his injur'd page,
He heeds or feels no more the ruthless critic's rage!
So, by some hedge, the gen'rous steed deceas'd,
For half-starv'd snarling curs a dainty feast;
By toil and famine wore to skin and bone,
Lies, senseless of each tugging bitch's son.

O Dulness! portion of the truly blest!
Calm shelter'd haven of eternal rest!
Thy sons ne'er madden in the fierce extremes
Of Fortune's polar frost, or torrid beams.
If mantling high she fills the golden cup,
With sober selfish ease they sip it up:
Conscious the bounteous meed they well deserve,
They only wonder 'some folks' do not starve.
The grave sage hern thus easy picks his frog
And thinks the mallard a sad worthless dog.
When disappointment snaps the clue of hope,
And thro' disastrous night they darkling grope,
With deaf endurance sluggishly they bear,
And just conclude that 'fools are fortune's care.'
So, heavy, passive to the tempest's shocks,
Strong on the signpost stands the stupid ox.

Not so the idle Muses' madcap train,
Not such the workings of their moonstruck brain;
In equanimity they never dwell,
By turns in soaring heav'n or vaulted hell.

[1] Alexander Monroe, Professor of Anatomy, Edinburgh.

I dread thee, Fate, relentless and severe,
With all a poet's, husband's, father's fear!
Already one strong hold of hope is lost—
Glencairn, the truly noble, lies in dust
(Fled, like the sun eclips'd as noon appears,
And left us darkling in a world of tears);
O! hear my ardent, grateful, selfish prayer!
Fintry, my other stay, long bless and spare!
Thro' a long life his hopes and wishes crown;
And bright in cloudless skies his sun go down!
May bliss domestic smooth his private path;
Give energy to life; and soothe his latest breath,
With many a filial tear circling the bed of death!

Additional Lines[1]

A little, upright, pert, tart, tripping wight,
And still his precious self his dear delight;
Who loves his own smart shadow in the streets,
Better than e'er the fairest she he meets.
Much specious lore, but little understood—
Veneering oft outshines the solid wood:
A man of fashion, too, he made his tour,
Learn'd 'vive la bagatelle et vive l'amour';
So travell'd monkeys their grimace improve,
Polish their grin—nay sigh for ladies' love.
His solid sense—by inches you must tell,
But mete his cunning by the Scottish ell;
His meddling vanity, a busy fiend,
Still making work his selfish craft must mend.

                    Crochallan came;
The old cock'd hat, the brown surtout the same;
His grisly beard just bristling in its might,
'Twas four long nights and days from shaving-night;
His uncomb'd, hoary locks, wild-staring, thatch'd,
A head for thought profound and clear, unmatch'd;
Yet, tho' his caustic wit was biting-rude,
His heart was warm, benevolent and good.

[1] On William Creech, the Edinburgh publisher, and the late Mr William Smellie, author of the *Philosophy of Natural History* and member of the Antiquarian and Royal Societies of Edinburgh.

THE SONG OF DEATH
Tune—*Oran an aoig*
Scene—A Field of Battle. Time of the day—evening. The wounded and dying of the victorious army are supposed to join in the following song

Farewell, thou fair day, thou green earth, and ye skies,
    Now gay with the broad setting sun!
Farewell, loves and friendships, ye dear tender ties—
    Our race of existence is run!
Thou grim king of terrors, thou life's gloomy foe!
    Go frighten the coward and slave!

Go teach them to tremble, fell tyrant! but know,
    No terrors hast thou to the brave!

Thou strik'st the dull peasant—he sinks in the dark,
    Nor saves e'en the wreck of a name;
Thou strik'st the young hero—a glorious mark!
    He falls in the blaze of his fame.
In the field of proud honour, our swords in our hands,
    Our king and our country to save,
While victory shines on life's last ebbing sands,
    O! who would not die with the brave!

On Sensibility
To my dear and much honoured friend, Mrs Dunlop of Dunlop
Tune—*Cornwallis' lament for Colonel Moorehouse*

Sensibility how charming,
    Dearest Nancy, thou canst tell;
But distress with horrors arming,
    Thou alas! hast known too well!

Fairest flower, behold the lily
    Blooming in the sunny ray.
Let the blast sweep o'er the valley,
    See it prostrate in the clay.

Hear the woodlark charm the forest,
    Telling o'er his little joys;
But alas! a prey the surest
    To each pirate of the skies.

Dearly bought the hidden treasure
    Finer feelings can bestow:
Chords that vibrate sweetest pleasure
    Thrill the deepest notes of woe.

The Toadeater

Of Lordly acquaintance you boast,
    And the Dukes that you dined wi' yestreen,
Yet an insect's an insect at most,
    Tho' it crawl on the curl of a Queen!

Another Version

No more of your titled acquaintances boast,
    Nor of the gay groups you have seen;
A crab louse is but a crab louse at last,
    Tho' stack to the   of a Queen.

In Lamington Kirk

As cauld a wind as ever blew,
A cauld kirk, an in 't but few:
As cauld a minister's ever spak;
Ye'se a' be het or I come back.

The Keekin' Glass
A lord in a state of inebriation, while dining in Mr Miller's of Dalswinton, asked about one of his daughters, 'Wha's yon howlet-faced thing in the corner?' Burns replied as follows:

How daur ye ca' me 'Howlet-face',
    Ye blear-e'ed, withered spectre?
Ye only spied the keekin' glass,
    An' there ye saw your picture.

A GRACE BEFORE DINNER, EXTEMPORE

O, Thou, who kindly dost provide
    For every creature's want!
We bless Thee, God of nature wide,
    For all Thy goodness lent:
And if it please Thee, Heavenly Guide,
    May never worse be sent;
But whether granted or denied,
    Lord bless us with content! Amen!

A GRACE AFTER DINNER, EXTEMPORE

O, Thou, in whom we live and move,
    Who mad'st the sea and shore,
Thy goodness constantly we prove,
    And grateful would adore.
And if it please Thee, Power above,
    Still grant us with such store;
The friend we trust, the fair we love,
    And we desire no more.

O MAY, THY MORN[1]
Tune—*The rashes*

O May, thy morn was ne'er so sweet
    As the mirk night o' December!
For sparkling was the rosy wine,
    And private was the chamber:
And dear was she I dare na name,
    But I will aye remember.
And here's to them that, like oursel,
    Can push about the jorum!
And here's to them that wish us weel,
    May a' that's guid watch o'er 'em!
And here's to them we dare na tell,
    The dearest o' the quorum!

[1] Alluding, it is thought, to one of his final meetings with Clarinda.

AE FOND KISS[1]
Tune—*Rory Dall's port*

Ae fond kiss, and then we sever;
Ae fareweel, alas, for ever!
Deep in heart-wrung tears I'll pledge thee,
Warring sighs and groans I'll wage thee.
Who shall say that Fortune grieves him,
While the star of hope she leaves him?
Me, nae cheerfu' twinkle lights me;
Dark despair around benights me.

I'll ne'er blame my partial fancy:
Naething could resist my Nancy!
But to see her was to love her,
Love but her, and love for ever.

[1] Written on his parting from Clarinda. The verses are beautiful, but the idea of either party being 'broken-hearted' is purely fanciful.

Had we never lov'd sae kindly,
Had we never lov'd sae blindly,
Never met—or never parted—
We had ne'er been broken-hearted.[1]

Fare-thee-weel, thou first and fairest!
Fare-thee-weel, thou best and dearest!
Thine be ilka joy and treasure,
Peace, enjoyment, love and pleasure!
Ae fond kiss, and then we sever!
Ae fareweel, alas, for ever!
Deep in heart-wrung tears I'll pledge thee,
Warring sighs and groans I'll wage thee.

[1] These four lines, Sir Walter Scott said, 'contain the essence of a thousand love tales'.

BEHOLD THE HOUR[1]
Tune—*Oran-gaoil*
First Version

Behold the hour, the boat arrive!
    My dearest Nancy, O fareweel!
Sever'd frae thee, can I survive,
    Frae thee whom I hae lov'd sae weel?

Endless and deep shall be my grief,
    Nae ray of comfort shall I see,
But this most precious, dear belief,
    That thou wilt still remember me!

Along the solitary shore
    Where flitting sea-fowl round me cry,
Across the rolling, dashing roar,
    I'll westward turn my wistful eye.

'Happy thou Indian grove,' I'll say,
    'Where now my Nancy's path shall be!
While thro' your sweets she holds her way,
    O, tell me, does she muse on me?'

[1] Clarinda is said to have been the inspirer of these verses. She was going to the West Indes.

BEHOLD THE HOUR
Second Version

Behold the hour, the boat arrive!
    Thou goest, thou darling of my heart!
Severed from thee, can I survive?
    But Fate has willed—and we must part.
I'll often greet the surging swell,
    Yon distant isle will often hail:
'E'en here I took the last farewell;
    There latest marked her vanished sail.'

Along the solitary shore,
    While flitting sea-fowl round me cry,
Across the rolling, dashing roar,
    I'll westward turn my wistful eye.
'Happy thou Indian grove,' I'll say,
    'Where now my Nancy's path shall be!
While thro' thy sweets she loves to stray,
    O tell me, does she muse on me?'

THOU GLOOMY DECEMBER

Ance mair I hail thee, thou gloomy December!
    Ance mair I hail thee wi' sorrow and care;
Sad was the parting thou makes me remember—
    Parting wi' Nancy,[1] oh, ne'er to meet mair!
Fond lovers' parting is sweet, painful pleasure,
    Hope beaming mild on the soft parting hour;
But the dire feeling, O farewell for ever!
    Is anguish unmingled and agony pure!

Wild as the winter now tearing the forest,
    Till the last leaf o' the summer is flown;
Such is the tempest has shaken my bosom
    Till my last hope and last comfort is gone.
Still as I hail thee, thou gloomy December,
    Still shall I hail thee wi' sorrow and care;
For sad was the parting thou makes me remember,
    Parting wi' Nancy, oh, ne'er to meet mair.

[1] Clarinda.

MY NATIVE LAND SAE FAR AWA
Tune—*Dalkeith maiden bridge*

O, sad and heavy, should I part,
    But for her sake, sae far awa;
Unknowing what my way may thwart,
    My native land sae far awa.

Thou that of a' things Maker art,
    That formed this Fair sae far awa,
Gie body strength, then I'll ne'er start
    At this my way sae far awa.

How true is love to pure desert!
    Like mine for her sae far awa;
And nocht can heal my bosom's smart,
    While, oh, she is sae far awa!

Nane other love, nane other dart,
    I feel but her's sae far awa;
But fairer never touch'd a heart
    Than her's, the Fair, sae far awa.

I DO CONFESS THOU ART SAE FAIR
Alteration of an Old Poem
Tune—*I do confess thou'rt smooth and fair*

I do confess thou art sae fair,
    I wad been o'er the lugs in luve,
Had I na found the slightest prayer
    That lips could speak thy heart could muve.

I do confess thee sweet, but find
    Thou art sae thriftless o' thy sweets,
Thy favours are the silly wind
    That kisses ilka thing it meets.

See yonder rose-bud, rich in dew,
    Amang its native briers sae coy,
How sune it tines its scent and hue,
    When pu'd and worn a common toy.

Sic fate ere lang shall thee betide,
    Though thou may gaily bloom awhile;
And sune thou shalt be thrown aside,
    Like onie common weed and vile.

LINES ON FERGUSSON, THE POET[1]

Ill-fated genius! Heaven-taught Fergusson,
    What heart that feels and will not yield a tear,
To think Life's sun did set e'er well begun
    To shed its influence on thy bright career.

O why should truest Worth and Genius pine
    Beneath the iron grasp of Want and Woe,
While titled knaves and idiot-greatness shine
    In all the splendour Fortune can bestow?

[1] *See also* page 197.

THE WEARY PUND O' TOW

Chorus: The weary pund, the weary pund,
    The weary pund o' tow;
I think my wife will end her life,
    Before she spin her tow.

I bought my wife a stane o' lint,
    As guid as e'er did grow,
And a' that she has made o' that
    Is ae puir pund o' tow.

There sat a bottle in a bole,
    Beyont the ingle low;
And aye she took the tither souk,
    To drouk the stourie tow.

Quoth I, 'For shame, ye dirty dame,
    Gae spin your tap o' tow!'
She took the rock, and wi' a knock,
    She brak it o'er my pow.

At last her feet—I sang to see 't!
    Gaed foremost o'er the knowe,
And or I wad anither jad,
    I'll wallop in a tow.

WHEN SHE CAM' BEN, SHE BOBBED

O, when she cam' ben she bobbéd fu' law,
O, when she cam' ben she bobbéd fu' law,
And when she cam' ben, she kiss'd Cockpen,
    And syne denied she did it at a'.

And was na Cockpen right saucy witha'?
And was na Cockpen right saucy witha'?
In leaving the daughter of a lord,
And kissin' a collier lassie an' a'!

O never look down, my lassie, at a'!
O never look down, my lassie, at a'!
Thy lips are as sweet, and thy figure complete,
As the finest dame in castle or ha'.

Tho' thou has nae silk and holland sae sma',
Tho' thou has nae silk and holland sae sma',
Thy coat and thy sark are thy ain handywark,
And Lady Jean was never sae braw.'

SCROGGAM, MY DEARIE

There was a wife wonn'd in Cockpen,
 Scroggam;
She brew'd guid ale for gentlemen;
 Sing auld Cowl, lay ye down by me,
 Scroggam, my dearie, ruffum.

The guidwife's dochter fell in a fever,
 Scroggam;
The priest o' the parish he fell in anither;
 Sing auld Cowl, lay ye down by me,
 Scroggam, my dearie, ruffum.

They laid the twa i' the bed thegither,
 Scroggam;
That the heat o' the tane might cool the tither;
 Sing Auld Cowl, lay ye down by me,
 Scroggam, my dearie, ruffum.

MY COLLIER LADDIE

'O, whare live ye, my bonnie lass?
 And tell me how they ca' ye!'
'My name,' she says, 'is Mistress Jean,
 And I follow the collier laddie.'

'O, see you not yon hills and dales
 The sun shines on sae brawlie?
They a' are mine, and they shall be thine,
 Gin ye'll leave your collier laddie!

'An' ye shall gang in gay attire,
 Weel buskit up sae gaudy;
And ane to wait on every hand,
 Gin ye'll leave your collier laddie!'

'Tho' ye had a' the sun shines on,
 And the earth conceals sae lowly,
I wad turn my back on you and it a',
 And embrace my collier laddie.

'I can win my five pennies in a day,
 An' spend it at night fu' brawlie,
And make my bed in the collier's neuk,
 And lie down wi' my collier laddie.

'Loove for loove is the bargain for me,
 Tho' the wee cot-house should haud me,
And the warld before me to win my bread—
 And fair fa' my collier laddie!'

SIC A WIFE AS WILLIE HAD
Tune—*The fowler o' the glen*

Willie Wastle dwalt on Tweed,
    The spot they ca'd it Linkumdoddie;
Willie was a wabster guid,
    Could stoun a clue wi' onie body:
He had a wife was dour and din,
    O, Tinkler Maidgie was her mither;
Sic a wife as Willie had,
    I wad na gie a button for her.

She has an e'e, she has but ane,
    The cat has twa the very colour;
Five rusty teeth, forbye a stump,
    A clapper tongue wad deave a miller:
A whiskin' beard about her mou',
    Her nose and chin they threaten ither;
Sic a wife as Willie had,
    I wadna gie a button for her.

She's bow-hough'd, she's hem-shin'd,
    Ae limpin' leg a hand-breed shorter;
She's twisted right, she's twisted left,
    To balance fair in ilka quarter:
She has a lump upon her breast,
    The twin o' that upon her shouther;
Sic a wife as Willie had,
    I wadna gie a button for her.

Auld baudrons by the ingle sits,
    An' wi' her loof her face a-washin';
But Willie's wife is nae sae trig,
    She dights her grunzie wi' a hushion;
Her walie nieves like midden creels,
    Her face wad fyle the Logan Water;
Sic a wife as Willie had,
    I wadna gie a button for her.

LADY MARY ANN
Tune—*Craigstone's growin'*

O, Lady Mary Ann looks o'er the castle wa',
She saw three bonnie boys playing at the ba',
The youngest he was the flower amang them a',
    My bonnie laddie's young, but he's growin' yet.

O father, O father, an ye think it fit,
We'll send him a year to the college yet,
We'll sew a green ribbon round about his hat,
    And that will let them ken he's to marry yet.

Lady Mary Ann was a flower in the dew,
Sweet was its smell and bonnie was its hue,
And the longer it blossom'd the sweeter it grew;
   For the lily in the bud will be bonnier yet.

Young Charlie Cochran was the sprout of an aik,
Bonnie and bloomin' and straight was its make;
The sun took delight to shine for its sake,
   And it will be the brag o' the forest yet.

The simmer is gane when the leaves they were green,
And the days are awa' that we hae seen,
But far better days I trust will come again;
   For my bonnie laddie's young, but he's growin' yet.

KELLYBURN BRAES

There lived a carl in Kellyburn Braes,
   Hey and the rue grows bonnie wi' thyme,
And he had a wife was the plague o' his days,
   And the thyme it is wither'd, and rue is in prime.

Ae day as the carl gaed up the lang glen,
   Hey and the rue grows bonnie wi' thyme,
He met wi' the Deil, wha said, 'How do you fen?'
   And the thyme it is wither'd, and rue is in prime.

'I've got a bad wife, sir, that's a' my complaint,'
   Hey and the rue grows bonnie wi' thyme,
'For, saving your presence, to her ye're a saint,'
   And the thyme it is wither'd, and rue is in prime.

'It's neither your stot nor your staig I shall crave,'
   Hey and the rue grows bonnie wi' thyme;
'But gie me your wife, man, for her I must have,'
   And the thyme it is wither'd, and rue is in prime.

'O, welcome most kindly!' the blythe carl said,
   Hey and the rue grows bonnie wi' thyme,
'But if ye can match her ye're waur than ye're ca'd,'
   And the thyme it is wither'd, and rue is in prime.

The devil has got the auld wife on his back,
   Hey and the rue grows bonnie wi' thyme,
And like a poor pedlar he's carried his pack,
   And the thyme it is wither'd, and rue is in prime.

He's carried her hame to his ain hallan door,
   Hey and the rue grows bonnie wi' thyme,
Syne bade her gae in, for a bitch and a whore,
   And the thyme it is wither'd, and rue is in prime.

Then straight he makes fifty, the pick o' his band,
    Hey and the rue grows bonnie wi' thyme:
Turn out on her guard in the clap o' a hand,
    And the thyme it is wither'd, and rue is in prime.

The carlin gaed thro' them like onie wud bear,
    Hey and the rue grows bonnie wi' thyme;
Whae'er she gat hands on cam ne'er her nae mair,
    And the thyme it is wither'd, and rue is in prime.

A reekit wee devil looks over the wa',
    Hey and the rue grows bonnie wi' thyme;
'O help, maister, help! or she'll ruin us a'.'
    And the thyme it is wither'd, and rue is in prime.

The devil he swore by the edge o' his knife,
    Hey and the rue grows bonnie wi' thyme;
He pitied the man that was tied to a wife.
    And the thyme it is wither'd, and rue is in prime.

The devil he swore by the kirk and the bell,
    Hey and the rue grows bonnie wi' thyme,
He was not in wedlock, thank Heav'n, but in hell.
    And the thyme it is wither'd, and rue is in prime.

Then Satan has travell'd again wi' his pack,
    Hey and the rue grows bonnie wi' thyme,
And to her auld husband he's carried her back.
    And the thyme it is wither'd, and rue is in prime.

'I hae been a devil the feck o' my life,'
    Hey and the rue grows bonnie wi' thyme,
'But ne'er was in hell till I met wi' a wife.'
    And the thyme it is wither'd, and rue is in prime.

THE SLAVE'S LAMENT

It was in sweet Senegal that my foes did me enthral,
    For the lands of Virginia-ginia, O;
Torn from that lovely shore, and must never see it more;
    And alas! I am weary, weary O!

All on that charming coast is no bitter snow and frost,
    Like the lands of Virginia-ginia, O;
There streams for ever flow, and there flowers for ever blow,
    And alas! I am weary, weary O!

The burden I must bear, while the cruel scourge I fear,
    In the lands of Virginia-ginia, O;
And I think on friends most dear, with the bitter, bitter tear,
    And alas! I am weary, weary O!

O Can Ye Labour Lea?
Tune—Auld lang syne

Chorus: O can ye labour lea, young man,
　　O can ye labour lea?
Gae back the gate ye came again—
　　Ye'se never scorn me!

I fee'd a man at Martinmas,
　　Wi' airle pennies three;
But a' the faut I had to him,
　　He could na labour lea,

O clappin's guid in Febarwar,
　　An' kissin' 's sweet in May;
But what signifies a young man's love,
　　An' 't dinna last for aye?

O, kissin' is the key o' love,
　　And clappin' is the lock;
An' makin' o' 's the best thing yet
　　That e'er a young thing got!

The Deuks Dang O'er My Daddie

The bairns gat out wi' an unco shout,
　　'The deuks dang o'er my daddie, O!'
'The fient-ma-care,' quo' the feirrie auld wife,
　　'He was but a paidlin' body, O!
He paidles out, and he paidles in,
　　An' he paidles late and early, O!
This seven lang years I hae lien by his side,
　　An' he is but a fusionless carlie, O!'

'O haud your tongue, my feirrie auld wife,
　　O haud your tongue now, Nansie, O!
I've seen the day, and sae hae ye,
　　Ye wadna been sae donsie, O.
I've seen the day ye butter'd my brose,
　　And cuddl'd me late and early, O;
But downa do's come o'er me now,
　　And och, I feel it sairly, O!'

The Deil's Awa' Wi' The Exciseman
Tune—'The Hemp-Dresser'

Chorus: The deil's awa', the deil's awa',
　　The deil's awa' wi' the Exciseman,
He's danc'd awa', he's danc'd awa',
　　He's danc'd awa' wi' the Exciseman.

The deil cam fiddlin' thro' the town,
　　And danc'd awa' wi' th' Exciseman;
And ilka wife cries, 'Auld Mahoun,
　　I wish you luck o' the prize, man.'

We'll mak our maut, and we'll brew our drink,
　　We'll laugh, sing and rejoice, man,
And monie braw thanks to the meikle black deil
　　That danc'd awa' wi' th' Exciseman.

There's threesome reels, there's foursome reels,
    There's hornpipes and strathspeys, man,
But the ae best dance e'er cam to the land
    Was—*The Deil's awa' wi' th' Exciseman.*

THE COUNTRY LASSIE

In simmer, when the hay was mawn,
    And corn wav'd green in ilka field,
While claver blooms white o'er the lea
    And roses blaw in ilka beild!
Blythe Bessie in the milking shiel,
    Says, 'I'll be wed, come o't what will!'
Out spake a dame in wrinkled eild;
    'O gude advisement comes nae ill.

'It's ye hae wooers monie ane,
    And lassie, ye're but young, ye ken;
Then wait a wee, and cannie wale
    A routhie butt, a routhie ben:
There's Johnie o' the Buskie Glen,
    Fu' is his barn, fu' is his byre;
Tak this frae me, my bonnie hen,
    It's plenty beets the luver's fire.'

'For Johnie o' the Buskie Glen,
    I dinna care a single flie;
He lo'es sae weel his craps and kye,
    He has nae loove to spare for me;
But blythe's the blink o' Robie's e'e,
    And weel I wat he lo'es me dear;
Ae blink o' him I wad na gie
    For Buskie Glen and a' his gear.'

'O thoughtless lassie, life's a faught!
    The canniest gate, the strife is sair;
But aye fu'-han't is fechtin' best,
    A hungry care's an unco care:
But some will spend and some will spare,
    An' wilfu' folk maun hae their will;
Syne as ye brew, my maiden fair,
    Keep mind that ye maun drink the yill.'

'O gear will buy me rigs o' land,
    And gear will buy me sheep and kye;
But the tender heart o' leesome loove,
    The gowd and siller canna buy;
We may be poor, Robie and I;
    Light is the burden loove lays on;
Content and loove brings peace and joy—
    What mair hae queens upon a throne?'

BESSY AND HER SPINNING WHEEL
Tune—*Sweet's the lass that loves me*

O leeze me on my spinnin' wheel,
And leeze me on my rock and reel;
Frae tap to tae that cleeds me bien,
And haps me biel and warm at e'en!
I'll set me down and sing and spin,
While laigh descends the simmer sun,
Blest wi' content, and milk and meal,
O leeze me on my spinnin' wheel.

On ilka hand the burnies trot,
And meet below my theekit cot;
The scented birk and hawthorn white
Across the pool their arms unite,
Alike to screen the birdie's nest,
And little fishes' caller rest;
The sun blinks kindly in the biel'
Where blythe I turn my spinnin' wheel.

On lofty aiks the cushats wail,
And Echo cons the doolfu' tale;
The lintwhites in the hazel braes,
Delighted, rival ither's lays.
The craik amang the claver hay,
The pairtrick whirring o'er the ley,
The swallow jinkin' round my shiel,
Amuse me at my spinnin' wheel.

Wi' sma' to sell and less to buy,
Aboon distress, below envy,
O wha wad leave this humble state,
For a' the pride of a' the great?
Amid their flairing, idle toys,
Amid their cumbrous, dinsome joys,
Can they the peace and pleasure feel
Of Bessy at her spinnin' wheel?

LOVE FOR LOVE
Tune—*Jockey fou and Jenny fain*

Ithers seek they kenna what,
Features, carriage and a' that;
Gie me loove in her I court—
Loove to loove maks a' the sport.

Let loove sparkle in her e'e;
Let her lo'e nae man but me;
That's the tocher-guid I prize,
There the luver's treasure lies.

SAW YE BONNIE LESLEY
Tune—The collier's bonnie lassie

O saw ye bonnie Lesley,
    As she gaed o'er the border?
She's gane, like Alexander,
    To spread her conquests farther.

To see her is to love her,
    And love but her for ever;
For Nature made her what she is,
    And never made anither!

Thou art a queen, fair Lesley,
    Thy subjects, we before thee;
Thou art divine, fair Lesley,
    The hearts o' men adore thee.

The deil he could na scaith thee,
    Or aught that wad belang thee;
He'd look into thy bonnie face,
    And say, 'I canna wrang thee!'

The powers aboon will tent thee,
    Misfortune sha'na steer thee;
Thou'rt like themsel sae lovely,
    That ill they'll ne'er let near thee.

Return again, fair Lesley,
    Return to Caledonie!
That we may brag we hae a lass
    There's nane again sae bonnie.

FRAGMENT OF SONG

No cold approach, no alter'd mien,
    Just what would make suspicion start;
No pause the dire extremes between,
    He made me blest—and broke my heart.

I'LL MEET THEE ON THE LEA RIG
Tune—The lea rig

When o'er the hill the eastern star
    Tells bughtin' time is near, my jo,
And owsen frae the furrow'd field
    Return sae dowf and weary, O;
Down by the burn, where scented birks
    Wi' dew are hangin clear, my jo,
I'll meet thee on the lea-rig,
    My ain kind dearie, O.

At midnight hour in mirkest glen
    I'd rove and ne'er be eerie, O,
If thro' that glen I gaed to thee,
    My ain kind dearie, O;
Although the night were ne'er sae wild,
    And I were ne'er sae weary, O,
I'll meet thee on the lea-rig,
    My ain kind dearie, O.

The hunter lo'es the morning sun;
    To rouse the mountain deer, my jo;
At noon the fisher seeks the glen
    Adown the burn to steer, my jo;
Gie me the hour o' gloamin' grey,
    It maks my heart sae cheery, O,
To meet thee on the lea-rig,
    My ain kind dearie, O.

THE WINSOME WEE THING
Air—*My wife's a wanton wee thing*

Chorus: She is a winsome wee thing,
    She is a handsome wee thing,
    She is a lo'esome wee thing,
      This sweet wee wife o' mine.

I never saw a fairer,
I never lo'ed a dearer,
And neist my heart I'll wear her,
    For fear my jewel tine,

The warld's wrack we share o't;
The warstle and the care o't;
Wi' her I'll blythely bear it,
    And think my lot divine.

HIGHLAND MARY
Tune—*Katherine Ogie*

Ye banks and braes and streams around
    The castle o' Montgomery!
Green be your woods and fair your flowers,
    Your waters never drumlie!
There simmer first unfauld her robes,
    And there the langest tarry;
For there I took the last fareweel
    O' my sweet Highland Mary.

How sweetly bloom'd the gay, green birk,
    How rich the hawthorn's blossom,
As underneath their fragrant shade,
    I clasp'd her to my bosom!
The golden hours on angel wings
    Flew o'er me and my dearie;
For dear to me, as light and life
    Was my sweet Highland Mary.

Wi' monie a vow and lock'd embrace,
    Our parting was fu' tender;
And pledging aft to meet again,
    We tore oursels asunder;
But Oh, fell death's untimely frost
    That nipt my flower sae early!
Now green's the sod and cauld's the clay
    That wraps my Highland Mary!

O pale, pale now those rosy lips
    I aft hae kiss'd sae fondly!
And clos'd for aye the sparkling glance
    That dwalt on me sae kindly!
And mouldering now in silent dust
    That heart that lo'ed me dearly!
But still within my bosom's core
    Shall live my Highland Mary.

AULD ROB MORRIS

There's Auld Rob Morris that wons in yon glen,
He's the king o' guid fellows and wale o' auld men;
He has gowd in his coffers, he has owsen and kine,
And ae bonnie lass, his dautie and mine.

She's fresh as the morning, the fairest in May;
She's sweet as the ev'ning amang the new hay;
As blythe and as artless as the lambs on the lea,
And dear to my heart as the light to my e'e.

But O, she's an heiress, Auld Robin's a laird,
And my daddie has nought but a cot-house and yard;
A wooer like me maunna hope to come speed;
The wounds I must hide that will soon be my dead.

The day comes to me, but delight brings me nane;
The night comes to me, but my rest it is gane;
I wander my lane like a night-troubled ghaist,
And I sigh as my heart it wad burst in my breast.

O had she but been of a lower degree,
I then might hae hop'd she'd ha'e smil'd upon me!
O, how past descriving had then been my bliss,
As now my distraction nae words can express.

THE RIGHTS OF WOMAN
An Occasional Address
Spoken by Miss Fontenelle[1] on her Benefit Night, 26 November 1792

While Europe's eye is fix'd on mighty things,
The fate of empires and the fall of kings;
While quacks of State must each produce his plan,
And even children lisp the Rights of Man;
Amid this mighty fuss just let me mention,
The Rights of Woman merit some attention.

First, in the sexes' intermix'd connection,
One sacred Right of Woman is Protection.
The tender flower that lifts its head, elate,
Helpless, must fall before the blasts of Fate,
Sunk on the earth, defac'd its lovely form,
Unless your shelter ward th' impending storm.

Our second Right—but needless here is caution,
To keep that right inviolate's the fashion;
Each man of sense has it so full before him,
He'd die before he'd wrong it—'tis Decorum.
There was, indeed, in far less polish'd days,
A time when rough rude man had naughty ways,
Would swagger, swear, get drunk, kick up a riot,

---

[1] A favourite actress in Dumfries.

Nay even thus invade a Lady's quiet.[1]
Now, thank our stars! these Gothic times are fled;
Now, well-bred men—and you are all well-bred—
Most justly think (and we are much the gainers)
Such conduct neither spirit, wit nor manners.

For Right the third, our last, our best, our dearest,
That right to fluttering female hearts the nearest;
Which even the Rights of Kings, in low prostration,
Most humbly own—'tis dear, dear Admiration!
In that blest sphere alone we live and move;
There taste that life of life—immortal love.
Smiles, glances, sighs, tears, fits, flirtations, airs;
'Gainst such an host what flinty savage dares,
When awful Beauty joins with all her charms,
Who is so rash as rise in rebel arms?

But truce with kings, and truce with constitutions,
With bloody armaments and revolutions;
Let Majesty your first attention summon,
Ah! *ça ira*! THE MAJESTY OF WOMAN!

[1] Ironical allusion to the Saturnalia of the Caledonian Hunt.

EPIGRAM ON SEEING MISS FONTENELLE IN A FAVOURITE CHARACTER

Sweet naïveté of feature,
    Simple, wild, enchanting elf,
Not to thee, but thanks to Nature,
    Thou art acting but thyself.

Wert thou awkward, stiff, affected,
    Spurning Nature, torturing art;
Loves and Graces all rejected,
    Then indeed thou'd'st act a part.

EXTEMPORE ON SOME COMMEMORATIONS OF THOMSON

Dost thou not rise, indignant Shade,
    And smile wi' spurning scorn,
When they wha wad hae starved thy life,
    Thy senseless turf adorn?

They wha about thee mak sic fuss
    Now thou art but a name,
Wad seen thee damn'd ere they had spar'd
    Ae plack to fill thy wame.

Helpless, alane, thou clamb the brae,
    Wi' meikle honest toil,
And claught th' unfading garland there,
    Thy sair-worn, rightful spoil.

And wear it thou! and call aloud
This axiom undoubted—
'Would thou hae Nobles' patronage?
First learn to live without it!'

'To whom hae much, more shall be given,'
Is every great man's faith;
But he, the helpless, needful wretch,
Shall lose the mite he hath.

DUNCAN GRAY

Duncan Gray cam' here to woo,
Ha, ha, the wooing o't,
On blythe Yule night when we were fu',
Ha, ha, the wooing o't!
Maggie coost her head fu' high,
Look'd asklent and unco skeigh,
Gart poor Duncan stand abeigh;
Ha, ha, the wooing o't.

Duncan fleech'd and Duncan pray'd;
Ha, ha, the wooing o't;
Meg was deaf as Ailsa Craig,[1]
Ha, ha, the wooing o't.
Duncan sigh'd baith out and in,
Grat his e'en baith bleer't and blin',
Spak o' lowpin' o'er a linn;
Ha, ha, the wooing o't.

Time and chance are but a tide,
Ha, ha, the wooing o't:
Slighted love is sair to bide,
Ha, ha, the wooing o't.
'Shall I, like a fool,' quoth he,
'For a haughty hizzie die?
She may gae to—France for me!'
Ha, ha, the wooing o't.

How it comes let doctors tell,
Ha, ha, the wooing o't;
Meg grew sick as he grew hale,
Ha, ha, the wooing o't.
Something in her bosom wrings,
For relief a sigh she brings:
And O, her een they spak sic things!
Ha, ha, the wooing o't.

Duncan was a lad o' grace,
Ha, ha, the wooing o't:
Maggie's was a piteous case,
Ha, ha, the wooing o't:
Duncan couldna be her death,
Swelling pity smoor'd his wrath;
Now they're crouse and canty baith,
Ha, ha, the wooing o't.

[1] A well-known island rock in the Firth of Clyde.

HERE'S A HEALTH TO THEM THAT'S AWA'[1]

Here's a health to them that's awa',
Here's a health to them that's awa';
And wha winna wish guid luck to our cause,
May never guid luck be their fa'!
It's guid to be merry and wise,
It's guid to be honest and true,
It's guid to support Caledonia's cause,
And bide by the buff and the blue.[2]

[1] Founded on an old favourite song.   [2] The colours of the Whig Party.

Here's a health to them that's awa',
Here's a health to them that's awa',
Here's a health to Charlie,[1] the chief o' the clan,
Altho' that his band be but sma'!
May Liberty meet wi' success!
May Prudence protect her frae evil!
May tyrants and tyranny tine i' the mist,
And wander their way to the devil!

Here's a health to them that's awa',
Here's a health to them that's awa';
Here's a health to Tammie,[2] the Norlan' laddie,
That lives at the lug o' the law!
Here's freedom to them that wad read,
Here's freedom to them that wad write,
There's nane ever fear'd that the truth should be heard,
But they whom the truth would indite.

Here's a health to them that's awa',
An' here's to them that's awa'!
Here's to Maitland and Wycombe, let wha doesna like 'em
Be built in a hole in the wa'!
Here's timmer that's red at the heart,
Here's fruit that is sound at the core;
And may he be that wad turn the buff and blue coat
Be turn'd to the back o' the door!

Here's a health to them that's awa',
Here's a health to them that's awa';
Here's chieftain McLeod,[3] a chieftain worth gowd,
Tho' bred amang mountains o' snaw!
Here's friends on baith sides o' the Forth,
And friends on baith sides o' the Tweed;
And wha wad betray old Albion's right,
May they never eat of her bread!

[1] Charles James Fox.
[3] MP for Inverness, a determined Reformer.
[2] Hon. Thomas Erskine, later Lord Erskine.

O Poortith Cauld And Restless Love[1]
Tune—*Cauld kail*

Chorus: O, why should Fate sic pleasure have,
Life's dearest bands untwining?
Or why sae sweet a flower as love
Depend on Fortune's shining?

O poortith cauld and restless Love,
Ye wrack my peace between ye;
Yet poortith a' I could forgive
An 'twere na for my Jeanie.

[1] Jean Lorimer of Kemmis Hall in Kirkmahoe is said to have been the subject of these verses.

This world's wealth, when I think on,
    Its pride and a' the lave o't;
My curse on silly coward man,
    That he should be the slave o't.

Her een sae bonnie blue betray
    How she repays my passion;
But prudence is her o'erword aye,
    She talks of rank and fashion.

O wha can prudence think upon,
    And sic a lassie by him?
O wha can prudence think upon,
    And sae in love as I am?

How blest the humble cotter's fate!
    He woos his artless dearie;
The silly bogles, Wealth and State,
    Can never make him eerie.

Braw Lads O' Galla Water

Braw, braw lads on Yarrow braes,
    They rove amang the blooming heather;
But Yarrow braes nor Ettrick shaws
    Can match the lads o' Galla Water.

But there is ane, a secret ane,
    Aboon them a' I lo'e him better;
And I'll be his, and he'll be mine,
    The bonnie lad o' Galla Water.

Although his daddie was nae laird,
    And though I hae nae meikle tocher,
Yet rich in kindest, truest love,
    We'll tent our flocks by Galla Water.

It ne'er was wealth, it ne'er was wealth,
    That coft contentment, peace or pleasure:
The bands and bliss o' mutual love,
    O that's the chiefest warld's treasure.

Sonnet—On Hearing A Thrush Sing
On A Morning Walk In January
Written on 25 January 1793, the Birthday of the Author

Sing on, sweet thrush, upon the leafless bough,
Sing on, sweet bird, I listen to thy strain;
See agéd Winter, 'mid his surly reign,
At thy blythe carol clears his furrowed brow.
So in lone Poverty's dominion drear
Sits meek Content with light, unanxious heart,
Welcomes the rapid moments, bids them part,
Nor asks if they bring ought to hope or fear.
I thank thee, Author of this opening day,
Thou whose bright sun now gilds yon orient skies!
Riches denied, thy boon was purer joys—
What wealth could never give nor take away!
But come, thou child of poverty and care,
The mite high heav'n bestow'd, that mite with thee I'll share.

WANDERING WILLIE
Tune—*Here awa', there awa'*

Here awa', there awa', wandering Willie,
    Here awa', there awa', haud awa' hame;
Come to my bosom, my ae only dearie,
    Tell me thou bring'st me my Willie the same.

Loud tho' the winter wind blew cauld on our parting,
    'Twas na the blast brought the tear in my e'e:
Welcome now, simmer, and welcome, my Willie,
    The simmer to nature, my Willie to me!

Rest, ye wild storms, in the cave o' your slumbers,
    How your dread howling a lover alarms!
Wauken, ye breezes, row gently, ye billows,
    And waft my dear laddie ance mair to my arms.

But O, if he's faithless, and minds na his Nannie,
    Flow still between us, thou wide-roaring main!
May I never see it, may I never trow it,
    But, dying, believe that my Willie's my ain!

LORD GREGORY

O mirk, mirk is this midnight hour,
    And loud the tempest's roar;
A waefu' wanderer seeks thy tower,
    Lord Gregory, ope thy door!

An exile frae her father's ha',
    And a' for loving thee;
At least some pity on me shaw,
    If love it may na be.

Lord Gregory, mind'st thou not the grove
    By bonnie Irwine side,
Where first I own'd that virgin love
    I lang, lang had denied?

How aften didst thou pledge and vow
    Thou wad for aye be mine;
And my fond heart, itsel' sae true,
    It ne'er mistrusted thine.

Hard is thy heart, Lord Gregory,
    And flinty is thy breast:
Thou dart of Heaven that flashest by,
    O wilt thou give me rest!

Ye mustering thunders from above,
    Your willing victim see!
But spare and pardon my false love,
    His wrangs to Heaven and me!

OPEN THE DOOR TO ME, O
Tune—*Open the door softly*

O, open the door, some pity to show,
    If love it may na be, O!
Tho' thou hast been false, I'll ever prove true—
    O, open the door to me, O!

Cauld is the blast upon my pale cheek,
    But caulder thy love for me, O!
The frost that freezes the life at my heart,
    Is nought to my pains frae thee, O!

The wan moon sets behind the white wave,
    And time is setting with me, O!
False friends, false love, farewell! for mair
    I'll ne'er trouble them, nor thee, O!

She has open'd the door, she has open'd it wide;
    She sees his pale corse on the plain, O!
'My true love!' she cried, and sank down by his side,
    Never to rise again, O!

YOUNG JESSIE
Tune—*Adew Dundee*

True-hearted was he, the sad swain o' the Yarrow,
    And fair are the maids on the banks o' the Ayr,
But by the sweet side o' the Nith's winding river
    Are lovers as faithful and maidens as fair;
To equal young Jessie, seek Scotia all over;
    To equal young Jessie you seek it in vain!
Grace, beauty and elegance fetter her lover,
    And maidenly modesty fixes the chain.

Fresh is the rose in the gay, dewy morning,
    And sweet is the lily at evening close;
But in the fair presence o' lovely young Jessie,
    Unseen is the lily, unheeded the rose.
Love sits in her smile, a wizard ensnaring;
    Enthron'd in her een he delivers his law:
And still to her charms she alone is a stranger,
    Her modest demeanour's the jewel of a'.

MEG O' THE MILL
Tune—*Jackie Hume's lament*

O ken ye what Meg o' the Mill has gotten,
An' ken ye what Meg o' the Mill has gotten?
She's gotten a coof wi' a claut o' siller
And broken the heart o' the barley miller.

The miller was strappin', the miller was ruddy,
A heart like a lord and a hue like a lady;
The laird was a widdifu', bleerit knurl;
She's left the guid fellow and taen the churl.

The miller he hecht her a heart leal and loving,
The laird did address her wi' matter mair moving:
A fine pacing-horse wi' a clear chainéd bridle,
A whip by her side and a bonnie side-saddle.

O wae on the siller, it is sae prevailing!
And wae on the love that's fixed on a mailen!
A tocher's nae word in a true lover's parle,
But gie me my love, and a fig for the warl'!

MEG O' THE MILL
Another Version

O ken ye what Meg o' the Mill has gotten,
An' ken ye what Meg o' the Mill has gotten?
A braw new naig wi' the tail o' a rottan,
And that's what Meg o' the Mill has gotten.

O ken ye what Meg o' the Mill loes dearly,
An' ken ye what Meg o' the Mill loes dearly?
A dram o' guid strunt in the morning early,
And that's what Meg o' the Mill loes dearly.

O ken ye how Meg o' the Mill was married,
An' ken ye how Meg o' the Mill was married?
The priest he was oxter'd, the clerk he was carried,
And that's how Meg o' the Mill was married.

O ken ye how Meg o' the Mill was bedded,
An' ken ye how Meg o' the Mill was bedded?
The groom gat sae fu' he fell awald beside it,
And that's how Meg o' the Mill was bedded.

THE SOLDIER'S RETURN
Air—*The mill, mill, O*

When wild War's deadly blast was blawn
 And gentle Peace returning,
Wi' monie a sweet babe fatherless
 And monie a widow mourning,
I left the lines and tented field,
 Where lang I'd been a lodger,
My humble knapsack a' my wealth,
 A poor and honest sodger.

A leal, light heart was in my breast,
 My hand unstain'd wi' plunder;
And for fair Scotia, hame again,
 I cheery on did wander.
I thought upon the banks o' Coil,
 I thought upon my Nancy,
I thought upon the witching smile
 That caught my youthful fancy.

At length I reach'd the bonnie glen
 Where early life I sported;
I pass'd the mill and trysting thorn
 Where Nancy aft I courted:
Wha spied I but my ain dear maid,
 Down by her mother's dwelling!
And turn'd me round to hide the flood
 That in my een was swelling.

Wi' alter'd voice, quoth I, 'Sweet lass,
　　Sweet as yon hawthorn's blossom,
O! happy, happy may he be,
　　That's dearest to thy bosom!
My purse is light, I've far to gang,
　　And fain would be thy lodger;
I've serv'd my king and country lang—
　　Take pity on a sodger.'

Sae wistfully she gaz'd on me,
　　And lovelier was than ever;
Quo' she, 'A sodger ance I lo'ed,
　　Forget him shall I never:
Our humble cot and hamely fare
　　Ye freely shall partake it;
That gallant badge—the dear cockade—
　　Ye're welcome for the sake o't.'

She gaz'd—she redden'd like a rose;
　　Syne pale like onie lily;
She sank within my arms, and cried,
　　'Art thou my ain dear Willie?'
'By Him who made yon sun and sky,
　　By whom true love's regarded,
I am the man! and thus may still
　　True lovers be rewarded.

'The wars are o'er, and I'm come hame,
　　And find thee still true-hearted.
Tho' poor in gear, we're rich in love,
　　And mair, we'se ne'er be parted.'
Quo' she, 'My grandsire left me gowd,
　　A mailen plenish'd fairly;
And come, my faithfu' sodger lad,
　　Thou'rt welcome to it dearly!'

For gold the merchant ploughs the main,
　　The farmer ploughs the manor;
But glory is the sodger's prize,
　　The sodger's wealth is honour:
The brave poor sodger ne'er despise,
　　Nor count him as a stranger;
Remember, he's his country's stay
　　In day and hour of danger.

YE TRUE LOYAL NATIVES

Ye true 'Loyal Natives', attend to my song!
In uproar and riot rejoice the night long!
From Envy and Hatred your corps is exempt,
But where is your shield from the darts of Contempt!

ON COMMISSARY GOLDIE'S BRAINS

Lord, to account who dares Thee call
    Or e'er dispute Thy pleasure?
Else why, within so thick a wall,
    Enclose so poor a treasure?

LINES INSCRIBED IN A LADY'S POCKET ALMANAC

Grant me, indulgent Heaven, that I may live,
To see the miscreants feel the pains they give;
Deal Freedom's sacred treasures free as air,
Till Slave and Despot be but things that were.

A TOAST[1]

Instead of a song, boys, I'll give you a toast:
Here's to the memory of those on the Twelfth that we lost!
That we lost, did I say?—nay, by Heav'n, that we found,
For their fame it will last while the world goes round.
The next in succession I'll give you—the King!
Whoe'er would betray him, on high may he swing!
And here's the grand fabric—our free Constitution,
As built on the base of our great Revolution!
And longer with Politics not to be cramm'd,
Be Anarchy curs'd, and be Tyranny damn'd!
And who would to Liberty e'er prove disloyal,
May his son be a hangman, and he his first trial!

---

[1] A meeting of the Dumfriesshire Volunteers was held in the King's Arms, Dumfries, on 12 April 1793 to commemorate the anniversary of Admiral Rodney's victory, 12 April 1782, at the Battle of Dominica in the West Indies. Burns was called on for a song, but instead he delivered these lines extempore.

THANKSGIVING FOR A NAVAL VICTORY
Lines Written on a Pane of Glass

Ye hypocrites! are these your pranks?
To murder men and give God thanks?
Desist, for shame! Proceed no further:
God won't accept your thanks for murther!

LINES WRITTEN ON A WINDOW
Of the Globe Tavern, Dumfries

The greybeard, old wisdom, may boast of his treasures;
    Give me with gay folly to live;
I grant him his calm-blooded, time-settled pleasures,
    But folly has raptures to give.

In politics if thou would'st mix,
  And mean thy fortunes be,
Bear this in mind, be deaf and blind,
  Let great folk hear and see.

My bottle is a holy pool
That heals the wounds o' care an' dool;
And pleasure is a wanton trout,
An ye drink it, ye'll find him out.

THE MAUCHLINE WEDDING

When Eighty-five was seven months auld
    And wearing thro' the aught,
When rolling rains and Boreas bauld
    Gied farmer-folks a faught;
Ae morning quondam Mason Will,
    Now Merchant Master Miller,
Gaed down to meet wi' Nansie Bell
    And her Jamaica siller
        To wed, that day.

The rising sun o'er Blacksideen
    Was just appearing fairly,
When Nell and Bess got up to dress
    Seven lang half-hours o'er early!
Now presses clink, and drawers jink,
    For linens and for laces;
But modest Muses only think
    What ladies' underdress is,
        On sic a day!

But we'll suppose the stays are lac'd,
    And bonnie bosoms steekit,
Tho' thro' the lawn—but guess the rest—
    An angel scarce durst keek it.
Then stockins fine o' silken twine
    Wi' cannie care are drawn up;
An' garten'd tight whare mortal wight—

    .   .   .   .

    .   .   .   .

But now the gown wi' rustling sound
    Its silken pomp displays;
Sure there's no sin in being vain
    O' siccan bonnie claes!
Sae jimp the waist, the tail sae vast—
    Trouth, they were bonnie birdies!
O Mither Eve, ye wad been grieve
    To see their ample hurdies
        Sae large that day!

Then Sandy, wi 's red jacket braw,
    Comes whip-jee-woa! about,
And in he gets the bonnie twa—
    Lord, send them safely out!
And auld John Trot wi' sober phiz,
    As braid and braw 's a Bailie,
His shouthers and his Sunday's jiz
    Wi' powther and wi' ulzie
        Weel smear'd that day.

The Hue And Cry Of John Lewars

A poor man ruined and undone by Robbery and Murder. Being an aweful WARNING to the young men of this age, how they look well to themselves in this dangerous, terrible WORLD

A Thief and a Murderer! stop her who can!
　　Look well to your lives and your goods!
Good people, ye know not the hazard you run,
　　'Tis the far-famed and much-noted Woods.[1]

While I looked at her eye, for the devil is in it,
　　In a trice she whipt off my poor heart:
Her brow, cheek and lip—in another sad minute
　　My peace felt her murderous dart.

Her features, I'll tell you them over—but hold!
　　She deals with your wizards and books;
And to peep in her face, if but once you're so bold,
　　There's witchery kills in her looks.

But softly—I have it—her hauts are well known,
　　At midnight so slily I'll watch her;
And sleeping, undrest, in the dark, all alone—
　　Good lord! the dear Thief how I'll catch her!

[1] Agnes Wood.

To Miss Isabella MacLeod[1]

The crimson blossom charms the bee,
　　The summer sun the swallow;
So dear this tuneful gift to me
　　From lovely Isabella.

Her portrait fair upon my mind
　　Revolving Time shall mellow,
And Mem'ry's latest effort find
　　The lovely Isabella.

No Bard nor lover's rapture this
　　In fancies vain and shallow!
She is, so come my soul to bliss,
　　The lovely Isabella!

[1] Isabella MacLeod, daughter of the laird of Raasay and sister of John MacLeod (*see* note page 207).

To William Stewart[1]

Brownhill Monday even.:
Dear Sir
　　In honest Bacon's ingle-neuk
　　　Here maun I sit and think,
　　Sick o' the warld and warld's folk,
　　　An' sick, damn'd sick o' drink!

[1] Factor in Nithsdale and brother-in-law of Bacon, owner of the Brownhill Inn (*see also* page 308).

I see, I see there is nae help,
　　But still down I maun sink,
Till some day *laigh enough*, I yelp,
　　'Wae worth that curséd drink!'

Yestreen, alas! I was. sae fu'
　　I could but yisk and wink;
And now, this day, sair, sair I rue
　　The weary, weary drink.

Satan, I fear thy sooty claws,
　　I hate thy brunstane stink,
And aye I curse the luckless cause,
　　The wicked soup o' drink.

In vain I would forget my woes
　　In idle rhyming clink,
For, past redemption damn'd in Prose,
　　I can do nought but drink.

To you my trusty, well-try'd friend,
　　May heaven still on you blink,
And may your life flow to the end,
　　Sweet as a dry man's drink!

THE TREE OF LIBERTY

Heard ye o' the tree o' France,
　　I watna what's the name o't;
Around it a' the patriots dance—
　　Weel Europe kens the fame o't.
It stands where ance the Bastile stood,
　　A prison built by kings, man,
When Superstition's hellish brood
　　Kept France in leading strings, man.

Upo' this tree there grows sic fruit,
　　Its virtues a' can tell, man:
It raises man aboon the brute,
　　It mak's him ken himsel', man.
Gif ance the peasant taste a bit,
　　He's greater than a lord, man,
And wi' the beggar shares a mite
　　O' a' he can afford, man.

This fruit is worth a' Afric's wealth,
　　To comfort us 'twas sent, man,
To gie the sweetest blush o' health,
　　And mak' us a' content, man.
It clears the een, it cheers the heart,
　　Mak's high and low guid friends, man,
And he wha acts the traitor's part,
　　It to perdition sends, man.

My blessings aye attend the chiel
    Wha pitied Gallia's slaves, man,
And staw a branch, spite o' the deil,
    Frae 'yont the western waves, man.
Fair Virtue water'd it wi' care,
    And now she sees wi' pride, man,
How weel it buds and blossoms there,
    Its branches spreading wide, man.

But vicious folk aye hate to see
    The works o' Virtue thrive, man.
The courtly vermin's bann'd the tree,
    And grat to see it thrive, man.
King Loui' thought to cut it down,
    When it was unco sma', man;
For this the watchman crack'd his crown,
    Cut aff his head and a', man.

A wicked crew syne, on a time,
    Did tak a solemn aith, man,
It ne'er should flourish to its prime—
    I wat they pledg'd their faith, man.
Awa' they gaed wi' mock parade,
    Like beagles hunting game, man,
But soon grew weary o' the trade
    And wish'd they'd been at hame, man.

Fair Freedom, standing by the tree,
    Her sons did loudly ca', man.
She sang a sang o' liberty,
    Which pleas'd them ane and a', man.
By her inspir'd, the new-born race
    Soon drew the avenging steel, man.
The hirelings ran—her foes gied chase,
    And bang'd the despot weel, man.

Let Britain boast her hardy oak,
    Her poplar and her pine, man,
Auld Britain ance could crack her joke,
    And o'er her neighbours shine, man.
But seek the forest round and round,
    And soon 'twill be agreed, man,
That sic a tree cannot be found
    'Twixt London and the Tweed, man.

Without this tree alake this life
    Is but a vale o' woe, man,
A scene o' sorrow mix'd wi' strife,
    Nae real joys we know, man.
We labour soon, we labour late,
    To feed the titled knave, man,

And a' the comfort we're to get,
　　Is that ayont the grave, man.

Wi' plenty o' sic trees, I trow,
　　The warld would live in peace, man.
The sword would help to mak a plough,
　　The din o' war wad cease, man.
Like brethren in a common cause,
　　We'd on each other smile, man;
And equal rights and equal laws
　　Wad gladden every isle, man.

Wae worth the loon wha wadna eat
　　Sic halesome, dainty cheer, man;
I'd gie the shoon frae aff my feet
　　To taste sic fruit, I swear, man.
Syne let us pray, Auld England may
　　Sure plant this far-fam'd tree, man;
And blythe we'll sing, and hail the day
　　That gave us liberty, man.

A SONNET UPON SONNETS

Fourteen, a sonneteer thy praises sings;
What magic myst'ries in that number lie!
Your hen hath fourteen eggs beneath her wings
That fourteen chickens to the roost may fly.
Fourteen full pounds the jockey's stone must be;
His age fourteen—a horse's prime is past.
Fourteen long hours too oft the Bard must fast;
Fourteen bright bumpers—bliss he ne'er must see!
Before fourteen, a dozen yields the strife;
Before fourteen—e'en thirteen's strength is vain.
Fourteen good years—a woman gives us life;
Fourteen good men—we lose that life again.
What lucubrations can be more upon it?
Fourteen good measur'd verses make a sonnet.

SKETCH FOR AN ELEGY

Craigdarroch,[1] fam'd for speaking art
And every virtue of the heart,
Stops short, nor can a word impart
　　To end his sentence,
When mem'ry strikes him like a dart
　　With auld acquaintance.

Black James—whase wit was never laith,
But, like a sword had tint the sheath,

---

[1] Alexander Fergusson, *see* The Whistle, page 270.

Aye ready for the work o' death—
    He turns aside,
And strains wi' suffocating breath
    His grief to hide.

Even Philosophic Smellie[1] tries
To choak the stream that floods his eyes:
So Moses wi' a hazel-rice
    Came o'er the stane;
But tho' it cost him speaking twice,
    It gush'd amain.

Go to your marble graffs, ye great,
In a' the tinkler-trash of state!
But by thy honest turf I'll wait,
    Thou man of worth,
And weep the ae best fallow's fate
    E'er lay in earth!

[1] William Smellie, Edinburgh printer and antiquarian (*see also* page 318).

THE CARES O' LOVE

He:
The cares o' Love are sweeter far
    Than onie other pleasure;
And if sae dear its sorrows are,
    Enjoyment, what a treasure!

She:
I fear to try, I dare na try
    A passion sae ensnaring;
For light's her heart and blythe's her song
    That for nae man is caring.

ON JOHNSON'S OPINION OF HAMPDEN

For shame!
Let Folly and Knavery
Freedom oppose:
'Tis suicide, Genius,
To mix with her foes.

AT WHIGHAM'S INN, SANQUHAR
Written on a Window Pane

Envy, if thy jaundiced eye
Through this window chance to spy,
To thy sorrow thou shalt find,
All that's generous, all that's kind,
Friendship, virtue, every grace,
Dwelling in this happy place.

DUMFRIES EPIGRAMS

On being told that Commissary Goldie did not seem disposed to push the Bottle

Friend Commissar, since we're met and are happy,
Pray why should we part without having more nappy?
Bring in t'other bottle, for faith I am dry—
Thy drink thou can't part with and neither can I.

On an Old Acquaintance who seemed to pass the Bard without Notice

Dost hang thy head, Billy, asham'd that thou knowest me?
'Tis paying in kind a just debt that thou owest me.

Dost blush, my dear Billy, asham'd of thyself,
    A Fool and a Cuckold together?
The fault is not thine, insignificant elf,
    Thou wast not consulted in either.

On James Swan
On his being elected Councillor and Baillie

Baillie Swan, Baillie Swan,
Let you do what you can—
God hae mercy on honest Dumfries;
But e'er the year's done,
Good Lord! Provost John
Will find that his *Swans* are but *Geese*.

On Edmund Burke By An Opponent
And a Friend to Warren Hastings

Oft have I wonder'd that on Irish ground
No poisonous Reptile has ever been found:
Revealed stands the secret of great Nature's work:
She preserved her poison to create a Burke!

On A Lady Of Amazonian Stature

Should he escape the slaughter of thine Eyes,
Within thy strong Embrace he struggling dies.

On William Copland of Collieston

Copland faithful likeness, friend Painter, would'st seize?
Keep out Worth, Wit and Wisdom: Put in what you please.

To The Dumfries Loyal Natives
A Club in Dumfries . . . who exhibited Violent Party Work and Intemperate Loyalty

Pray, who are these Natives the Rabble so ven'rate?
They're our true ancient Natives, and they breed undegen'rate
The ignorant savage that weather'd the storm,
When the man and the Brute differed but in form.

Epitaph For John Hunter, Writer In Ayr

Here lies a Scots mile of a chiel,
If he's in heaven, Lord, fill him weel!

On Mr Pitt's Hair-Powder Tax

Pray, Billy Pitt, explain thy rigs,
This new poll-tax of thine!
'I mean to mark the GUINEA pigs
From other common SWINE.'

To The Honourable Wm R. Maule Of Panmure
Extempore
On seeing the Honourable William Ramsay Maule of Panmure 'driving away in his fine
and elegant Phaeton on the Race Ground at Tinwald Downs'

Thou fool, in thy Phaeton towering.
Art proud when that Phaeton's prais'd?
'Tis the pride of a Thief's exhibition
When higher his pillory's rais'd.

To Captain Gordon
On being asked why I was not to be of the Party with him
and his Brother Kenmure at Syme's

Dost ask, dear Captain, why from Syme
   I have no invitation,
When well he knows he has with him
   My first friends in the nation?

Is it because I love to toast,
   And round the bottle hurl?
No! there conjecture wild is lost,
   For Syme, by God, 's no churl!

Is 't lest with bawdy jests I bore,
   As oft the matter of fact is?
No! Syme the theory can't abhor—
   Who loves so well the practice.

Is it a fear I should avow
   Some heresy seditious?
No! Syme (but this is *entre nous*)
   Is quite an old Tiresias.

In vain Conjecture thus would flit
   Thro' mental clime and season:
In short, dear Captain, Syme's a Wit—
   Who asks of Wits a reason?

Yet must I still the *sort* deplore
   That to my griefs adds one more,
In balking me the social hour
   With you and noble Kenmure.

On Marriage

That hackney'd judge of human life,
   The Preacher and the King,
Observes: 'The man that gets a wife
   He gets a noble thing.'

But how capricious are mankind,
   Now loathing, now desirous!
We married men, how oft we find
   The best of things will tire us!

Elegy On William Cruikshank[1]

Now honest William's gaen to Heaven,
    I wat na gin 't can mend him:
The fauts he had in Latin lay,
    For nane in English kent them.

[1] Latin master at Edinburgh High School with whose family Burns lodged for a while.

Epitaph On Robert Muir[1]

What man could esteem, or what woman could love,
    Was he who lies under this sod:
If such Thou refusest admission above,
    Then whom wilt Thou favour, Good God?

[1] Wine merchant in Kilmarnock and an old friend of Burns.

For Mr Walter Riddell[1]

So vile was poor Wat, such a miscreant slave,
That the worms ev'n damn'd him when laid in his grave.
'In his scull there's a famine,' a starved reptile cries;
'And his heart, it is poison,' another replies.

[1] The husband of Maria Riddell and brother of Robert Riddell.

Weary Fa' You, Duncan Gray

Weary fa' you, Duncan Gray!
    (Ha, ha, the girdin o't!)
Wae gae by you, Duncan Gray!
    (Ha, ha, the girdin o't!)
When a' the lave gae to their play,
Then I maun sit the lee-lang day,
And jeeg the cradle wi' my tae,
    And a' for the girdin o't!

Bonnie was the Lammas moon
    (Ha, ha, the girdin o't!)
Glowrin a' the hills aboon,
    (Ha, ha, the girdin o't!)
The girdin brak, the beast cam down,
I tint my curch and baith my shoon,
And Duncan, ye're an unco loon—
    Wae on the bad girdin o't!

But Duncan, gin ye'll keep your aith
    (Ha, ha, the girdin o't!)
I'se bless you wi' my hindmost breath
    (Ha, ha, the girdin o't!)
Duncan, gin ye'll keep your aith,
The beast again can bear us baith,
And auld Mess John will mend the skaith
    And clout the bad girdin o't.

THE PLOUGHMAN

Chorus: Then up wi't a', my ploughman lad,
    And hey, my merry ploughman!
Of a' the trades that I do ken,
    Commend me to the ploughman!

The ploughman, he's a bonnie lad,
    His mind is ever true, jo!
His garters knit below his knee,
    His bonnet it is blue, jo.

My ploughman he comes hame at e'en,
    He's aften wat and weary:
Cast off the wat, put on the dry,
    And gae to bed, my dearie.

I will wash my ploughman's hose,
    And I will dress his o'erlay;
I will mak my ploughman's bed,
    And cheer him late and early.

I hae been east, I hae been west,
    I hae been at Saint Johnston;
The bonniest sight that e'er I saw
    Was the ploughman laddie dancin.

Snaw-white stockings on his legs
    And siller buckles glancin,
A guid blue bonnet on his head,
    And O, but he was handsome!

Commend me to the barn-yard
    And the corn mou, man!
I never got my coggie fou
    Till I met wi' the ploughman.

LANDLADY, COUNT THE LAWIN
Tune—*Hey tuiti taiti*

Chorus: Hey tutti, taiti, How tutti, taiti,
Hey tutti, taiti, Wha's fou now?

    Landlady, count the lawin,
    The day is near the dawin;
    Ye're a' blind drunk, boys
        And I'm but jolly fou.

    Cog, an ye were aye fou,
    Cog, an ye were aye fou,
    I wad sit and sing to you,
        If ye were aye fou!

    Weel may ye a' be!
    Ill may ye never see!
    God bless the king
        And the companie!

O'ER THE WATER TO CHARLIE

Chorus: We'll o'er the water, we'll o'er the sea,
    We'll o'er the water to Charlie;
Come weal, come woe, we'll gather and go,
    And live and die wi' Charlie.

Come boat me o'er, come row me o'er,
    Come boat me o'er to Charlie;
I'll gie John Ross anither bawbee
    To boat me o'er to Charlie.

I lo'e weel my Charlie's name,
  Tho' some there be abhor him;
But O, to see Auld Nick gaun hame,
  And Charlie's faes before him!

I swear and vow by moon and stars,
  And sun that shines so early,
If I had twenty thousand lives,
  I'd die as aft for Charlie.

AS I WAS A-WAND'RING
Tune—*Rinn m'eudial mo mhealladh*

Chorus: Weel, since he has left me, may pleasure gae wi' him;
  I may be distress'd but I winna complain:
I'll flatter my fancy I may get anither
  My heart it shall never be broken for ane.

As I was a-wand'ring ae midsummer e'enin
  The pipers and youngsters were making their game,
Amang them I spyed my faithless fause luver,
  Which bled a' the wounds o' my dolour again.

I could na get sleepin till dawin, for greetin;
  The tears trickl'd down like the hail and the rain:
Had I na got greetin, my heart wad a broken,
  For O, luve forsaken's a tormenting pain!

Although he has left me for greed o' the siller,
  I dinna envy him the gains he can win:
I rather wad bear a' the lade o' my sorrow,
  Than ever hae acted sae faithless to him.

THE SHEPHERD'S WIFE

The shepherd's wife cries o'er the knowe,
  'Will ye come hame, will ye come hame?'
The shepherd's wife cries o'er the knowe,
  'Will ye come hame again e'en, jo?'

'O, what will ye gie me to my supper,
  Gin I come hame, gin I come hame,
O, what will ye gie me to my supper,
  Gin I come hame again e'en, jo?'

'Ye'se get a panfu' o' plumpin parridge,
  And butter in them, and butter in them,
Ye'se get a panfu' o' plumpin parridge,
  Gin ye'll come hame again e'en, jo?'

'Ha, ha, how! that's naething that dow,
  I winna come hame, I canna come hame;

Ha, ha, how! that's naething that dow,
 I winna come hame gin e'en, jo.'

The shepherd's wife cries o'er the knowe, etc.
'O, what will ye gie me to my supper, etc.

'A reekin fat hen, weel fryth'd i' the pan,
 Gin ye'll come hame, gin ye'll come hame,
A reekin fat hen weel fryth'd i' the pan,
 Gin ye'll come hame again e'en, jo.'

'Ha, ha, how! that's naething that dow, etc.
The shepherd's wife cries o'er the knowe, etc.
'O, what will ye gie me to my supper, etc.

'A weel-made bed and a pair o' clean sheets,
 Gin ye'll come hame, gin ye'll come hame,
A weel-made bed and a pair o' clean sheets,
 Gin ye'll come hame again e'en, jo.'

'Ha, ha, how! that's naething that dow, etc.
The shepherd's wife cries o'er the knowe, etc.
'O, what will ye gie me to my supper, etc.

'A luving wife in lily-white linens,
 Gin ye'll come hame, gin ye'll come hame,
A luving wife in lily-white linens,
 Gin ye'll come hame again e'en, jo.'

'Ha, ha, how! that's something that dow,
 I will come hame, I will come hame:
Ha, ha, how! that's something that dow,
 I will come hame again e'en, jo.'

Green Sleeves

Green sleeves and tartan ties
Mark my true love where she lies:
I'll be at her or she rise,
 My fiddle and I thegither.

Be it by the crystal burn,
Be it by the milk-white thorn;
I shall rouse her in the morn,
 My fiddle and I thegither.

I'll Mak You Be Fain To Follow Me

As late by a sodger I chancéd to pass,
I heard him a-courtin a bonnie young lass,
'My hinny, my life, my dearest,' quo he,
'I'll mak you be fain to follow me.'
'Gin I should follow you, a poor sodger lad,
Ilk ane o' my cummers wad think I was mad.
For battles I never shall lang to see,
I'll never be fain to follow thee.'

'To follow me, I think ye may be glad,
A part o' my supper, a part o' my bed,
A part o' my bed, wherever it be,
I'll mak ye be fain to follow me.
Come try my knapsack on your back,
Alang the king's high-gate we'll pack,
Between Saint Johnston and bonnie Dundee,
I'll mak you be fain to follow me.'

O Dear Minny, What Shall I Do?

Chorus: O dear minny, what shall I do?
O dear minny, what shall I do?
O dear minny, what shall I do?
'Daft thing, doylt thing, do as I do.'

If I be black, I canna be lo'ed;
If I be fair I canna be guid;
If I be lordly, the lads will look by me:
O dear minny, what shall I do?

The Bob O' Dumblane

Lassie, lend me your braw hemp heckle,
    And I'll lend you my thrippling kame:
My heckle is broken, it canna be gotten,
    And we'll gae dance the Bob o' Dumblane.

Twa gaed to the wood, to the wood, to the wood,
    Twa gaed to the wood—three cam hame:
An 't be na weel bobbit, weel bobbit, weel bobbit,
    An 't be na weel bobbit, we'll bob it again.

Galloway Tam

O, Galloway Tam cam here to woo;
I'd rather we'd gi'en him the brawnit cow;
For our lass Bess may curse and ban
The wanton wit o' Galloway Tam.

O, Galloway Tam cam here to shear;
I'd rather we'd gi'en him the guid grey mare;
He kist the guidwife and strack the guidman,
And that's the tricks o' Galloway Tam.

My Wife's A Wanton Wee Thing

Chorus: My wife's a wanton, wee thing,
My wife's a wanton, wee thing,
My wife's a wanton, wee thing,
    She winna be guided by me.

She play'd the loon or she was married,
She play'd the loon or she was married,
She play'd the loon or she was married,
    She'll do it again or she die.

She sell'd her coat and she drank it,
She sell'd her coat and she drank it,
She row'd hersel in a blanket—
    She winna be guided by me.

She mind 't na when I forbade her,
She mind 't na when I forbade her,
I took a rung and I claw'd her,
    And a braw guid bairn was she.

Up And Warn A', Willie

Up and warn a', Willie,
    Warn, warn a';
To hear my canty Highland sang
    Relate the thing I saw, Willie.

When we gaed to the braes o' Mar,
    And to the wapon-shaw, Willie,
Wi' true design to serve the king
    And banish Whigs awa, Willie.
Up and warn a', Willie,
Warn, warn a';
For lords and lairds came there bedeen,
    And wow but they were braw, Willie.

But when the standard was set up,
    Right fierce the wind did blaw, Willie;
The royal nit upon the tap
    Down to the ground did fa', Willie.
Up and warn a', Willie,
Warn, warn a';
Then second-sighted Sandie said
    We'd do nae guid at a', Willie.

But when the army join'd at Perth,
    The bravest e'er ye saw, Willie,
We didna doubt the rogues to rout,
    Restore our king an a', Willie.
Up and warn a', Willie,
Warn, warn a';
The pipers play'd frae right to left
    O, whirry Whigs awa, Willie.

But when we march'd to Sherramuir
    And there the rebels saw, Willie;
Brave Argyle attack'd our right,
    Our flank, and front and a', Willie;

U, and warn a', Willie,
Warn, warn a';
Traiter Huntly soon gave way,
    Seaforth, St Clair and a', Willie.

But brave Glengary on our right
    The rebels' left did claw, Willie;
He there the greatest slaughter made
    That ever Donald saw, Willie.
Up and warn a', Willie,
    Warn, warn a';
And Whittam shat his breeks for fear,
    And fast did rin awa', Willie.

For he ca'd us a Highland mob,
    And soon he'd slay us a', Willie;
But we chas'd him back to Stirling brig—
    Dragoons, and foot, and a', Willie.
Up and warn a', Willie,
    Warn, warn a';
At length we rallied on a hill,
    And briskly up did draw, Willie.

But when Argyle did view our line,
    And them in order saw, Willie,
He straight gaed to Dumblane again,
    And back his left did draw, Willie.
Up and warn a', Willie,
    Warn, warn a';
Then we to Auchterairder march'd
    To wait a better fa', Willie.

Now if ye spier wha wan the day,
    I've tell'd you what I saw, Willie,
We baith did fight, and baith did beat,
    And baith did rin awa, Willie.
Up and warn a', Willie,
    Warn, warn a';
For second-sighted Sandie said
    We'd do nae guid at a', Willie.

JOHNIE COPE

Chorus: Hey, Johnie Cope, are ye wauking yet?
Or are ye sleeping I would wit;
O haste ye get up, for the drums do beat;
O fye, Cope, rise in the morning!

Sir John Cope trode the north right far,
Yet ne'er a rebel he cam naur
Until he landed at Dunbar
Right early in a morning.

He wrote a challenge from Dunbar,
'Come fight me, Charlie, an ye daur,
If it be not by the chance of war
I'll give you a merry morning.'

When Charlie look'd the letter upon,
He drew his sword the scabbard from—
'So Heaven restore to me my own,
I'll meet you, Cope, in the morning.'

Cope swore, with many a bloody word,
That he would fight them gun and sword,
But he fled frae his nest like an ill-scar'd bird,
And Johnie he took wing in the morning.

It was upon an afternoon,
Sir Johnie march'd to Preston town;
He says, 'My lads, come lean you down,
And we'll fight the boys in the morning.'

But when he saw the Highland lads
Wi' tartan trews and white cockauds,
Wi' swords, and guns, and rungs, and gauds,
O, Johnie, he took wing in the morning.

On the morrow when he did rise,
He looked between him and the skies;
He saw them wi' their naked thighs,
Which fear'd him in the morning.

O then he flew into Dunbar,
Crying for a man of war;
He thought to have pass'd for a rustic tar,
And gotten awa' in the morning.

Sir Johnie into Berwick rade,
Just as the devil had been his guide;
Gi'en him the warld he would na stay'd
To foughten the boys in the morning.

Says the Berwickers unto Sir John:
'O what's become of all your men?'
'In faith,' says he, 'I dinna ken—
I left them a' this morning.'

Says Lord Mark Car, 'Ye are na blate
To bring us the news o' your ain defeat;
I think you deserve the back o' the gate,
Get out o' my sight this morning!'

Johnie Blunt

There liv'd a man in yonder glen,
    And John Blunt was his name, O;
He maks guid maut, and he brews guid ale,
    And he bears a wondrous fame, O.

The wind blew in the hallan ae night,
    Fu' snell out o'er the moor, O;
'Rise up, rise up, auld Luckie,' he says,
    'Rise up and bar the door, O.'

They made a paction 'tween them twa,
    They made it firm and sure, O,
Whae'er sud speak the foremost word,
    Should rise and bar the door, O.

Three travellers that had tint their gate,
    As thro' the hills they foor, O,
They airted by the line o' light
    Fu' straught to Johnie Blunt's door, O.

They haurl'd auld Luckie out o' her bed,
    And laid her on the floor, O;
But never a word auld Luckie wad say,
    For barrin o' the door, O.

'Ye've eaten my bread, ye hae druken my ale,
    And ye'll mak my auld wife a whore, O.'—
'Aha, Johnie Blunt! ye hae spoke the first word—
    Get up and bar the door, O.'

The Campbells Are Comin

Chorus: The Campbells are comin, Oho! Oho!
    The Campbells are comin, Oho! Oho!
The Campbells are comin to bonnie Lochleven,
    The Campbells are comin, Oho! Oho!

Upon the Lomonds I lay, I lay,
Upon the Lomonds I lay, I lay,
I looké́d down to bonnie Lochleven
    And saw three bonnie perches play.

Great Argyle he goes before;
He maks his cannons and guns to roar,
Wi' sound o' trumpet, pipe and drum;
    The Campbells are comin, Oho! Oho!

The Campbells they are a' in arms,
Their loyal faith and truth to show,
Wi' banners rattling in the wind,
    The Campbells are comin, Oho! Oho!

SANDY AND JOCKIE
Tune—*Jenny's lamentation*

Twa bonnie lads were Sandy and Jockie;
Jockie was lo'ed but Sandy unlucky;
Jockie was laird baith of hills and of valleys,
But Sandy was nought but the king o' guid fellows.

Jockie lo'ed Madgie, for Madgie had money,
And Sandy lo'ed Mary for Mary was bonnie;
Ane wedded for love, ane wedded for treasure,
So Jockie had siller and Sandy had pleasure.

SOUTERS O' SELKIRK

It's up wi' the Souters o' Selkirk,
    And down wi' the Earl o' Hume;
And here is to a' the braw laddies
    That wear the single-sol'd shoon.
It's up wi' the Souters o' Selkirk,
    For they are baith trusty and leal,
And up wi' the lads o' the Forest,
    And down wi' the Merse to the deil!

HUGHIE GRAHAM
Tune—*Druimionn dubh*

Our lords are to the mountains gane,
    A-hunting o' the fallow deer;
And they hae gripet Hughie Graham,
    For stealing o' the bishop's mare.

And they hae tied him hand and foot,
    And led him up thro' Stirling town;
The lads and lassies met him there,
    Cried, 'Hughie Graham thou art a loon.'

'O, lowse my right hand free,' he says,
    'And put my braid sword in the same.
He's no in Stirling town this day,
    Daur tell the tale to Hughie Graham.'

Up then bespake the brave Whitefoord,
    As he sat by the bishop's knee;
'Five hundred white stots I'll gie you,
    If ye'll let Hughie Graham gae free.'

'O haud your tongue,' the bishop says,
    'And wi' your pleading let me be;
For tho' ten Grahams were in his coat,
    Hughie Graham this day shall die.'

Up then bespake the fair Whitefoord,
    As she sat by the bishop's knee,
'Five hundred white pence I'll gie you,
    If ye'll gie Hughie Graham to me.'

'O haud your tongue now, lady fair,
    And wi' your pleading let it be;
Altho' ten Grahams were in his coat,
    It's for my honour he maun die.'

They've ta'en him to the gallows knowe,
    He lookéd to the gallows tree,
Yet never colour left his cheek,
    Nor ever did he blin' his e'e.

At length he looked round about,
    To see whatever he could spy,
And there he saw his auld father,
    And he was weeping bitterly.

'O haud your tongue, my father dear,
    And wi' your weeping let it be;
Thy weeping's sairer on my heart
    Than a' that they can do to me.

'And ye may gie my brother John
    My sword that's bent in the middle clear,
And let him come at twelve o'clock,
    And see me pay the bishop's mare.

'And ye may gie my brother James
    My sword that's bent in the middle brown,
And bid him come at four o'clock,
    And see his brother Hugh cut down.

'Remember me to Maggy, my wife,
    The niest time ye gang o'er the moor;
Tell her she staw the bishop's mare,
    Tell her she was the bishop's whore.

'And ye may tell my kith and kin
    I never did disgrace their blood;
And when they meet the bishop's cloak,
    To make it shorter by the hood.'

As I Cam Down By Yon Castle Wa'

As I cam down by yon castle wa',
    And in by yon garden green,
O, there I spied a bonnie, bonnie lass,
    But the flower borders were us between.

A bonnie, bonnie lassie she was,
　　As ever mine eyes did see:
'O, five hundred pounds would I give
　　For to have such a pretty bride as thee.'

'To have such a pretty bride as me,
　　Young man, ye are sairly mista'en;
Tho' ye were king o' fair Scotland,
　　I wad disdain to be your queen.'

'Talk not so very high, bonnie lass,
　　O talk not so very, very high:
The man at the fair that wad sell,
　　He maun learn at the man that wad buy.

'I trust to climb a far higher tree,
　　And herry a far richer nest:
Tak this advice o' me, bonnie lass,
　　Humility wad set thee best.'

LORD RONALD, MY SON

'O, where hae ye been, Lord Ronald, my son?
O, where hae ye been, Lord Ronald, my son?'
'I hae been wi' my sweetheart, mother, make my bed soon,
For I'm weary wi' the hunting, and fain wad lie down.'

'What got ye frae your sweetheart, Lord Ronald, my son?
What got ye frae your sweetheart, Lord Ronald, my son?'
'I hae got deadly poison, mother, make my bed soon,
For life is a burden that soon I'll lay down.'

AS I WENT OUT AE MAY MORNING

As I went out ae May morning,
　　A May morning it chanc'd to be;
There I was aware of a weel-far'd maid
　　Cam linkin o'er the lea to me.

O, but she was a weel-far'd maid,
　　The bonniest lass that's under the sun;
I spier'd gin she could fancy me,
　　But her answer was, 'I am too young.

'To be your bride I am too young,
　　To be your loon wad shame my kin,
So therefore pray, young man, begone,
　　For you never, never shall my favour win.'

But amang yon birks and hawthorns green,
　　Where roses blaw and woodbines hing,
O, there I learn'd my bonnie lass,
　　That she was not a single hour too young.

The lassie blush'd, the lassie sigh'd,
    And the tear stood twinklin in her e'e;
'O kind Sir, since ye hae done me this wrang,
    It's pray when will ye marry me.'

'It's of that day tak ye nae heed,
    For that's a day ye ne'er shall see;
For ought that pass'd between us twa,
    Ye had your share as weel as me.'

She wrang her hands, she tore her hair,
    She cried out most bitterlie,
'O, what will I say to my mammie
    When I gae hame wi' my big bellie!'

'O, as ye maut, so maun ye brew,
    And as ye brew, so maun ye tun:
But come to my arms, my ae bonnie lass,
    For ye never shall rue what ye now hae done.'

Geordie—An Old Ballad

There was a battle in the north,
    And nobles there was many,
And they hae kill'd Sir Charlie Hay,
    And they laid the wyte on Geordie.

O, he has written a lang letter—
    He sent it to his lady—
'Ye maun cum up to Enbrugh town
    To see what words o' Geordie.'

When first she look'd the letter on,
    She was baith red and rosy;
But she had na read a word but twa,
    Till she wallow't like a lily.

'Gar get to me my guid grey steed,
    My menzie a' gae wi' me;
For I shall neither eat nor drink
    Till Enbrugh town shall see me.'

And she has mountit her guid grey steed,
    Her menzie a' gaed wi' her;
And she did neither eat nor drink
    Till Enbrugh town did see her.

And first appear'd the fatal block,
    And syne the aix to head him,
And Geordie cumin down the stair,
    And bands o' airn upon him.

But tho' he was chain'd in fetters strang,
    O' airn and steel sae heavy,
There was na ane in a' the court
    Sae bra' a man as Geordie.

O, she's down on her bended knee,
    I wat she's pale and weary;
'O pardon, pardon, noble king,
    And gie me back my Dearie!

'I hae born seven sons to my Geordie dear,
    The seventh ne'er saw his daddie:
O, pardon, pardon, noble king,
    Pity a waefu' lady!'

'Gar bid the headin'-man mak haste!'
    Our king reply'd fu' lordly.
'O noble king, tak a' that's mine
    But gie me back my Geordie.'

The Gordons cam and the Gordons ran,
    And they were stark and steady;
And aye the word amang then a'
    Was, 'Gordons, keep you ready.'

An agéd lord at the king's right hand
    Says: 'Noble king, but hear me—
Gar her tell down five thousand pound,
    And gie her back her Dearie.'

Some gae her marks, some gae her crowns,
    Some gae her dollars many;
And she's tell'd down five thousand pound,
    And she's gotten again her Dearie.

She blinkit blythe in her Geordie's face,
    Says: 'Dear I've bought thee, Geordie,
But there sud been bluidy bouks on the green
    Or I had tint my laddie.'

He claspit her by the middle sma',
    And he kist her lips sae rosy,
'The fairest flower o' womankind
    Is my sweet bonnie Lady.'

TAM LIN

O, I forbid you, maidens a',
    That wear gowd on your hair,
To come or gae by Carterhaugh,
    For young Tam Lin is there.

There's nane that gaes by Carterhaugh
    But they leave him a wad;
Either their rings, or green mantles,
    Or else their maidenhead.

Janet has kilted her green kirtle
    A little aboon her knee;
And she has broded her yellow hair
    A little aboon her bree;
And she's awa to Carterhaugh
    As fast as she can hie.

But when she cam to Carterhaugh,
    Tam Lin was at the well,
And there she fand his steed standing,
    But away was himsel'.

She had na pu'd a double rose,
    A rose but only twae,
Till up then started young Tam Lin,
    Says, 'Lady, thou's pu' nae mae.

'Why pu's thou the rose, Janet,
    And why breaks thou the wand!
Or why comes thou to Carterhaugh
    Withoutten my command?'

'Carterhaugh it is my ain;
    My daddie gave it me;
I'll come and gang by Garterhaugh,
    And ask nae leave at thee.'

Janet has kilted her green kirtle
    A little aboon her knee,
And she has snooded her yellow hair
    A little aboon her bree,
And she is to her father's ha'
    As fast as she can hie.

Four and twenty ladies fair
    Were playing at the ba',
And out then cam the fair Janet,
    Ance the flower amang then a'.

Four and twenty ladies fair
    Were playing at the chess,
And out then cam the fair Janet,
    As green as onie glass.

Out then spak an auld grey knight
    Lay o'er the castle wa';
And says: 'Alas! fair Janet for thee,
    But we'll be blaméd a'.'

'Haud your tongue, ye auld fac'd knight,
    Some ill death may ye die,
Father my bairn on whom I will,
    I'll father nane on thee.'

Out then spak her father dear,
    And he spak meek and mild,
'And ever alas! Sweet Janet,' he says,
    'I think thou gaes wi' child.'

'If that I gae wi' child, father,
    Mysel' maun bear the blame,
There's ne'er a laird about your ha',
    Shall get the bairn's name.

'If my love were an earthly knight,
    As he's an elfin grey,
I wadna gie my ain true love
    For nae lord that ye hae.

'The steed that my true love rides on
    Is lighter than the wind;
Wi' siller he is shod before,
    Wi' burning gowd behind.'

Janet has kilted her green kirtle
    A little aboon her knee;
And she has snooded her yellow hair
    A little aboon her bree;
And she's awa to Carterhaugh
    As fast as she can hie.

When she cam to Carterhaugh,
    Tam Lin was at the well;
And there she fand his steed standing,
    But away was himsel'.

She had na pu'd a double rose,
    A rose but only twae,
Till up then started young Tam Lin
    Says, 'Lady, thou pu's nae mae.

'Why pu's thou the rose, Janet,
    Amang the groves sae green,
And a' to kill the bonnie babe
    That we gat us between?'

'O, tell me tell me, Tam Lin,' she says,
    'For 's sake that died on tree,
If e'er ye was in holy chapel
    Or Christendom did see.'

'Roxbrugh he was my grandfather,
    Took me with him to bide,
And ance it fell upon a day,
    That wae did me betide.

'Ance it fell upon a day,
    A cauld day and a snell,
When we were frae the hunting come
    That frae my horse I fell.

'The queen o' Fairies she caught me
    In yon green hill to dwell,
And pleasant is the fairyland—
    But an eerie tale to tell!

'Aye, at the end o' seven years
    We pay a tiend to hell;
I am sae fair and fu' o' flesh
    I'm fear'd it be mysel'.

'But the night is Hallowe'en, lady,
    The morn is Hallowday;
Then win me, win me, an ye will,
    For weel I wat ye may.

'Just at the mirk and midnight hour
    The fairy folk will ride;
And they that wad their true love win
    At Milecross they maun bide.'

'But how shall I thee ken, Tam Lin,
    Or how my true love know,
Amang sae monie unco knights
    The like I never saw.'

'O first let pass the black, lady,
    And syne let pass the brown;
But quickly run to the milk-white steed,
    Pu' ye his rider down.

'For I'll ride on the milk-white steed,
    And aye nearest the town,
Because I was an earthly knight
    They gie me that renown.

'My right hand will be glov'd, lady,
    My left hand will be bare;
Cockt up shall my bonnet be
    And kaim'd down shall my hair;
And thae's the tokens I gie thee—
    Nae doubt I will be there:

'They'll turn me in your arms, lady,
  Into an esk and adder,
But hold me fast and fear me not—
  I am your bairn's father.

'They'll turn me to a bear sae grim
  And then a lion bold;
But hold me fast and fear me not,
  As ye shall love your child.

'Again they'll turn me in your arms
  To a red-het gaud of airn;
But hold me fast and fear me not,
  I'll do to you nae harm.

'And last they'll turn me in your arms
  Into the burning lead;
Then throw me into well water;
  O, throw me in wi' speed!

'And then I'll be your ain true love,
  I'll turn a naked knight;
Then cover me wi' your green mantle,
  And cover me out o' sight.'

Gloomy, gloomy was the night,
  And eerie was the way,
As fair Jenny in her green mantle
  To Milecross she did gae.

About the middle o' the night
  She heard the bridles ring;
This lady was as glad at that
  As any earthly thing.

First she let the black pass by,
  And syne she let the brown,
But quickly she ran to the milk-white steed
  And pu'd the rider down.

Sae weel she minded what he did say
  And young Tam Lin did win;
Syne cover'd him wi' her green mantle,
  As blythe 's a bird in spring.

Out then spak the queen o' fairies,
  Out of a bush o' broom;
'Them that has gotten young Tam Lin
  Has gotten a stately groom.'

Out then spak the queen o' fairies,
  And an angry queen was she:

'Shame betide her ill-far'd face,
　　And an ill death may she die,
For she's ta'en awa' the bonniest knight
　　In a' my companie.

'But had I kend, Tam Lin,' she says,
　　'What now this night I see,
I wad hae ta'en out thy twa grey een,
　　And put in twa een o' tree.'

THE RANTIN LADDIE

Aften hae I play'd at the cards and the dice,
　　For the love of a bonnie rantin laddie;
But now I maun sit in my father's kitchen neuk,
　　And balou a bastard babie.

For my father he will not me own,
　　And my mother she neglects me,
And a' my friends hae lightlied me,
　　And their servants they do slight me.

But had I a servant at my command,
　　As aft times I've had many,
That wad rin wi' a letter to bonnie Glenswood,
　　Wi' a letter to my rantin laddie.

'O, is he either a laird or a lord,
　　Or is he but a cadie,
That ye do him ca' sae aften by name,
　　Your bonnie, bonnie rantin laddie.'

'Indeed he is baith a laird and a lord,
　　And he never was a cadie,
But he is the Earl o' bonnie Aboyne,
　　And he is my rantin laddie.'

'O ye'se get a servant at your command,
　　As aft times ye've had many,
That sall rin wi' a letter to bonnie Glenswood—
　　A letter to your rantin laddie.'

When Lord Aboyne did the letter get,
　　O, but he blinket bonnie;
But or he had read three lines of it,
　　I think his heart was sorry.

'O, wha is he daur be sae bauld,
　　Sae cruelly to use my lassie?'

　　·　　　　　·　　　　　·　　　　　·

　　·　　　　　·　　　　　·　　　　　·

'For her father he will not her know,
    And her mother she does slight her;
And a' her friends hae lightlied her,
    And their servants they neglect her.'

'Go raise to me my five hundred men,
    Make haste and make them ready;
With a milk-white steed under every ane
    For to bring hame my lady.'

As they came in through Buchan shire,
    They were a company bonnie,
With a guid claymore in every hand
    And O, but they shin'd bonnie.

THE ROWIN 'T IN HER APRON

Our young lady's a-huntin gane,
Sheets nor blankets has she ta'en,
But she's born her auld son or she cam hame,
    And she's row'd him in her apron.

Her apron was o' the hollan fine,
Laid about wi' laces nine;
She thought it a pity her babie should tyne,
    And she's row'd him in her apron.

Her apron was o' the hollan sma',
Laid about wi' laces a',
She thought it a pity her babe to let fa',
    And she row'd him in her apron.

Her father says within the ha',
Among the knights and nobles a',
'I think I hear a babie ca'
    In the chamber among our young ladies.'

'O father dear, it is a bairn,
I hope it will do you nae harm,
For the laddie I lo'ed, and he'll lo'e me again,
    For the rowin 't in my apron.'

'O, is he a gentleman or is a clown
That has brought thy fair body down?
I would not for a' this town
    The rowin 't in thy apron.'

'Young Terreagles he's nae clown,
He is the toss of Edinborrow town,
And he'll buy me a braw new gown
    For the rowin 't in my apron.'

'It's I hae castles, I hae towers,
I hae barns, and I hae bowers;
A' that is mine it shall be thine
    For the rowin 't in thy apron.'

GUID WALLACE

'O, for my ain king,' quo' guid Wallace,
    'The rightfu' king of fair Scotland,
Between me and my sovereign bluid,
    I think I see ill seed sawn.'

Wallace out over yon river he lap,
    And he has lighted low down on yon plain,
And he was aware of a gay ladie,
    As she was at the well washing.

'What tydins, what tydins, fair lady,' he says,
    'What tydins hast thou to tell unto me;
What tydins, what tydins, fair lady,' he says,
    'What tydins hae ye in the south countrie?'

'Low down in yon wee Ostler house
    There is fyfteen Englishmen,
And they are seekin for guid Wallace;
    It's him to take, and him to hang.'

'There's nocht in my purse,' quo' guid Wallace,
    'There's nocht, not even a bare pennie;
But I will down to yon wee Ostler house
    Thir fyfteen Englishmen to see.'

And when he cam in to yon wee Ostler house
    He bad benedicite be there;

    .   .   .   .
    .   .   .   .

'Where was ye born, auld crookit carl,
    Where was ye born—in what countrie?'
'I am a true Scot born and bred,
    And an auld crookit carl just sic as ye see.'

'I wad gie fyfteen shillings to onie crookit carl—
    To onie crookit carl just sic as ye,
If ye will get me guid Wallace,
    For he is the man I wad very fain see.'

He hit the proud captain alang the chaft blade
    That never a bit o' meal he ate mair;
And he sticket the rest at the table where they sat,
    And he left them a' lyin sprawlin there.

'Get up, get up, guidwife,' he says,
  'And get to me some dinner in haste;
For it will soon be three lang days
  Sin I a bit o' meat did taste.'

The dinner was na weel readie,
  Nor was it on the table set,
Till other fyfteen Englishmen
  Were a' lighted about the yett.

'Come out, come out, now guid Wallace,
  This is the day that thou maun die.'
'I lippen nae sae little to God,' he says,
  'Altho' I be but ill wordie.'

The guidwife had an auld guidman,
  By guid Wallace he stiffly stood,
Till ten o' the fyfteen Englishmen
  Before the door lay in their bluid.

The other five to the greenwood ran,
  And he hang'd these five upon a grain;
And on the morn wi' his merry men a'
  He sat at dine in Lochmaben town.

THE GERMAN LAIRDIE

Chorus: Sing heedle liltie, teedle liltie,
    Andum, tandum, tandie,
  Sing fal de dal, de dal lal lal,
    Sing howdle liltie dandie.

What merriment has ta'en the Whigs
  I think they be gaen mad, Sir,
Wi' playing up their Whiggish jigs,
  Their dancin may be sad, Sir.

The Revolution principles
  Has put their heads in bees, Sir;
They're a' fa'en out amang themsels—
  Deil tak the first that grees, Sir.

WHERE HELEN LIES

O, that I were where Helen lies!
Night and day on me she cries;
O, that I were where Helen lies
  In fair Kirkconnel lee.
O Helen fair! beyond compare,
A ringlet of thy flowing hair,
I'll wear it still for evermair
  Until the day I die.

Curs'd be the hand that shot the shot,
And curs'd the gun that gave the crack!
Into my arms bird Helen lap,
  And died for sake o' me.
O think na ye but my heart was sair;
My love fell down and spake nae mair,
There did she swoon wi' meikle care
  On fair Kirkconnel lee.

I lighted down, my sword did draw,
I cutted him in pieces sma';
I cutted him in pieces sma'
  On fair Kirkconnel lee.

O Helen chaste, thou wert modest.
If I were with thee I were blest,
Where thou lies low, and takes thy rest
    On fair Kirkconnel lee.

I wish my grave was growing green,
A winding sheet put o'er my een,
And I in Helen's arms lying
    In fair Kirkconnel lee!
I wish I were where Helen lies!
Night and day on me she cries;
O, that I were where Helen lies
    On fair Kirkconnel lee.

CAULD FROSTY MORNING

'Twas past ane o'clock in a cauld frosty morning
    When cankert November blaws over the plain,
I heard the kirk bell repeat the loud warning
    As restless I sought for sweet slumber in vain:
Then up I arose, the silver moon shining bright,
    Mountains and valleys appearing all hoary white;
Forth I would go amid the pale, silent night
    To visit the fair one, the cause of my pain.

Sae gently I staw to my lovely maid's chamber,
    And rapp'd at her window, low down on my knee,
Begging that she would awauk from sweet slumber,
    Awauk from sweet slumber and pity me:
For, that a stranger to a' pleasure, peace and rest,
    Love into madness had fired my tortur'd breast,
And that I should be of a' men the maist unblest,
    Unless she would pity my sad miserie!

My true love arose and whispered to me
    (The moon looked in and envy'd my love's charms),
'An innocent maiden, ah, would you undo me!'
    I made no reply but leapt into her arms:
Bright Phoebus peep'd over the hills and found me there;
    As he has done, now, seven lang years and mair,
A faithfuller, constanter, kinder, more loving pair,
    His sweet chearing beam nor enlightens nor warms.

BROOM BESOMS

Chorus: Buy broom besoms! Wha will buy them now?
Fine heather ringers, better never grew.

I maun hae a wife, whatsoe'er she be;
An she be a woman, that's eneugh for me.

If that she be bonnie, I shall think her right:
If that she be ugly, where's the odds at night?

O, an she be young, how happy shall I be!
If that she be auld, the sooner she will die.

If that she be fruitfu', O, what joy is there!
If she should be barren, less will be my care.

If she like a drappie, she and I'll agree;
If she dinna like it, there's the mair for me.

Be she green or grey, be she black or fair,
Let her be a woman, I shall seek nae mair.

Alternative Verses

Chorus: Buy broom besoms! Wha will buy them now?
Fine heather ringers, better never grew.

Young and souple was I, when I lap the dyke;
Now I'm auld and frail, I douna step a syke.

Young and souple was I, when at Lautherslack,
Now I'm auld and frail, and lie at Nansie's back.

Had she gien me butter, when she gae me bread,
I wad looked baulder, wi' my beld head.

THE TAILOR FELL THRO' THE BED
Tune—*Beware o' the ripells*

The tailor fell thro' the bed, thimble an' a',
The tailor fell thro' the bed, thimble an' a';
The blankets were thin, and the sheets they were sma',
The tailor fell thro' the bed, thimble an' a'!

The sleepy bit lassie, she dreaded nae ill,
The sleepy bit lassie, she dreaded nae ill;
The weather was cauld, and the lassie lay still:
She thought that a tailor could do her nae ill!

Gie me the groat again, cannie young man,
Gie me the groat again, cannie young man;
The day it is short, and the night it is lang,
The dearest siller that ever I wan!

There's somebody weary wi' lying her lane,
There's somebody weary wi' lying her lane,
There's some that are dowie, I trow wad be fain
To see the bit tailor come skippin again.

AYE WAUKIN, O

Chorus: Aye waukin, O,
    Waukin still and weary:
Sleep I can get nane
    For thinking on my dearie.

Simmer's a pleasant time,
    Flowers of every colour;
The water rins o'er the heugh,
    And I long for my true lover.

When I sleep I dream,
    When I wauk I'm eerie,
Sleep I can get nane
    For thinkin on my dearie.

THE WHITE COCKADE

Chorus: O, he's a ranting, roving lad,
He is a brisk an' a bonnie lad;
Betide what may, I will be wed
And follow the boy wi' the White Cockade!

My love was born in Aberdeen,
The bonniest lad that e'er was seen,
But now he makes our hearts fu' sad—
He takes the field wi' his White Cockade.

I'll sell my rock, my reel, my tow,
My guid grey mare and hawkit cow,
To buy mysel' a tartan plaid,
To follow the boy wi' the White Cockade.

JOHN, COME KISS ME NOW

Chorus: O John, come kiss me now, now, now;
    O John, my love, come kiss me now;
O John, come kiss me by and by,
    For weel ye ken the way to woo!

O, some will court and compliment,
    And ither some will kiss and daut;
But I will mak o' my guidman,
    My ain guidman—it is nae faut!

O, some will court and compliment,
    And ither some will prie their mou',
And some will hause in ither's arms,
    And that's the way I like to do!

O, AN YE WERE DEAD, GUIDMAN

Chorus: O, an ye were dead, guidman,
A green turf on your head, guidman,
I wad bestow my widowhood
Upon a rantin Highlandman.

There's sax eggs in the pan, guidman,
There's sax eggs in the pan, guidman;
There's ane to you, and twa to me,
And three to our John Highlandman.

A sheep-head's in the pot, guidman,
A sheep-head's in the pot, guidman;
The flesh to him, the broo to me,
An' the horns become your brow, guidman.

Chorus to last verse:
Sing round about the fire wi' a rung she ran,
An' round about the fire wi' a rung she ran:
'Your horns shall tie you to the staw,
An' I shall bang your hide, guidman!'

COMIN THRO' THE RYE
Tune—*Miller's Wedding*

Chorus: O, Jenny's a' weet, poor body,
    Jenny's seldom dry:
She draigl't a' her petticoatie,
    Comin thro' the rye!

Comin thro' the rye, poor body,
    Comin thro' the rye,
She draigl't a' her petticoatie,
    Comin thro' the rye!

Gin a body meet a body
    Comin thro' the rye,
Gin a body kiss a body,
    Need a body cry?

Gin a body meet a body
    Comin thro' the glen,
Gin a body kiss a body,
    Need the warld ken?

Gin a body meet a body
    Comin thro' the grain;
Gin a body kiss a body,
    The thing's a body's ain.

THERE'S THREE TRUE GUID FELLOWS
Tune—*Three guid fellows ayont the glen*

There's three true guid fellows,
There's three true guid fellows,
There's three truc guid fellows,
    Down ayont yon glen!

It's now the day is dawin,
But or night do fa' in,
Whase cock's best at crawin,
    Willie, thou sall ken!

THE REEL O' STUMPIE

Wap and rowe, wap and rowe,
    Wap and rowe the feetie o't,
I thought I was a maiden fair,
    Till I heard the greetie o 't!

My daddie was a fiddler fine,
    My minnie she made mantie, O,
And I myself a thumpin quine,
    And danc'd the reel o' Stumpie, O.

AS I CAME O'ER THE CAIRNEY MOUNT

Chorus: O, my bonnie Highland lad,
    My winsome, weel-faur'd Highland laddie;
Wha wad mind the wind and rain
    Sae weel row'd in his tartan plaidie!

As I cam o'er the Cairney mount
    And down among the blooming heather,
Kindly stood the milking-shiel
    To shelter frae the stormy weather.

Now Phoebus blinkit on the bent,
    And o'er the knowes the lambs were bleating;
But he wan my heart's consent
    To be his ain at the neist meeting.

HIGHLAND LADDIE

She
The bonniest lad that e'er I saw,
    Bonnie laddie, Highland laddie,
Wore a plaid and was fu' braw,
    Bonnie Highland laddie.

On his head a bonnet blue,
    Bonnie laddie, Highland laddie;
His royal heart was firm and true
    Bonnie Highland laddie.

He
Trumpets sound and cannons r'
    Bonnie lassie, Lawland lass
And a' the hills wi' echoes roar,
    Bonnie Lawland lassie.

Glory, Honour, now invite,
    Bonnie lassie, Lawland lassie,
For freedom and my King to fight,
    Bonnie Lawland lassie.

She
The sun a backward course shall take,
    Bonnie laddie, Highland laddie,
Ere aught thy manly courage shake,
    Bonnie Highland laddie.

Go, for yoursel' procure renown,
    Bonnie laddie, Highland laddie,
And for your lawful King his crown,
    Bonnie Highland laddie.

THE TAILOR

The tailor he cam here to sew,
    And weel he kend the way to woo,
For aye he pree'd the lassie's mou',
    As he gaed but and ben, O,
        For weel he kenn'd the way, O,
        The way, O, the way, O,
        For weel he kenn'd the way, O,
    The lassie's heart to win, O!

The tailor rase and sheuk his duds,
    The flaes they flew awa' in cluds!
And them that stay'd gat fearfu' thuds
    The tailor prov'd a man, O,
        For now it was the gloamin,
        The gloamin, the gloamin,
        For now it was the gloamin,
    When a' the rest are gaun, O!

THERE GROWS A BONNIE BRIER BUSH

There grows a bonnie brier bush in our kailyard,
There grows a bonnie brier bush in our kailyard;
And below the bonnie brier bush there's a lassie and a lad,
And they're busy, busy courting in our kailyard.

We'll court nae mair below the buss in our kailyard,
We'll court nae mair below the buss in our kailyard;
We'll awa' to Athole's green, and there we'll no be seen,
Whare the trees and the branches will be our safeguard.

Will ye go to the dancin in Carlyle's ha',
Will ye go to the dancin in Carlyle's ha',
Whare Sandy and Nancy I'm sure will ding them a'?
I winna gang to the dance in Carlyle-ha'!

What will I do for a lad when Sandie gangs awa'?
What will I do for a lad when Sandie gangs awa'?
I will awa' to Edinburgh, and win a pennie fee,
And see an onie lad will fancy me.

He's comin frae the north that's to marry me,
He's comin frae the north that's to marry me;
A feather in his bonnet and a ribbon at his knee,
He's a bonnie, bonnie laddie, and yon be he!

WE'RE A' NODDIN

Chorus: We're a' noddin, nid nid noddin,
　　　　We're a' noddin at our house at hame,
　　We're a' noddin, nid nid noddin,
　　　　We're a' noddin at our house at hame,

'Guid e'en to you, kimmer,
　And how do ye do?'
'Hiccup!' quo' kimmer,
　'The better that I'm fou!'

Kate sits i' the neuk,
　Suppin hen broo.
Deil tak Kate
　An she be na noddin too!

'How's a' wi' you, kimmer?
　And how do you fare?'
'A pint o' the best o't,
　And twa pints mair!'

'How's a' wi' you, kimmer?
　And how do ye thrive?
How monie bairns hae ye?'
　Quo' kimmer, 'I hae five.'

'Are they a' Johnie's?
　'Eh! atweel no:
Twa o' them were gotten
　When Johnie was awa!'

Cats like milk,
　And dogs like broo;
Lads like lasses weel,
　And lasses lads too.

WHEN FIRST I SAW
Tune—*Maggie Lauder*

Chorus: She's aye, aye sae blithe, sae gay,
　　She's aye sae blithe and cheerie,
　She's aye sae bonnie, blithe and gay,
　　O gin I were her dearie!

When first I saw fair Jeanie's face,
I couldna tell what ail'd me:
My heart went fluttering pit-a-pat,
My een they almost fail'd me.
She's aye sae neat, sae trim, sae tight,
All grace does round her hover!
Ae look depriv'd me o' my heart,
And I became her lover.

Had I Dundas's whole estate,
　Or Hopetoun's wealth to shine in;
Did warlike laurels crown my brow,
　Or humbler bays entwining;
I'd lay them a' at Jeanie's feet,
　Could I but hope to move her,
And, prouder than a belted knight,
　I'd be my Jeanie's lover.

But sair I fear some happier swain,
　Has gain'd sweet Jeanie's favour,
If so, my every bliss be hers,
　Though I maun never have her!
But gang she east, or gang she west,
　'Twixt Forth and Tweed all over,
While men have eyes, or ears, or taste,
　She'll always find a lover.

THE PRIMROSE
Tune—*Todlin hame*

Dost ask me, why I send thee here,
The firstling of the infant year?
Dost ask me what this primose shows,
Bepearled thus with morning dew?

  I must whisper to thy ears,
  The sweets of love are wash'd with tears.

This lovely native of the vale,
Thou seest how languid, pensive, pale:
Thou seest this bending stalk so weak,
That each way yielding doth not break?

  I must tell thee, these reveal,
  The doubts and fears a lover feels.

LEEZIE LINDSAY—A FRAGMENT

Will ye go to the Hielands, Leezie Lindsay,
  Will ye go to the Hielands wi' me?
Will ye go to the Hielands, Leezie Lindsay,
  My pride and my darling to be.

THE WREN'S NEST—A FRAGMENT

The Robin cam to the Wren's nest
  And keekit in and keekit in;
O weel's me on your auld pow,
  Wad ye be in, wad ye be in?

Ye'se ne'er get leave to lie without,
  And I within, and I within,
Sae lang's I hae an auld clout
  To row ye in, to row ye in.

A TIPPLING BALLAD
On the Duke of Brunswick's breaking up his Camp and the defeat of the
Austrians by Dumourier

When Princes and Prelates and hot-headed zealots,
A' Europe had set in a low, a low,
The poor man lies down, nor envies a crown,
And comforts himself as he dow, as he dow,
  And comforts himself as he dow.

The black-headed eagle, as keen as a beagle,
He hunted o'er height and o'er howe,
In the braes o' Gemappe, he fell in a trap,
E'en let him come out as he dow, dow, dow,
  E'en let him come out as he dow.

But truce with commotions, and new-fangled notions,
A bumper, I trust you'll allow;
Here's George our good king, and Charlotte his queen,
And lang may they ring as they dow, dow, dow,
  And lang may they ring as they dow.

Epitaph For Hugh Logan, Esq., Of Logan

Here lyes Squire Hugh—ye harlot crew,
Come mak your water on him,
I'm sure that he weel pleas'd would be
To think ye pish'd upon him.

On A Dog Of Lord Eglinton's

I never barked when out of season,
I never bit without a reason;
I ne'er insulted weaker brother,
Nor wronged by force or fraud another.
We brutes are placed a rank below;
Happy for man could he say so.

Lassie, Lie Near Me

Chorus: Near me, near me,
Lassie, lie near me;
Lang hast thou lien thy lane,
Lassie, lie near me.

Lang hae we parted been,
Lassie, my dearie;
Now we are met again,
Lassie, lie near me.

A' that I hae endur'd,
Lassie, my dearie,
Here in thy arms is cur'd,
Lassie, lie near me.

Sweetest May

Sweetest May, let love inspire thee;
Take a heart which he designs thee;
As thy constant slave regard it;
For its faith and truth reward it.

Proof o' shot to Birth or Money,
Not the wealthy but the bonnie;
Not high-born but noble-minded,
In Love's silken band can bind it.

Tibbie Fowler

Chorus: Wooin at her, pu'in at her,
Courtin at her, canna get her:
Filthy elf, it's for her pelf,
That a' the lads are wooin at her.

Tibbie Fowler o' the glen,
There's o'er monie wooin at her,
Tibbie Fowler o the glen,
There's o'er monie wooin at her.

She's got pendles in her lugs,
Cockleshells wad set her better;
High-heel'd shoon and siller tags,
And a' the lads are wooin at her.

Ten came east, and ten cam west,
Ten cam rowin o'er the water;
Twa came down the lang dyke side,
There's twa and thirty wooin at her.

Be a lassie e'er sae black,
An she hae the name o' siller,
Set her upo' Tintock-tap,
The wind will blaw a man till her.

There's seven but, and seven ben,
Seven in the pantry wi' her;
Twenty head about the door,
There's ane and forty wooin at her.

Be a lassie e'er sae fair,
An she want the pennie siller;
A flie may fell her in the air,
Before a man be even till her.

I Murder Hate

I murder hate by flood or field,
    Tho' glory's name may screen us;
In wars at home I'll spend my blood—
    Life-giving wars of Venus.
The deities that I adore
    Are social Peace and Plenty;
I'm better pleas'd to make one more
    Than be the death of twenty.

I would not die like Socrates,
    For all the fuss of Plato;
Nor would I with Leonidas,
    Nor yet would I with Cato:
The zealots of the Church and State
    Shall ne'er my mortal foes be;
But let me have bold Zimri's fate,
    Within the arms of Cosbi![1]

[1] *Vide* Numbers, Chap. 25, verses 8–15.—R.B.

Kirk And State Excisemen
Lines Written on a Window at the King's Arms, Dumfries

Ye men of wit and wealth, why all this sneering
'Gainst poor Excisemen? Give the cause a hearing:
What are your landlord's rent rolls? Taxing ledgers;
What premiers? What even monarchs? Mighty gaugers!
Nay, what are priests, those seeming godly wise men,
What are they, pray, but spiritual Excisemen?

Extempore Reply To An Invitation

The King's most humble servant, I
    Can scarcely spare a minute;
But I'll be wi' you by an' by,
    Or else the deil's be in it.

Grace After Meat

Lord, Thee we thank, and Thee adore,
    For temporal gifts we little merit;
At present we will ask no more—
    Let William Hislop[1] give the spirit.

[1] William Hislop of the Globe Tavern, Dumfries.

Grace Before And After Meat

O Lord, when hunger pinches sore,
    Do Thou stand us in stead,
And send us from Thy bounteous store
    A tup or wether head! Amen.

O Lord, since we have feasted thus,
    Which we so little merit,
Let Meg[1] now take away the flesh,
    And Jock bring in the spirit! Amen.

[1] Jock and Meg Hislop of the Globe Tavern.

ON GENERAL DUMOURIER'S DESERTION[1]

You're welcome to Despots, Dumourier!
You're welcome to Despots, Dumourier!
  How does Dampiere do?
  Ay, and Bournonville too?
Why did they not come along with you, Dumourier?

I will fight France with you, Dumourier.
I will fight France with you, Dumourier.
  I will fight France with you,
  I will take my chance with you,
By my soul, I'll dance with you, Dumourier.

Then let us fight about, Dumourier!
Then let us fight about, Dumourier!
  Then let us fight about,
  Till Freedom's spark be out,
Then we'll be damn'd, no doubt, Dumourier.

[1] Chanted extempore when he heard of Dumourier deserting the French Republican cause, 5 April 1793.

LOGAN BRAES
Tune—*Logan Water*

O Logan, sweetly didst thou glide,
The day I was my Willie's bride!
And years sinsyne hae o'er us run,
Like Logan to the simmer sun.
But now thy flow'ry banks appear
Like drumlie winter, dark and drear,
While my dear lad maun face his faes,
Far, far frae me and Logan braes.

Again the merry month o' May
Has made our hills and valleys gay;
The birds rejoice in leafy bowers,
The bees hum round the breathing flowers;
Blithe morning lifts his rosy eye,
And evening's tears are tears o' joy:
My soul, delightless, a' surveys,
While Willie's far frae Logan braes.

Within yon milk-white hawthorn bush,
Amang her nestlings sits the thrush;
Her faithfu' mate will share her toil,
Or wi' his song her cares beguile:
But I, wi' my sweet nurslings here,
Nae mate to help, nae mate to cheer,
Pass widow'd nights and joyless days,
While Willie's far frae Logan braes.

O wae upon you, men o' state,
That brethren rouse to deadly hate!
As ye make monie a fond heart mourn,
Sae may it on your heads return!
How can your flinty hearts enjoy
The widow's tears, the orphan's cry?
But soon may peace bring happy days
And Willie hame to Logan braes!

BLYTHE HAE I BEEN
Tune—The Quaker's wife

Blythe hae I been on yon hill,
   As the lambs before me;
Careless ilka thought and free,
   As the breeze flew o'er me;
Now nae langer sport and play,
   Mirth or sang can please me;
Lesley is sae fair and coy,
   Care and anguish seize me.

Heavy, heavy is the task,
   Hopeless love declaring:
Trembling, I dow nought but glow'r,
   Sighing, dumb despairing!
If she winna ease the thraws
   In my bosom swelling;
Underneath the grass-green sod,
   Soon maun be my dwelling.

O WERE MY LOVE YON LILAC FAIR
Tune—Hughie Graham

O were my love yon lilac fair,
   Wi' purple blossoms to the spring,
And I, a bird to shelter there,
   When weary on my little wing!
How I wad mourn when it was torn
   By autumn wild and winter rude!
But I wad sing on wanton wing
   When youthfu' May its bloom renew'd.

O gin my love were yon red rose
   That grows upon the castle wa'!
And I mysel' a drap o' dew
   Into her bonnie breast to fa'!
O, there beyond expression blest,
   I'd feast on beauty a' the night;
Seal'd on her silk-saft faulds to rest
   Till fley'd awa by Phoebus' light!

BONNIE JEAN[1]—A BALLAD

There was a lass, and she was fair,
   At kirk or market to be seen;
When a' our fairest maids were met,
   The fairest maid was bonnie Jean.

---

[1] Jean McMurdo, daughter of John McMurdo of Drumlanrig (*see* note page 245), is said to have been the heroine of this ballad song.

And aye she wrought her mammie's wark,
    And aye she sang sae merrilie;
The blythest bird upon the bush
    Had ne'er a lighter heart than she.

But hawks will rob the tender joys
    That bless the little lintwhite's nest;
And frost will blight the fairest flowers,
    And love will break the soundest rest.

Young Robie was the brawest lad,
    The flower and pride of a' the glen;
And he had owsen, sheep and kye,
    And wanton naigies nine or ten.

He gaed wi' Jeanie to the tryste,
    He danc'd wi' Jeanie on the down;
And, lang ere witless Jeanie wist,
    Her heart was tint, her peace was stown.

As in the bosom o' the stream
    The moonbeam dwells at dewy e'en;
So trembling, pure, was tender love
    Within the breast o' bonnie Jean.

And now she works her mammie's wark,
    And aye she sighs wi' care and pain;
Yet wist na what her ail might be
    Or what wad mak her weel again.

But did na Jeanie's heart loup light,
    And didna joy blink in her e'e,
As Robie tauld a tale o' love
    Ae e'ening on the lily lea?

The sun was sinking in the west,
    The birds sang sweet in ilka grove;
His cheek to hers he fondly prest,
    And whisper'd thus his tale o' love:

'O Jeanie fair, I lo'e thee dear;
    O canst thou think to fancy me!
Or wilt thou leave thy mammie's cot
    And learn to tent the farms wi' me?

'At barn or byre thou shalt na drudge,
    Or naething else to trouble thee;
But stray amang the heather-bells,
    And tent the waving corn wi' me.'

Now what could artless Jeanie do?
    She had nae will to say him na:
At length she blush'd a sweet consent,
    And love was aye between them twa.

LINES ON JOHN McMURDO, ESQ.[1]

Blest be McMurdo to his latest day!
No envious cloud o'ercast his evening ray;
No wrinkle furrow'd by the hand of care,
Nor ever sorrow add one silver hair!
O, may no son the father's honour stain,
Nor ever daughter give the mother pain!

[1] The steward of the Duke of Queensberry. *See* note page 245.

EPITAPH ON A LAP-DOG
Named Echo[1]

In wood and wild, ye warbling throng,
　　Your heavy loss deplore;
Now half extinct your powers of song,
　　Sweet Echo is no more.

Ye jarring, screeching things around,
　　Scream your discordant joys;
Now half your din of tuneless sound
　　With Echo silent lies.

[1] Belonging to Mrs Gordon of Kenmure Castle.

EPIGRAMS AGAINST THE EARL OF GALLOWAY

What dost thou in that mansion fair?
　　Flit, Galloway, and find
Some narrow, dirty, dungeon cave,
　　The picture of thy mind.

No Stewart art thou, Galloway,
　　The Stewarts all were brave;
Besides, the Stewarts were but fools,
　　Not one of them a knave.

Bright ran thy line, O Galloway,
　　Thro' many a far-fam'd sire!
So ran the far-fam'd Roman way,
　　And ended in a mire.

Spare me thy vengeance, Galloway!
　　In quiet let me live;
I ask no kindness at thy hand,
　　For thou hast none to give.

EPIGRAM ON THE LAIRD OF LAGGAN

When Morine, deceas'd, to the devil went down,
'Twas nothing would serve him but Satan's own crown;
'Thy fool's head,' quoth Satan, 'that crown shall wear never,
I grant thou'rt as wicked—but not quite so clever.'

PHILLIS THE FAIR[1]
Tune—*Robin Adair*

While larks with little wing fann'd the pure air,
Tasting the breathing Spring, forth I did fare.
    Gay the sun's golden eye
    Peep'd o'er the mountains high;
'Such thy morn!' did I cry, 'Phillis the fair!'

In each bird's careless song, glad I did share;
While yon wild flowers among, chance led me there.
    Sweet to the opening day,
    Rosebuds bent the dewy spray;
'Such thy bloom!' did I say, 'Phillis the fair!'

Down in a shady walk, doves cooing were;
I mark'd the cruel hawk, caught in a snare:
    So kind may fortune be,
    Such make his destiny,
He who would injure thee, Phillis the fair!

[1] A tribute to Miss Phillis McMurdo, written at the request of Mr Stephen Clarke. She was his pupil, and he had a passion for her. She later became Mrs Lockhart of Carnwath.

HAD I A CAVE
Tune—*Robin Adair*

Had I a cave on some wild distant shore,
Where the winds howl to the waves' dashing roar:
    There would I weep my woes,
    There seek my lost repose,
    Till grief my eyes should close,
        Ne'er to wake more!

Falsest of womankind, can'st thou declare
All thy fond, plighted vows fleeting as air!
    To thy new lover hie,
    Laugh o'er thy perjury;
    Then in thy bosom try
        What peace is there!

BY ALLAN STREAM
Tune—*Allan Water*

By Allan stream I chanc'd to rove,
    While Phoebus sank beyond Benledi;[1]
The winds were whispering thro' the grove,
    The yellow corn was waving ready:
I listen'd to a lover's sang,
    An' thought on youthfu' pleasures monie;
And aye the wild-wood echoes rang—
    'O, dearly do I lo'e thee, Annie!

[1] A mountain west of Strath-Allan, 3009 feet high.—R.B.

O, happy be the woodbine bower,
　Nae nightly bogle make it eerie;
Nor ever sorrow stain the hour,
　The place and time I met my dearie!
Her head upon my throbbing breast,
　She, sinking, said, 'I'm thine for ever!'
While monie a kiss the seal imprest,
　The sacred vow we ne'er should sever.

The haunt o' Spring's the primrose brae,
　The Simmer joys the flocks to follow;
How cheery thro' her short'ning day
　Is Autumn in her weeds o' yellow;
But can they melt the glowing heart,
　Or chain the soul in speechless pleasure,
Or thro' each nerve the rapture dart,
　Like meeting her, our bosom's treasure?

WHISTLE, AND I'LL COME TO YOU, MY LAD

Chorus: O, whistle, and I'll come to ye, my lad,
O, whistle, and I'll come to ye, my lad;
Tho' father and mother and a' should gae mad,
　O, whistle, and I'll come to ye, my lad.

But warily tent when ye come to court me,
And come nae unless the back yett be a-jee;
Syne up the back stile and let naebody see,
And come as ye were na comin' to me,
　And come as ye were na comin' to me.

At kirk, or at market, whene'er ye meet me,
Gang by me as tho' that ye car'd nae a flie;
But steal me a blink o' your bonnie black e'e,
Yet look as ye were na lookin' at me,
　Yet look as ye were na lookin' at me.

Aye vow and protest that ye care na for me,
And whyles ye may lightly my beauty a wee;
But court nae anither, though jokin' ye be,
For fear that she wyle your fancy frae me,
　For fear that she wyle your fancy frae me.

PHILLIS, THE QUEEN O' THE FAIR[1]
Tune—*The muckin o' Geordie's byre*

Chorus: Awa' wi' your belles and your beauties,
　They never wi' her can compare,
Wha-ever has met wi' my Phillis,
　Has met wi' the queen o' the fair.

[1] *See* note on previous page regarding Phillis McMurdo

Adown winding Nith I did wander,
    To mark the sweet flowers as they spring;
Adown winding Nith I did wander,
    Of Phillis to muse and to sing.

The daisy amus'd my fond fancy,
    So artless, so simple, so wild;
'Thou emblem,' said I, 'o' my Phillis!'
    For she is simplicity's child.

The rosebud's the blush o' my charmer,
    Her sweet balmy lip when 'tis prest:
How fair and how pure is the lily,
    But fairer and purer her breast.

Yon knot of gay flowers in the arbour,
    They ne'er wi' my Phillis can vie;
Her breath is the breath o' the woodbine,
    Its dewdrop o' diamond her eye.

Her voice is the song o' the morning,
    That wakes thro' the green-spreading grove
When Phoebus peeps over the mountains,
    On music, and pleasure, and love.

But beauty, how frail and how fleeting,
    The bloom of a fine summer's day!
While worth in the mind o' my Phillis
    Will flourish without a decay.

COME, LET ME TAKE THEE TO MY BREAST
Tune—Cauld kail

Come, let me take thee to my breast,
    And pledge we ne'er shall sunder;
And I shall spurn as vilest dust
    The warld's wealth and grandeur:
And do I hear my Jeanie own
    That equal transports move her?
I ask for dearest life alone,
    That I may live to love her.

Thus in my arms, wi' a' her charms,
    I clasp my countless treasure;
I seek nae mair o' Heaven to share
    Than sic a moment's pleasure:
And by thy e'en, sae bonnie blue,
    I swear I'm thine for ever!
And on thy lips I seal my vow,
    And break it shall I never!

DAINTY DAVIE

Chorus: Meet me on the warlock knowe,
    Dainty Davie, dainty Davie;
There I'll spend the day wi' you,
    My ain dear dainty Davie.

Now rosy May comes in wi' flowers,
To deck her gay, green-spreading bowers;
And now comes in the happy hours,
    To wander wi' my Davie.

The crystal waters round us fa',
The merry birds are lovers a',
The scented breezes round us blaw,
    A wandering wi' my Davie.

As purple morning starts the hare,
To steal upon her early fare,
Then thro' the dews I will repair,
    To meet my faithfu' Davie.

When day, expiring in the west,
The curtain draws o' Nature's rest,
I'll flee to his arms I lo'e the best,
    And that's my ain dear Davie.

BRUCE'S ADDRESS TO HIS ARMY AT BANNOCKBURN
Tune—*Hey tutti taiti*

Scots, wha hae wi' Wallace bled,
Scots, wham Bruce has aften led,
Welcome to your gory bed—
    Or to Victorie!

Now's the day, and now's the hour;
See the front o' battle lour;
See approach proud Edward's power—
    Chains and Slaverie!

Wha will be a traitor knave?
Wha can fill a coward's grave?
Wha sae base as be a slave?
    Let him turn and flie!

Wha for Scotland's king and law,
Freedom's sword will strongly draw,
Freeman stand, or Freeman fa',
    Let him follow me!

By Oppression's woes and pains!
By your sons in servile chains!
We will drain our dearest veins,
    But they *shall* be free!

Lay the proud usurpers low!
Tyrants fall in every foe!
Liberty's in every blow!
    Let us do—or die!

DOWN THE BURN, DAVIE

As down the burn they took their way,
    And thro' the flowery dale;
His cheek to hers he aft did lay,
    And love was aye the tale.

With 'Mary, when shall we return,
    Sic pleasure to renew?'
Quoth Mary—'Love, I like the burn,
    And aye shall follow you.'

THOU HAST LEFT ME EVER, JAMIE
Tune—*Fee him, father, fee him*

Thou hast left me ever, Jamie,
    Thou hast left me ever.
Thou has left me ever, Jamie,
    Thou hast left me ever:
Aften hast thou vow'd that Death
    Only should us sever;
Now thou's left thy lass for aye—
    I maun see thee never, Jamie,
    I'll see thee never.

Thou hast me forsaken, Jamie,
Thou hast me forsaken!
Thou hast me forsaken, Jamie,
Thou hast me forsaken.
Thou canst love anither jo,
While my heart is breaking;
Soon my weary een I'll close,
Never mair to waken, Jamie,
Never mair to waken!

WHERE ARE THE JOYS I HAVE MET?
Tune—*Saw ye my father*

Where are the joys I have met in the morning,
That danc'd to the lark's early song?
Where is the peace that awaited my wand'ring,
At evening the wild woods among?

No more a-winding the course of yon river,
And marking sweet flowerets so fair:
No more I trace the light footsteps of pleasure,
But sorrow and sad-sighing care.

Is it that summer's forsaken our valleys,
And grim, surly winter is near?
No, no! the bees, humming round the gay roses
Proclaim it the pride of the year.

Fain would I hide what I fear to discover,
Yet long, long too well have I known:
All that has caused the wreck in my bosom,
Is Jenny, fair Jenny alone.

Time cannot aid me, my griefs are immortal,
Nor hope dare a comfort bestow;
Come then, enamour'd and fond of my anguish,
Enjoyment I'll seek in my woe.

DELUDED SWAIN, THE PLEASURE
Tune—*The collier's daughter*

Deluded swain, the pleasure
The fickle Fair can give thee,
Is but a fairy treasure,
Thy hopes will soon deceive thee:
The billows on the ocean,
The breezes idly roaming,
The clouds' uncertain motion,
They are but types of Woman.

O! art thou not ashamed
To doat upon a feature?
If Man thou wouldst be named,
Despise the silly creature.
Go, find an honest fellow;
Good claret set before thee;
Hold on till thou art mellow,
And then to bed in glory!

THINE AM I, MY FAITHFUL FAIR
Tune—*The Quaker's wife*

Thine am I, my Faithful fair,
    Thine, my lovely Nancy;
Ev'ry pulse along my veins,
    Ev'ry roving fancy.

To thy bosom lay my heart,
    There to throb and languish;
Tho' despair had wrung its core,
    That would heal its anguish.

Take away those rosy lips,
    Rich with balmy treasure;
Turn away thine eyes of love,
    Lest I die with pleasure.

What is life when wanting love?
    Night without a morning:
Love's the cloudless summer sun,
    Nature gay adorning.

IMPROMPTU ON MRS RIDDELL'S BIRTHDAY
4 November 1793

Old Winter, with his frosty beard,
Thus once to Jove his prayer preferred.
'What have I done of all the year
To bear this hated doom severe?
My cheerless suns no pleasure know;
Night's horrid car drags dreary slow;
My dismal months no joys are crowning,
But spleeny English hanging, drowning.

'Now Jove, for once be mighty civil,
To counterbalance all this evil;
Give me, and I've no more to say,
Give me Maria's natal day!
That brilliant gift will so enrich me,
Spring, Summer, Autumn, cannot match me.'
''Tis done!' says Jove; so ends my story,
And Winter once rejoiced in glory.

MY SPOUSE, NANCY
Tune—*My jo Janet*

'Husband, husband, cease your strife,
    Nor longer idly rave, Sir;
Tho' I am your wedded wife
    Yet I am not your slave, Sir.'
'One of two must still obey,
    Nancy, Nancy;
Is it man or woman, say,
    My spouse, Nancy?'

'If 'tis still the lordly word,
    Service and obedience;
I'll desert my sov'reign lord,
    And so, good bye, allegiance!'
'Sad shall I be, so bereft,
    Nancy, Nancy;
Yet I'll try to make a shift,
    My spouse, Nancy.'

'My poor heart then break it must,
    My last hour I am near it:
When you lay me in the dust,
    Think how you will bear it.'
'I will hope and trust in heaven,
    Nancy, Nancy;
Strength to bear it will be given,
    My spouse, Nancy.'

'Well, sir, from the silent dead,
    Still I'll try to daunt you;
Ever round your midnight bed
    Horrid sprites shall haunt you!'
'I'll wed another like my dear
    Nancy, Nancy;
Then all hell will fly for fear,
    My spouse, Nancy.'

ADDRESS

Spoken by Miss Fontenelle[1] on her Benefit Night,
4 December 1793, at the Theatre, Dumfries.

Still anxious to secure your partial favour,
And not less anxious, sure, this night, than ever,
A Prologue, Epilogue, or some such matter,
'Twould vamp my bill, said I, if nothing better;
So sought a poet, roosted near the skies,
Told him I came to feast my curious eyes;
Said, nothing like his works was ever printed;
And last, my prologue-business slily hinted.
'Ma'am, let me tell you,' quoth my man of rhymes,
'I know your bent—these are no laughing times:
Can you—but, Miss, I own I have my fears—
Dissolve in pause, and sentimental tears;
With laden sighs, and solemn-rounded sentence,
Rouse from his sluggish slumbers, fell Repentance;
Paint Vengeance as he takes his horrid stand,
Waving on high the desolating brand,
Calling the storms to bear him o'er a guilty Land?'

I could no more—askance the creature eyeing,
'D'ye think,' said I, 'this face was made for crying?
I'll laugh, that's pos—nay more, the world shall know it;
And so, your servant! gloomy Master Poet!'

Firm as my creed, Sirs, 'tis my fix'd belief
That Misery's another word for Grief:
I also think—so may I be a bride!
That so much laughter, so much life enjoy'd.

Thou man of crazy care and ceaseless sigh,
Still under bleak Misfortune's blasting eye;
Doom'd to that sorest task of man alive—
To make three guineas do the work of five;
Laugh in Misfortune's face—the beldam witch!
Say, you'll be merry tho' you can't be rich.

Thou other man of care, the wretch in love,
Who long with jiltish arts and airs hast strove;
Who, as the boughs all temptingly project,
Measur'st in desperate thought—a rope—thy neck—
Or, where the beetling cliff o'erhangs the deep,
Peerest to meditate the healing leap:
Would'st thou be cur'd, thou silly, moping elf?
Laugh at her follies—laugh e'en at thyself:
Learn to despise those frowns now so terrific,
And love a kinder—that's your grand specific.

To sum up all, be merry, I advise;
And as we're merry, may we still be wise.

[1] *See* note page 333.

EPIGRAM ON MARIA RIDDELL

'Praise Woman still,' his lordship roars,
    'Deserv'd or not, no matter?'
But thee, whom all my soul adores,
    Ev'n Flattery cannot flatter:
Maria, all my thought and dream,
    Inspires my vocal shell;
The more I praise my lovely theme,
    The more the truth I tell.

TO A GENTLEMAN WHOM HE HAD OFFENDED

The friend who, wild from wisdom's way,
    The fumes of wine infuriate send
(Not moony madness more astray)
    Who but deplores that hapless friend?

Mine was th' insensate frenzied part,
    Ah! why should I such scenes outlive?
Scenes so abhorrent to my heart!—
    'Tis thine to pity and forgive.

WILT THOU BE MY DEARIE?
Tune—*The sutor's dochter*

Wilt thou be my dearie?
When sorrow wrings thy gentle heart,
    O wilt thou let me cheer thee!
By the treasure of my soul,
    That's the love I bear thee!
I swear and vow that only thou
    Shall ever be my dearie!
Only thou, I swear and vow,
    Shall ever be my dearie!

Lassie, say thou lo'es me;
Or if thou wilt na be my ain,
    O say na thou'lt refuse me!
If it winna, canna be,
    Thou for thine may choose me,
Let me, lassie, quickly die,
    Trusting that thou lo'es me!
Lassie, let me quickly die,
    Trusting that thou lo'es me!

AMANG THE TREES
Tune—*The king of France, he rade a race*

Amang the trees, where humming bees,
    At buds and flowers were hinging, O!
Auld Caledon drew out her drone,
    And to her pipe was singing, O!
'Twas pibroch, sang, strathspeys and reels,
    She dirl'd them aff fu' clearly, O!
When there cam a yell o' foreign squeels
    That dang her tapsalteerie, O!

Their capon craws an' queer 'ha, ha's',
    They made our lugs grow eerie, O!
The hungry bike did scrape and fyke,
    Till we were wae and weary, O!

But a royal ghaist, wha ance was cas'd,
  A prisoner, aughteen year awa',
He fir'd a fiddler in the North,
  That dang them tapsalteerie, O!

As I Stood By Yon Roofless Tower
Tune—*Cumnock Psalms*

Chorus: A lassie all alone, was making her moan,
  Lamenting our lads beyond the sea;
'In the bluidy wars they fa', and our honour's gane an' a',
  And broken-hearted we maun die.'

As I stood by yon roofless tower,[1]
  Where the wa'flower scents the dewy air,
Where the houlet mourns in her ivy bower,
  And tells the midnight moon her care.

The winds were laid, the air was still,
  The stars they shot along the sky;
The tod was howling on the hill,
  And the distant-echoing glens reply.

The burn, adown its hazelly path,
  Was rushing by the ruin'd wa',
Hasting to join the sweeping Nith,
  Whase roarings seem'd to rise and fa'.

The cauld blae North was streaming forth
  Her lights, wi' hissing, eerie din,
Athort the lift they start and shift,
  Like Fortune's favours, tint as win.

Now, looking over frith and fauld,
  Her horn the pale-faced Cynthia rear'd,
When lo! in form of minstrel auld,
  A stern and stalwart ghaist appear'd.

And frae his harp sic strains did flow,
  Might rous'd the slumbering dead to hear;
But oh, it was a tale of woe,
  As ever met a Briton's ear!

He sang wi' joy his former day,
  He, weeping, wail'd his latter times;
But what he said—it was nae play,
  I winna venture 't in my rhymes.

---

[1] Lincluden Abbey, Dumfriesshire.

A RED, RED ROSE
Tune—*Major Graham*

O, my luve's like a red, red rose,
    That's newly sprung in June.
O, my luve's like the melodie,
    That's sweetly play'd in tune.

As fair art thou, my bonnie lass,
    So deep in luve am I;
And I will luve thee still, my dear,
    Till a' the seas gang dry.

Till a' the seas gang dry, my dear,
    And the rocks melt wi' the sun;
I will luve thee still, my dear,
    While the sands o' life shall run.

And fare thee weel, my only luve!
    And fare-thee-weel, a while!
And I will come again, my luve,
    Tho' it were ten thousand mile!

YOUNG JAMIE, PRIDE OF A' THE PLAIN
Tune—*The carlin of the glen*

Young Jamie, pride of a' the plain,
Sae gallant and sae gay a swain,
Thro' a' our lasses he did rove,
And reign'd resistless King of Love.

But now, wi' sighs and starting tears,
He strays amang the woods and breers;
Or in the glens and rocky caves,
His sad complaining dowie raves—

'I wha sae late did range and rove,
And chang'd with every moon my love,
I little thought the time was near,
Repentance I should buy sae dear.

'The slighted maids my torments see,
And laugh at a' the pangs I dree;
While she, my cruel, scornful Fair,
Forbids me e'er to see her mair.'

BANKS OF CREE

Here is the glen, and here the bower,
    All underneath the birchen shade;
The village bell has toll'd the hour,
    O what can stay my lovely maid?

'Tis not Maria's whispering call;
    'Tis but the balmy breathing gale,
Mixt with some warbler's dying fall,
    The dewy star of eve to hail!

It is Maria's voice I hear!
    So calls the woodlark in the grove
His little faithful mate to cheer;
    At once 'tis music—and 'tis love.

And art thou come? And art thou true?
    O welcome dear to love and me!
And let us all our vows renew,
    Along the flowery banks of Cree!

MONODY ON MARIA, FAMED FOR HER CAPRICE[1]

How cold is that bosom which folly once fired,
    How pale is that cheek where the rouge lately glisten'd;

[1] Written on Mrs Riddell after a rift in their relationship.

How silent that tongue which the echoes oft tired,
  How dull is that ear which to flatt'ry so listen'd!

If sorrow and anguish their exit await,
  From friendship and dearest affection remov'd;
How doubly severer, Maria, thy fate,
  Thou diedst unwept, as thou livedst unlov'd.

Loves, Graces and Virtues, I call not on you;
  So shy, grave and distant, ye shed not a tear:
But come, all ye offspring of Folly so true,
  And flowers let us cull for Maria's cold bier.

We'll search through the garden for each silly flower,
  We'll roam through the forest for each idle weed;
But chiefly the nettle, so typical, shower,
  For none e'er approach'd her but rued the rash deed.

We'll sculpture the marble, we'll measure the lay;
  Here Vanity strums on her idiot lyre;[1]
There keen Indignation shall dart on his prey,
  Which spurning Contempt shall redeem from his ire.

The Epitaph

Here lies, now a prey to insulting Neglect,
  What once was a butterfly gay in life's beam:
Want only of goodness denied her respect,
  Want only of goodness denied her esteem.

  [1] *NB* The lady affects to be a poetess.—R.B.

Pinned To Mrs Walter Riddell's Carriage

If you rattle along like your Mistress' tongue,
  Your speed will outrival the dart;
But a fly for your load, you'll break down on the road,
  If your stuff be as rotten 's her heart.

Epistle From Esopus To Maria[1]

From those drear solitudes and frowsy cells,
Where Infamy with sad repentance dwells;
Where turnkeys make the jealous portal fast,
And deal from iron hands the spare repast;
Where truant 'prentices, yet young in sin,
Blush at the curious stranger peeping in;
Where strumpets, relics of the drunken roar,
Resolve to drink—nay half, to whore—no more;
Where tiny thieves not destin'd yet to swing,
Beat hemp for others, riper for the string:
From these dire scenes my wretched lines I date,
To tell Maria her Esopus' fate.

[1] James Williamson, an actor, supposed to address Mrs Riddell from a House of Correction.

'Alas! I feel I am no actor here!'
'Tis real hangmen real scourges bear.
Prepare, Maria, for a horrid tale
Will turn thy very rouge to deadly pale;
Will make thy hair, tho' erst from gipsy poll'd,
By barber woven and by barber sold,
Tho' twisted smooth by Harry's[1] nicest care,
Like hoary bristles to erect and stare.
The hero of the mimic scene, no more
I start in Hamlet, in Othello roar;
Or haughty chieftain, 'mid the din of arms,
In Highland bonnet, woo Malvina's charms;
While sans-culottes stoop up the mountain high,
And steal from me Maria's prying eye.

Blest Highland bonnet! once my proudest dress,
Now prouder still, Maria's temples press;
I see her wave thy towering plumes afar,
And call each coxcomb to the wordy war:
I see her face the first of Ireland's sons,[2]
And even out-Irish his Hibernian bronze;
The crafty colonel[3] leaves the tartan'd lines;
For other wars, where he a hero shines:
The hopeful youth, in Scottish senate bred,
Who owns a Bushby's[4] heart without the head,
Comes 'mid a string of coxcombs, to display
That *Veni, vidi, vici* is his way:
The shrinking bard adown the alley skulks,
And dreads a meeting worse than Woolwich hulks;
Tho' there, his heresies in Church and State
Might well award him Muir and Palmer's fate:
Still she, undaunted, reels and rattles on,
And dares the public like a noontide sun!

What scandal call'd Maria's jaunty stagger
The ricket reeling of a crooked swagger?
What slander nam'd her seeming want of art
The flimsy wrapper of a rotten heart.
Whose spleen e'en worse than Burns' venom, when
He dips in gall unmix'd his eager pen,
And pours his vengeance in the burning line,
Who christen'd thus Maria's lyre divine
The idiot strum of vanity bemus'd,
And even the abuse of Poesy abus'd?
Who called her verse a parish workhouse, made
For motley, foundling fancies, stolen or strayed?

[1] Her servant.
[2] Gillespie.
[3] Colonel M'Dowal of Logan, the Lothario of his day.
[4] Bushby Maitland, son of Mr John Maitland of Tinwald-downs, a writer and banker with whom Burns had been on terms of intimacy.

A workhouse! Ah, that sound awakes my woes,
And pillows on the thorn my rack'd repose!
In durance vile here must I wake and weep,
And all my frowsy couch in sorrow steep!
That straw where many a rogue has lain of yore,
And vermin'd gipsies litter'd heretofore.
Why, Lonsdale, thus thy wrath on vagrants pour?
Must earth no rascal save thyself endure?
Must thou alone in guilt immortal swell,
And make a vast monopoly of hell?
Thou knowest the Virtues cannot hate thee worse;
The Vices also, must they club their curse?
Or must no tiny sin to others fall,
Because thy guilt's supreme enough for all?

Maria, send me too thy griefs and cares;
In all of thee, sure, thy Esopus shares.
As thou at all mankind the flag unfurls,
Who on my fair one Satire's vengeance hurls?
Who calls thee, pert, affected, vain coquette,
A wit in folly and a fool in wit!
Who says that Fool alone is not thy due,
And quotes thy treacheries to prove it true?
Our force united on thy foes we'll turn,
And dare the war with all of woman born:
For who can write and speak as thou and I?
My periods that decyphering defy,
And thy still matchless tongue that conquers all reply!

EPITAPHS

On A Noted Coxcomb—Captain William Roddick of Corbiston

Light lay the earth on Billy's breast,
    His chicken heart so tender;
But build a castle on his head,
    His scull will prop it under.

On Captain Lascelles[1]

When Lascelles thought fit from this world to depart,
Some friends warmly thought of embalming his heart;
A bystander whispers— 'Pray don't make so much o't,
The subject is poison, no reptile will touch it.'

[1] Later 1st Earl of Harewood.

On William Graham, Esq., Of Mossknowe

'Stop thief!' dame Nature call'd to Death,
    As Willy drew his latest breath;
'How shall I make a fool again?
    My choicest model thou hast ta'en.'

On John Bushby, Esq., Tinwald Downs

Here lies John Bushby—honest man!
Cheat him, Devil—if you can.

Sonnet On The Death Of Robert Riddell
Of Glenriddell and Friars Carse[1]

No more, ye warblers of the wood, no more;
    Nor pour your descant grating on my soul;
    Thou young-eyed Spring, gay in thy verdant stole,
More welcome were to me grim Winter's wildest roar.

How can ye charm, ye flowers, with all your dyes?
    Ye blow upon the sod that wraps my friend.
    How can I to the tuneful strain attend?
That strain flows round th' untimely tomb where Riddell lies.

Yes, pour, ye warblers, pour the notes of woe,
    And soothe the Virtues weeping on this bier:
    The man of worth—and has not left his peer—
Is in his 'narrow house', for ever darkly low.

Thee, Spring! again with joy shall others greet;
Me, memory of my loss will only meet.

[1] Who died 21 April 1794.

The Lovely Lass O' Inverness

The lovely lass o' Inverness,
    Nae joy nor pleasure can she see;
For e'en to morn she cries, 'Alas!'
    And aye the saut tear blin's her e'e.

'Drumossie moor, Drumossie day—[1]
    A waefu' day it was to me!
For there I lost my father dear,
    My father dear, and brethren three!

'Their winding sheet the bluidy clay,
    Their graves are growin' green to see;
And by them lies the dearest lad
    That ever blest a woman's e'e!

'Now wae to thee, thou cruel lord,[2]
    A bluidy man I trow thou be;
For monie a heart thou has made sair
    That ne'er did wrang to thine or thee!'

[1] The Battle of Culloden.   [2] The Duke of Cumberland.

CHARLIE, HE'S MY DARLING

Chorus: An' Charlie, he's my darling,
    My darling, my darling,
Charlie, he's my darling,
    The young Chevalier.

'Twas on a Monday morning,
    Right early in the year,
That Charlie came to our town,
    The young Chevalier.

As he was walking up the street,
    The city for to view,
O there he spied a bonnie lass
    The window looking thro'.

Sae light 's he jumped up the stair,
    And tirl'd at the pin;
And wha sae ready as hersel'
    To let the laddie in.

He set his Jenny on his knee,
    All in his Highland dress;
For brawly well he kenn'd the way
    To please a bonnie lass.

It's up yon heathery mountain,
    An' down yon scroggie glen,
We daur na gang a milking,
    For Charlie and his men.

BANNOCKS O' BEAR MEAL
Tune—*The Killogie*

Chorus: Bannocks o' bear meal,
    Bannocks o' barley,
Here's to the Highlandman's
    Bannocks o' barley!

Wha in a brulyie will
    First cry 'a parley?'
Never the lads wi' the
    Bannocks o' barley!

Wha in his wae days
    Were loyal to Charlie?
Wha but the lads wi' the
    Bannocks o' barley!

THE HIGHLAND BALOU

Hee balou! my sweet wee Donald,
Picture o' the great Clanronald;
Brawlie kens our wanton chief
Wha got my wee Highland thief.

Leeze me on thy bonnie craigie,
An thou live, thou'll steal a naigie,
Travel the country thro' and thro',
And bring hame a Carlisle cow.

Thro' the Lawlands, o'er the Border,
Weel, my babie, may thou furder;
Herry the louns o' the laigh countrie,
Syne to the Highlands hame to me.

THE HIGHLAND WIDOW'S LAMENT
Tune—*Gaelic air*

O, I am come to the low countrie,
    Ochon, ochon, ochrie!
Without a penny in my purse,
    To buy a meal to me.

It was na sae in the Highland hills,
    Ochon, ochon, ochrie!
Nae woman in the country wide,
    Sae happy was as me.

For then I had a score o' kye,
    Ochon, ochon, ochrie!
Feeding on you hill sae high,
    And giving milk to me.

And there I had three score o' yowes,
    Ochon, ochon, ochrie!
Skipping on yon bonnie knowes,
    And casting woo to me.

I was the happiest of a' the clan,
    Sair, sair may I repine;
For Donald was the brawest man,
    And Donald he was mine.

Till Charlie Stewart cam at last,
    Sae far to set us free;
My Donald's arm was wanted then
    For Scotland and for me.

Their waefu' fate what need I tell,
    Right to the wrang did yield;
My Donald and his country fell,
    Upon Culloden field.

Ochon! O Donald, O!
    Ochon, ochon, ochrie!
Nae woman in the warld wide,
    Sae wretched now as me.

IT WAS A' FOR OUR RIGHTFU' KING

It was a' for our rightfu' king
    We left fair Scotland's strand;
It was a' for our rightfu' king
    We e'er saw Irish land, my dear,
    We e'er saw Irish land.

Now a' is done that men can do,
    And a' is done in vain;
My Love and Native Land fareweel,
    For I maun cross the main, my dear,
    For I maun cross the main.

He turn'd him right and round about,
    Upon the Irish shore;
And gae his bridle reins a shake,
    With adieu for evermore, my dear,
    And adieu for evermore.

The soger frae the wars returns,
    The sailor frae the main;
But I hae parted frae my love,
    Never to meet again, my dear,
    Never to meet again.

When day is gane, and night is come,
    And a' folk bound to sleep;
I think on him that's far awa,
    The lee-lang night and weep, my dear,
    The lee-lang night and weep.

ODE FOR GENERAL WASHINGTON'S BIRTHDAY

No Spartan tube, no Attic shell,
    No lyre Aeolian I awake;
'Tis liberty's bold note I swell,
    Thy harp, Columbia, let me take!

See gathering thousands, while I sing,
A broken chain exulting bring,
    And dash it in a tyrant's face,
And dare him to his very beard,
And tell him he no more is feared—
      No more the despot of Columbia's race!
A tyrant's proudest insults brav'd,
They shout—a People freed! They hail an Empire saved.

Where is man's god-like form?
    Where is that brow erect and bold—
    That eye that can unmov'd behold
The wildest rage, the loudest storm
That e'er created Fury dared to raise?
Avaunt! thou caitiff, servile, base,
That tremblest at a despot's nod,
Yet, crouching under the iron rod,
Canst laud the hand that struck th' insulting blow!
Art thou of man's Imperial line?
Dost boast that countenance divine?
    Each skulking feature answers, No!
But come, ye sons of Liberty,
Columbia's offspring, brave as free,
In danger's hour still flaming in the van,
Ye know, and dare maintain, the Royalty of Man!

Alfred! on thy starry throne,
    Surrounded by the tuneful choir,
    The bards that erst have struck the patriot lyre
    And rous'd the freeborn Briton's soul of fire,
No more thy England own!
Dare injured nations form the great design
    To make detested tyrants bleed?
    Thy England execrates the glorious deed!
    Beneath her hostile banners waving,
    Every pang of honour braving,
England in thunder calls, 'The tyrant's cause is mine!'

    That hour accurst how did the fiends rejoice,
    And hell, thro' all her confines, raise the exulting voice,
    That hour which saw the generous English name
Linkt with such damnéd deeds of everlasting shame!

Thee, Caledonia! thy wild heaths among,
Fam'd for the martial deed, the heaven-taught song,
    To thee I turn with swimming eyes;
Where is that soul of Freedom fled?
Immingled with the mighty dead,
    Beneath that hallow'd turf where Wallace lies
Hear it not, WALLACE! in thy bed of death!
    Ye babbling winds! in silence sweep,
    Disturb not ye the hero's sleep,

Nor give the coward secret breath!
Is this the ancient Caledonian form,
Firm as the rock, resistless as the storm?
Show me that eye which shot immortal hate,
    Blasting the Despot's proudest bearing;
Show me that arm which, nerv'd with thundering fate,
    Crush'd Usurpation's boldest daring!
Dark-quench'd as yonder sinking star,
No more that glance lightens afar;
That palsied arm no more whirls on the waste of war.

LINES WRITTEN ON A COPY OF THOMSON'S SONGS
Presented to Miss Graham of Fintry

Here, where the Scottish Muse immortal lives,
    In sacred strains and tuneful numbers join'd,
Accept the gift; though humble he who gives,
    Rich is the tribute of the grateful mind.

So may no ruffian feeling in my breast
    Discordant jar thy bosom-chords among;
But Peace attune thy gentle soul to rest,
    Or love ecstatic wake his seraph song.

Or Pity's notes, in luxury of tears,
    As modest want the tale of woe reveals;
While conscious Virtue all the strains endears,
    And heaven-born Piety her sanction seals.

ON THE SEAS AND FAR AWAY
Tune—*O'er the hills and far awa'*

How can my poor heart be glad,
When absent from my sailor lad?
How can I the thought forego,
He's on the seas to meet the foe?
Let me wander, let me rove,
Still my heart is with my love!
Nightly dreams, and thoughts by day,
Are with him that's far away.
    On the seas and far away,
    On stormy seas and far away;
    Nightly dreams and thoughts by day,
    Are aye with him that's far away.

When in summer noon I faint,
As weary flocks around me pant,
Haply in this scorching sun
My sailor's thund'ring at his gun;
Bullets, spare my only joy!
Bullets, spare my darling boy!

Fate, do with me what you may,
Spare but him that's far away,
    On the seas and far away,
    On stormy seas and far away;
    Fate, do with me what you may,
    Spare but him that's far away.

At the starless midnight hour
When winter rules with boundless power;
As the storms the forests tear,
And thunders rend the howling air,
Listening to the doubling roar,
Surging on the rocky shore,
All I can—I weep and pray
For his weal that's far away,
    On the seas and far away,
    On stormy seas and far away;
    All I can—I weep and pray,
    For his weal that's far away.

Peace, thy olive wand extend,
And bid wild war his ravage end,
Man with brother Man to meet,
And as a brother kindly greet:
Then may Heaven with prosperous gales,
Fill my sailor's welcome sails,
To my arms their charge convey—
My dear lad that's far away.
    On the seas and far away,
    On stormy seas and far away;
    To my arms their charge convey,
    My dear lad that's far away.

SHE[1] SAYS SHE LO'ES ME BEST OF A'
Tune—*Onagh's waterfall*

Sae flaxen were her ringlets,
    Her eyebrows of a darker hue,
Bewitchingly o'er-arching
    Twa laughing e'en o' bonnie blue;
Her smiling sae wyling
    Wad make a wretch forget his woe;
What pleasure, what treasure,
    Unto these rosy lips to grow:
Such was my Chloris' bonnie face,
    When first that bonnie face I saw,
And aye my Chloris' dearest charm—
    She says she lo'es me best of a'.

[1] Jean Lorimer.

Like harmony her motion;
    Her pretty ankle is a spy,
Betraying fair proportion
    Wad make a saint forget the sky.
Sae warming, sae charming,
    Her fauteless form and gracefu' air;
Ilk feature—auld Nature
    Declar'd that she could do nae mair:
Hers are the willing chains o' love,
    By conquering beauty's sovereign law;
And aye my Chloris' dearest charm—
    She says she lo'es me best of a'.

Let others love the city,
    And gaudy show at sunny noon;
Gie me the lonely valley,
    The dewy eve and rising moon,
Fair beaming and streaming
    Her silver light the boughs amang;
While falling, recalling,
    The amorous thrush concludes his sang;
There, dearest Chloris, wilt thou rove,
    By wimpling burn and leafy shaw,
And hear my vows o' truth and love,
    And say, thou lo'es me best of a'.

To Dr Maxwell[1] On Miss Jessie Staig's Recovery[2]

Maxwell, if merit here you crave,
    That merit I deny:
You save fair Jessie from the grave?
    An Angel could not die!

[1] Dr Maxwell was later the poet's physician at his death bed.
[2] Afterwards married to a Major Miller but died young.

To The Beautiful Miss Eliza J——N
On her Principles of Liberty and Equality

How Liberty, girl, can it be by thee nam'd?
Equality too! Hussey, art not asham'd?
Free and Equal indeed; while mankind thou enchainest,
And over their hearts a proud Despot so reignest.

On Chloris[1]
Requesting me to give her a Sprig of blossomed Thorn

From the white-blossom'd sloe my dear Chloris requested
    A sprig, her fair breast to adorn:
'No, by Heavens!' I exclaim'd, 'let me perish, if ever
    I plant in that bosom a thorn!'

[1] Jean Lorimer.

ON SEEING MRS KEMBLE IN THE CHARACTER OF YARICO

Kemble, thou cur'st my unbelief
Of Moses and his rod;
At Yarico's sweet note of grief
The rock with tears had flow'd.

EPIGRAM ON A GALLOWAY LAIRD[1]
Not quite so wise as Solomon

Bless Jesus Christ, O Cardoness,
With grateful, lifted eyes,
Who taught that not the soul alone,
But body too shall rise.

For had He said 'the soul alone
From death I will deliver,'
Alas, alas! O Cardoness,
Then hadst thou lain for ever.

[1] Sir David Maxwell of Cardoness.

ON BEING SHOWN A BEAUTIFUL COUNTRY SEAT
Belonging to the same Laird

We grant they're thine, those beauties all,
So lovely in our eye;
Keep them, thou eunuch, Cardoness,
For others to enjoy!

ON HEARING THAT THERE WAS FALSEHOOD
In the Rev. Dr Babington's Very Looks

That there is falsehood in his looks,
I must and will deny:
They tell their Master is a knave,
And sure they do not lie.

EPITAPHS

On A Suicide

Here lies in earth a root of Hell,
Set by the Deil's ain dibble;
This worthless body damned himsel',
To save the Lord the trouble.

On A Swearing Coxcomb

Here cursing, swearing Burton lies,
A buck, a beau, or 'Dem my eyes!'
Who in his life did little good,
And his last words were, 'Dem my blood!'

On An Innkeeper Nicknamed 'The Marquis'

Here lies a mock Marquis, whose titles were shamm'd,
If ever he rise, it will be to be damn'd.

On Andrew Turner[1]

In se'enteen hunder'n forty-nine,
The deil gat stuff to mak a swine,
An' coost it in a corner;
But wilily he chang'd his plan,
An' shap'd it something like a man,
An' ca'd it Andrew Turner.

[1] A man who patronised Burns and asked for a specimen of his verse.

Pretty Peg

As I gaed up by yon gate-end,
When day was waxin' weary,
Wha did I meet come down the street,
But pretty Peg, my dearie!

Her air sae sweet, an' shape complete,
Wi' nae proportion wanting,
The Queen of Love did never move
Wi' motion mair enchanting.

Wi' linkéd hands we took the sands,
Adown yon winding river;
And O, that hour and shady bower,
Can I forget it? Never!

Ah Chloris

Ah, Chloris, since it may not be,
That thou of love wilt hear;
If from the lover thou maun flee,
Yet let the friend be dear.

Altho' I love my Chloris, mair
Than ever tongue could tell;
My passion I will ne'er declare—
I'll say, I wish thee well.

Tho' a' my daily care thou art,
And a' my nightly dream,
I'll hide the struggle in my heart,
And say it is esteem.

Saw Ye My Dear, My Philly[1]
Tune—*When she cam' ben she bobbit*

O saw ye my dear, my Philly?
O saw ye my dear, my Philly,
She's down i' the grove, she's wi' a new love,
She winna come hame to her Willy.

What says she my dear, my Philly?
What says she my dear, my Philly?
She lets thee to wit that she has thee forgot,
And forever disowns thee, her Willy.

O had I ne'er seen thee, my Philly!
O had I ne'er seen thee, my Philly!
As light as the air, and fause as thou's fair,
Thou's broken the heart o' thy Willy.

[1] The subjects of this song were Miss Phillis McMurdo and her 'despairing swain', Stephen Clarke, the musician. *See also* note page 386.

How Lang And Dreary Is The Night[1]
Tune—*Cauld kail*

Chorus: For O, her lanely nights are lang!
    And O, her dreams are eerie;
And O, her widow'd heart is sair,
    That's absent frae her dearie.

How lang and dreary is the night
    When I am frae my dearie!
I restless lie frae e'en to morn,
    Though I were ne'er sae weary.

When I think on the lightsome days
    I spent wi' thee, my dearie;
And now what seas between us roar—
    How can I be but eerie?

How slow ye move, ye heavy hours;
    The joyless day how dreary!
It was na sae ye glinted by,
    When I was wi' my dearie!

[1] *See* first version, page 226.

Inconstancy In Love
Tune—*Duncan Gray*

Let not Woman e'er complain
    Of inconstancy in love;
Let not Woman e'er complain
    Fickle Man is apt to rove:
Look abroad through Nature's range,
Nature's mighty law is Change;
Ladies, would it not seem strange
    Man should then a monster prove?

Mark the winds, and mark the skies,
    Ocean's ebb, and ocean's flow.
Sun and moon but set to rise;
    Round and round the seasons go.
Why then ask of silly Man
To oppose great Nature's plan?
We'll be constant while we can—
    You can be no more, you know.

The Lover's Morning Salute To His Mistress
Tune—*Deil tak the wars*

Sleep'st thou, or wauk'st thou, fairest creature?
    Rosy morn now lifts his eye,
Numbering ilka bud which Nature
    Waters wi' the tears o' joy.
    Now, to the streaming fountain,
    Or up the heathy mountain,
The hart, hind and roe, freely, wildly-wanton stray;
    In twining hazel bowers,
    His lay the linnet pours,
    The lav'rock to the sky
    Ascends, wi' sangs o' joy,
While the sun and thou arise to bless the day.

Phoebus gilding the brow o' morning,
 Banishes ilk darksome shade,
Nature, gladdening and adorning;
 Such to me my lovely maid.
 When frae my Chloris parted,
 Sad, cheerless, broken-hearted,
The night's gloomy shades, cloudy, dark, o'ercast my sky:
 But when she charms my sight,
 In pride of Beauty's light—
 When through my very heart
 Her burning glories dart;
'Tis then—'tis then I wake to life and joy!

THE WINTER OF LIFE
Tune—*Chevy chase*

But lately seen in gladsome green,
 The woods rejoic'd the day,
Thro' gentle showers the laughing flowers
 In double pride were gay:
But now our joys are fled
 On winter blasts awa;
Yet maiden May, in rich array,
 Again shall bring them a'.

But my white pow, nae kindly thowe
 Shall melt the snaws of Age;
My trunk of eild, but buss or beild,
 Sinks in Time's wintry rage.
O, Age has weary days,
 And nights o' sleepless pain:
Thou golden time, o' Youthfu' prime,
 Why comes thou not again!

BEHOLD, MY LOVE, HOW GREEN THE GROVES
Tune—*Doun the burn, Davie*

Behold, my love, how green the groves,
 The primrose banks how fair;
The balmy gales awake the flowers,
 And wave thy flaxen hair.
The lav'rock shuns the palace gay,
 And o'er the cottage sings:
For Nature smiles as sweet, I ween,
 To shepherds as to kings.

Let minstrels sweep the skilfu' string,
 In lordly lighted ha',
The shepherd stops his simple reed,
 Blythe in the birken shaw.

The princely revel may survey
    Our rustic dance wi' scorn;
But are their hearts as light as ours,
    Beneath the milk-white thorn?

The shepherd in the flowery glen
    In homely phrase, will woo;
The courtier tells a finer tale,
    But is his heart as true?
These wild-wood flowers I've pu'd to deck
    That spotless breast o' thine:
The courtier's gems may witness love,
    But, 'tis na love like mine.

THE CHARMING MONTH OF MAY
Altered from an Old English Song
Tune—*Daintie Davie*

Chorus: Lovely was she by the dawn,
    Youthful Chloe, charming Chloe,
Tripping o'er the pearly lawn,
    The youthful, charming Chloe.

It was the charming month of May,
When all the flowers were fresh and gay.
One morning, by the break of day,
    The youthful, charming Chloe,
From peaceful slumber she arose,
Girt on her mantle and her hose,
And o'er the flowery mead she goes,
    The youthful, charming Chloe.

The feather'd people you might see
Perch'd all around on every tree,
In notes of sweetest melody
    They hail the charming Chloe;
Till, painting gay the eastern skies,
The glorious sun began to rise,
Outrivall'd by the radiant eyes
    Of youthful, charming Chloe.

LASSIE WI' THE LINT-WHITE LOCKS[1]
Tune—*Rothiemurchie's rant*

Chorus: Lassie wi' the lint-white locks,
    Bonnie lassie, artless lassie,
Wilt thou wi' me tent the flocks?
    An' wilt thou be my dearie, O?

[1] Jean Lorimer.

Now Nature cleeds the flowery lea,
And a' is young and sweet like thee,
O wilt thou share its joys wi' me,
    And say thou'lt be my dearie, O?

The primrose bank, the wimpling burn,
The cuckoo on the milk-white thorn,
The wanton lambs at early morn,
    Shall welcome thee, my dearie, O.

And when the welcome simmer shower
Has cheer'd ilk drooping little flower,
We'll to the breathing woodbine bower,
    At sultry noon, my dearie, O.

As Cynthia lights, wi' silver ray,
The weary shearer's hameward way,
Through yellow waving fields we'll stray,
    And talk o' love, my dearie, O.

And should the howling wintry blast
Disturbs my lassie's midnight rest,
I'll fauld thee to my faithfu' breast,
    And comfort thee, my dearie, O.

O PHILLY, HAPPY BE THAT DAY
Tune—*The sow's tail*

Both
Chorus: For a' the joys that gowd can gie,
    I dinna care a single flie!
    The lad I love's the lad for me,
    The lass I love's the lass for me,
        And that's my ain dear Willy.
        And that's my ain dear Philly.

Willy
O Philly, happy be that day,
When roving thro' the gather'd hay,
My youthfu' heart was stown away,
    And by thy charms, my Philly.

Philly
O Willy, aye I bless the grove
Where first I own'd my maiden love,
Whilst thou did pledge the Powers above,
    To be my ain dear Willy.

Willy
As songsters of the early year,
Are ilka day mair sweet to hear,
So ilka day to me mair dear
    And charming is my Philly.

Philly
As on the brier the budding rose
Still richer breathes and fairer blows,
So in my tender bosom grows
    The love I bear my Willy.

Willy
The milder sun and bluer sky
That crown my harvest cares wi' joy,
Were ne'er sae welcome to my eye
    As is a sight o' Philly.

Philly
The little swallow's wanton wing,
Tho' wafting o'er the flowery spring,
Did ne'er to me sic tidings bring,
    As meeting o' my Willy.

Willy
The bee that thro' the sunny hour
Sips nectar in the opening flower,
Compar'd wi' my delight is poor,
    Upon the lips o' Philly.

Philly
The woodbine in the dewy weet,
When evening shades in silence meet,
Is nocht sae fragrant or sae sweet
    As is a kiss o' Willy.

Willy
Let Fortune's wheel at random rin,
And fools may tyne and knaves may win;
My thoughts are a' bound up in ane,
    And that's my ain dear Philly.

Philly
What's a' the joys that gowd can gie?
I dinna care a single flie;
The lad I love's the lad for me,
    And that's my ain dear Willy.

CONTENTED WI' LITTLE AND CANTIE WI' MAIR
Tune—*Lumps o' puddins*

Contented wi' little, and cantie wi' mair,
Whene'er I forgather wi' sorrow and care,
I gie them a skelp, as they're creeping alang,
Wi' a cog o' guid swats and an auld Scottish sang.

I whyles claw the elbow o' troublesome thought;
But Man is a soger, and Life is a faught;
My mirth and guid humour are coin in my pouch,
And my freedom's my lairdship nae monarch dare touch.

A townmond o' trouble, should that be may fa',
A night o' guid fellowship southers it a';
When at the blythe end o' our journey at last,
Wha the deil ever thinks o' the road he has past?

Blind Chance, let her snapper and stoyte on her way;
Be 't to me, be 't frae me, e'en let the jade gae:
Come Ease, or come Travail, come Pleasure or Pain,
My warst word is—'Welcome, and welcome again!'

FAREWELL, THOU STREAM[1]
Tune—*Nancy's to the greenwood gane*

Farewell, thou stream that winding flows
    Around Eliza's dwelling!
O mem'ry! spare the cruel thoes
    Within my bosom swelling:
Condemn'd to drag a hopeless chain,
    And yet in secret languish;
To feel a fire in every vein,
    Nor dare disclose my anguish.

Love's veriest wretch, unseen, unknown,
    I fain my griefs would cover;
The bursting sigh, th' unweeting groan,
    Betray the hapless lover.
I know thou doom'st me to despair,
    Nor wilt, nor canst relieve me;
But, O! Eliza, hear one prayer—
    For pity's sake forgive me!

The music of thy voice I heard,
    Nor wist while it enslav'd me;
I saw thine eyes, yet nothing fear'd,
    Till fears no more had sav'd me:
Th' unwary sailor thus aghast,
    The wheeling torrent viewing,
'Mid circling horrors sinks at last,
    In overwhelming ruin.

[1] See the song in its first and best dress given on page 408 with the title of 'The Lover's Morning Salute to his Mistress'. Burns remarks upon it, 'I could easily throw this into an English mould; but, to my taste, in the simple and the tender of the pastoral song, a sprinkling of the old Scottish has an inimitable effect.'

CANST THOU LEAVE ME THUS, MY KATY
Tune—*Roy's wife*

Chorus: Canst thou leave me thus, my Katy?
    Canst thou leave me thus, my Katy?
Well thou know'st my aching heart,
    And canst thou leave me thus, for pity?

Is this thy plighted, fond regard,
　　Thus cruelly to part, my Katy?
Is this thy faithful swain's reward—
　　An aching, broken heart, my Katy!

Farewell! and ne'er such sorrows tear
　　That fickle heart of thine, my Katy!
Thou may'st find those will love thee dear—
　　But not a love like mine, my Katy.

My Nannie's Awa'[1]
Tune—*There'll never be peace*

Now in her green mantle blythe Nature arrays,
And listens the lambkins that bleat o'er the braes,
While birds warble welcome in ilka green shaw,
But to me it's delightless—my Nannie's awa'.

The snawdrap and primrose our woodlands adorn,
And violets bathe in the weet o' the morn;
They pain my sad bosom, sae sweetly they blaw,
They mind me o' Nannie—and Nannie's awa'.

Thou lav'rock that springs frae the dews of the lawn,
The shepherd to warn o' the grey-breaking dawn,
And thou mellow mavis that hails the night-fa',
Give over for pity—my Nannie's awa'.

Come Autumn, sae pensive, in yellow and grey,
And soothe me wi' tidings o' Nature's decay:
The dark, dreary Winter, and wild-driving snaw
Alane can delight me—now Nannie's awa'.

[1] Clarinda is said to have been the subject of this lyric.

Wae Is My Heart

Wae is my heart, and the tear's in my e'e;
Lang, lang joy's been a stranger to me:
Forsaken and friendless, my burden I bear,
And the sweet voice o' pity ne'er sounds in my ear.

Love, thou hast pleasures, and deep hae I lov'd;
Love, thou hast sorrows, and sair hae I prov'd:
But this bruiséd heart that now bleeds in my breast,
I can feel by its throbbings will soon be at rest.

O, if I were—where happy I hae been—
Down by yon stream and yon bonnie castle-green!
For there he is wand'ring and musing on me
Wha wad soon dry the tear frae his Phillis's e'e.

For The Sake O' Somebody

My heart is sair—I darena tell—
    My heart is sair for Somebody;
I could wake a winter night
    For the sake o' Somebody.
      O-hon! for Somebody!
      O-hey! for Somebody!
I could range the world around,
    For the sake o' Somebody.

Ye Powers that smile on virtuous love,
    O, sweetly smile on Somebody!
Frae ilka danger keep him free,
    And send me safe my Somebody!
      O-hon! for Somebody!
      O-hey! for Somebody!
I wad do—what wad I not?—
    For the sake o' Somebody.

A Man's A Man For A' That
Tune—*For a' that*

Is there, for honest poverty
    That hangs his head, and a' that;
The coward slave, we pass him by,
    We dare be poor for a' that!
For a' that, and a' that,
    Our toils obscure, and a' that,
The rank is but the guinea's stamp,
    The Man's the gowd for a' that.

What though on hamely fare we dine,
    Wear hoddin grey, and a that;
Gie fools their silks, and knaves their wine,
    A man's a man for a' that!
For a' that, and a' that,
    Their tinsel show, and a' that;
The honest man, though e'er sae poor,
    Is king o' men for a' that!

Ye see yon birkie, ca'd a lord,
    Wha struts, and stares, and a' that;
Though hundreds worship at his word,
    He's but a coof for a' that.
For a' that, and a' that,
    His riband, star, and a' that,
The man of independent mind
    He looks and laughs at a' that.

A king can mak a belted knight,
    A marquis, duke, and a' that;
But an honest man's aboon his might,
    Guid faith, he maunna fa' that!
For a' that, and a' that,
    Their dignities, and a' that,
The pith o' sense, and pride o' worth,
    Are higher rank than a' that.

Then let us pray that come it may—
    As come it will for a' that—

That sense and worth, o'er a' the earth,
    May bear the gree, and a' that.
For a' that, and a' that,
    It's coming yet for a' that,
That man to man, the world o'er,
    Shall brothers be for a' that!

THE SOLEMN LEAGUE AND COVENANT[1]

The Solemn League and Covenant
    Now brings a smile, now brings a tear;[2]
But sacred Freedom, too, was theirs:
    If thou'rt a slave, indulge thy sneer.

[1] Spoken in reply to a gentleman who sneered at the Covenant.
[2] Alternate line: 'Cost Scotland blood—cost Scotland tears'.

TO JOHN SYME OF RYEDALE
Lines sent with a Present of a Dozen of Porter

O had the malt thy strength of mind,
    Or hops the flavour of thy wit,
'Twere drink for first of human kind,
    A gift that e'en for Syme were fit.
Jerusalem Tavern, Dumfries

INSCRIPTION ON A GOBLET BELONGING TO MR SYME

There's Death in the cup, sae beware!
    Nay, more—there is danger in touching;
But wha can avoid the fell snare?
    The man and his wine's sae bewitching!

TO JOHN SYME
On refusing to dine with him, after having been promised the
First of Company and the First of Cookery

No more of your guests, be they titled or not,
    And cookery the first in the nation:
Who is proof to thy personal converse and wit,
    Is proof to all other temptation.

EPITAPH FOR MR GABRIEL RICHARDSON

Here Brewer Gabriel's fire's extinct,
    And empty all his barrels:
He's blest—if, as he brew'd, he drink—
    In upright, honest morals.

EPIGRAM ON MR JAMES GRACIE

Gracie, thou art a man of worth,
    O be thou Dean for ever!
May he be damned to hell henceforth,
    Who fauts thy weight or measure!

BONNIE PEG-A-RAMSAY

Cauld is the e'enin' blast,
   O' Boreas o'er the pool,
An' dawin' it is dreary,
   When birks are bare at Yule.

O cauld blaws the e'enin' blast,
   When bitter bites the frost,
And in the mirk and dreary drift
   The hills and glens are lost.

Ne'er sae murky blew the night
   That drifted o'er the hill,
But bonnie Peg-a-Ramsay
   Gat grist to her mill.

INSCRIPTION AT FRIARS CARSE HERMITAGE
To the Memory of Robert Riddell

To Riddell, much lamented man,
   This ivied cot was dear;
Reader, dost value matchless worth?
   This ivied cot revere.

THERE WAS A BONNIE LASS

There was a bonnie lass, and a bonnie, bonnie lass,
   And she lo'ed her bonnie laddie dear;
Till War's loud alarms tore her laddie frae her arms,
   Wi' monie a sigh and tear.

Over sea, over shore, where the cannons loudly roar,
   He still was a stranger to fear;
And nocht could him quail, or his bosom assail,
   But the bonnie lass he lo'ed sae dear.

WEE WILLIE GRAY
Tune—*Wee totum Fogg*

Wee Willie Gray an' his leather wallet,
Peel a willow wand to be him boots and jacket.
The rose upon the breer will be him trews an' doublet,
The rose upon the breer will be him trews an' doublet!

Wee Willie Gray and his leather wallet,
Twice a lily-flower will be him sark and cravat.
Feathers of a flee wad feather up his bonnet,
Feathers of a flee wad feather up his bonnet!

O AYE MY WIFE SHE DANG ME
Tune—*My wife she dang me*

Chorus: O aye my wife she dang me,
   An' aft my wife she bang'd me!
If ye gie a woman a' her will,
   Guid faith, she'll soon o'er-gang ye!

On peace an' rest my mind was bent,
    And, fool I was! I married;
But never honest man's intent
    Sae cursedly miscarried.

Some sairie comfort at the last,
    When a' thir days are done, man,
My 'pains o' hell' on earth is past,
    I'm sure o' bliss aboon, man.

GUID ALE KEEPS THE HEART ABOON

Chorus: O guid ale comes and guid ale goes;
Guid ale gars me sell my hose,
Sell my hose and pawn my shoon,
Guid ale keeps my heart aboon!

I had sax owsen in a pleugh,
And they drew a' weel eneugh:
I sald them a' just ane by ane;
Guid ale keeps the heart aboon!

Guid ale hauds me bare and busy,
Gars me moop wi' the servant hizzie,
Stand i' the stool when I hae dune—
Guid ale keeps the heart aboon!

O STEER HER UP AN' HAUD HER GAUN

O steer her up an' haud her gaun,
    Her mither's at the mill, jo;
An' gin she winna tak a man,
    E'en let her tak her will, jo.
First shore her wi' a gentle kiss,
    And ca' anither gill, jo;
An' gin she tak the thing amiss,
    E'en let her flyte her fill, jo.

O steer her up and be na blate,
    An' gin she tak it ill, jo,
Then leave the lassie till her fate,
    And time nae langer spill, jo:
Ne'er break your heart for ae rebute,
    But think upon it still, jo,
That gin the lassie winna do 't,
    Ye'll find anither will, jo.

THE LASS O' ECCLEFECHAN
Tune—*Jack o' Latin*

Gat ye me, O gat ye me,
    O gat ye me wi' naething?
Rock an' reel an' spinning wheel,
    A mickle quarter basin:
Bye attour, my gutcher has
    A heich house and a laigh ane,
A' forbye my bonnie sel',
    The toss o' Ecclefechan!

O haud your tongue now, Luckie Lang,
    O haud your tongue and jauner;
I held the gate till you I met,
    Syne I began to wander:

I tint my whistle and my sang,
    I tint my peace and pleasure,
But your green graff, now Luckie Lang,
    Wad airt me to my treasure.

O Lassie, Art Thou Sleeping Yet
Tune— *Will ye lend me your loom*

Chorus: O let me in this ae night,
This ae, ae, ae night;
For pity's sake this ae night,
    O rise, and let me in, jo!

O Lassie, art thou sleeping yet,
Or art thou wakin', I wad wit?
For love has bound me hand an' fit,
    And I would fain be in, jo.

Thou hear'st the winter wind an' weet?
Nae star blinks thro' the driving sleet;
Tak pity on my weary feet,
    And shield me frae the rain, jo.

The bitter blast that round me blaws,
Unheeded howls, unheeded fa's;
The cauldness o' thy heart's the cause
    Of a' my care and pine, jo.

Her Answer

Chorus: I tell you now this ae night,
This ae, ae, ae night;
And ance for a' this ae night,
I winna let ye in, jo.

O tell na me o' wind an' rain,
Upbraid na me wi' cauld disdain,
Gae back the gait ye cam again,
    I winna let ye in, jo.

The snellest blast, at mirkest hours,
That round the pathless wand'rer pours
Is nocht to what poor She endures,
    That's trusted faithless Man, jo.

The sweetest flower that deck'd the mead,
Now trodden like the vilest weed;
Let simple maid the lesson read,
    The weird may be her ain, jo.

The bird that charm'd his summer day,
Is now the cruel fowler's prey;
Let that to witless woman say—
    How aft her fate's the same, jo!

I'LL AYE CA' IN BY YON TOWN
Tune—I'll gang nae mair to yon town

Chorus: I'll aye ca' in by yon town,
        And by yon garden-green again;
I'll aye ca' in by yon town,
        And see my bonnie Jean again.

There's nane sall ken, there's nane sall guess
        What brings me back the gate again,
But she, my fairest faithfu' lass,
        And stownlins we sall meet again.

She'll wander by the aiken tree,
        When trystin' time draws near again;
And when her lovely form I see,
        O haith! she's doubly dear again!

O WAT YE WHA'S IN YON TOWN
Tune—I'll gang nae mair to yon town

Chorus: O wat ye wha's in yon town,
        Ye see the e'enin' sun upon,
The dearest maid's in yon town,
        That e'ening sun is shining on.

Now haply down yon gay green shaw,
        She wanders by yon spreading tree;
How blest ye flowers that round her blaw,
        Ye catch the glances o' her e'e!

How blest ye birds that round her sing,
        And welcome in the blooming year,
And doubly welcome be the Spring,
        The season to my Jeanie dear!

The sun blinks blythe on yon town,
        Amang the broomy braes sae green;
But my delight in yon town,
        And dearest pleasure, is my Jean.

Without my Fair, not a' the charms
        O' Paradise could yield me joy;
But give me Jeanie in my arms
        And welcome Lapland's dreary sky!

My cave wad be a lover's bower,
        Tho' raging Winter rent the air;
And she a lovely little flower,
        That I wad tent and shelter there.

O sweet is she in yon town,
        The sinking Sun's gane down upon;

A fairer than's in yon town,
    His setting beam ne'er shone upon.

If angry Fate is sworn my foe,
    And suff'ring I am doom'd to bear;
I careless quit aught else below,
    But spare, O spare me Jeanie dear.

For while life's dearest blood is warm,
    Ae thought frae her shall ne'er depart,
And she—as fairest is her form,
    She has the truest, kindest heart.

BALLADS ON MR HERON'S ELECTION, 1795
Ballad First
Tune—*For a' that*

Wham will we send to London town,
    To Parliament, and a' that?
Or who in a' the country roun'
    The best deserves to fa' that?
      For a' that, and a' that,
      Thro' Galloway and a' that,
    Where is the laird or belted knight
      Thay best deserves to fa' that?

Wha sees Kerroughtree's[1] open yett,
    (And wha is 't never saw that?)
Wha ever wi' Kerroughtree met,
    And has a doubt of a' that?
      For a' that, and a' that,
      Here's Heron yet for a' that!
    The independent patriot,
      The honest man, and a' that.

Tho' wit and worth, in either sex,
    Saint Mary's Isle can shaw that,
Wi' lords and dukes let Selkirk[2] mix,
    And weel does Selkirk fa' that.
      For a' that, and a' that,
      Here's Heron yet for a' that!
    An independent commoner
      Shall be the man for a' that.

But why should we to nobles jouk,
    And is 't against the law, that?
For why, a lord may be a gowk,
    Wi' ribband, star, and a' that,
      For a' that, and a' that,
      Here's Heron yet for a' that!
    A lord may be a lousy loun,
      Wi' ribband, star, and a' that.

[1] Patrick Heron of Kerroughtree, the Whig candidate.   [2] Earl of Selkirk.

Yon beardless boy[1] comes o'er the hills,
　　Wi' uncle's[2] purse, and a' that;
But we'll hae ane frae 'mang oursels,
　　A man we ken, and a' that.
　　　　For a' that, and a' that,
　　　　Here's Heron yet for a' that!
　　We are na to be bought and sold,
　　　　Like naigs, and nowte, and a' that.

Then let us drink—The Stewartry,[3]
　　Kerroughtree's laird, and a' that,
Our representative to be,
　　For weel he's worthy a' that.
　　　　For a' that, and a' that,
　　　　Here's Heron yet for a' that!
　　A House o' Commons such as he,
　　　　They wad be blest that saw that!

[1] Thomas Gordon of Balmaghie, the Tory candidate.　　[3] Kirkcudbrightshire.
[2] James Murray of Broughton.

BALLAD SECOND—ELECTION DAY
Tune—*Fy, let us a' to the bridal*

Fy, let us a' to Kirkcudbright,
　　For there will be bickerin' there;
For Murray's light horse are to muster,
　　And O, how the heroes will swear!
And there will be Murray, commander,
　　And Gordon, the battle to win;
Like brothers they'll stand by each other,
　　Sae knit in alliance and kin.

And there will be black-nebbit Johnie,[1]
　　The tongue o' the trump to them a';
An he get na Hell for his haddin',
　　The Deil gets na justice ava.
And there will be Kempleton's birkie,[2]
　　A boy no sae black at the bane;
But as to his fine Nabob fortune,
　　We'll e'en let the subject alane.

And there will be Wigton's new Sheriff;[3]
　　Dame Justice fu' brawly has sped;
She's gotten the heart of a Bushby,
　　But, Lord! what's become o' the head?
And there will be Cardoness, Esquire,[4]
　　Sae mighty in Cardoness' eyes;
A wight that will weather damnation,
　　The Devil the prey will despise.

[1] John Bushby. *See* note, page 424.　　　　　　　　　　[3] Maitland Bushby, son of John Bushby.
[2] William Bushby of Kempleton, who had made his fortune in India.　[4] David Maxwell of Cardoness.

And there will be Douglasses doughty,[1]
    New christening towns far and near;
Abjuring their democrat doings,
    By kissin' the arse of a peer.
And there will be folk frae Saint Mary's,[2]
    A house o' great merit and note;
The Deil ane but honours them highly—
    The Deil ane will gie them his vote!

And there will be Kenmure, sae gen'rous,[3]
    Whose honour is proof to the storm,
To save them from stark reprobation,
    He lent them his name in the Firm.
And there will be lads o' the gospel,
    Muirhead[4] wha's as guid as he's true;
And there will be Buittle's Apostle,[5]
    Wha's mair o' the black than the blue.

And there will be Logan M'Dowall,[6]
    Sculdudd'ry an' he will be there,
And also the Wild Scot o' Galloway,
    Sogering, gunpowder Blair.[7]
But we winna mention Redcastle,[8]
    The body, e'en let him escape!
He'd venture the gallows for siller,
    An 'twere na the cost o' the rape!

But where is the Doggerbank hero,
    That made 'Hogan Mogan' to skulk?
Poor Keith's gane to hell to be fuel,
    The auld rotten wreck of a Hulk.
And where is our King's Lord Lieutenant,
    Sae fam'd for his gratefu' return?
The birkie is gettin' his questions
    To say in St Stephen's the morn.

But mark ye! there's trusty Kerroughtree,[9]
    Whose honour was ever his law;
If the Virtues were pack'd in a parcel,
    His worth might be sample for a';
And strang an' respectfu' 's his backing,
    The maist o' the lairds wi' him stand;
Nae gipsy-like nominal barons,
    Wha's property's paper—not land.

And there, frae the Niddisdale borders,
    The Maxwells will gather in droves,

[1] Messrs Douglas of Carlinwark, called by them 'Castle Douglas'.
[2] Seat of the Earl of Selkirk.
[3] Gordon of Kenmure.
[4] Muirhead of Ure.
[5] Rev. George Maxwell of Buittle.
[6] Logan M'Dowall, the Lothario of 'Ye banks and Braes o' Bonnie Doon'.
[7] Mr Blair of Dunskey.
[8] William Sloan Lawrie.
[9] Patrick Heron of Kerroughtree.

Teugh Jockie,[1] staunch Geordie,[2] an' Wellwood,[3]
 That griens for the fishes and loaves;
And there will be Heron, the Major,[4]
 Wha'll ne'er be forgot in the Greys;
Our flatt'ry we'll keep for some other,
 Him, only it's justice to praise.

And there will be maiden Kilkerran,[5]
 And also Barskimming's guid Knight,[6]
And there will be roarin' Birtwhistle,[7]
 Yet luckily roars i' the right.
And there'll be Stamp Office Johnnie,[8]
 (Tak tent how ye purchase a dram!)
And there will be gay Cassencarry,
 And there'll be gleg Colonel Tam.[9]

And there'll be wealthy young Richard,[10]
 Dame Fortune should hing by the neck
For prodigal, thriftless bestowing—
 His merit had won him respect.
And there will be rich brother Nabobs,[11]
 (Though Nabobs, yet men not the worst,)
And there will be Collieston's whiskers,[12]
 And Quintin—a lad o' the first.[13]

Then hey! the chaste Interest o' Broughton,
 And hey! for the blessin's 'twill bring;
It may send Balmaghie to the Commons,
 In Sodom 'twould make him a king;
And hey! for the sanctified Murray,
 Our land wha wi' chapels has stor'd;
He founder'd his horse among harlots,
 But gied the auld naig to the Lord.

[1] John Maxwell, Esq., of Terraughty.
[2] George Maxwell of Carruchan.
[3] Mr Wellwood Maxwell.
[4] Major Heron, brother of the Whig candidate.
[5] Sir Adam Fergusson of Kilkerran.
[6] Sir William Miller of Barskimming, afterwards Lord Glenlee.
[7] Mr Alexander Birtwhistle of Kirkcudbright.
[8] John Syme, distributor of stamps for Dumfries.
[9] Colonel Goldie of Goldielea.
[10] Richard Oswald of Auchincruive.
[11] Messers Hannay.
[12] Mr Copeland of Collieston.
[13] Mr Quintin M'Adam of Cragingillan.

BALLAD THIRD—JOHN BUSHBY'S LAMENTATION[1]
Tune—*Babes o' the wood*

'Twas in the seventeen hunder year
 O' grace, and ninety-five,
That year I was the wae'est man
 Of onie man alive.

In March the three-an'-twentieth morn,
 The sun raise clear an' bright;

[1] John Bushby of Tinwald Downs.

But O! I was a waefu' man,
    Ere to-fa' o' the night.

Earl Galloway lang did rule this land,
    Wi' equal right and fame,
And thereto was his kinsmen join'd,
    The Murray's noble name.

Earl Galloway's man o' men was I,
    And chief o' Broughton's host;
So twa blind beggars, on a string,
    The faithfu' tyke will trust.
But now Earl Galloway's sceptre's broke,
    And Broughton's wi' the slain,
And I my ancient craft may try,
    Sin' honesty is gane.

'Twas on the bonnie banks o' Dee,
    Beside Kirkcudbright's towers,
The Stewart and the Murray there,
    Did muster a' their powers.

Then Murray on his auld grey yaud,
    Wi' wingéd spurs[1] did ride,
That auld grey yaud a' Nidsdale rade,
    He staw upon Nidside.

An there had na been the Earl himsel',
    O, there had been nae play;
But Garlies was to London gane,
    And sae the kye might stray.

And there was Balmaghie, I ween,
    In front rank he wad shine;
But Balmaghie had better been
    Drinkin' Madeira wine.

And frae Glenkens cam to our aid
    A chief o' doughty deed;
In case that worth should wanted be,
    O' Kenmure we had need.

And by our banners march'd Muirhead,
    And Buittle was na slack;
Whase haly priesthood nane could stain,
    For wha could dye the black?

And there was grave squire Cardoness,
    Look'd on till a' was done;
Sae in the tower o' Cardoness
    A howlet sits at noon.

[1] An allusion to the woman that Murray of Broughton had eloped with—Johnstone, whose crest was winged spurs.

And there led I the Bushby clan,
    My gamesome billie, Will,
And my son Maitland, wise as brave,
    My footsteps follow'd still.

The Douglas and the Heron's name,
    We set nought to their score;
The Douglas and the Heron's name,
    Had felt our weight before.

But Douglasses o' weight had we,
    The pair o' lusty lairds,
For building cot-houses sae fam'd,
    And christenin' kail-yards.

And then Redcastle drew his sword,
    That ne'er was stain'd wi' gore,
Save on a wand'rer lame and blind,
    To drive him frae his door.

And last cam creepin' Collieston,
    Was mair in fear than wrath;
Ae knave was constant in his mind—
    To keep that knave frae scaith.

HERON ELECTION BALLAD FOURTH
The Trogger
Tune—*Buy broom besoms*

Chorus: Buy braw troggin frae the banks o' Dee;
Wha wants troggin let him come to me.

Wha will buy my troggin, fine election ware,
Broken trade o' Broughton, a' in high repair?

Here's a noble Earl's[1] fame and high renown,
For an auld sang—it's thought the gudes were stown—

Here's the worth o' Broughton[2] in a needle's e'e;
Here's a reputation tint by Balmaghie.[3]

Here's its stuff and lining, Cardoness' head,[4]
Fine for a soger, a' the wale o' lead.

Here's a little wadset, Buittle's[5] scrap o' truth,
Pawn'd in a gin-shop, quenching holy drouth.

Here's an honest conscience might a prince adorn;
Frae the downs o' Tinwald,[6] so was never worn.

Here's armorial bearings frae the manse o' Urr;
The crest, a sour crab-apple, rotten at the core.[7]

[1] Earl of Galloway.
[2] Mr Murray of Broughton.
[3] Gordon of Balmaghie.
[4] Maxwell of Cardoness.
[5] Rev. George Maxwell of Buittle.
[6] John Bushby of Tinwald.
[7] Muirhead of Urr.

Here is Satan's picture, like a bizzard gled,
Pouncing poor Redcastle,[1] sprawlin' like a taed.

Here's the font where Douglas[2] stane and mortar names;
Lately used at Caily christening Murray's crimes.

Here's the worth and wisdom Collieston[3] can boast;
By a thievish midge they had been nearly lost.

Here is Murray's fragments o' the ten commands;
Gifted by black Jock[4] to get them aff his hands.

Saw ye e'er sic troggin? if to buy ye're slack,
Hornie's turnin chapman—he'll buy a' the pack.

[1] Walter Sloan Lawrie.   [3] Copeland of Collieston.
[2] Douglas of Carlinwark.   [4] John Bushby.

POETICAL INSCRIPTION FOR AN ALTAR OF INDEPENDENCE
At Kerroughtree, the Seat of Mr Heron

Thou of an independent mind,
With soul resolv'd, with soul resign'd;
Prepar'd Power's proudest frown to brave,
Who wilt not be, nor have a slave;
Virtue alone who dost revere,
Thy own reproach alone dost fear—
Approach this shrine, and worship here.

THE CARDIN O'T, THE SPINNIN O'T
Tune—*Salt fish and dumplings*

Chorus: The cardin' o't, the spinnin' o't,
The warpin' o't, the winnin' o't;
When ilka ell cost me a groat,
The tailor staw the lynin' o't.

I coft a stane o' haslock woo,
To mak a wab to Johnie o't;
For Johnie is my only jo,
I lo'e him best of onie yet.

For tho' his locks be lyart grey,
And tho' his brow be beld aboon,
Yet I hae seen him on a day,
The pride of a' the parishen.

THE COOPER O' CUDDIE
Tune—*Bab at the bowster*

Chorus: We'll hide the cooper behint the door,
Behint the door, behint the door,
We'll hide the cooper behint the door,
And cover him under a mawn, O.

The cooper o' Cuddie cam here awa',
He ca'd the girrs out o'er us a'—
An' our guid wife has gotten a ca',
That anger'd the silly guidman, O.

He sought them out, he sought them in,
    Wi' 'Deil hae her!' and 'Deil hae him!'
But the body he was sae doited and blin',
    He wist na where he was gaun, O.

They cooper'd at e'en, they cooper'd at morn,
    Till our guidman has gotten the scorn;
On ilka brow she's planted a horn,
    And swears that there they sall stan', O.

THE LASS THAT MADE THE BED TO ME

When Januar' wind was blawing cauld,
    As to the north I took my way,
The mirksome night did me enfauld,
    I knew na where to lodge till day:
By my guid luck a maid I met,
    Just in the middle o' my care,
And kindly she did me invite
    To walk into a chamber fair.

I bow'd fu' low unto this maid,
    And thank'd her for her courtesie;
I bow'd fu' low unto this maid,
    An' bade her make a bed to me;
She made the bed baith large and wide,
    Wi' twa white hands she spread it doun;
She put the cup to her rosy lips,
    And drank—'Young man, now sleep ye soun'.'

She snatch'd the candle in her hand,
    And frae my chamber went wi' speed;
But I call'd her quickly back again,
    To lay some mair below my head:
A cod she laid below my head,
    And servéd me with due respect,
And, to salute her wi' a kiss,
    I put my arms about her neck.

'Haud aff your hands, young man!' she said,
    'And dinna sae uncivil be;
Gif ye hae onie luve for me,
    O wrang na my virginitie!'
Her hair was like the links o' gowd,
    Her teeth were like the ivorie,
Her cheeks like lilies dipt in wine,
    The lass that made the bed to me.

Her bosom was the driven snaw,
    Twa drifted heaps sae fair to see;
Her limbs the polish'd marble stane,
    The lass that made the bed to me.

I kiss'd her o'er and o'er again,
    And aye she wist na what to say;
I laid her 'tween me and the wa';
    The lassie thocht na lang till day.

Upon the morrow when we raise,
    I thank'd her for her courtesie;
But aye she blush'd and aye she sigh'd,
    And said, 'Alas, ye've ruin'd me!'
I clasp'd her waist, and kiss'd her syne,
    While the tear stood twinkling in her e'e;
I said, 'My lassie, dinna cry.
    For ye aye shall make the bed to me.'

She took her mither's holland sheets
    An' made them a' in sarks to me;
Blythe and merry may she be,
    The lass that made the bed to me.
The bonnie lass made the bed to me,
    The braw lass made the bed to me.
I'll ne'er forget till the day I die,
    The lass that made the bed to me.

HAD I THE WYTE? SHE BADE ME

Had I the wyte, had I the wyte,
    Had I the wyte? she bade me;
She watch'd me by the hie-gate side,
    And up the loan she shaw'd me.
And when I wadna venture in,
    A coward loon she ca'd me:
Had Kirk an' State been in the gate,
    I'd lighted when she bade me.

Sae craftilie she took me ben,
    And bade me mak nae clatter;
'For our ramgunshoch, glum guidman
    Is o'er ayont the water.'
Whae'er shall say I wanted grace,
    When I did kiss and dawte her,
Let him be planted in my place,
    Syne say, I was the fautor.

Could I for shame, could I for shame,
    Could I for shame refus'd her?
And wadna manhood been to blame,
    Had I unkindly used her!
He claw'd her wi' the ripplin' kame,
    And blae and bluidy bruis'd her;
When sic a husband was frae hame,
    What wife but wad excus'd her!

I dighted aye her e'en sae blue,
    An' bann'd the cruel randy,
And weel I wat, her willin' mou
    Was sweet as sugar-candie.
At gloamin'-shot, it was I wat,
    I lighted on the Monday;
But I cam through the Tyseday's dew,
    To wanton Willie's brandy.

DOES HAUGHTY GAUL INVASION THREAT?

Tune—*Push about the jorum*

Does haughty Gaul invasion threat?
    Then let the louns beware, Sir;
There's Wooden Walls upon our seas,
    And Volunteers on shore, Sir:
The Nith shall run to Corsincon,[1]
    And Criffel sink in Solway,
Ere we permit a Foreign Foe
    On British ground to rally!
We'll ne'er permit a Foreign Foe
    On British ground to rally!

O let us not, like snarling curs,
    In wrangling be divided,
Till, slap! come in an unco loon,
    And wi' a rung decide it!
Be Britain still to Britain true,
    Amang oursels united;
For never but by British hands
    Maun British wrangs be righted!
No! never but by British hands
    Shall British wrangs be righted!

The kettle o' the Kirk and State,
    Perhaps a clout may fail in 't;
But deil a foreign tinkler loon
    Shall ever ca' a nail in 't.
Our Fathers' bluid the kettle bought,
    And wha wad dare to spoil it,
By Heavens! the sacrilegious dog
    Shall fuel be to boil it!
By Heavens! the sacrilegious dog
    Shall fuel be to boil it!

The wretch that would a tyrant own,
    And the wretch, his true-born brother,
Who'd set the mob above the throne,
    May they be damn'd together!

[1] A high hill at the source of the River Nith.

Who will not sing 'God save the King',
  Shall hang as high 's the steeple;
But while we sing 'God save the King',
  We'll ne'er forget The People!
But while we sing 'God save the King',
  We'll ne'er forget The People!

ADDRESS TO THE WOODLARK
Tune—*Loch Erroch-side*

O stay, sweet warbling woodlark, stay,
Nor quit for me the trembling spray,
A hapless lover courts thy lay,
  Thy soothing, fond complaining.
Again, again, that tender part,
That I may catch thy melting art;
For surely that wad touch her heart
  Wha kills me wi' disdaining.

Say, was thy little mate unkind,
And heard thee as the careless wind?
O, nocht but love and sorrow join'd,
  Sic notes o' woe could wauken!
Thou tells o' never-ending care;
O' speechless grief, and dark despair:
For pity's sake, sweet bird, nae mair!
  Or my poor heart is broken.

ON CHLORIS[1] BEING ILL
Tune—*Ay waukin, O*

Chorus: Long, long the night,
  Heavy comes the morrow,
While my soul's delight
  Is on her bed of sorrow.

Every hope is fled,
  Every fear is terror,
Slumber ev'n I dread,
  Every dream is horror.

Can I cease to care?
  Can I cease to languish,
While my darling fair
  Is on the couch of anguish?

Hear me, Powers divine!
  O, in pity hear me!
Take aught else of mine,
  But my Chloris spare me!

[1] Jean Lorimer.

HOW CRUEL ARE THE PARENTS
Altered from an Old English Song.
Tune—*John Anderson, my jo*

How cruel are the parents
  Who riches only prize,
And to the wealthy booby
  Poor Woman sacrifice!
Meanwhile the hapless daughter
  Has but a choice of strife;

> To shun a tyrant father's hate,
>> Become a wretched wife.

> The ravening hawk pursuing,
>> The trembling dove thus flies,
> To shun impelling ruin
>> Awhile her pinions tries;
> Till of escape despairing,
>> No shelter or retreat,
> She trusts the ruthless falconer,
>> And drops beneath his feet.

MARK YONDER POMP OF COSTLY FASHION
Tune—*Deil tak the wars*

Mark yonder pomp of costly fashion
  Round the wealthy, titled bride:
But when compar'd with real passion,
  Poor is all that princely pride.
  What are the showy treasures,
  What are the noisy pleasures?
The gay, gaudy glare of vanity and art:
  The polish'd jewels' blaze
  May draw the wond'ring gaze,
  And courtly grandeur bright
  The fancy may delight,
But never, never can come near the heart.

But did you see my dearest Chloris
  In simplicity's array;
Lovely as yonder sweet opening flower is,
  Shrinking from the gaze of day,
  O then, the heart alarming,
  And all resistless charming,
In Love's delightful fetters she chains the willing soul!
  Ambition would disown
  The world's imperial crown,
  Even Av'rice would deny,
  His worshipp'd deity,
And feel thro' ev'ry vein love's raptures roll.

'TWAS NA HER BONNIE BLUE E'E
Tune—*Laddie, lie near me*

'Twas na her bonnie blue e'e was my ruin,
Fair tho' she be, that was ne'er my undoing;
'Twas the dear smile when naebody did mind us,
'Twas the bewitching, sweet, stown glance o' kindness.

Sair do I fear that to hope is denied me,
Sair do I fear that despair maun abide me;
But tho' fell fortune should fate us to sever,
Queen shall she be in my bosom for ever.

Chloris, I'm thine wi' a passion sincerest,
And thou hast plighted me love o' the dearest!
And thou'rt the angel that never can alter,
Sooner the sun in his motion would falter.

THEIR GROVES O' SWEET MYRTLE
Tune—*Humours of glen*

Their groves o' sweet myrtle let foreign lands reckon,
    Where bright-beaming summers exalt the perfume;
Far dearer to me yon lone glen o' green breckan,
    Wi' the burn stealing under the lang, yellow broom.
Far dearer to me are yon humble broom bowers
    Where the bluebell and gowan lurk lowly, unseen;
For there, lightly tripping amang the wild flowers,
    A-list'ning the linnet, aft wanders my Jean.[1]

Tho' rich is the breeze in their gay, sunny valleys,
    And cauld Caledonia's blast on the wave.
Their sweet-scented woodlands that skirt the proud palace,
    What are they?—The haunt o' the tyrant and slave!
The slave's spicy forests, and gold-bubbling fountains,
    The brave Caledonian views wi' disdain;
He wanders as free as the winds o' his mountains,
    Save love's willing fetters—the chains o' his Jean.

[1] The poet's wife, who so charmed him by singing it with taste and feeling that he declared it to be one of his luckiest lyrics.

FORLORN, MY LOVE, NO COMFORT NEAR
Tune—*Let me in this ae night*

Chorus: O wert thou, love, but near me;
But near, near, near me;
How kindly thou wouldst cheer me,
    And mingle sighs with mine, love.

Forlorn, my Love, no comfort near,
Far, far from thee, I wander here;
Far, far from thee, the fate severe,
    At which I most repine, love.

Cold, alter'd friendship's cruel part,
To poison fortune's ruthless dart—
Let me not break thy faithful heart,
    And say that fate is mine, love.

Around me scowls a wintry sky,
Blasting each bud of hope and joy;
And shelter, shade, nor home have I,
    Save in these arms of thine, love.

But dreary tho' the moments fleet,
    O let me think we yet shall meet!
That only ray of solace sweet
    Can on thy Chloris shine, love.

WHY, WHY TELL THY LOVER
Tune—*Caledonian Hunt's delight*

Why, why tell thy lover,
    Bliss he never must enjoy?
Why, why undeceive him,
    And give all his hopes the lie?

O why, while fancy, raptur'd, slumbers,
    'Chloris, Chloris' all the theme,
Why, why would'st thou, cruel,
    Wake thy lover from his dream?

THE BRAW WOOER
Tune—*The Lothian lassie*

Last May a braw wooer cam down the lang glen,
    And sair wi' his love he did deave me.
I said there was naething I hated like men,
    The deuce gae wi'm, to believe me, believe me,
    The deuce gae wi'm to believe me.

He spak o' the darts in my bonnie black een,
    And vow'd for my love he was dying.
I said he might die when he liked for Jean,
    The Lord forgi'e me for lying, for lying,
    The Lord forgi'e me for lying!

A weel-stockéd mailen—himsel' for the laird—
    And marriage aff-hand were his proffers:
I never loot on that I kenn'd it, or car'd,
    But thought I might hae waur offers, waur offers,
    But thought I might hae waur offers.

But what wad ye think? In a fortnight or less—
    The Deil tak his taste to gae near her!—
He up the Gate-slack to my black cousin, Bess,
    Guess ye how, the jad! I could bear her, could bear her;
    Guess ye how, the jad! I could bear her.

But a' the niest week, as I fretted wi' care,
    I gaed to the tryst o' Dalgarnock;
And wha but my fine fickle wooer was there!
    I glowr'd as I'd seen a warlock, a warlock,
    I glowr'd as I'd seen a warlock.

But owre my left shouther I gae him a blink,
    Lest neebors might say I was saucy;
My wooer he caper'd as he'd been in drink,
    And vow'd I was his dear lassie, dear lassie,
    And vow'd I was his dear lassie.

I spier'd for my cousin fu' couthy and sweet,
    Gin she had recover'd her hearin',
And how her new shoon fit her auld schachl't feet,
    But heavens! how he fell a swearin', a swearin',
    But heavens! how he fell a swearin'.

He beggéd, for Gudesake! I wad be his wife,
    Or else I wad kill him wi' sorrow;
So e'en to preserve the poor body in life,
    I think I maun wed him tomorrow, tomorrow;
    I think I maun wed him tomorrow.

THIS IS NO MY AIN LASSIE
Tune—*This is no my ain house*

Chorus: O, this is no my ain lassie,
    Fair tho' the lassie be;
    Weel ken I my ain lassie,
    Kind love is in her e'e.

I see a form, I see a face,
Ye weel may wi' the fairest place:
It wants, to me, the witching grace,
    The kind love that's in her e'e.

She's bonnie, blooming, straight and tall,
And lang has had my heart in thrall;
And aye it charms my very saul,
    The kind love that's in her e'e.

A thief sae pawkie is my Jean,
To steal a blink by a' unseen;
But gleg as light are lover's een,
    When kind love is in her e'e.

It may escape the courtly sparks,
It may escape the learnéd clerks;
But well the watching lover marks
    The kind love that's in her eye.

O BONNIE WAS YON ROSY BRIER
Tune—*I wish my love were in a mire*

O bonnie was yon rosy brier,
    That blooms sae far frae haunt o' man;
And bonnie she, and ah, how dear!
    It shaded frae the e'enin sun.

Yon rosebuds in the morning dew,
    How pure amang the leaves sae green;
But purer was the lover's vow
    They witness'd in their shade yestreen.

All in its rude and prickly bower,
    That crimson rose how sweet and fair!
But love is far a sweeter flower,
    Amid life's thorny path o' care.

The pathless wild, and wimpling burn,
    Wi' Chloris in my arms, be mine;
And I the world nor wish nor scorn,
    Its joys and griefs alike resign.

NOW SPRING HAS CLAD THE GROVE IN GREEN
Tune—*The hopeless lover*

Now spring has clad the grove in green,
    And strew'd the lea wi' flowers;
The furrow'd, waving corn is seen
    Rejoice in fostering showers.
While ilka thing in Nature join
    Their sorrows to forego,
O why thus all alone are mine
    The weary steps of woe!

The trout within yon wimpling burn
    Glides swift, a silver dart,
And safe beneath the shady thorn
    Defies the angler's art;
My life was once that careless stream,
    That wanton trout was I;
But love, wi' unrelenting beam,
    Has scorch'd my fountains dry.

That little floweret's peaceful lot,
    In yonder cliff that grows—
Which, save the linnet's flight, I wot,
    Nae ruder visit knows—
Was mine; till love has o'er me past,
    And blighted a' my bloom,
And now beneath the withering blast
    My youth and joy consume.

The waken'd lav'rock warbling springs
    And climbs the early sky,
Winnowing blythe his dewy wings
    In morning's rosy eye;
As little reckt I sorrow's power,
    Until the flowery snare
O' witching love, in luckless hour,
    Made me the thrall o' care.

O, had my fate been Greenland snows,
    Or Afric's burning zone,
Wi' Man and Nature leagu'd my foes,
    So Peggy ne'er I'd known!
The wretch whase doom is 'hope nae mair',
    What tongue his woes can tell!
Within whase bosom, save despair,
    Nae kinder spirits dwell.

O, THAT'S THE LASSIE O' MY HEART
Tune—*Morag*

Chorus: O that's the lassie o' my heart,
    My lassie ever dearer;
O that's the queen o' womankind,
    And ne'er a ane to peer her.

O wat ye wha that lo'es me,
    And has my heart a-keeping?
O sweet is she that lo'es me,
    As dews o' simmer weeping,
    In tears the rosebuds steeping!

If thou shalt meet a lassie,
    In grace and beauty charming,

That e'en thy chosen lassie,
>   Erewhile thy breast sae warming,
>   Had ne'er sic powers alarming;

If thou hast heard her talking,
>   And thy attention's plighted,
That ilka body talking
>   But her, by thee is slighted,
>   And thou art all delighted;

If thou hast met this fair one,
>   When frae her thou hast parted,
If every other fair one
>   But her, thou hast deserted,
>   And thou art broken-hearted.

To Chloris

'Written on the blank leaf of a copy of the last edition of my poems, presented to the Lady whom, in so many fictitious reveries of passion, but with the most ardent sentiments of real friendship, I have so often sung under the name of—"Chloris".'[1]—R.B.

'Tis Friendship's pledge, my young, fair Friend,
>   Nor thou the gift refuse,
Nor with unwilling ear attend
>   The moralising Muse.

Since thou, in all thy youth and charms,
>   Must bid the world adieu,
(A world 'gainst Peace in constant arms)
>   To join the Friendly Few.

Since, thy gay morn of life o'ercast,
>   Chill came the tempest's lour;
(And ne'er Misfortune's eastern blast
>   Did nip a fairer flower.)

Since life's gay scenes must charm no more;
>   Still much is left behind;
Still nobler wealth hast thou in store—
>   The comforts of the mind!

Thine is the self-approving glow,
>   On conscious Honour's part;
And (dearest gift of Heaven below)
>   Thine Friendship's truest heart.

The joys refin'd of Sense and Taste,
>   With every Muse to rove:
And doubly were the Poet blest,
>   These joys could he improve.

[1] Jean Lorimer.

THERE'S NEWS, LASSES, NEWS
Tune—*I winna gang to my bed until I get a man*

Chorus: The wean wants a cradle,
    An' the cradle wants a cod:
An' I'll no gang to my bed,
    Until I get a nod.

There's news, lasses, news,
    Guid news I've to tell!
There's a boatfu' o' lads
    Come to our town to sell.

'Father,' quo' she, 'Mither,' quo she,
    'Do what you can,
I'll no gang to my bed,
    Until I get a man.'

I hae as guid a craft rig
    As made o' yird and stane;
And waly fa' the ley-crap,
    For I maun till 't again.

CROWDIE EVER MAIR

Chorus: Ance crowdie, twice crowdie,
    Three times crowdie in a day;
Gin ye 'Crowdie' onie mair,
    Ye'll crowdie a' my meal away.

O that I had ne'er been married,
    I wad never had nae care,
Now I've gotten wife an' bairns,
    An' they cry 'Crowdie' evermair.

Waefu' Want and Hunger fley me,
    Glowrin' by the hallan en';
Sair I fecht them at the door,
    But aye I'm eerie they come ben.

MALLY'S MEEK, MALLY'S SWEET

Chorus: O Mally's meek, Mally's sweet,
    Mally's modest and discreet;
Mally's rare, Mally's fair,
    Mally's ev'ry way complete.

As I was walking up the street,
    A barefit maid I chanc'd to meet,
But O, the road was very hard
    For that fair maiden's tender feet.

It were mair meet that those fine feet
    Were weel lac'd up in silken shoon,
An' 'twere more fit that she should sit
    Within yon chariot gilt aboon,

Her yellow hair beyond compare
    Comes trinklin' down her swan-like neck,
And her two eyes like stars in skies
    Would keep a sinking ship frae wreck,

JOCKEY'S TA'EN THE PARTING KISS
Tune—*Bonnie lass tak a man*

Jockey's ta'en the parting kiss,
    O'er the mountains he is gane,
And with him is a' my bliss,
    Nought but griefs with me remain.
Spare my love, ye winds that blaw,
    Plashy sleets and beating rain!
Spare my love, thou feath'ry snaw,
    Drifting o'er the frozen plain!

When the shades of evening creep
    O'er the day's fair, gladsome e'e,
Sound and safely may he sleep,
    Sweetly blythe his waukening be.
He will think on her he loves,
    Fondly he'll repeat her name;
For whare'er he distant roves,
    Jockey's heart is still the same.

TO COLLECTOR MITCHELL[1]

Friend of the Poet, tried and leal,
Wha, wanting thee, might beg or steal;
Alake, alake! the meikle deil
        Wi' a' his witches
Are at it, skelpin jig and reel,
        In my poor pouches?

I modestly fu' fain wad hint it,
That One-pound-one, I sairly want it;
If wi' the hizzie down ye sent it,
        It would be kind;
And while my heart wi' life-blood dunted,
        I'd bear 't in mind.

So may the Auld Year gang out moanin'
To see the New come laden, groanin',
Wi' double plenty o'er the loanin',
        To thee and thine;
Domestic peace and comforts crownin'
        The hale design.

Postscript

Ye've heard this while how I've been licket,
And by fell Death was nearly nicket;
Grim loon! he got me by the fecket,
        And sair he sheuk;
But by guid luck I lap a wicket,
        And turn'd a neuk.

[1] John Mitchell, Collector of Excise, Dumfries.

But by that health, I've got a share o't,
But by that life, I'm promis'd mair o't,
My hale and wee, I'll tak a care o't
    A tentier way:
So farewell, folly, hide and hair o't,
      For ance and aye!

THE DEAN OF FACULTY[1]—A NEW BALLAD
Tune—*The dragon of Wantley*

Dire was the hate at old Harlaw,
    That Scot to Scot did carry;
And dire the discord Langside saw
    For beauteous, hapless Mary:
But Scot to Scot ne'er met so hot,
    Or were more in fury seen, Sir,
Than 'twixt Hal and Bob for the famous job,
    Who should be the Faculty's Dean, Sir.

This Hal for genius, wit and lore,
    Among the first was number'd;
But pious Bob, 'mid learning's store,
    Commandment the tenth remember'd.
Yet simple Bob the victory got
    And wan his heart's desire,
Which shows that heaven can boil the pot,
    Though the devil piss in the fire.

Squire Hal, besides, had in this case
    Pretensions rather brassy,
For talents to deserve a place
    Are qualifications saucy.
So their worships of the Faculty,
    Quite sick of merit's rudeness,
Chose one who should owe it all, d'ye see,
    To their gratis grace and goodness.

As once on Pisgah purg'd was the sight
    Of a son of Circumcision,
So may be, on this Pisgah height,
    Bob's purblind mental vision—
Nay, Bobby's mouth may be opened yet,
    Till for eloquence you hail him,
And swear that he has the angel met
    That met the ass of Balaam.

In your heretic sins may you live and die,
    Ye heretic Eight-and-thirty!
But accept, ye sublime Majority,
    My congratulations hearty.

---

[1] These verses allude to the victory gained by the Tory Lord Advocate, Robert Blair, over the famous wit, Henry Erskine, brother of Thomas, Lord Erskine.

With your honours, as with a certain king,
    In your servants this is striking,
The more incapacity they bring,
    The more they're to your liking.

POEM ON LIFE
Addressed to Colonel De Peyster,[1] Dumfries

My honour'd Colonel, deep I feel
Your interest in the Poet's weal;
Ah! now sma' heart hae I to speel
        The steep Parnassus,
Surrounded thus by bolus pill
        And potion glasses.

O what a canty warld were it,
Would pain and care and sickness spare it;
And Fortune favour worth and merit
        As they deserve;
And aye a rowth o' roast-beef and claret,
        Syne wha wad starve?
Dame Life, tho' fiction out may trick her,
And in paste gems and frippery deck her;
O! flickering, feeble and unsicker
        I've found her still,
Aye wavering like the willow wicker,
        'Tween good and ill.

Then that curst carmagnole,[2] auld Satan,
Watches like baudrons by a ratton
Our sinfu' saul to get a claut on,
        Wi' felon ire;
Syne, whip! his tail ye'll ne'er cast saut on,
        He's aff like fire.

Ah Nick! ah Nick! it is na fair,
First showing us the tempting ware,
Bright wines and bonnie lasses rare,
        To put us daft;
Syne weave, unseen, thy spider snare
        O' hell's damned waft.

Poor Man, the flie, aft bizzes by,
And aft as chance he comes thee nigh,
Thy damn'd auld elbow yeuks wi' joy
        And hellish pleasure;
Already in thy fancy's eye,
        Thy sicker treasure.

[1] A military man who had served in Canada and lived to be ninety-six, dying in Dumfries in 1822.
[2] A French Revolutionary nickname.

Soon, heels o'er gowdie, in he gangs,
And, like a sheep-head on a tangs,
Thy girning laugh enjoys his pangs
      And murdering wrestle,
As dangling in the wind he hangs,
      A gibbet's tassel.

But lest you think I am uncivil
To plague you with this draunting drivel,
Abjuring a' intentions evil,
      I quat my pen.
The Lord preserve us frae the devil!
      Amen! Amen!

HEY FOR A LASS WI' A TOCHER
Tune—*Balinamona and ora*

Chorus: Then hey for a lass wi' a tocher,
Then hey for a lass wi' a tocher,
Then hey for a lass wi' a tocher,
    The nice yellow guineas for me!

Awa' wi' your witchcraft o' beauty's alarms,
The slender bit beauty you grasp in your arms,
O, gie me the lass that has acres o' charms,
O, gie me the lass wi' the weel-stockit farms.

Your beauty's a flower in the morning that blows
And withers the faster, the faster it grows;
But the rapturous charm o' the bonnie green knowes,
Ilk spring they're new deckit wi' bonnie white yowes.

And e'en when this beauty your bosom hath blest,
The brightest o' beauty may cloy when possest;
But the sweet, yellow darlings wi' Geordie imprest,
The langer ye hae them, the mair they're caresst.

COMPLIMENTARY VERSICLES TO JESSIE LEWARS

The Toast

Fill me with the rosy wine,
Call a toast, a toast divine;
Give the Poet's darling flame,
Lovely Jessie be her name;
Then thou mayest freely boast,
Thou hast given a peerless toast.

The Menagerie

Talk not to me of savages,
    From Afric's burning sun;
No savage e'er could rend my heart,
    As Jessie, thou hast done.

But Jessie's lovely hand in mine,
    A mutual faith to plight,
Not even to view the heavenly choir
    Would be so blest a sight.

On Jessie's Illness

Say, sages, what's the charm on earth
    Can turn Death's dart aside?
It is not purity and worth,
    Else Jessie had not died.

On the Recovery of Jessie

But rarely seen since Nature's birth,
    The natives of the sky;
Yet still one seraph's left on earth,
    For Jessie did not die.

O Lay Thy Loof In Mine, Lass
Tune—*The cordwainer's march*

Chorus: O lay thy loof in mine, lass,
In mine, lass, in mine, lass,
And swear on thy white hand, lass,
    That thou wilt be my ain.

A slave to Love's unbounded sway,
He aft has wrought me meikle wae;
But now he is my deadly fae,
    Unless thou be my ain.

There's monie a lass has broke my rest,
That for a blink I hae lo'ed best;
But thou art queen within my breast,
    For ever to remain.

Here's A Health To Ane I Lo'e Dear
Tune—*Here's a health to them that's awa'*

Chorus: Here's a health to ane I lo'e dear,
    Here's a health to ane I lo'e dear;
Thou art sweet as the smile when fond lovers meet,
    And soft as their parting tear, Jessy—[1]
    And soft as their parting tear.

Altho' thou maun never be mine,
    Altho' even hope is denied;
'Tis sweeter for thee despairing,
    Than aught in the world beside, Jessy,
    Than aught in the world beside!

I mourn thro' the gay, gaudy day,
    As, hopeless, I muse on thy charms;
But welcome the dream o' sweet slumber,
    For then I am lockt in thine arms, Jessy,
    For then I am lockt in thine arms!

I guess by the dear angel smile,
    I guess by the love-rolling e'e;
But why urge the tender confession,
    'Gainst fortune's fell, cruel decree, Jessy,
    'Gainst fortune's fell, cruel decree!

[1] Jessy Lewars, afterwards Mrs James Thomson, Dumfries.

O WERT THOU IN THE CAULD BLAST[1]
Tune—*Lennoxlove to Blantyre*

O wert thou in the cauld blast,
    On yonder lea, on yonder lea,
My plaidie to the angry airt,
    I'd shelter thee, I'd shelter thee;
Or did misfortune's bitter storms
    Around thee blaw, around thee blaw,
Thy bield should be my bosom,
    To share it a', to share it a'.

Or were I in the wildest waste,
    Sae black and bare, sae black and bare,
The desert were a paradise,
    If thou wert there, if thou wert there;
Or were I monarch o' the globe,
    Wi' thee to reign, wi' thee to reign,
The brightest jewel in my crown
    Wad be my queen, wad be my queen.

[1] Written for music played by Jessy Lewars, who nursed him in his last illness.

TO MISS JESSY LEWARS
With Books which the Bard Presented Her[1]

Thine be the volumes, Jessy fair,
And with them take the Poet's prayer,
That Fate may in her fairest page,
With every kindliest, best presage
Of future bliss, enroll thy name:
With native worth and spotless fame,
And wakeful caution, still aware
Of ill—but chief, Man's felon snare;
All blameless joys on earth we find,
And all the treasures of the mind—
These be thy guardian and reward;
So prays thy faithful friend, the Bard.

[1] A copy of the *Scots Musical Museum*, in four volumes.

FAIREST MAID[1] ON DEVON BANKS
Tune—*Rothiemurchie*

Chorus: Fairest maid on Devon banks,
Crystal Devon, winding Devon,
Wilt thou lay that frown aside
    And smile as thou wert wont to do?

Full well thou know'st I love thee dear,
Couldst thou to malice lend an ear?
O, did not love exclaim, 'Forbear,
    Nor use a faithful lover so.'

Then come, thou fairest of the fair,
Those wonted smiles, O let me share;
And, by thy beauteous self I swear,
    No love but thine my heart shall know.

[1] Charlotte Hamilton, sister of Gavin Hamilton.

Glossary

A

a' all; every.

a-back behind, away; ago.

abiegh aloof; off, at a distance.

ablins perhaps.

aboon above; overhead; up; beyond.

abread abroad.

abreed in breadth.

ae one.

aff off.

aff-hand at once.

aff-loof off-hand.

a-fiel afield.

afore before.

aft oft.

aften often.

agley awry.

ahin behind.

aiblins perhaps.

aidle foul water; the urine of cattle.

aik an oak.

aiken made of oak.

ain own.

air early.

airle, arle earnest money, a nominal sum of money given as confirmation of a contract.

airn iron.

airt a direction, way.

airt to direct.

aith an oath.

aits oats.

aiver an old horse.

aizle a cinder.

a-jee ajar; to one side.

alake alas.

alane alone.

alang along.

amaist almost.

amang among.

an if.

an' and.

ance once.

ane one.

aneath beneath.

anes once.

anither another.

aqua-fontis spring water.

aqua-vitae whisky.

arle *same as* **airle**.

ase ashes.

asklent askew, askance.

aspar aspread.

asteer astir.

a'thegither altogether.

athort athwart.

atweel in truth.

atween between.

aught eight.

aught possessed of.

aughten eighteen.

aughtlins at all; in any degree.

auld old.

auld-farran, auld-farrant old-fashioned; sagacious; shrewd.

Auld Nick a nickname for the Devil.

Auld Reekie Edinburgh.

auld-warld old-world.

aumous alms; a good deed.

ava at all.

awa', awa away; around.

awald backways and doubled up.

awauk awake.

awauken awaken.

awe owe.

awkart awkward.

awnie bearded.

ay yes.

aye always.

ayont beyond.

B

ba' a ball.

backet a bucket; a box.

backit backed.

backlins-comin coming back.

back-yett a back gate.

bade endured.

bade asked.

baggie the stomach.

baig'net a bayonet.

baillie, bailie a magistrate of a Scots burgh.

bainie bony.

bairn a child.

bairntime the time during which a woman bears children; a woman's whole birth of children; childhood.

baith both.

bake a small biscuit.

ballat a ballad.

balou a lullaby.

ban to curse, swear.

ban' a band (particularly of Presbyterian clergyman).

bane a bone.
bang an effort; a blow; a large number.
bang to thump.
banie *same as* **bainie**.
bannet a bonnet.
bannock, bonnock a thick oatmeal cake.
bardie a minor poet; a humble poet.
barefit barefooted.
barket barked.
barley-brie *or* **bree** barley-brew ale or whisky.
barm yeast.
barmie yeasty.
barn-yard a stackyard.
Bartie the Devil.
bashing abashing.
batch a number.
batts botts, a disease in horses or dogs; colic.
bauckie-bird the bat.
baudrons, baudrans a cat.
bauk a crossbeam.
bauk a field path.
bauk-en' a beam end.
bauld bold.
bauldest boldest.
bauldly boldly.
baumy balmy.
bawbee a halfpenny.
bawdrons *same as* **baudrons**.
bawk a field path.
baws'nt white-streaked.
bear barley.
beas' beasts, vermin.
beastie the diminutive of beast, used to express sympathy or affection.
beck a curtsy.
beet to feed, supply; to kindle.
befa' to befall.
beild *same as* **biel**.
belang to belong.
beld bald.
bellum an assault.
bellys bellows.
belyve by and by.
ben a parlour, an inner room; into the parlour.
benmost inmost.
be-north to the north of.
be-south to the south of.
bestead circumstanced.
bethankit grace after meat.
beuk a book.
bicker a beaker, a wooden cup.
bicker a short run.
bicker to flow swiftly and with a slight noise.
bickerin a noisy contention.
bickering hurrying.
bid to ask; to wish; to offer.

bide to abide, endure.
biel, bield a shelter; a sheltered spot.
biel comfortable.
bien comfortable.
bien, bienly comfortably.
big to build.
biggin a building.
bike *same as* **byke**.
bill a bull.
billie a fellow, comrade, brother.
bing a heap.
birdie the diminutive of bird; a girl.
birk the birch.
birken made of birch.
birkie a fellow.
birr force, vigour.
birring a whirring.
birse a bristle.
birth berth.
bit small, used contemptuously or endearingly.
bit the nick of time.
bitch a term of contempt applied to a man.
bitch-fou completely drunk.
bizz a flurry.
bizz to buzz.
bizzard the buzzard.
bizzie busy.
black-bonnet a Presbyterian elder.
black-nebbit black-beaked.
blad *same as* **blaud**.
blae blue; livid.
blastit, blastet blasted.
blastie a damned creature; a little wretch.
blate modest, bashful.
blather the bladder.
blaud a large quantity.
blaud to slap, pelt.
blaw a blow.
blaw to brag.
blawing blowing.
blawn blown.
bleer to blear.
bleer't bleared.
bleeze to blaze.
bleeze a blaze.
blellum a babbler, railer, blusterer.
blether blethers, nonsense.
blether to talk nonsense.
bletherin' talking nonsense.
blin' blind.
blink a glance; a moment.
blink to glance; to shine.
blinker a spy; an ogler.
blinkin smirking, leering.
blin't blinded.
blitter the snipe.

blue-gown the livery of a licensed beggar.
bluid, blude blood.
bluidy bloody.
blume to bloom.
blunt a stupid fellow.
bluntie a stupid fellow.
blype a shred of skin when it peels off.
bobbed curtsied.
bocked vomited.
boddle a farthing.
bode to look for.
bodkin a tailor's needle.
body, bodie a person.
boggie the diminutive of bog.
bogle a bogie, a hobgoblin.
bole a hole or small recess in a wall.
bonnie, bonie pretty, beautiful.
bonnilie, bonilie prettily.
bonnock *same as* **bannock**.
'boon above.
boord a board; a surface.
boord-en' a board end.
boortress elders.
boost must needs.
boot what is given into the bargain or to equalise an exchange.
bore a chink, recess.
botch an angry tumour.
bouk a human trunk; bulk.
bountith a bounty, a bonus.
'bout about.
bow-hough'd bow-legged.
bow-kail cabbage.
bow't bent.
brachen a fern.
brae the slope of a hill.
braid broad.
broad-claith broadcloth.
braik a harrow.
braing't plunged.
brak broke.
brak's broke his.
brankie finely dressed, gaudy.
branks a wooden curb, a bridle.
bran'y brandy.
brash a short attack.
brat a small piece, a rag.
brat a small child.
brattle a scamper.
brattle a noisy onset.
braw handsome; fine; gaily dressed.
brawlie finely; perfectly; heartily.
braxie a sheep that has died of braxie, a internal inflammation, or other natural death.
breastie the diminutive of breast.
breastit sprang forward.

brechan a fern.
bree *same as* **barley brie**.
bree *same as* **brie**.
breeks breeches, trousers.
breer a briar.
brent brand.
brent straight, steep; (*of the forehead*) lofty, unwrinkled.
brie, bree *same as* **barley brie**.
brie, bree eyebrow.
brief a writ.
brier a briar.
brig a bridge.
brisket the breast.
brither a brother.
brock a badger.
brogue a trick.
broo soup, broth, water; liquid in which anything is cooked.
brooses wedding races from the church to the home of the bride.
brose a thick mixture of meal and warm water; porridge.
browster wives ale wives.
brugh a burgh.
brulzie, brulyie a brawl.
brunstane brimstone.
brunt burned.
brust burst.
buckie the diminutive of buck; a smart youngster.
buckle a curl.
buckskin Virginian; American.
budget a tinker's bag of tools.
buff to bang, to thump.
bughtin folding.
buirdly stalwart.
bum the buttocks.
bum to hum.
bum-clock a humming flying beetle.
bummle a drone; a useless fellow.
bunker a seat.
bunter a harlot.
burd a maiden; a young lady.
burdie the diminutive of bird or burd, a term of endearment or of irony used to a young man or woman.
bure bore.
burn a stream, rivulet.
burnewin burn the wind, a blacksmith.
burnie the diminutive of burn.
burr-thistle the spear-thistle.
busk to dress; to garb; to dress up; to adorn.
buss a bush.
bussle bustle.
but without.

butt, but without, outside; out, outside of; **butt the house** in the kitchen.

by past, aside.

by beside.

by himsel beside himself.

bye attour beside and at a distance.

byke a bees' nest, a hive; a swarm; a crowd.

byre a cow house.

C

ca' a call, summons by voice or instrument; a knock; a drive of cattle.

ca' to call; to knock; to drive cattle.

cadger a carrier; a hawker (especially of fish).

cadie, caddie a fellow.

caff chaff.

caird a tinker.

calf-ward a small enclosure for grazing calves.

callant, callan a stripling.

caller cool, refreshing.

callet a trull.

cam came.

canie *same as* **cannie**.

cankrie crabbed.

canna cannot.

cannie, canny cautious, prudent; shrewd; crafty; gentle; quiet; useful; soft, easy, slow in motion; comfortable, cosy.

canniest quietest.

cannilie, cannily quietly; prudently, cautiously.

canny *same as* **cannie**.

cant a merry story; a canter; a spree.

cantie cheerful, lively, jolly, merry.

cantraip magic, witching.

capestane a copestone.

capon to castrate.

care na by do not care.

carl, carle a man, an old man.

carl-hemp the largest stalk of hemp; mental vigour, firmness.

carlie a little man; a precocious boy.

carlin, carline a middle-aged or old woman; a witch.

carte a playing card.

cartie the diminutive of cart.

catch-the-plack the hunt for money.

caudron a caldron.

cauf a calf.

cauf-leather calfskin.

cauk chalk.

cauld cold.

cauldron a caldron.

caup a wooden drinking vessel.

causey a causeway, street.

cavie a hen coop.

chamer a chamber.

change-house an alehouse, tavern.

chanter the fingering part of a bagpipe that produces the melody; a song.

chap a fellow, a young fellow.

chap to strike.

chapman a pedlar.

chaumer a chamber.

chaup, chap a stroke, a blow.

chear to cheer.

chearfu' cheerful.

chearless cheerless.

cheary cheery.

cheek-for-chow cheek-by-jowl.

cheep a chirp, cry of a young bird; a squeak, like that of a mouse; to creak.

cheep to chirp; to squeak; to creak.

chiel, child a fellow, a young fellow.

chimla a chimney.

chittering shivering.

chow to chew.

chuck a hen; a term of endearment.

chuckie the diminutive of chuck; a mother hen, an old dear.

chuffie fat-faced.

chuse to choose.

cit the civet.

cit a citizen; a merchant.

clachan a small village.

claeding clothing.

claise, claes clothes.

claith cloth.

claithing clothing.

clankie a severe knock.

clap the clapper of a mill.

clark a clerk.

clark clerkly, scholarly.

clarkit, clerked wrote.

clarty dirty.

clash an idle tale; gossip.

clash to tattle.

clatter noise, tattle, talk, disputation, babble.

clatter to make a noise by striking; to babble; to prattle.

claught clutched, seized.

claughtin clutching, grasping.

claut a clutch, a handful.

claut to scrape.

claver clover.

clavers gossip; nonsense.

claw a scratch; a blow.

claw to scratch; to strike.

clay-cauld clay-cold.

claymore a two-handed Highland sword.

cleckin a brood.

cleed to clothe.

cleek to snatch.

cleek to link arms, walk arm in arm.
cleg gadfly.
clink a sharp stroke; jingle.
clink money, coin.
clink to chink.
clink to rhyme.
clinkin with a smart motion.
clinkum, clinkumbell a beadle; a bell-ringer.
clips shears.
clish-ma-claver idle talk; gossip, tale-telling; nonsense.
clockin-time the hatching of eggs already laid.
cloot a hoof.
Clootie, Cloots the Devil).
clour a bump or swelling after a blow.
clout a cloth; a patch.
clout to patch.
clud a cloud.
clunk to make a hollow sound.
coble a broad, flat boat.
cock a fellow, a good fellow.
cock the tee in a curling rink.
cockie the diminutive of cock, applied to a crony or an old man.
cod a pillow.
coft bought.
cog a wooden vessel for holding milk, ale, porridge, broth, etc; a pail; a corn measure for horses.
coggie a little dish.
collieshangie a squabble.
cood the cud.
coof a simpleton, a fool.
cook to appear and disappear by fits; to hide oneself.
cookit hid.
coor to cover.
cooser a courser, a stallion.
coost looped; cast, threw off; tossed; chucked.
cootie a small pail.
cootie leg-plumed.
corbie a raven; a crow.
core a choir, company of singers or musicians; a convivial company; friendly terms.
corn mou a stack of corn; the place where corn is stacked.
corn't fed with corn.
corse a corpse.
corss a cross; a marketplace.
cou'dna, couldna couldn't.
countra rustic, country.
coup to capsize.
couthie, couthy loving, affable, cosy, comfortable.
cowe to scare, to daunt.
cowe to lop.

cowp to capsize.
crack a tale; a chat; talk.
crack to chat, to talk.
craft a croft.
craft-rig a croft ridge.
craig the throat.
craig a crag, a rocky place.
craigie the diminutive of craig.
craigy craggy.
craik the corncrake, the landrail.
crambo-clink a rhyme.
crambo-jingle rhyming.
cran a support for a pot or kettle.
crank a harsh creaking noise.
crankous fretful.
cranreuch hoar-frost.
crap to crop; to lop.
crap a crop, produce.
craw a crow; the crop of a bird.
creel an osier basket.
creepie-chair the stool of repentance for public penitents.
creeshie greasy, oily.
crock an old ewe.
cronie an intimate friend.
crood to coo.
crood a coo.
crookit deformed.
croon a moan; the lowing of cattle.
croon to moan; (*of cattle*) to low; (*of a bell*) to toll.
crooning humming.
croose *same as* **crouse**.
crouchie hunchbacked.
crouse, croose bold; eager; brisk; conceited; happy; proud.
crousely confidently.
crowdie meal and cold water, meal and milk, porridge.
crowdie-time porridge-time, breakfast-time.
crowlin crawling.
crummie a horned cow.
crummock, cummock a cudgel, a crooked staff.
crump crisp.
crunt a blow.
cuddle to fondle.
cuif, coof a simpleton, a fool.
cummock *same as* **crummock**.
curch a kerchief for the head.
curchie a curtsy.
curler one who plays at curling.
curmurring a commotion.
curpin, curple the crupper, the part of a horse's rump behind the saddle.
cushat the wood pigeon.
custock the pith of the colewort.
cute the ankle; the foot.

cutty short.

cutty-stool a short three-legged stool, the stool of repentance.

D

dad, daddie father.

daez't dazed.

daffin larking, fun.

daft mad, foolish.

dail a plank of wood.

daimen icker an ear of corn met occasionally.

daintie, dainty a treat, a delicacy.

daintie, dainty large; thriving; pleasant; good-natured; worthy; excellent.

dam pent-up water, urine.

damie the diminutive of dame.

dang beat, drove.

danton *same as* **daunton**.

darena dare not.

darg labour; a task; a day's work.

darklins in the dark.

daud a large piece.

daud to pelt.

daunder to stroll, saunter.

daunder a saunter; a drunken frolic.

daunton to daunt.

daur to dare.

daurna dare not.

daur't dared.

daut, dawte to fondle.

daviely spiritless.

daw to dawn.

dawd a lump.

dawtingly prettily; caressingly.

dead death.

dead-sweer extremely reluctant.

deave to deafen.

deil, deevil devil, the Devil; **deil-haet** nothing at all; deil-ma-care devil-may-care; **deil's picture beuks** playing cards.

deleeret delirious, mad.

delvin digging.

dern to hide.

descrive to describe.

deuk a duck.

devel a stunning blow.

diddle to move quickly.

didna did not, didn't.

dight to wipe.

dight winnowed, sifted.

din (*of the complexion*) muddy.

ding to beat, to surpass.

dint an occasion; an opportunity.

dink trim, neat, finely dressed.

dinna do not, don't.

dirl to vibrate; to ring.

diz'n, dizzen a dozen.

dochter a daughter.

doited muddled, doting; stupid, bewildered.

donsie vicious, bad-tempered; restive; testy.

dook *same as* **douk**.

dool woe, sorrow.

doolfu' doleful, woeful.

dorty pettish.

douce, douse sedate, sober, prudent.

douce, doucely, dousely sedately, prudently.

doudl'd dandled.

dought could.

douk to duck; to plunge or dip into water.

doup the bottom, buttocks.

doup-skelper bottom-smacker.

dour, doure stubborn, obstinate; cutting.

dow, dowe to be able to; to dare.

dow a dove.

dowf, dowff dull.

dowie drooping, mournful.

dowilie drooping.

downa cannot.

downa-do lack of potency.

doylt stupid, stupefied.

doytin doddering.

dozen'd torpid.

dozin torpid.

draigle to draggle; to trail in the mud.

drant prosing.

drap a drop.

drappie a small drink.

draunting tedious.

dree to endure, suffer.

dreigh *same as* **dreight**.

dribble (to) drizzle.

driddle to toddle.

dreigh tedious, dull.

droddum the breech, bottom.

drone the bass part of a bagpipe.

droop-rumpl't (*of a horse*) short-rumped.

drouk to wet, to drench.

droukit wetted.

drouth thirst.

drouthy thirsty.

drucken, druken drunken.

drumlie muddy, turbid.

drummock a mixture of raw meal and cold water.

drunt the huff.

dry thirsty.

dub a puddle; slush; mud, mire.

duddie ragged.

duddies rags.

duds rags, clothes.

dun (*of the complexion*) muddy.

dung beat, drove.

dunt to throb; to beat.
dunt a blow.
durk a dagger, dirk.
dusht pushed or thrown down violently.
dwalling a dwelling.
dwalt dwelt.
dyke a fence of stone or turf; a wall.
dyvor a bankrupt.

E

ear' early.
earn the eagle.
eastlin eastern.
e'e an eye.
e'ebrie the eyebrow.
een the eyes.
e'en even.
e'en evening.
e'enin' evening.
e'er ever.
eerie apprehensive; inspiring ghostly fear.
eild old age.
eke also.
elbuck the elbow.
eldritch unearthly, haunted, fearsome.
elekit elected.
ell a unit of measurement, 37 inches.
eller a church elder.
en' end.
eneugh enough.
enfauld infold.
enow enough.
Erse Gaelic.
ether-stane adder-stone.
ettle an aim, intent.
evermair evermore.
e'vn even.
ev'n down downright, sheer, positive.
eydent diligent.

F

fa' fall.
fa' lot, portion.
fa' to get; suit; to claim.
facket a waistcoat, under-jacket; a shirt.
faddom'd fathomed.
fae a foe.
faem foam.
faiket let off, excused.
fain fond, affectionate; glad.
fainness fondness, love, affection.
fair fa' good befall! welcome.
fairin a present from a fair.
fallow a fellow.
fa'n fallen.
fand found.

far-aff far-off.
farl an oatcake.
fash annoyance.
fash to trouble, worry.
fash'd, fash't bothered, irked.
fashious troublesome.
Fasten-e'en, Fasten's Even Shrove Tuesday evening.
faught a fight.
fauld a sheepfold.
fauld folded.
faulding sheep-folding.
faun fallen.
fause false.
fause-house a vacant space in a cornstack for ventilation.
faut fault.
fautor an offender, transgressor.
fawsont seemly, well-doing; good-looking.
feat spruce.
fecht to fight.
fecht disputatious, fighting.
feck the bulk, the most part.
feck value, return.
fecket a waistcoat, under-jacket; a shirt.
feckless weak, pithless, feeble.
feckly mostly.
feg a fig.
fegs faith!
feide a feud.
feint *same as* **fient**.
feirrie lusty.
fell keen, cruel, dreadful, deadly; pungent.
fell the cuticle under the skin.
felly relentless.
fen' a shift.
fen', fend to look after; to care for; to keep off.
fenceless defenceless.
ferlie, ferly a wonder.
ferlie to marvel.
fetch to draw a long breath, gasp.
fetch't stopped suddenly.
fey fated to death.
fidge to fidget, to wriggle.
fidgin-fain eager, excited.
fiel well.
fient, feint a fiend, a petty oath; **fient a** not a, devil a; **fient haet** nothing; **fient haet o'** not one of; **fient-ma-care** the fiend may care (I don't!).
fier, fiere a companion.
fier sound, active.
fin' to find.
fissle to tingle, fidget with delight.
fit the foot.
fittie-lan' the near horse of the hindmost pair in a plough.

flae a flea.
flaffin flapping.
flainin flannen, flannel.
flang flung.
flee to fly.
fleech to wheedle.
fleesh a fleece.
fleg a scare, blow, jerk.
fleth'rin flattering.
flewit a sharp lash.
fley to scare.
flichterin fluttering.
flinders shreds, broken pieces.
flinging kicking out in dancing; capering.
flingin-tree a piece of timber hung as a partition between two horses in a stable; a flail.
flisk to make restless, uneasy.
flit to shift.
flittering fluttering.
flyte to scold.
fock, focks folk.
fodgel dumpy.
foor fared, travelled.
Foorsday Thursday.
forbear, forebear a forefather, ancestor.
forby, forbye besides.
forfairn worn-out; forlorn.
forfoughten exhausted.
forgather to meet with for a special purpose.
forgie to forgive.
forjesket jaded.
forrit forward.
fother fodder.
fou, fow drunk.
foughten troubled.
foumart a polecat.
foursome a quartet.
fouth fullness, abundance.
fow *same as* **fou**.
fow a bushel.
frae from.
freath to froth,.
freen, frien' friend.
fremit estranged, hostile.
fu' full.
fu'-han't full-handed.
fud a short tail; the backside
fuff't puffed.
fur a furrow.
fur-ahin the hindmost plough-horse in the furrow.
furder success.
furder to succeed.
furm a wooden form.
furr a furrow.
fusionless pithless, sapless, tasteless,.

fyke fret.
fyke to fuss; fidget.
fyle to defile, to foul.

G

gab the mouth.
gab to talk.
gabs talk.
gae gave.
gae to go; **gae your gate** go your way.
gaed went.
gaen gone.
gaets ways, manners.
gair a strip of cloth, gusset.
gane gone.
gang to go.
gangrel a vagrant.
gar to cause, to make, to compel.
garcock the moorcock.
garten a garter.
gash wise, sagacious; well-prepared; talkative.
gashing talking, gabbing.
gat got.
gate way, road; manner; **gae your gate** go your way.
gatty enervated.
gaucie *same as* **gawsie**.
gaud a goad.
gaudsman, goadsman the driver of a plough team.
gaun going.
gau'n gave.
gaunted gaped, yawned.
gawky a foolish woman or lad.
gawky foolish.
gawsie buxom; jolly.
gaylies in fair health; pretty well.
gear money, wealth; goods; stuff.
geck to sport; to toss the head.
ged the pike.
gentles gentry.
genty trim and elegant.
Geordie, George a guinea.
get issue, offspring, breed.
ghaist a ghost.
gie to give.
gied gave.
gien given.
gif if.
giftie the diminutive of gift.
giglet a giggling youngster or girl.
gillie the diminutive of gill (of whisky).
gilpey a young girl.
gimmer a young ewe.
gin if, whether should; by.
girdle a circular metal plate for baking oatcakes, scones, bannocks, etc.

girn to grin; to twist the face in rage or scorn.
gizz a wig.
glaikit foolish, silly; thoughtless, giddy.
glaive a sword.
glaizie glossy, shiny.
glaum to grasp, clutch.
gled the buzzard; the kite.
gleede a glowing coal.
gleg nimble, sharp, keen-witted.
gleg smartly.
glieb a portion of land.
glib-gabbet smooth-tongued.
glint to twinkle; to go quickly.
gloamin twilight.
gloamin-shot sunset.
glow'r (to) stare.
glunch to frown; to grumble.
goavin looking dazedly.
gotten got.
goud *same as* **gowd**.
gowan the wild or mountain daisy.
gowany covered with wild daisies.
gowd, goud gold.
gowdie the head; **heels-o'er-gowdie** topsy-turvy.
gowff to strike, as in the game of golf.
gowk the cuckoo; a fool, dolt.
gowling howling, growling.
graff a grave, a vault.
graine, grane (to) groan.
graip a dung fork.
graith implements, gear; furniture; attire.
graithing gearing, vestments.
graine, grane (to) groan.
grannie, graunie grandmother.
grape to grope.
grat wept.
gree prize, palm, highest honours.
gree to agree.
greet to weep.
groanin maut ale brewed for a lying-in.
grozet a gooseberry.
grumphie the pig.
grun' the ground.
gruntie the diminutive of grunt, a pig.
gruntle the snout; the face in general.
grunzie growing.
grutten wept.
Gude God.
guid, gude good.
guid e'en good evening.
guid-father father-in-law.
guidman husband.
guidwife mistress of the house.
guid-willie hearty, full of goodwill.
gullie, gully a large knife.
gulravage riotous play.

gumlie muddy.
gumption wisdom.
gusty tasty.
gutcher grandfather.

H

ha' hall.
ha' folk servants.
haddin a holding of house or land, inheritance.
hae have.
haet a an atom, whit, particle, used generally with negatives.
haffet, hauffet the temple, the side of the head; (*pl*) sidelocks.
hafflins half, partly.
hag, hagg a moss, a broken bog.
haggis the minced lungs, heart and liver of a sheep, mixed and cooked with oatmeal, suet, onions, pepper and salt, formerly cooked in the sheep's stomach.
hain to spare, to save.
hairst, har'st harvest.
haith! an exclamation of surprise, faith!
haivers *same as* **havers**.
hal', hald holding, possession.
hale health.
hale, hail whole, healthy.
hale, hail the whole.
halesome wholesome.
hallan a partition wall in a cottage between the door and the fireplace; a porch, outer door.
Halloween All Saints' Eve, 31 October.
Hallowmas All Saints' Day, 1 November.
haly holy.
hame home,.
han' hand.
han-darg *same as* **darg**.
hand-wal'd hand-picked.
Aangie hangman, nickname for the Devil.
hansel, handsel a first gift for luck; an auspicious beginning, good omen; the first money received for sale of goods; reward.
hansel, handsel to give money; to inaugurate.
hap a wrap, a covering against cold.
hap to shelter.
hap to hop.
happer the hopper of a mill.
hap-step-an'-loup hop, step and jump.
harkit hearkened.
harn coarse cloth of flax or hemp.
hash a foolish person, an oaf.
haslock woo the fine wool on the throat of a sheep.
haud to hold;to keep.
hauf half.
haugh low, level and fertile land by a river.
haun a hand.

haurl to trail.
hause to cuddle, embrace.
haveril, hav'rel a person who talks nonsense.
havers nonsense.
havins manners, conduct.
hawkie a white-faced cow; a cow.
heal *same as* **hale**.
healsome *same as* **halesome**.
hecht to promise; to threaten.
heckle a comb with steel teeth for dressing flax and hemp.
heels-o'er-gowdie topsy-turvy.
heeze to hoist.
heich, heigh high.
held away took away.
hellim a helm.
hem-shin'd crooked-shinned.
herd a herd-boy.
here awa' hereabout.
herry to harry.
herryment spoliation.
hersel herself.
het hot.
heugh a hollow or pit; a crag, a steep bank.
heuk a hook.
hilch to hobble.
hiltie-skiltie helter-skelter.
himsel himself.
hiney, hinny honey, a term of endearment.
hing to hang.
hirple to move unevenly; to limp.
hissel as many cattle or sheep as one person can attend.
histie bare.
hizzie a hussy, a wench.
hoast (to) cough.
hoddin riding heavily.
hoddin-grey coarse grey woollen cloth.
hoggie the diminutive of hog, a lamb.
hog-score the distance line in curling.
hog-shouther to jostle, as in a game in which the players push each other with the shoulder.
hoodie-craw the hooded crow, the carrion crow.
hoodock foul and greedy, like a hoodie-craw, miserly.
hool an outer case, sheath, shell.
hoolie softly.
hoord hoard; **hoordet** hoarded.
horn a spoon made of horn; a comb of horn.
Hornie a nickname for the Devil.
host *same as* **hoast**.
hotch to jerk.
houghmagandie fornication.
houlet the owl.
houpe hope.
hove to swell; to rise up.

howdie, howdy a midwife.
howe a hollow; a valley.
howk to dig.
howlet the owl.
hoyse a hoist.
hoy't urged.
hoyte to amble crazily.
hullion a clumsy person; a sloven.
hunder a hundred.
hunkers hams resting on the legs near the heels.
hurcheon the hedgehog.
hurchin an urchin.
hurdies the buttocks.
hurl to trundle.
hushion a footless stocking.
hyte furious, raging.

I

i' in.
icker an ear of corn.
ier-oe a great-grandchild.
ilk, ilka each, every.
ill evil; **ill o't** bad at it; **ill-taen** ill-taken; **ill-willie** ill-natured, niggardly.
Ill-thief a nickname for the Devil.
indentin indenturing.
ingine genius, ingenuity; wit.
ingle a fire in a room; the fireside.
ingle-cheek the fireside.
ingle-lowe, ingle-low the flame of a fire.
I'se I shall, I will.
itsel' itself.
ither other, another.

J

jad a jade.
Janwar January.
jauk to trifle, to dally.
jauner gabber.
jauntie the diminutive of jaunt, a little journey.
jaup to splash.
jaw talk, impudence.
jaw to throw, to dash.
jeeg to jog.
jillet a jilt.
jimp small, slender.
jimply neatly.
jimps stays, open in front.
jink the slip, an escape.
jink to frisk, to sport, to dodge.
jinker a lively, giddy girl; a fast horse.
jirkinet a bodice.
jirt a jerk.
jiz a wig.
jo a sweetheart.
jocteleg a clasp-knife.

jouk to duck, to cover, to dodge.

jow to ring or toll a bell ('a verb which includes both the swinging motion and pealing sound of a large bell'—R.B.)

jumpet, jumpit jumped.

jundie to jostle.

jurr a servant girl.

K

kae the jackdaw.

kail, kale the cabbage; broth made of kail and other greens; food, dinner.

kail-blade the leaf of the cabbage.

kail-gullie a cabbage knife.

kail-runt the stem of the cabbage.

kail-whittle a cabbage knife.

kail-yard a kitchen garden.

kain rent in kind.

kale *same as* **kail**.

kame a comb.

kane rent in kind.

kebar a rafter.

kebbuck a cheese; **kebbuck heel** the last crust of a cheese.

keckle to cackle, to giggle.

keek a look, glance.

keekin glass a looking glass.

keel red chalk.

kelpie a water sprite.

ken to know.

kenna know not.

kennin a small portion of anything; a very little.

kep to catch.

ket the fleece on a sheep.

key quay.

kiaugh anxiety.

kilt to tuck up.

kimmer a wench; a gossip; a wife.

kin' kind.

king's-hood the second stomach in a ruminant.

kintra (of the) country.

Kirk the Church of Scotland.

kirk a church.

kirn a churn.

kirn the harvest home festival.

kirsen to christen.

kist a chest, box; a shop counter.

kitchen to give relish to food.

kittle difficult, ticklish; delicate; fickle.

kittle to tickle.

kittlin a kitten.

kiutle to fondle; to embrace.

knag a knob or peg on which to hang articles; the projection of a knot in a tree.

knaggie having protuberances like rock, wood, etc, knobby.

knappin-hammer a hammer for breaking stones.

knowe a knoll.

knurl, knurlin a dwarf.

kye cows.

kyles skittles.

kyte the belly.

kythe to show.

L

laddie the diminutive of lad, a term of affection for a boy or youth; a boy; a male sweetheart.

lade a load.

lag backward, late; slow, sluggish.

laggen the angle formed by the side and bottom of a wooden dish, barrel, etc.

laigh low.

laik lack.

lair lore; learning; education.

lair to sink in mud or snow, etc; to stick fast in mud, snow, etc.

laird a landowner.

laith loath.

laithfu' bashful, sheepish.

Lallan belonging to the Lowlands of Scotland.

Lallans the Lowlands of Scotland; the Scots Lowland vernacular.

Lammas the beginning of August.

lammie the diminutive of lamb, a term of endearment; a young lamb; a kid.

lan' land.

lan'-afore the foremost horse on the unploughed land side of a plough.

lan'-ahin the hindmost horse on the unploughed land side of a plough.

lane lone.

lanely lonely.

lang long.

lang syne long since, long ago.

length length.

lap leapt.

lass a girl, a young woman; a female sweetheart; a daughter; a maidservant.

lassie the diminutive of lass, a term of endearment.

lave the rest.

lav'rock, laverock the lark.

lawin a tavern bill, the reckoning.

lea grass, untilled land.

lear lore; learning; education.

lea'e to leave.

leddy lady.

lee-lang live-long.

leesome lawful.

leeze, leese to be pleased to; **leeze me on** an expression of great pleasure; dear is to me; commend me to; blessings on.

leister a fish spear with prongs.
len' to lend.
leugh laughed.
leuk (to) look.
ley-crap lea crop.
libbet castrated.
licks a beating.
lien lain.
lieve lief.
lift the sky.
lift a load.
lightly to disparage, to scorn.
lilt to sing.
limmer a rascal, rogue; a prostitute; a mistress.
linn, lin a waterfall.
lint flax.
lint-white flax-coloured.
lintwhite the linnet.
lippen to trust.
lippie the diminutive of lip.
loan a lane.
loanin a private road leading to a farm.
lo'e (to) love.
lo'ed loved.
Lon'on London.
loof (*pl* **looves**) the palm of the hand; help; a hoof.
loon, loun, lown a fellow; a rascal; a peasant; a loose woman.
loosome lovable.
loot permitted, let.
loove (to) love.
looves *see* **loof**.
losh! a corrupt form of 'Lord', used as an exclamation of surprise or wonder.
lough a pond, loch or lake.
loun *same as* **loon**.
loup, lowp to leap.
louse to untie, let loose.
low, lowe a flame.
lowin, lowing flaming, burning.
lown *same as* **loon**.
lowp *same as* **loup**.
lowse to untie, let loose.
lucky a familiar term of address to an elderly woman; a midwife; a grandmother; a wife, mistress; a helpmate; a landlady of an ale-house.
lug the ear.
lugget having ears.
luggie a small dish with a handle.
lum a chimney.
lume a loom.
lunch a large piece of food.
lunt (to) smoke; (to) steam.
lunzie the loin.

luve love.
lyart (*of hair*) streaked with grey, hoary; (*of fallen leaves*) variegated, changed in colour; streaked with red and white.
lynin lining.

M

madden to anger, vex.
mae more.
Mailie Molly, the name for a pet ewe; a pet ewe.
mailin, mailen a farm or holding.
mair more.
maist most.
maist almost.
mak to make; to compose poetry; **mak o'** to pet, fondle; **mak to through** to make good.
'mang among.
manteel, manteele a mantle.
mark, merk an old Scots coin worth 13s 4d Scots, $13^1/_3$d sterling (7p).
mashlum mixed meal; the flour or meal of different kinds of grain.
maskin-pat a teapot.
maukin a hare.
maun must.
maund *same as* **mawn**.
maunna must not, mustn't.
maut malt.
mavis the song-thrush.
maw to mow.
mawin the quantity mowed in a day.
mawn mown.
mawn, maund a large basket, hamper.
mear, meer, meere a mare.
meikle much; great.
melancholious melancholic.
melder the quantity of oats ground at one time.
mell to mix; to be intimate; to meddle, interfere; to join battle; to match, equal.
melvie to cover or soil with meal.
men' to mend.
mense tact; discretion; politeness, good manners.
menseless unmannerly, ill-bred.
mercies whisky, etc.
merk *same as* **mark**.
merle the blackbird.
Merran Marian.
Mess John Mass John, the parish priest, the minister.
messin a cur, a mongrel.
mickle much; great.
midden a dunghill.
midden-creel a basket for manure.
midden-dub a dunghill pool.
midden-hole a gutter at the bottom of the dunghill.

milking shiel a milking shed.

mim prudish, prim, affectedly meek.

mim-mou'd affectedly proper in speech or action.

min' mind, remembrance.

mind to remember, bear in mind.

minnie a mother; a pet name for 'mother'.

mirk dark.

mirksome rather dark.

misca' to miscall, abuse.

mishanter a mishap.

mislear'd mischievous, unmannerly.

mistak to mistake.

misteuk mistook.

mither mother.

mixtie-maxtie confused, jumbled.

monie, mony many.

mools a grave; the earth of a grave, dust.

moop to nibble; to keep company with; to meddle.

mottie dusty.

mou' the mouth.

moudiewort a mole.

muckle much; great.

muir a moor.

muslin-kail broth made simply of water, barley and greens.

mutchkin a liquid measure equal to an English pint.

mysel myself.

N

na, nae no; not.

naething, naithing nothing.

naig a horse, nag.

nane none,.

nappy strong ale; any alcoholic drink.

natch a notching implement; a notch.

neebour a neighbour.

needna need not, needn't.

ne'er never.

neibour a neighbour.

neist next.

neuk, newk a nook, corner.

new-ca'd (*of a cow*) lately calved; pregnant.

nick to sever, slit; to nail; to seize away.

nick a cut; one of the rings on a cow's horns.

Nickie-ben a nickname for the Devil.

nick-nacket a trinket, curiosity.

nieve the fist.

nieve-fu' a handful, fistful.

niffer an exchange, barter.

nit a nut; a hazelnut.

no not.

nocht nought, nothing.

norland northern.

notion a fancy that may lead to love-making; a liking for; a whim.

nowt, nowte cattle.

O

o' of.

och! an exclamation of sorrow, surprise, etc.

ochon! alas!

o'er over; too.

o'ergang to overcome, master.

o'erlay a cravat, necktie.

o'erword a refrain; a catchword.

onie, ony any.

oorie *same as* **ourie**.

or ere, before ; until.

orra extra; odd, unmatched; spare, superfluous.

o't of it.

ought aught, anything at all.

oughtlins, aughtlins at all; in any degree.

ourie, oorie melancholy, depressing; drooping, sickly-looking; bleak; chilly.

oursel' ourselves.

outcast a quarrel, disagreement.

outler (*of an animal*) not housed in winter.

outowre, out-owre out from any place; across, beyond.

owre over; too.

owsen oxen.

owthor author.

oxter'd held up under the arms.

P

pack an' thick confidential.

paidle to paddle, wade; to walk with a weak action.

paidle a nail bag.

painch a paunch.

paitrick a partridge; a girl.

palaver idle talk, nonsense.

pang to cram, stuff full.

parishen, parishon a parish.

parritch oatmeal porridge.

pat a pot.

pat put.

pattle, pettle a plough staff, a small long-handled spade used for cleaning a plough.

paughty haughty, proud; insolent.

paukie, pauky, pawkie cunning; knowing, artful; sly.

pay to beat, drub.

pech to pant, puff; to breathe hard.

pechan, peghan the stomach.

pendle a pendant; an earring.

penny-fee, pennie-fee wages in money.

penny-wheep very weak beer sold at a penny a bottle.

pettle *same as* **pattle**.

philibeg the kilt.

phrase, phraise to flatter, wheedle.

pickle a few, a little.

pike to pick.

pint a measure equal to two English quarts.

pit to put.

placad a proclamation.

plack a copper coin worth one third of an old penny sterling or four pennies Scots.

plackless penniless, poor.

plaid coarse woollen twilled cloth; plaid used as a blanket or covering.

plaiden made of plaid.

plaister (to) plaster.

plenish'd stocked.

pleugh, pleuch a plough.

pliskie, plisky a trick, prank.

pliver the plover.

plumpet, plumpit sank, plunged.

poacher-court a nickname for a kirk session.

pock a bag, wallet, poke, sack.

poind to distrain, impound.

poortith poverty.

poosie a cat; a hare.

pot a small still.

pou to pull.

pouch a pocket; a purse.

pouk to poke.

poupit a pulpit.

pouse a push; a blow.

poussie a cat; a hare.

pout a chicken, pullet.

pouther powder.

pow the head, the poll.

pow to pull.

pownie a pony.

powt a chicken, pullet.

pow't pulled.

powther powder.

pree to prove, experience; to taste, partake of; to kiss.

preef proof.

preen a pin.

prent (to) print.

prie to prove, experience; to taste, partake of; to kiss.

prief proof.

priggin haggling; entreaty.

primsie, primpsie the diminutive of prim, demure, precise; affected.

proves a provost, the chief officer of a burgh.

pu' to pull.

puddock-stool a toadstool.

puir poor.

pun', pund a pound in money or weight.

pursy, pursie the diminutive of purse; purse-proud.

pussie a cat; a hare.

pyet the magpie.

pyke to pick.

pyle a blade or stalk of grass; a single grain of corn.

Q

quarrel to challenge, reprove, check.

quat quit, quitted.

quaukin quaking.

quean a young woman, a lass.

queir a choir.

quey a young cow, a heifer until she has a calf.

quietlin-wise, quietlinswise quietly.

quo', quod quoth.

quine *same as* **quean**.

R

rab to rob.

rade rode.

raep, rape a rope.

ragweed the ragwort.

raible to speak confusedly; to gabble.

rair to roar.

rairin roaring.

rair't roared.

raise rose.

raize to excite; to anger.

ramfeezl'd exhausted.

ramgunshoch morose, surly.

ram-stam headlong; headstrong, heedless.

randie lawless, obstreperous.

randie, randy a scoundrel, a rascal.

rant to frolic, romp; to revel.

rant merrymaking; a rough noisy frolic; a lively story or song.

rape *same as* **raep**.

raploch coarse woollen cloth, homespun and undyed.

rase rose.

rash a rush.

rash-buss a clump of rushes.

rashy, rashie covered with rushes.

rattan, rattoon a rat.

rattlin rollicking; lively.

raucle rough, coarse; sturdy.

raught reached.

raw a row, a rank.

rax to extend, stretch.

ream cream; froth, foam.

ream to foam.

reave to rob, plunder.

rebute a rebuff.

red advised; afraid.

red, rede to advise, counsel.

red-wat-shod shod with wet blood.

red-wud raging mad; insane; furious; eager.

reek (to) smoke.

reekie, reeky smoky.

reestit, reestet smoke-dried; shrivelled up.

reestit, reestet (*of a horse*) refused to go.

reif robbery, plunder.

remead remedy.

rickle a small stack of corn in a field.

rief robbery, plunder.

rig, rigg a ridge; a long narrow hill; a section of a ploughed field; the first furrow turned in ploughing; a drill for potatoes, etc.

riggin the roof-tree, the roof.

rigwoodie lean, bony.

rin to run.

ripp a handful of unthreshed corn or hay.

ripplin-kame a toothed instrument for separating the seed of flax from the stalks.

risk to make a harsh, grating sound, like the tearing of roots.

rive to split, tear; to tug; to burst; to take by force.

rock a distaff, the rod on which flax, wool, etc, is wound before spinning.

rockin a friendly gathering of neighbours with their rocks and spindles.

roon a shred; a round, circuit.

roose, rouse to praise, flatter.

roose, rouse reputation.

roosty rusty.

rottan a rat.

roun' round.

roupet hoarse.

rouse *same as* **roose**.

routh *same as* **rowth**.

routhie well-stocked.

row, rowe to roll; to wrap; to flow, as a river.

rowte to low, bellow, roar.

rowth plenty, abundance; a store.

rozet resin.

run-deil a thorough devil, incorrigible villain.

rung a cudgel.

runkl'd wrinkled.

runt a cabbage stalk.

ryke to reach.

S

's is; are; as; us.

sab to sob.

sae so.

saft soft; simple, silly; lazy.

sair sore, aching; sad, sorrowful; hard, severe; strong.

sair to suffice; to satisfy sexually; to treat.

sair, sairly sorely.

sairie sorrowful; sorry.

sall shall.

Sandy, Sannack diminutives of the name Alexander.

sark a shirt; a chemise; a nightdress.

saugh a willow.

saul soul; spirit; mettle.

saumont a salmon.

saunt a saint.

saut salt.

saut-backet a box made of wood for holding salt.

saw to sow.

sawmont a salmon.

Sawney *same as* **Sandy**.

sax six.

saxpence sixpence.

scaith, scathe injury; loss; damage.

scandal-potion a sarcastic name for tea.

scar to scare, frighten.

scar *same as* **scaur**.

scathe *same as* **scaith**.

scaud to scald.

scaul, scauld to scold.

scaul, scauld a scold; a scolding.

scaur afraid.

scaur, scar a cliff, precipice; a bare place on the side of a steep hill.

scho she.

sclate a slate.

scone a flat, round cake of flour, etc, baked on a girdle.

sconner disgust.

sconner to disgust; to loathe.

scraichin calling hoarsely; screaming.

screed a rip, tear, rent.

screed to recite rapidly, to reel off.

scriech a scream.

scriechin screeching.

scriegh to scream; to whinny.

scrievin careering.

scrimpit scanty, niggardly.

scroggie, scroggy abounding in stunted bushes or underwood.

sculdudd'ry, sculduddery bawdry; grossness; fornication.

see'd saw.

seisins freehold possessions.

sel, sel', sell self.

sell'd, sell't sold.

semple simple.

sen' to send.

set to set off; to start.

set sat.

sets becomes.

shachl'd shapeless.

shaird a shred; a shard; a fragment.

shangan, shanagan a stick cleft at one end for putting on a do's tail.

shank to travel on foot.

shanna shall not, shan't.

shaul shallow.

shaver a funny fellow, a wag.

shavie a trick; a practical joke.

shaw a grove.

shaw to show.

shearer a reaper.

sheep-shank a sheep's trotter; **nae sheep-shank bane** a person of no small importance.

sheerly surely; wholly.

sheers scissors.

sheugh, sheuch a ditch, drain; a furrow, trench, gutter.

sheuk shook.

shiel a hut, cottage; a shepherd's summer shelter.

shill shrill, loud, noisy.

shog a shake; a push, nudge.

shool a shovel, spade.

shoon shoes.

shore to threaten; to offer.

shouldna should not, shouldn't.

shouther, showther the shoulder.

shure sheared, shore.

sic such.

siccan such a, such an.

sicker secure, safe; firm; sure, certain; steady, unyielding; **sicker score** strict conditions.

sidelins sideways; with legs on one side; alongside; aside.

siller silver; money; payment; price.

simmer summer.

sin a son.

sin' since.

sindry sundry, several.

singet singed, shrivelled.

sinn the sun.

sinny sunny.

sinsyne ago, since then.

skaith injury; loss; damage.

skaith to damage.

skeigh, skiegh 'mettlesome, fiery, proud'—R.B.

skellum a rascal, scamp, scoundrel.

skelp a slap, a smack, blow.

skelp to strike with the open hand, spank; to move quickly; **skelpin at it** driving at it.

skelpie-limmer's-face 'a technical term in female scolding'—R. B.

skelvy having various layers; shelving.

skiegh *same as* **skeigh**.

skinking thin, liquid, watery.

skinklin glittering, sparkling.

skirl to cry or sing shrilly.

sklent a slant, a turn; a glance; a squint.

sklent to slope; to slant, to look obliquely or askance; to squint; to cheat.

skouth abundance, scope.

skriech a scream.

skriegh to scream; to whinny.

skyrin making a great show; gaudy.

skyte a slap.

slade slid, did slide.

slae the blackthorn; the sloe, the fruit of the blackthorn.

slap a gap or temporary opening in a fence, etc.

slaw slow.

slee sly; clever; skilful.

sleekit smooth and glossy; crafty, sly.

slidd'ry, sliddery slippery, smooth.

sloken to slake; to spend money on drink.

slype 'to fall over as a wet furrow from the plough'—R.B.

slypet slipped.

sma' small; young.

smeddum a powder; mettle, spirit; intelligence.

smeek smoke.

smiddie, smiddy a smithy.

smoor to smother, suffocate.

smoutie obscene, smutty.

smytrie a collection of small individuals, children, etc.

snakin exulting and sneering.

snap quick, active; smart, acute.

snapper to stumble, trip.

snash abusive language; impudence.

snaw snow.

snaw-broo melted snow.

snaw-drap snowdrop.

snawy snowy.

sned to prune; to lop off.

sneeshin mill a snuffbox.

snell keen, eager; cold, bitter, biting.

snick a latch; **he weel a snick can draw** he is good at cheating.

snick-drawing latch-lifting; stealthy; scheming.

snirtle to laugh in a suppressed way, snigger.

snood a ribbon or band for confining the hair.

snool 'one whose spirit is broken with oppressive slavery'—R.B.

snool to cringe; to snub.

snoove to move smoothly and steadily; to walk with a steady step.

snore to snort.

snowk to snuff, as a dog.

sodger, soger a soldier.

sonsie, sonsy pleasant, good-natured; cheerful, jolly; plump, buxom.

soom to swim; to float.

soor sour.

sough *same as* **sugh**.

sough a sigh; a deep breath; the sound of wind; a rumour.

souk a suck.

soup, soupe a sip, mouthful; a small quantity of liquid.

souple supple; flexible.

souter a shoemaker, cobbler.

sowens a porridge made of oats and water.

sowps sups.

sowth 'to try over a tune with a low whistle'—R.B.

sowther to solder.

spae to foretell; to prophesy.

spail a splinter, chip or shaving of wood.

spair spare, thin.

spairge to splash; to scatter; to roughcast a wall.

spak spoke.

spate a flood.

spavie the spavin in horses.

spavit, spavet spavined.

spean to wean.

speat a flood.

speel to climb, ascend.

speer to ask, inquire, question.

speet to spit.

speir, spier to ask, inquire, question.

spence a country parlour.

spleuchan a tobacco pouch; a large purse or pouch.

splore a frolic, spree, revel; a carousal, debauch.

sprachle to clamber.

sprattle to scramble.

spreckled speckled.

spring a quick lively tune; a dance to this.

sprittie, spritty full of rushes or tough roots.

sprush spruce, neat, smart.

spunk a match; a spark of fire; the spark of life, spirit.

spunkie full of spirit.

spunkie a will-o'-the-wisp; liquor, spirits.

spurtle a wooden rod for stirring porridge, etc.

spurtle-blade a sword.

squad a number of people, company.

squatter to flap or flutter in water, as a duck.

squattle to squat, settle down.

stacher to stagger, totter.

stack stuck.

staggie the diminutive of staig.

staig a young horse.

stammer to stagger, stumble.

stan' to stand.

stane stone; a measure of weight.

stang (to) sting; (to) goad.

stang a long wooden bar or pole.

stang to cause to ride the stang—to punish a wife-beater or unfaithful husband by carrying him from place to place astride a pole borne on the shoulders of others.

stank 'a pool of standing water'—R.B.

stan't stood.

stap to stop; to stuff.

stapple a stopper, plug.

stark strong; potent.

starn a star.

starnie the diminutive of starn, a little star; a very small quantity.

startle to take fright.

staumrel half-witted.

staw a stall.

staw to surfeit, satiate; to sicken.

staw stole.

stech to stuff, cram.

steek a stitch; a loop in knitting.

steek to shut; to close; to touch, meddle with.

steeve stiff, firm; strong, sturdy.

stell a still for distillation.

stell to prop, fix.

sten a leap; a spring.

stent to erect; to place on high.

stent an assessment, rate, tax.

sten't sprang.

stey steep; hard to climb.

stibble stubble.

stibble-rig a stubble field; the leading reaper on a ridge.

stick-an-stowe completely.

stilt a crutch; the handle of a plough.

stimpart a quarter of a peck, a measure of grain.

stir sir.

stirk a young bullock.

stock the stem of a cabbage plant.

stockit, stocket stocked.

stoit, stoiter to stagger, stumble, totter.

stoor harsh, stern; 'sounding hollow, strong and hoarse'—R.B.

stoun' a pang, throb.

stour strife; adversity; dust.

stourie dusty.

stown stolen.

stownlins by stealth.

stoyte to stagger, stumble, totter.

strae straw; **strae death** a death in bed in contrast to a violent one.

straik to stroke; to smooth.

strak struck.

strang strong.

straucht, straught to stretch; to make straight.

straucht, straught straight.

streekit stretched.

striddle to straddle, sit astride.

stroan't, stron't urinated.

strunt any kind of spiritous liquor.
strunt to walk with dignity.
studdie an anvil.
stumpie the diminutive of stump; a worn quill.
sturt strife; vexation.
sturt to vex, trouble.
sturtin frightened.
styme the faintest form of an object.
sucker sugar.
sud should, should have.
sugh a sigh; a deep breath; the sound of wind; a rumour.
sumph a simpleton; a surly, sulky person.
sune soon.
sup a sip, mouthful; a small quantity of liquid.
suthron southern.
sutor a shoemaker, cobbler.
swaird sward.
swall'd swelled.
swank supple, pliant.
swanky a smart active, strapping lad or girl.
swap to exchange.
swarf to swoon.
swat sweated.
swatch a sample, pattern.
swats new ale.
sweer slow, lazy, reluctant.
swirl 'a curve, an eddying blast or pool, a knot in wood'—R.B.
swirlie full of twists or knots.
swith begone! quick!
swither doubt, hesitation.
swoom to swim.
swoor swore.
sybow a young union; a shallot.
syne ago, since; from that time; then; **lang syne** long ago; **short syne** a little while ago.

T

tack a lease, holding, farm.
tacket a hobnail.
tae to.
tae a toe.
taed a toad.
tae'd toed; pronged.
taen, ta'en taken.
taet a small quantity; a lock of hair or wool.
tairge to keep under discipline.
tak to take.
tald told.
tane the one (in contrast to the other).
tangs tongs.
tap the top; the head; the quantity of flax put on the distaff.
tapetless senseless.
tapmaist, tapmost topmost, uppermost.

tappet-hen a bottle in the shape of a hen, holding three quarts of claret.
tap-pickle the uppermost grain in a stalk of oats.
tapsalteerie topsy-turvy, upside-down.
targe a shield.
targe to cross-question, examine.
tarrow to tarry, linger; to be reluctant, to murmur.
tassie a small glass, a goblet.
tauk (to) talk.
tauld told.
tawie tame, tractable.
tawpie a foolish, awkward girl.
tawted matted.
teat a tuft; a small quantity of anything.
teen vexation, annoyance.
tell'd told.
temper-pin a fiddle peg; a wooden screw for tightening the band of a spinning wheel.
ten-hours bite a slight feed given to horses in the yoke in the forenoon.
tent heed, care, attention.
tent to attend to; to heed, take care; to notice.
tentie, tenty careful, heedful, cautious, watchful.
tentier more watchful.
tentless careless, heedless, inattentive.
tester an old coin, about sixpence in value.
teuch, teugh tough; hard; pertinacious.
teuk took.
thack (to) thatch; **thack and rape** a cover for stacks agains wind and rain; home comforts.
thae those, these.
thairm the belly of man or beast; catgut; a fiddle-string.
theckit thatched.
thegither together.
themsel themselves.
thick friendly, intimate; rapid.
thieveless cold, lacking warmth; forbidding, spiteful.
thig to beg, borrow.
thir these; those.
thirl to perforate, drill; to pierce.
thole to endure, suffer.
thou'se thou shalt.
thowe a thaw.
thowless lacking energy, lazy; useless.
thrang a throng, crowd of people.
thrang to throng, crowd.
thrang crowded, busy.
thrapple the windpipe, neck, throat.
thrave twenty-four sheaves of grain.
thraw a twist, wrench; a sprain; (*pl*) throes.
thraw to throw, cast; to twist, wrench; to sprain; to turn; to thwart.
threap to argue, wrangle.
threesome three together, a trio.

thretteen thirteen.
thretty thirty.
thrissle a thistle.
thrist to thirst.
throu'ther unmethodical; pell-mell.
thrum to strum; to hum.
thummart a polecat.
thy lane alone.
thysel thyself, yourself.
tight neat, trim; well-shaped; good-looking; tidy; able, ready for action; prepared.
till to.
till't to it.
timmer timber, wood.
tine to lose; to be lost.
tinkler a tinker, gipsy.
tint lost.
tip a ram.
tippence twopence.
tirl to strip, denude; to make a rattling or scraping sound so as to attract attention at a door.
tither the other.
tittlin whispering.
tocher a dowry.
tocher to give a dowry.
tocher-gude a marriage portion.
tod a fox.
to-fa', toofa' the close of day or night.
toom empty.
toop a ram.
toss a toast; a belle frequently toasted.
toun a town; a farm steading.
tousie shaggy.
tout blast.
tow flax or hemp in a prepared state; a rope.
towmond, towmont a twelvemonth, year.
towsing a ruffling.
toyte to totter.
tozie muddled; tipsy; snug, warm.
tram a shaft of a barrow, cart, carriage, etc.
transmugrify metamorphose, transform.
trashtrie trashy food or drink.
trews trousers.
trig neat, tidy, trim.
trinklin flowing.
trin'le a wheel.
trogger a packman, pedlar.
troggin pedlars' wares.
troke to barter, exchange.
trot (*of a stream*) to flow briskly.
trouse trousers.
trowth in truth.
trump a Jew's harp.
tryst, tryste a meeting; a fair; a cattle-market; a betrothal.
trysted appointed.

trysting meeting.
tulyie, tulzie a squabble, brawl, contest.
tup a ram.
twa two.
'twad it would.
twafauld twofold, double.
twal twelve; **the twal** twelve o'clock at night.
twalpennie worth the value of a penny sterling.
twang twinge.
twa-three two or three.
tway two.
twin, twine to rob, deprive; to bereave.
twistle a twist, sprain.
tyke a dog.
tyne *same as* **tine**.
Tysday, Tyesday Tuesday.

U

ulzie oil.
unchancy unlucky; dangerous.
unco unknown, strange; foreign; uncommon; extraordinary, very great.
unco extremely, unusually, very.
uncos news, strange tidings.
under, un'er under pretence of.
unkend, unkenned, unkent unknown, unknowable; innumerable.
unsicker insecure; not to be depended upon.
unskaithed uninjured.
usquabae, usquebae whisky.

V

vauntie, vaunty boastful, proud.
vera very.
virl an encircling band or ring of metal or ivory.
vittle grain, fodder.
vogie vain.
vow an exclamation of suprise, admiration, etc.

W

wa', waw a wall.
wab a web.
wabster a weaver.
wad (to) wager.
wad to marry, wed.
wad would, would have.
wad'a would have.
wadna would not, wouldn't.
wadset a mortgage; a deed from a debtor to a creditor assigning the rents of land until the debt is paid.
wae woe; **wae's me** woe is to me; **waesucks** alas! **wae worth** woe befall.
wae woeful, sorrowful.
wair to spend.
wale to choose, select, pick out.

wale choice; choosing; the choicest, the pick.
walie, wawlie ample, large, handsome.
wallop to dance; to gallop; to kick about; to dangle loosely.
waly fa' good luck to.
wame the belly; the stomach.
wamefou a bellyful.
wan won.
wanchancie unlucky; dangerous.
wanrestfu' restless.
ware to spend.
ware worn.
wark work, labour.
wark-lume, warklum a tool, implement.
warl', warld the world.
warlock a wizard.
warl'y, warly, warldly worldly.
warran to warrant; to assure.
warse worse.
warsle, warstle to wrestle; to strive.
warsle, warstle a struggle; a tussle.
washen washed.
wast west.
waste the waist.
wastrie waste; extravagance.
wat wet.
wat to know; to inform; to assure; to be sensible of.
water-fit the mouth of a river.
water-kelpies a water sprite.
watna don't know.
wattle a twig, switch.
wauble to wobble.
waught a copious draught, a big drink.
wauk, wauken to awake; to awaken; to become animated.
waukin awake; disinclined for sleep.
waukit (*of the hands*) hardened, calloused.
waukrife wakeful.
waulie jolly.
waur worse.
waur to worst.
waurst worst.
waur't worsted, beat.
wean a child, an infant.
weanies infants.
weason the gullet, windpipe.
wecht a weight.
wee little, small; **a wee** a short space or time.
wee thing a child.
weel well, fine, satisfied.
weel-faured, weel-far'd well-favoured, good-looking.
weel-gaun well-going.
weel-hain'd well-kept, saved to good purpose.
weel-tocher'd, well-tochered well-dowered.

weepers strips of muslin or cambric stitched on the cuffs of a coat or gown as a sign of mourning.
weet wet.
weet to wet.
weet rain; dew.
werena were not, weren't.
we'se we shall.
westlin western.
wha who.
whaizle, whaisle to wheeze.
whalpet whelped.
wham whom.
whan when.
whang a a large piece or slice of cheese.
whang to beat, thrash, flog.
whar, whare where; whither.
wha's whose; who is.
whase, wha's whose.
what for, whatfore wherefore.
whatna what kind of.
whatreck nevertheless; what matter?
whatt whittled, whetted.
whaup a curlew.
whaur where; whither.
wheep *same as* **penny-wheep**.
wheep to jerk.
whid a fib, lie.
whid (*of a hare*) to move nimbly and noiselessly.
whids gambols.
Whig an old name for a Covenanter, a Presbyterian or a dissenter from the established Church of Scotland.
whigmeleerie a fantastic, useless ornament.
whiles sometimes; at other times; now and then.
whin gorse.
whinge to whine.
whingin whining.
whirlygigum, whirligigum a whirligig, a fanciful ornament.
whist silence, hush.
whissle, whissel (to) whistle.
whitter a hearty draught of liquor.
whittle a knife.
whyles sometimes; at other times; now and then.
wi' with.
wick a bore to drive a curling stone at an angle through an opening.
wicker a twig, a switch.
widdifu' deserving to be hanged.
widdle (to) wriggle.
wiel an eddy.
wight a fellow.
wight stout, mighty; clever.
wighter more influential.
willcat, wil-cat the wildcat.

willyart, wilyart shy, bashful.
wimble a gimlet; the penis.
wimple to wind, meander.
win won.
win' wind.
winn to winnow.
winna will not, won't.
winnin winding.
winnock a window.
winnock-bunker a window-seat.
win't did wind.
winter-hap winter covering.
wintle to stagger, reel; to swing to and fro; to wriggle.
winze a curse.
wi's with his.
wiss to wish.
wi't with it.
won to dwell, reside, live.
wonner a wonder; a prodigy; a term of contempt.
woo' wool.
woodie, woody a withe, a flexible twig of willow; a halter or rope for the gallows originally made from withes.
wooer-bab a love-knot; a garter with a couple of knots worn below the knee by a suitor.
woor wore.
wordy, wordie worthy.
worset worsted.
wot to know; to inform; to assure; to be sensible of.
wraith 'a spirit, a ghost; an apparition exactly like a living person, whose appearance is said to forbode the person's approaching death'—R.B.
wrang wrong; wronged.

wreath, wreeth a snowdrift.
wud angry, mad.
wumble *same as* **wimble**.
wyliecoat, wylecoat an undervest.
wyte to blame; to reproach.

Y

yad an old mare.
yard a garden.
yaud an old mare.
ye you; yourself.
yealing a coeval, one contemporary in age.
yearn an eagle.
yearth earth.
yell barren; dry, milkless.
yerd a yard, garden; earth; the grave.
yerkit jerked.
yerl an earl.
ye'se you shall.
yestreen last night.
yett a gate.
yeuk, yeuck to itch.
yill ale.
yill-caup a horn or wooden cup from which ale is drunk.
yird earth.
yirr the growl of a dog.
yokin, yoking a spell at the plough; a day's work; a bout, contest; a coupling.
yon yonder.
'yont beyond.
youngker a youngster.
yoursel yourself, yourselves.
yowe a ewe.
yowie the diminutive of ewe; a pet ewe.
Yule Christmas.

Index of Titles

Index of First Lines